The

Jewish Targums

and John's

Logos Theology

The
Jewish Targums
and John's
Logos Theology

John Ronning

Baker Academic

a division of Baker Publishing Group
Grand Rapids, Michigan

© 2010 by John L. Ronning

Published by Baker Academic
a division of Baker Publishing Group
P.O. Box 6287, Grand Rapids, MI 49516-6287
www.bakeracademic.com

Baker Academic edition published 2010
ISBN 978-0-8010-4759-6

Previously published in 2010 by Hendrickson Publishers

Printed in the United States of America

The Library of Congress has cataloged the original edition as follows:
Ronning, John L., 1954–
    The Jewish Targums and John's logos theology / John L. Ronning.
      p. cm.
    Includes bibliographical references and indexes.
    ISBN 978-1-59856-306-1 (alk. paper)
    1. Logos (Christian theology) 2. Bible. N.T. John—Theology. 3. Bible. O.T. Aramaic—Criticism, interpretation, etc. 4. Bible—Criticism, interpretation, etc. I. Title.
    BS2615.52.R66 2009
    232'.2—dc22
                                  2009032076

10 11 12 13 14 15 16   7 6 5 4 3 2 1

For Martin McNamara:
in vindication

When they were fully awake, they saw his glory. (Luke 9:32)

Table of Contents

Preface

This book grew out of a sabbatical in the United States in the fall of 2002. I had actually intended to do some writing on the OT historical books at that time, but I first wanted to follow up on something I had been thinking about from a course in Aramaic I had taken long before. Some reading I did for that course argued that the Logos title in John was rooted in the Targums—the Aramaic translations of the Hebrew OT. I thought that such a view made good sense in light of echoes in John 1:14 of the OT theme of the manifestation of God's glory in the tabernacle and temple. I figured that "the Word" must be a way of referring to the OT name of God and that this argued for a targumic origin. So before doing my other writing, I decided to write a paper for the Evangelical Theological Society annual convention that year, covering basically the material in ch. 2 of the present book in the section, The Manifestation of the Glory of the Lord in the Tabernacle and the Temple.

In researching this paper, it was not long before I realized I was on to something big. Thankfully, I had no one warning me that I might be going down a blind alley—I might have listened, and, as so many others have, been discouraged from looking seriously at the Targums to explain the Logos title.[1] Far from roaming a blind alley, I was discovering that the concept of the divine Word in the Targums was a vital key to understanding John's Gospel. As an OT scholar, I was quite stunned (and still am) to discover to what extent this subject had been neglected in Johannine studies.

I decided to write a longer paper for a journal article, but soon realized that there was enough material for a book. Along the way I wrote two more papers. Again on sabbatical in the fall of 2006, I wrote a paper for the ETS annual convention entitled "Caiaphas Prophecies in the Targums," which is the subject of ch. 10 in this book. I also eventually did write a journal article, which basically distills the portions of the present book dealing with *Targum Isaiah*.[2] The time seems to have been right for my discoveries; the Targums have become more and more accessible in English translation, and electronic Aramaic texts with parsing information

---

[1]C. K. Barrett's comment is typical: "*Memra* is a blind alley in the study of the biblical background of John's logos doctrine" (C. K. Barrett, *The Gospel According to St. John* [2d ed.; Philadelphia: Westminster, 1978], 153).

[2]John L. Ronning, "The *Targum of Isaiah* and the Johannine Literature," *WTJ* 69 (2007): 247–78. Because this article was published at quite a late stage in the production of this book, I have not referred to it.

have been made readily available. Etheridge's nineteenth-century translations of *Targum Onqelos* and *Targum Pseudo-Jonathan* (covering the Pentateuch) are online, so one can easily search by keyword to find passages of interest.

I am conscious of the fact that the present book could be improved by a few more years of research, but if I wait any longer I will feel like the lepers outside the gates of Samaria during famine, who discovered the abandoned spoils left behind by the Aramaeans who fled in panic. After helping themselves to the spoils for a while, they said, "We are not doing what is right. Today is a day of good news, but we are keeping silent. If we wait until morning light, punishment will find us. Now come, let us go and tell the house of the king" (2 Kgs 7:9). Likewise, I invite the reader to participate in these surprising discoveries, since an understanding of the Targums helps us to experience what the apostle John experienced and described for us: "We saw his glory."

I take a conventional view of the authorship and date of John's Gospel. That John the Apostle is the author has been ably defended by others and I have nothing to add, and it seems clear that John is familiar with the synoptic tradition and expects his readers to be as well, and that he is writing after the destruction of Jerusalem, which is much on his mind as he writes.

While I will not argue at length that John is dependent on the Synoptics, I will here give what I think is a rather compelling example of such dependence. After his resurrection, around a charcoal fire, Jesus asks Peter three times, "Do you love me?" (John 21:15–17). The threefold question is commonly related to Peter's threefold denial, which in John's Gospel also took place around a charcoal fire (18:18). The first time the question is "Do you love me more than these?" When we look at the definitions of love given by Jesus in the upper room, we can see that when Peter boasted that he would give his life for Jesus, he was boasting of having what Jesus said is the greatest love: "greater love than this no one has, that one lay down his life for his friends" (15:13). In saying that he would lay his life down for Jesus (13:37), Peter was saying, "I have that greatest love." Further, in saying that even if the rest of the disciples were to forsake Jesus, Peter would lay his life down for Jesus, he was in effect saying to Jesus, "I love you more than these do." Around the first charcoal fire, Peter's boast of this love proved untrue. Around the second charcoal fire, Jesus asks him if he would repeat this boast: "Do you love me more than these (do)?" Peter is willing to affirm that he loves Jesus, but he is unwilling to affirm his previous boast, proven wrong at the first charcoal fire, that he loves Jesus more than the other disciples do.

The point in all of this is that in John's Gospel there is no record of Peter comparing himself to the other disciples in this matter of the greatest love. This information is found only in the Synoptics (Matt 26:33–35; Mark 14:29–31). Thus it is only by combining the record in John (love means laying one's life down for his friends, and Peter's claim that he will do so for Jesus) with that of the Synoptics (Peter boasting that he would lay his life down for Jesus even if all the rest of the disciples forsake him) that we can see that in the Lord's question in John 21:15, he is asking Peter if he will repeat his boast of love that was disproved by his denial. Thus if John omits something in his gospel that is mentioned in the Synoptics, it does not follow that he is unaware of it. It may be rather that he takes for granted his reader's knowledge of it.

A note on translations: Much of this book is based on comparison of original English translations of Hebrew (OT) texts with Greek (NT, and sometimes LXX) texts, and both of these with Aramaic texts. I have facilitated such comparison by using a literal, formal equivalence type of translation. Thus the translations are my own, unless otherwise indicated, although for OT and NT texts my translations are usually close to NASB. For the Aramaic texts the translations are usually close to those which appear in The Aramaic Bible series (exact quotes are footnoted, as are substantive differences). The translation method in The Aramaic Bible is also literal, but I have not followed several of the translation practices in this series, such as the use of italics to indicate changes or additions to the Hebrew text, and the transliteration of *Memra* and *Dibbera* (which I translate as "Word," relating them to the Logos title in John). Furthermore, I have uniformly translated קבּיל as "receive" and סעד as "help" because of how I believe these words relate to John's Gospel.

In quoting from the various texts, I have frequently used italics to emphasize particular words and phrases. Unless otherwise noted, all italicized text in such quotations should be understood as indicating my particular emphases rather than as an integral part of the translation. When citing texts I have used curly braces {} to indicate variant readings from the same tradition (e.g., different MS readings from *Tg. Onq.*), square brackets [ ] to indicate marginal glosses (*Tg. Neof.*), and angle brackets <> to indicate where the translation represents wording missing from the original texts that has been supplied from somewhere else. Simple parentheses are used for comparing one text to another, whether a translated text to its original (such as comparing a Targum text to the MT text upon which it is based, or an LXX reading to MT), an original to a translated text, or one translated text to another. Where the verse numbering in English translation differs from the Hebrew and Aramaic or LXX, I have elected to use the English numbering, even when the discussion focuses exclusively on the MT, Targum, or LXX.

Quotes from the Talmud are from the Soncino edition.[3] Quotes from the Mishnah are from Danby.[4] Quotes from Philo are from the Loeb Classical Library (LCL) edition.

---

[3] I. Epstein, *The Babylonian Talmud* (35 vols.; London: Soncino, 1935–1952; 18-vol. ed., 1961).

[4] Herbert Danby, *The Mishnah: Translated from the Hebrew with Introduction and Brief Explanatory Notes* (New York: Oxford University Press, 1933).

Acknowledgments

Two scholars have had significant roles in leading me along the path that has led to the present work, Moises Silva and Martin McNamara. I took an elective course in Aramaic from Silva (more than twenty years ago now) while in the course of my doctoral studies at Westminster Theological Seminary in Philadelphia. The course included a discussion and comparison of all the Targums of Gen 3:15 that was useful for me at the time as a help in research for my dissertation on Gen 3:15. The course also dealt with Martin McNamara's discussion of the dependence of Rev 12:16–17 on the Palestinian Targums of Gen 3:15 and Exod 15:12, and served to introduce me to his writings on the Targums.[1] The course readings also got me interested in the Targums as the source of the Logos title in John's Gospel. I revisited the notes and bibliography for that class when starting out on the present project, and I was glad to be able to "meet" Dr. McNamara by e-mail along the way. Both Drs. Silva and McNamara were kind enough to review aspects of my work at an early stage and to provide encouragement and recommendations to prospective publishers. I am hopeful that at last Dr. McNamara's advocacy of the Targum background for the Logos title will find the acceptance that it has long deserved, and I am pleased to dedicate this work to him in vindication of this thesis.

Stephen Kaufman of the Comprehensive Aramaic Lexicon project of the Hebrew Union College was always prompt and thorough in answering my occasional query concerning Targum texts.

Thanks also go to the trustees and faculty of the John Wycliffe Theological College for encouraging and facilitating me in all of my research and writing interests, and likewise to my wife Linda. Linda and our daughter Laurel also helped with indexing. Thanks are also due to all those over the years who have supported us as a missionary family in South Africa. Finally, thanks to associate editor Mark House of Hendrickson Publishers and copyeditor Scott Brown for all of their careful work and for a smooth process leading up to the present publication. I ask the reader's indulgence for any errors that remain.

---

[1] Martin McNamara, *The New Testament and the Palestinian Targum to the Pentateuch* (AnBib 27A; Rome: Biblical Institute Press, 1978), 221–22.

Abbreviations

General

B.C.E.	before the Common Era
C.E.	Common Era
cf.	compare
ch(s).	chapter(s)
ed(s).	editor(s), edited by, edition(s)
e.g.	*exempli gratia*, for example
esp.	especially
et al.	and others
Heb.	Hebrew
ibid.	*ibidem*, in the same place
i.e.	*id est*, that is
int.	interlinear gloss
LXX	Septuagint (Greek OT)
MS(S)	Manuscript(s)
mg.	marginal gloss
MT	Masoretic Text (Hebrew OT), or a literal translation thereof
n(n).	note(s)
no(s).	number(s)
NT	New Testament
OT	Old Testament
p(p).	page(s)
pl.	plural
repr.	reprint
rev.	revised
trans.	translated by
v(v).	verse(s)
vol(s).	volume(s)

Biblical and Apocryphal Books

Gen	Genesis
Exod	Exodus

Lev	Leviticus
Num	Numbers
Deut	Deuteronomy
Josh	Joshua
Judg	Judges
1–2 Sam	1–2 Samuel
1–2 Kgs	1–2 Kings
1–2 Chr	1–2 Chronicles
Neh	Nehemiah
Esth	Esther
Ps	Psalms
Prov	Proverbs
Song	Song of Songs, Song of Solomon
Isa	Isaiah
Jer	Jeremiah
Ezek	Ezekiel
Dan	Daniel
Hos	Hosea
Mic	Micah
Hag	Haggai
Zech	Zechariah
Mal	Malachi
Bar	Baruch
Sir	Sirach/Ecclesiasticus
Wis	Wisdom of Solomon
Matt	Matthew
Rom	Romans
1–2 Cor	1–2 Corinthians
Gal	Galatians
Eph	Ephesians
Phil	Philippians
Col	Colossians
1 Thess	1 Thessalonians
1 Tim	1 Timothy
Heb	Hebrews
Jas	James
1 Pet	1 Peter
Rev	Revelation

Targumic Texts

CTg.	*Cairo Genizah Targum* manuscript fragments (of *Palestinian Targums*), followed by ᴍꜱ identifier.
Frg. Tg(s).	*Fragmentary Targum(s)* (of the Pentateuch)

Pal. Tg(s).	*Palestinian Targum(s)* (of the Pentateuch)
Tg. Isa., etc.	*Targum Isaiah,* etc. (from *Targum Jonathan* of the Prophets)
Tg. Jon.	*Targum Jonathan* (of the Prophets)
Tg. Josh.	*Targum Joshua* (from *Targum Jonathan* of the Prophets)
Tg. Neof.	*Targum Neofiti* (of the Pentateuch)
Tg. Neof. [mg.]	*Targum Neofiti* marginal gloss
Tg. Neof. [int.]	*Targum Neofiti* interlinear gloss
Tg. Onq.	*Targum Onqelos* (of the Pentateuch)
Tg. Ps.-J.	*Targum Pseudo-Jonathan* (of the Pentateuch)
Tg. Ps., etc.	*Targum Psalms* (of the Writings)
Tos. Tg(s).	*Tosefta Targum(s)* (of the Prophets)

Mishnah, Talmud, and Rabbinic Sources

b.	Babylonian Talmud (e.g., *b. Berakot*)
m.	Mishnah (e.g., *m. Sukkah*)
Pirqe R. El.	*Pirqe Rabbi Eleazer*

Modern Bible Versions

ESV	English Standard Version
KJV	King James Version
NASB	New American Standard Bible
NIV	New International Version
NJB	New Jerusalem Bible
NLT	New Living Translation
REB	Revised English Bible
NRSV	New Revised Standard Version

Secondary Sources

ABD	*Anchor Bible Dictionary*
AnBib	Analecta biblica
ArBib	The Aramaic Bible
BHS	*Biblia Hebraica Stuttgartensia.* Edited by K. Elliger and W. Rudolph. Stuttgart, 1983
BN	*Biblische Notizen*
BZAW	Beihefte zur Zeitschrift für die alttestamentliche Wissenschaft
CAD	*The Assyrian Dictionary of the Oriental Institute of the University of Chicago.* Chicago, 1956–
CAL	Comprehensive Aramaic Lexicon project, Hebrew Union College, Cincinnati

CBQ	*Catholic Biblical Quarterly*
GNS	Good News Studies
HTR	*Harvard Theological Review*
ICC	International Critical Commentary
JBL	*Journal of Biblical Literature*
JBLMS	Journal of Biblical Literature Monograph Series
JSNTSup	Journal for the Study of the New Testament: Supplement Series
LCL	Loeb Classical Library
NIBCOT	New International Biblical Commentary on the Old Testament
NICNT	New International Commentary on the New Testament
RB	*Revue biblique*
SBL	Society of Biblical Literature
SNTSMS	Society for New Testament Studies Monograph Series
Str-B	Strack, H. L., and P. Billerbeck. *Kommentar zum Neuen Testament aus Talmud und Midrasch.* 6 vols. Munich, 1922–1961
TWNT	*Theologische Wörterbuch zum Neuen Testament.* Edited by G. Kittel and G. Friedrich. Stuttgart, 1932–1979
TWOT	*Theological Wordbook of the Old Testament.* Edited by R. L. Harris and G. L. Archer Jr. 2 vols. Chicago, 1980
WTJ	*Westminster Theological Journal*
WUNT	Wissenschaftliche Untersuchungen zum Neuen Testament
ZNW	*Zeitschrift für die neutestamentliche Wissenschaft und die Kunde der älteren Kirche*

1

Why John Calls Jesus "the Word"

Introduction

This book depends entirely on, and argues for, the view that John's decision to call Jesus "the Word," the Logos (ὁ λόγος), was influenced by the Targums, the Aramaic translations of the Hebrew Scriptures, many or most of which were prepared for recitation in the synagogue after the reading of the Hebrew text. In hundreds of cases in these Targums, where the MT refers to God, the corresponding Targum passage refers to the divine *Word*. Considered against this background, calling Jesus "the Word" is a way of identifying him with the God of Israel. This book also argues that understanding the Logos title as based on the Targums is crucial to understanding not only John's Prologue, but the body of the Gospel as well, for if we understand the Logos as a divine title, we can see that John's statements about the Word (the Word was with God, the Word was God, and the Word became flesh) presage themes throughout the Gospel.

My reader is probably more familiar with other explanations for the Logos title: (1) that it is based on "the word of the LORD" in the OT, through which God reveals himself and accomplishes his will in the world, just as he does through his Son in the NT, (2) that it is developed from the idea of Wisdom personified in the OT and in the intertestamental Wisdom literature, and (3) that it is adapted from the Greek philosophical concept of the Logos, especially as found in the writings of the Alexandrian Jew Philo. Each of these views is plausible, and each is described in the next section. A fourth view, Bultmann's gnostic hypothesis, is not considered plausible and will not be discussed here.[1]

Three Plausible Proposals

OT Word of the LORD

In the first view, the OT use of "the word of the LORD" (דְּבַר־יהוה) is considered sufficient to explain John's use of "the Word" for Christ. For instance, C. H.

---

[1] For a refutation of the gnostic view, see Craig A. Evans, *Word and Glory: On the Exegetical and Theological Background of John's Prologue* (JSNTSup 89; Sheffield: JSOT Press, 1993).

Dodd, though an advocate of the third view, nevertheless noted that there is "a very strong case to be made out, stronger than has sometimes been recognized, for the view that the Logos of the Prologue is the [OT] Word of the Lord."[2] Likewise, William Hendriksen wrote, "Already in the Old Testament the Word of God is represented as a Person," citing Ps 33:6, which can be related to John 1:1 ("by the word of the LORD the heavens were made").[3] In addition, Donald A. Carson suggested that John chose the title as fitting Christ's work of revelation, to which he was uniquely suited, being the only one to have been to heaven; he paraphrases John 1:1, "In the beginning God expressed himself." Carson contends that God's word is so important in the OT in creation, revelation, and deliverance; that John 1:1 ("In the beginning") alludes directly to Gen 1, where the phrase "and God said" is so prominent that this word is sometimes personified (e.g., Ps 107:20). All this makes "it suitable for John to apply [the Word] as a title to God's ultimate self-disclosure, the person of his own Son."[4]

Franklin W. Young pointed to Isa 55:10–11 as an attractive possibility for an OT background to Christ as God's Word, with a focus more on agency:

> As the rain and the snow *come down* from heaven, And do not return there without watering the earth, . . . and furnishing . . . *bread to the eater,* So shall *my word* be which *goes forth* from my mouth; It shall not *return to me* empty, without *accomplishing what I desire.*[5]

Young noted that one could view "my word" here as a description of Christ's work as described in John 6: he came down from heaven to do the Father's will (v. 38); he is the bread upon whom people must feed to have life (vv. 48, 50); and he will not return until he accomplishes the Father's will (v. 44). The LXX for "accomplish" in Isa 55:11 is a form of συντελέω, which Young compares to the Lord's final saying on the cross, "It is finished" (τετέλεσται; John 19:30).[6] The LXX of Isa 55:10 has ῥῆμα for "word," but λόγος could have been used just as well, and John does not necessarily use the LXX for his OT citations and allusions.[7]

Delbert Burkett gave further support for this view by relating John 7:34, "You will seek me but will not find me . . ." (similarly 8:21) to Amos 8:11–12, which

---

[2] C. H. Dodd, *The Interpretation of the Fourth Gospel* (Cambridge: Cambridge University Press, 1953), 273.

[3] William Hendriksen, *The Gospel of John* (Edinburgh: Banner of Truth Trust, 1954), 70.

[4] Donald A. Carson, *The Gospel according to John* (Grand Rapids: Eerdmans, 1991), 96, 115–16.

[5] Franklin W. Young, "A Study of the Relation of Isaiah to the Fourth Gospel," *ZNW* 46 (1955): 228.

[6] Ibid. Similarly, Delbert Burkett, *The Son of the Man in the Gospel of John* (JSNTSup 56; Sheffield: JSOT Press, 1991), 131–32.

[7] See Günter Reim, *Studien zum alttestamentlichen Hintergrund des Johannesevangeliums* (Cambridge: Cambridge University Press, 1974), 1–98, which studies OT quotations in John as designated by the author. In these quotations John does not necessarily follow the LXX, and it follows that the same would hold for allusions, as we will see in ch. 2. Consider, for example, "full of grace and truth" in John 1:14, which depends on a non-LXX rendition of Exod 34:6.

predicts a famine for hearing the words of the LORD: "They will wander from sea to sea . . . to seek the word of the LORD, but they will not find it."[8] This passage is especially striking in that the context indicates that the sign of the fulfillment of this judgment is that "I will make the sun go down at noon, and darken the earth in broad daylight" (Amos 8:9; cf. Matt 27:45; Mark 15:33; Luke 23:44). That John does not mention this darkening of the land does not necessarily count against this allusion if (as I assume) John's intended audience is already familiar with the synoptic tradition.

As impressive as Burkett's argument is, John 7:34 can also be used to furnish equally striking support for each of the other views to be discussed. Support for the notion that the Logos title is based on the OT "word of the LORD" can also be found in John 14:6, where Jesus calls himself "the truth" and later says that the Father's "word is truth" (17:17), echoing Ps 119:60, "the sum of your words is truth." Thus, "Jesus is the truth" implies "Jesus is the [OT] word."

Andreas J. Köstenberger offered four lines of support for the idea that the OT word of the LORD is preferable to either Wisdom or Philo's Logos as a basis for the Logos title:

> (1) the evangelist's deliberate effort to echo the opening words of the Hebrew Scriptures by the phrase "in the beginning"; (2) the reappearance of several significant terms from Gen 1 in John 1 ("light," "darkness," "life"); (3) the Prologue's OT allusions, be it to Israel's wilderness wanderings (1:14: "pitched his tent") or to the giving of the law (1:17–18); and (4) the evangelist's adaptation of Isa. 55:9–11 for his basic Christological framework.[9]

Wisdom in the Wisdom Literature

Interpreters have also made a reasonable case for the second view—that the idea of Wisdom as developed in Proverbs, Sirach, Baruch, and Wisdom of Solomon provides a possible background to John's Logos.[10] Thomas H. Tobin, though an advocate of the third view, summarized the connection to Wisdom as follows:

> Both the logos of the hymn in the Prologue [of John] and wisdom in Jewish wisdom literature are with God in the beginning; both are involved in the creation of the world; both seek to find a place among humankind; both are within a Jewish tradition of speculation about the deeper meanings of the early chapters of Genesis. In addition, many of the parallels between the logos in the hymn and the figure of wisdom are found in passages which like the hymn are poetic in character (Prov 8:22–31; Sir 24). The parallels are not simply conceptual but also stylistic.[11]

---

[8] Burkett, *Son of the Man in the Gospel of John,* 151.

[9] Andreas J. Köstenberger, *John* (Baker Exegetical Commentary on the New Testament; Grand Rapids: Baker, 2004), 27.

[10] This view was initially proposed by J. Rendel Harris, *The Origin of the Prologue to St. John's Gospel* (Cambridge: Cambridge University Press, 1917).

[11] Thomas H. Tobin, "Logos," *ABD* 4:354. Tobin made similar comments in an article "The Prologue of John and Hellenistic Jewish Speculation," *CBQ* 52 (1990): 252–69. As many

Especially of interest in connection with John 1:14 is Sirach's image of Wisdom as dwelling in a tent among men:

> I (Wisdom) dwelt in the highest heavens,
>   and my throne was in a pillar of cloud.
> Alone I compassed the vault of heaven
>   and traversed the depths of the abyss.
> Over waves of the sea, over all the earth,
>   and over every people and nation I have held sway.
> Among all these I sought a resting place;
>   in whose territory should I abide?
> "Then the Creator of all things gave me a command,
>   and my Creator chose the place for my tent.
> He said, 'Make your dwelling in Jacob,
>   and in Israel receive your inheritance.'" (Sir 24:4–8 NRSV)

"Dwelt" in v. 4 and "make your dwelling" in v. 8 are from κατασκηνόω, often used in the LXX to translate the Hebrew verb שָׁכַן, used for God's dwelling among his people. John 1:14 uses the similar verb σκηνόω. Likewise, "tent" in v. 8 is σκηνή, used in the LXX for the tabernacle. Similarities to John 1:14 are thus obvious. Of course, there is a major difference as well, since John says that all things were created through the Word, whereas in the wisdom passage, Wisdom is said to be "created" by "the Creator of all things."

Baruch 3:36–37 also is reminiscent of John 1:14: "(God) found the whole way to knowledge, and gave her to his servant Jacob and to Israel, whom he loved. Afterward she appeared on earth and lived [συναναστρέφω] with humankind" (NRSV).

The view that John's Word depends on Wisdom in the Wisdom Literature has much in common with the view that the Logos title depends on the OT word of God, since Wisdom is specifically equated with God's written word. Immediately following the quote just given about Wisdom living with humankind, we read of Wisdom, "She is the book of the commandments of God, the law that endures forever. All who hold her fast will live, and those who forsake her will die" (Bar 4:1 NRSV). Thus, Wisdom "appeared upon earth" as the Torah given to Israel.

In Proverbs the message of Wisdom is essentially the same as that of the Law and the Prophets: fear God, heed his commandments, and live. Craig Keener thinks that John combined the idea of Torah (OT word in its most complete sense) and Wisdom to present Jesus as Torah, because his life exhibited perfect obedience to (thus was a revelation of) the Torah.[12]

In terms of the close verbal parallels to John's Prologue, the Wisdom background can be seen as an improvement over the OT word background. There is

---

do, Tobin regards the sections of John's Prologue that mention the Logos as part of an originally independently circulating hymn to which some material was later added before it was incorporated in the Gospel.

[12]Craig S. Keener, *The Gospel of John: A Commentary* (2 vols.; Peabody, Mass.: Hendrickson, 2003), 360–63.

nothing as explicit as "and Wisdom became flesh," but Dodd notes that the fact that Wisdom is immanent among men "provides a kind of matrix in which the idea of incarnation might be shaped." In addition, he notes that the Wisdom literature comes closer to the proposition "the Word was God" because "the functions assigned to Wisdom are often clearly those which are elsewhere assigned to God Himself."[13] For example, while the passages quoted above speak of Wisdom dwelling among humankind (specifically, Israel), the OT speaks of the LORD himself dwelling among humankind.

Glory is an attribute of Wisdom, and Wisdom is associated with the glory of God (Wis 7:25; 9:11; Sir 14:27). Wisdom is also unique (Wis 7:22, using μονο-γενής as in John 1:14, 18), which leads Martin Scott to conclude, "Just as the glory of the unique Sophia is seen as she comes into the world, so too the glory of the unique Logos is seen as he comes among human beings as a human."[14] However, Wis 7:22 says that Wisdom has a *spirit* that is μονογενής, and there is no Wisdom text that uses phraseology anything like "the glory of the unique Wisdom is seen as she comes into the world."

Other texts in John could be used to support a personified Wisdom background to "the Word" in John. In 15:10, Jesus says, "If you keep my commandments, you will abide in my love." Because Jesus defines love for him as keeping his commandments (14:15, 21; 15:14), 15:10 could also be interpreted, "If you love me, you will abide in my love," agreeing with Prov 8:17, where Wisdom says, "I love those who love me, and those who diligently seek me shall find me." This last phrase could also be connected to John 7:34 ("You [the Jews] will seek me but will not find me"), the same verse Burkett connected to Amos 8:11–12 to support the OT word view (see above). John 7:34 could support the view that outside the Prologue, the Gospel of John depicts Jesus as Wisdom; they will not find him because they do not seek diligently. Proverbs 14:6 makes a similar point about wisdom, though the verb "find" is not actually used: "The scornful seeks wisdom, but there is none." With Jesus understood as Wisdom, this verse would imply that they do not find him because they are scoffers (cf. Luke 16:14, where the Pharisees are scoffing at him).

While the personified Wisdom interpretation might be preferable to the OT word interpretation, as it accords better with the statement "the Word was God," it has the disadvantage that John uses "Word," not "Wisdom." The switch to "word" is sometimes explained as due to the avoidance of the feminine gender of the word "wisdom" (both in Greek and Hebrew, not to mention Aramaic). Further, "word" is an appropriate substitute for "wisdom" on the grounds that either (1) personified Wisdom is the wisdom of the OT word or (2) Philo's Logos incorporates Wisdom and brings us closer to "the Word was God." This leads us to a discussion of the Logos in Philo.

---

[13] Dodd, *Fourth Gospel*, 275.

[14] Martin Scott, *Sophia and the Johannine Jesus* (JSNTSup 71; Sheffield: JSOT Press, 1992), 107.

The Logos in Philo

One of the most prominent advocates of the third view was C. H. Dodd, who wrote that "With Wisdom we are already half-way to Philo's Logos." Dodd argued for the following parallels between the Logos in Philo and John's Prologue:[15]

In the beginning was the Word.

"Before creation, God conceived in His mind the κόσμος νοητός [the world perceptible to the mind], which is His λόγος." This plan of the world is analogous to that of an architect before he builds a city. "Discerned only by the intellect," this plan can only be called "the Word of God" (*On the Creation of the World* 24).

The Word was with [πρὸς] God.

"God sent forth His younger son, the κόσμος αἰσθητός, but kept the elder, κόσμος νοητός = λόγος (see above), παρ' ἑαυτῷ (with him)." God decided that this older son "should remain in His own keeping" (*That God Is Unchangeable* 31).

The Word was God.

"The anarthrous θεός may be used of the λόγος while ὁ θεός is reserved for the Self-existent." Dodd cites *On Dreams* 1.229–30 where Philo is commenting on Gen 31:13, which in the LXX reads, "I am (the) God [ὁ θεός] who appeared to you (Jacob) in the place of God" (ἐν τόπῳ θεοῦ, without the definite article, for MT Bethel). What Moses calls "God" without the article is "His chief Word." Dodd could have cited this text also under "the Word was with God," since Philo is wondering why God does not say to Jacob "in my place," but rather "'in the place of God,' as though it were another's" (*On Dreams* 1.228). This apparent "other" is the Logos.

All things came into being through him.

In *On the Cherubim* 127 Philo says that God is the cause of the world coming into existence, while "its instrument (is) the word of God, through which it was framed."

In him was life.

Dodd did not find a direct parallel, but pointed to *On Flight and Finding* 97, where Philo interprets the command to flee to a city of refuge as a command to flee "to the supreme Divine Word, who is the fountain of Wisdom, in order that he may draw from the stream and, released from death, gain life eternal as his prize."

---

[15] Dodd, *Fourth Gospel*, 276–77. In what follows, the quoted summaries of Philo are from Dodd, and the quotes from Philo are from LCL (in these quotes "word" always stands for *logos*).

In *On the Posterity of Cain* 68–69, Philo says, "he that lives an irrational [ἀλόγως] life has been cut off from the life of God."

The Word is true light.

In *On Dreams* 1.75, Philo refers to God as light, and the highest model of light: "For the model or pattern was the Word which contained all His fullness—light, in fact." *On the Creation of the World* 33 speaks of the adversary relationship between light and darkness. In *On the Confusion of Tongues* 60–63, Philo calls the incorporeal light "the eldest son," elsewhere called "His first-born" which is also elsewhere called the Logos.

To those who received him, he gave the right to become children of God.

Philo notes that Moses calls the Israelites "sons of God" in Deut 14:1: "But if there be any as yet unfit to be called a Son of God, let him press to take his place under God's First-born, the Word" who is called by many names, such as "the Name of God, and His Word, and the Man after His image," so that at least "we may be sons of His invisible image, the most holy Word" (*On the Confusion of Tongues* 145–47).

No man has seen God at any time . . .

Commenting on Exod 24:10, which in the LXX reads, "they saw the place where the God of Israel stood" (cf. the MT: "they saw the God of Israel"), Philo says that those who choose Moses as their guide will see this place. It is natural to "desire to see the Existent if they may, but, if they cannot, to see at any rate his image, the most holy Word" (*On the Confusion of Tongues* 96–97).

Tobin has also advocated Philo's Logos over wisdom as the source of John's Logos title. He reasons that the fact that we find λόγος and not σοφία in John 1 shows that the author has moved beyond wisdom speculation to the kind of Logos speculation found in Philo, in which the "*logos* overshadows wisdom in importance," is "a reality which existed with God before creation," is described with "the anarthrous *theos* (God)" connected to "in the beginning" from Gen 1:1, was the instrument of creation, and is associated with light and with becoming children of God.[16]

Despite these parallels, Philo's Logos falls short in providing a complete explanation for the Logos of John 1, specifically, "the Word became flesh." Dodd maintains, however, that this sentiment is more understandable in Philo than in the Wisdom literature since in Philo the Logos is not a word but "creative reason," which in some sense is "immanent in man, as the equivalent of the divine, essential humanity."[17]

---

[16] Tobin, "Logos," 4:354. Tobin had already noted, however, that not just the λόγος in Philo, but wisdom in the wisdom speculation was light and was associated with life and with becoming children (actually, "friends") of God (ibid.).

[17] Dodd, *Fourth Gospel*, 281.

Dodd also explained why the word λόγος is not used in this Philonic sense in the Gospel itself: "It is only in the Prologue that the evangelist deals with cosmology." Even so, he maintained that the Logos theology pervaded the Gospel. As evidence, he noted: (1) "truth" as used in the Gospel is very close to λόγος in Philo; (2) the metaphysics of John is not unlike Philo (Jesus' use of ἀληθινός for true light, true bread, true vine); (3) the term "Son of Man" is best understood as true man (ἄνθρωπος ἀληθινός) or "the Idea of Man," identified in Philo with the Logos. Thus, "the substance of a Logos-doctrine similar to that of Philo is present all through the gospel."[18]

Returning to John 7:34, we have noted previously how this text ("You will seek me, but will not find me") can be related either to OT Word or to wisdom texts so as to provide striking support for either of the two previously discussed views. But if one was inclined to explain the Logos title as deriving from Philo, one can also find support for this view in John 7:34.

In *Questions and Answers on Genesis* 3.27, Philo explains the meaning of Gen 16:7 ("An angel of the Lord found her by a spring of water . . ."), in the course of which he says, "If the divine Logos is to be found, he seeks it"—"he" being "the soul that progresses" who is not "completely foolish." In *On Flight and Finding* 5, Philo identifies the angel of the LORD who found Hagar (Gen 21:17) as the divine Word [θεῖος λόγος].

In *On Flight and Finding* 120, Philo discusses the possible combinations of seeking and finding: (1) some neither seek nor find; (2) some both seek and find; (3) some seek but do not find; (4) some do not seek yet find. John 7:34 would put Jesus' hearers in the third category, but Philo's discussion of the second category is actually more pertinent to John's Gospel. In a discussion of the manna in the wilderness, Philo says that the Israelites' question concerning the manna (Exod 16:15, "What is it?") was an inquiry of those seeking to know about "What it is that nourishes the soul," adding that they "became learners and found it to be a saying of God [ῥῆμα θεοῦ], that is the Divine Word [καὶ λόγον θεῖον], from which all kinds of instruction and wisdom flow in perpetual stream" (*On Flight and Finding*, 137). Such a view of the manna as divine word could be seen as underlying John 6, where Jesus, called the divine Word in the Prologue, presents himself as the true manna (vv. 32ff.), after being both sought and found (vv. 24–25). In closing his discussion of seeking and finding, Philo quotes Moses from Deut 4:29, that if Israel seeks the LORD with all their soul, they will find him (*On Flight and Finding*, 142). Deuteronomy 4:29 assumes that Israel has been exiled for their sins, and promises restoration, which is of relevance to John if, as most interpreters believe, the Gospel is also written from a post-AD 70 perspective, so that Palestinian Jews have experienced a recent exile and would naturally hope for a restoration such as Deut 4:29 anticipates.

While Philo ascribes spiritual motives to the Israelites' seeking to know what the manna is, implying that this is why they found what they sought, Jesus says that his hearers seek him for baser motives: "You seek me, not because you saw

---

[18] Dodd, *Fourth Gospel*, 278–79.

miracles, but because you ate of the loaves, and were filled" (John 6:26). He goes on to direct their attention to spiritual nourishment and their need to feed upon him, the one whom John has called "the Word." Their rejection of this invitation means that they will fall not into Philo's second category but into his third: "You will seek me but will not find me."

Summary

In this chapter, we have reviewed the plausible arguments for three views of the source of John's Logos title. A wrong hypothesis will typically be harder to recognize as wrong, the closer it is to the correct one. It is easy to assume that data which is *consistent* with a particular hypothesis confirms that hypothesis and thereby to overlook the fact that the data might also be consistent with another hypothesis. We saw that John 7:34 could be interpreted to support any of these three views, which diminishes its value in supporting any one of them in particular. Further, John 7:34 can just as plausibly be interpreted as consistent with a Targum derivation of the Logos title. I make the case for such an understanding in ch. 8, but at this point I will simply mention that the Targum view takes "the Word" as a divine title denoting the name of God. Consequently, one may, for example, relate John 7:34 directly to Deut 4:29 (the passage mentioned by Philo, and noted above, which promises that if Israel seeks the LORD with all their heart, they will find him) or Isa 55:6 ("Seek the LORD while he may be found"), two passages that imply the possibility of seeking God but not finding him.

Methodologically, when faced with multiple possible interpretations, one must identify the one that best explains all the data. When there are competing views, it is necessary to explain why one's favored view is better than the others. As we have seen, Dodd did so when advocating Philo's Logos, except that he did not consider the "Word" language of the Targums, even though (as we shall see) he acknowledged that the targumic Word was conceptually similar to Philo's Logos. Often interpreters completely overlook the Targum view. We will address the arguments of those who do consider this view in ch. 12, when we will be in a better position to critique them.

A PRELIMINARY CASE FOR DERIVING THE LOGOS TITLE FROM THE TARGUMS

What Are the Targums?

"Targum" is a Hebrew word (also used in Aramaic) meaning "translation," and it is used especially for Aramaic translations of the Hebrew Scriptures that were read in the synagogues on the Sabbath and on feast or fast days. Scholars usually assume that the practice of translation was necessitated by the loss of Hebrew fluency by Jews growing up in exile. Nehemiah 8:7–8 says that after Ezra's reading of the law, the Levites explained the law to the people: "They read from the book, from the law of God, translating [or explaining] to give the sense so that they understood the reading" (v. 8 NASB). Other versions say not that they translated, but that they made clear, or read clearly or distinctly.[19] In any case, the NASB translation of Neh 8:8 seems to be a good summary of the goal of the Targums. Translations developed over time, and at some point began to be written down, though in the synagogue they were recited, not read, so as not to be put at the same level as the Hebrew Scriptures. The written Targums were subject to modification from one generation to another, while the Hebrew Scriptures were preserved as they were received. All of the extant Targums seem to date from the second century C.E. and later, yet a number of the translations would preserve readings that were current in the first century, as is evident from various passages from the NT itself.[20] For the Targums of individual books or sets of books described below, the relevant volumes of The Aramaic Bible provide suitable introductions with bibliographies (Collegeville, Minn., Liturgical Press; Edinburgh, T&T Clark). This ongoing project, started in 1987, aims to provide English translations for all the Targums.

Targums Jonathan and Onqelos

Targum Jonathan (*Tg. Jon.*) covers the Former and Latter Prophets (Joshua, Judges, Samuel, Kings, Isaiah, Jeremiah, Ezekiel, and the minor prophets). Tradition ascribed this Targum to Jonathan ben Uzziel, who lived in the first century C.E., although it is more likely a product of many hands and continued to be modified into the fourth century. *Targum Onqelos* (*Tg. Onq.*) covers the Pentateuch and, like *Jonathan*, probably has many authors. *Onqelos* and *Jonathan* are considered "official" Targums in the sense that they are supposed to represent rabbinic Judaism after C.E. 70. They apparently originated in Palestinian Judaism, but their latest editions were done in Babylon.

The Palestinian Targums of the Pentateuch[21]

Targums considered "Palestinian" (*Pal. Tgs.*) are *Neofiti 1* (*Tg. Neof.*), *Pseudo-Jonathan* (*Tg. Ps.-J.*), and the *Fragmentary Targums* (*Frg. Tgs.*). In the case of *Tg. Ps.-J.*, both "Palestinian" and "Targum" need qualification. Michael Maher suggests that *Ps.-J.*, though based on a Targum, is not a proper "Targum" in that (1)

---

[19] The Hebrew is מְפֹרָשׁ (*pual*), "to be made distinct."

[20] See, e.g., J. T. Forestell, *Targumic Traditions and the New Testament: An Annotated Bibliography with a New Testament Index* (SBL Aramaic Studies 4; Chico, Calif.: Scholars Press, 1979).

[21] For introductory material for *Tg. Neof.*, see Martin McNamara, *Targum Neofiti 1: Genesis* (ArBib 1A; Collegeville, Minn.: Liturgical Press, 1992), ix–50, 231–49; also see Alejandro Díez Macho, *Neophyti 1: Targum Palestinense* MS de la Biblioteca Vaticana (5 vols.; Madrid: Consejo Superior de Investigaciones Científicas, 1968, 1970, 1971, 1974, 1978), for the Aramaic text of *Tg. Neof.*, various introductory studies, and Spanish (Díez Macho), French (Roger Le Déaut), and English (Martin McNamara and Michael Maher) translations. For *Tg. Ps.-J.*, see Michael Maher, *Targum Pseudo-Jonathan: Genesis* (ArBib 1B; Collegeville, Minn.: Liturgical Press, 1992), 9–14, 167–85.

it shows signs of being a scholarly work meant to be read and studied in private by other scholars rather than recited publicly in the synagogue as a translation of the Hebrew Scriptures; and (2) it approaches the genre "rewritten Bible" because of the extensive embellishments which have little or nothing to do with translating the relevant Hebrew text. "Palestinian" is also problematic because that term is supposed to distinguish these Targums from the "official" Targum of the Pentateuch, namely, *Tg. Onq.* Yet it is clear that in a great many cases *Tg. Ps.-J.* agrees with *Tg. Onq.* against the *Pal. Tgs.*[22] This fact underscores the importance of the discovery of *Tg. Neof.* sixty years ago; until then we did not have "Palestinian" renderings of a great number of passages in the Pentateuch.

The name *Pseudo-Jonathan* came about due to the fact that at one time (e.g., J. W. Etheridge's nineteenth-century translation) the author was considered to be the same Jonathan who was thought to have authored *Tg. Jon.*, the Targum of the Prophets. This conclusion seems to have resulted from mistaking the initials TJ (תי), likely meaning "*Targum Jerusalem*," for "*Targum Jonathan*." When the mistake was realized, the text then became known as *Targum Pseudo-Jonathan*. Of course, as noted above, Jonathan did not write the Targum of the Prophets, either, but the Targum of the Prophets is not called *Pseudo-Jonathan*.

The *Frg. Tgs.* are not fragments of manuscripts of complete Targums but rather portions of Palestinian Targums of the Pentateuch that were selected and copied out according to some unknown principle. The two major types are called P (after the Paris MS 110) and V (after MSS from the Vatican, Nürnberg, and Leipzig).[23] In this book, *Frg. Tg. V* indicates a reading found in one or more of the MSS of this type.

Targum Neofiti, thought to be a copy of a Targum from about the fourth century, is therefore the only complete Palestinian Targum of the Pentateuch. Actually, as Martin McNamara notes, because of the extensive marginal and interlinear glosses (*Tg. Neof.* [mg.] / [int.]), it is a witness also to three other types of Palestinian Targums.[24] *Neofiti* glosses tend to agree with the *Frg. Tgs.* (where extant) more closely than does the body of the text. *Neofiti* was discovered in the Vatican library in 1949, about the same time as the Dead Sea scrolls were discovered in the caves of Judea. It had been overlooked for some time because it was considered to be just another copy of *Tg. Onq. Neofiti*, so called because it was produced by a college for Jewish converts to Catholicism (thus neophytes).

Fragments of Targum manuscripts from the famous Cairo Synagogue Genizah (*CTgs.*), not to be confused with the *Frg. Tgs.*, often agree with one or more of the Palestinian Targum readings.[25] McNamara's volumes on *Tg. Neof.* in The Aramaic Bible series include readings of interest from these fragments.

---

[22] Maher, *Pseudo-Jonathan: Genesis,* 1–8.

[23] See Michael L. Klein, *The Fragment-Targums of the Pentateuch according to Their Extant Sources* (2 vols.; AnBib 76; Rome: Biblical Institute Press, 1980), 1:12–42.

[24] McNamara, *Neofiti 1: Genesis,* 15.

[25] These fragments are published in Michael L. Klein, *Genizah Manuscripts of Palestinian Targum to the Pentateuch* (2 vols.; Cincinnati: Hebrew Union College, 1986).

Besides having odd-sounding names, the Palestinian Targums are character-ized by more paraphrase and inclusion of legendary material than *Tg. Onq.* They also tend to be of more significance for NT studies, including (as we shall see) the concept of the divine Word.

Other Targums

Targums of the other OT books, with the exception of Ezra-Nehemiah and Daniel (originally written partly in Aramaic), also exist and are relevant for our study. The *Tosefta Targum of the Prophets* (*Tos. Tg.*) consists of Targums of in-dividual verses in the Prophets which have a more "Palestinian" character than *Tg. Jon.* and may be witnesses to a now (mostly) lost Palestinian Targum of the Prophets.[26]

> There is some evidence that there may once have been a Palestinian Targum to the Prophets that contained large units of material added into the translation. The evi-dence is that some manuscripts of the known Targum to the Prophets preserve such additional material in their margins. Similarly, medieval scholars such as Rashi and Kimḥi cite prophetic traditions in Aramaic designated as Targum Yerushalmi (i.e., Palestinian Targum) as do some manuscripts such as Codex Reuchlinianus. The best explanation for this material is that they once belonged to a complete Palestinian Tar-gum to the Prophets, but during the early middle ages when the more literal Jonathan Targum to the Prophets became the dominant targum in the West, the aggadic ma-terial was extracted to preserve it alongside the newly authoritative translation, while the Palestinian Targum itself was lost.[27]

The Aramaic texts of the Targums are available online, through the "Compre-hensive Aramaic Lexicon" project (CAL) of the Hebrew Union College in Cincin-nati. The texts are displayed a verse or chapter at a time, with some morphological information. Online dictionaries and concordance searches are also available on the website.[28] Etheridge's nineteenth-century English translations of *Tg. Onq., Tg.*

---

[26] Rimon Kasher published 150 such texts in *Toseftot Targum to the Prophets* [Hebrew; תוספתות תרגום לנביאים] (Sources for the Study of Jewish Culture 2; Jerusalem: World Union of Jewish Studies, 1996).

[27] Paul V. M. Flesher, ed., "Palestinian Targum to the Prophets," in *Dictionary of Ju-daism in the Biblical Period: 450 B.C.E. to 600 C.E.* (ed. Jacob Neusner and William Scott Green; 2 vols.; New York: Simon & Schuster Macmillan, 1996), 2:467. Articles in this dic-tionary are unsigned, but p. ix indicates that Flesher was responsible for editing articles on the Targums.

[28] Online: http://call.cn.huc.edu/; accessed June 30, 2009. Users of the CAL text should be aware that marginal readings in *Tg. Neof.* that only indicate the addition of *Memra* are not indicated in that text (or in programs such as BibleWorks that use this text). Therefore some of the marginal readings in *Tg. Neof.* noted in this book will not be found in the CAL text. The CAL texts were produced independently and thus may differ on occasion from published texts. *BibleWorks 7* has the Aramaic texts of the Targums, although version 6 omitted the *Pal. Tgs.* of the Pentateuch. *Accordance 8* has the Aramaic texts and is in the process of producing English translations. *Logos Bible Software* has a Targum module based on the CAL material, including the *Pal. Tgs.*, for use in the Libronix Digital Library System. Public domain English translations of *Tg. Song* (Adam Clarke) and *Tg. Isa.* (C. W. H. Pauli)

Ps.-J., and *Frg. Tg. V* (labeled "Jerusalem"),[29] along with recent English translations of the Targums of Psalms, Lamentations, Ruth, and Song of Songs, are available online through "The Newsletter for Targumic and Cognate Studies."[30]

The Divine Word in the Targums

In the Targums, the divine Word is usually indicated by a form of the Aramaic word מֵימְרָא (*Memra*), which, when so used, is not a translation of anything in the Hebrew text; rather, the phrase "the Word of the LORD," is often a circumlocution, or substitute, for the Tetragrammaton (the "four letters," יהוה, or YHWH), the pre-eminent OT name for God.[31] "The Word of the LORD" is actually more than a circumlocution, since "Lord" by itself was already in use as a substitute for the divine name, as is clear from a comparison of the MT and the LXX. In recitation of the Targums, when the Hebrew *'Adonay* was used, rather than another Hebrew word meaning "Lord," the hearers would know that the Tetragrammaton was meant.[32]

"*Memra*" is the emphatic (definite) form of מֵימַר (*memar*), from the root אמר. Aramaic *memar* may be used simply as a translation of a Hebrew word for "word" (usually the etymologically related אֵמֶר or אִמְרָה). When the word is used as a circumlocution for the divine name, it is of particular interest with relation to the Logos title. When so used, in English translations of the Targums it is often transliterated consistently as *Memra*, even though the underlying Aramaic spelling changes depending on whether or not the word is emphatic or has pronominal suffixes.

Another important word used in "the Word of the LORD" as a way of rendering MT "the LORD" is דִּבֵּרָא (*Dibbera*), also spelled דִּבּוּרָא (*Dibbura*). This word is

---

have been compiled and made available as user databases for *BibleWorks* by Jay Palmer: see http://bibleworks.oldinthenew.org/?cat=37 (Accessed: July 21, 2009).

[29] J. W. Etheridge, *The Targums of Onkelos and Jonathan Ben Uzziel on the Pentateuch, with Fragments of the Jerusalem Targum from the Chaldee* (2 vols.; London: Longman, Green, Longman, 1862, 1865; repr., 2 vols. in 1, New York: Ktav, 1968).

[30] Online: http://targum.info/; accessed June 30, 2009. The site has links to various English translations of Targums; these include Etheridge, *Targums of Onkelos and Jonathan Ben Uzziel;* Edward M. Cook, "The Psalms Targum: An English Translation" (2001); Christian M. M. Brady, "Targum Lamentations" (print ed.: *The Rabbinic Targum of Lamentations: Vindicating God* [Studies in the Aramaic Interpretation of Scripture 3; Leiden: Brill, 2003]); Samson H. Levey, "Targum to Ruth" (1998); and Jay C. Treat, "The Aramaic Targum to Song of Songs" (2001).

[31] In English translations of the Hebrew Bible, the Tetragrammaton is traditionally rendered LORD, with capital letters indicating the name of God as opposed to the Hebrew word *Adonai,* "Lord." In the Targums the Tetragrammaton is represented in various ways besides יהוה, such as ה, יוי, יי or ייי. The י seems to be used as a syllable place holder, such that ייי represents the 3 syllables of Hebrew *Adonay,* יי represents the 2 written vowels of the Tetragrammaton as it is usually found in MT, while the ו in יוי indicates the long ō vowel of *Adonay.* ה would represent the Hebrew definite article and be an abbreviation for "the Name."

[32] Aramaic רִבּוֹן is used for human masters in the Targums but sometimes also for God (e.g. *Tg. Neof.* Exod 23:17). "Marana-tha" ("Lord come!") in 1 Cor 16:22 is based on another Aramaic word, מָר, or מָרֵי, also found in the Targums occasionally for God, e.g. *Tg. Ps.* 35:23.

used primarily in the *Pal. Tgs.* of the Pentateuch and appears infrequently compared to מֵימְרָא. Yet, among its relatively few uses are several that give key support to the view that the Logos title in John does in fact depend on the Word of the LORD terminology from the Targums. *Dibbera/Dibbura* is generally overlooked by those considering the Targums as possible background for the Logos title, though its use was noted as long ago as the nineteenth century by Ferdinand Weber and B. F. Westcott.[33]

To some extent, *Memra* and *Dibbera* are used interchangeably, as can be seen from several examples: (1) Gen 3:8 says that Adam and Eve heard the sound of the LORD God walking about in the garden; in v. 10 Adam says, "I heard the sound of you." In *Pal. Tgs.* Gen 3:8, 10, Adam and Eve hear the sound/voice of "the Word of the LORD" strolling about in the garden. Both *Memra* (*Tgs. Neof.* and *Ps.-J.* Gen 3:8, 10; *Frg. Tg. P* Gen 3:8) and *Dibbera* (*Tg. Neof.* [mg.] and *Frg. Tg. P* Gen 3:10) are used. (2) In giving instructions for the building of the ark of the covenant, the LORD says, "there I will meet with you, and from above the mercy seat, from between the two cherubim that are on the ark of the testimony, I will speak with you about all that I will command you concerning the sons of Israel" (Exod 25:22). In place of "I will meet you," *Tg. Neof.*, *Tg. Ps.-J.*, and *Tg. Onq.* all read "I will appoint my *Memra*."[34] In reporting the fulfillment of this purpose in Num 7:89, *Tgs. Neof.* and *Ps.-J.* say that from above the mercy seat, between the two cherubim, the *Dibbera* used to speak to Moses. Also, in Num 17:[4] God describes the place before the ark as the place where he meets with Moses, and again *Tg. Neof.*, *Tg. Ps.-J.*, and *Tg. Onq.* say that his *Memra* meets Moses there. (3) Leviticus 1:1 says, "The LORD called to Moses and spoke to him." The *Tg. Ps.-J.* Lev 1:1 says the *Dibbera* of the LORD called to him and the *Memra* of the LORD spoke to him. *Targum Neofiti* and *Frg. Tg. V* also use *Dibbera* as subject of the verb "call," and both of the *Frg. Tg.* traditions use *Memra* as subject of the verb "spoke." When "Word" (capitalized) appears in Targum passages in this book, *Memra* is meant, unless otherwise indicated (e.g. by adding *Dibbera/Dibbura* in brackets).

But despite the overlap between the two terms, *Dibbera* is used in a more specialized sense than *Memra*. Etan Levine notes that *Memra* is used for more or less the full range of God's activities in the world; *Memra* "conveys the *being* and *doing* of YHWH, across the entire spectrum."[35] Samson H. Levey notes the *Memra* "is

---

[33] Ferdinand Weber, *System der Altsynagogalen palästinischen Theologie aus Targum, Midrasch, und Talmud* (1880); repr. in *Jüdische Theologie auf Grund des Talmud und verwandter Schrifen* (ed. Franz Delitzsch and Georg Schnedermann; 2d ed.; Leipzig: Dörfling & Francke, 1897), 180, cited in Robert Hayward, *Divine Name and Presence: The Memra* (Totowa, N.J.: Allenheld, Osmun, 1981), 2, 11 n. 5; B. F. Westcott, *The Gospel according to St. John: With Introduction and Notes* (1880; repr., London: James Clarke & Co., 1958), xvi. Westcott noted that in *Tg. Onq.* "the action of God is constantly though not consistently referred to 'His Word.' . . . It may be noticed that the term *Debura* (רבורא) occurs in this sense as well as *Memra*" (ibid.).

[34] Evans noted the association of the *Memra* with the tabernacle in *Tg. Neof.* Exod 25:22; 29:43; 30:6, 36 (*Word and Glory*, 118).

[35] Etan Levine, *The Aramaic Version of the Bible: Contents and Context* (BZAW 174; Berlin: de Gruyter, 1988), 59–60.

everything that God is supposed to be, and its manifold activity encompasses the entire spectrum of divine endeavor," but "the *Dibbur* is the divine word, limited to speech, articulation, proclamation."[36]

Since *Dibbera* by itself means divine speech, it is not necessary to say "the *Dibbera* of LORD." Thus, in Num 7:89, cited above, the *Pal. Tgs.* say, "From there the *Dibbera* (*not* the *Dibbera* of the LORD) used to speak with (Moses)." This is potentially significant since in the Prologue John calls Jesus "the Word," not "the Word of the Lord" or "the Word of God" (although this term is used for Jesus in Rev 19:13). George Foot Moore argued against the idea of relating *Memra* to John's Logos because

> *memra* does not occur without a genitive—"the word of the Lord," "my word," etc., or a circumlocution for the genitive, "a *memar* from before the LORD." "The *Memra*," "the Word," is not found in the Targums, notwithstanding all that is written about it by authors who have not read them.[37]

However, John called Jesus "the Word" based on both *Memra* and *Dibbera*, this objection loses its force. As shown below, several passages in John 1 seem to be illumined by passages in the *Pal. Tgs.* of the Pentateuch, where Jesus in the NT corresponds to the *Dibbera*, "the Word," of the Targums.

In its "common" meaning, דִּבֵּר is used for the Ten Commandments, which are the ten "words" in Hebrew, rendered in the LXX with both λόγοι (Exod 34:28; Deut 10:4) and ῥήματα (Deut 4:13). *Targum Pseudo-Jonathan* Deut 4:12–13 illustrates the two usages: "You heard the voice of the Word [דבורא] . . . And he declared to you his covenant, . . . the ten words [דבוריא]."[38] *Dibbera* is also not used in pronominal expressions such as "my Word." דִּבֵּיר is also found once as a biblical Hebrew word, if the pointing is correct, where again it has the connotation of divine speech: "The word [הַדִּבֵּר] is not in them (the false prophets)" (Jer 5:13).

An objection to examining targumic passages containing *Dibbera* with passages in John could be made on the basis that "*Dibbura* is usually held to be a late and secondary insertion within the Targumic versions."[39] Against this view I would draw attention to the use of *Dibbura* in *Tg. Ezek.* 1:25. Levey notes how *Tg. Ezek.* (part of *Tg. Jon.* of the Prophets) avoids use of the term "Messiah," despite a

---

[36] Samson H. Levey, *The Targum of Ezekiel* (ArBib 13; Collegeville, Minn.: Liturgical Press, 1987), 15.

[37] George Foot Moore, "Intermediaries in Jewish Theology: *Memra, Shekinah*, Metatron," *HTR* 15 (1922): 61 n.24.

[38] Cf. Ernest G. Clarke, *Targum Pseudo-Jonathan: Deuteronomy* (ArBib 5B; Collegeville, Minn.: Liturgical Press, 1998), 18, where v. 13 is mistakenly rendered "the ten *Memras*."

[39] Andrew Chester, *Divine Revelation and Divine Titles in the Pentateuchal Targumim* (Texte und Studien zum antiken Judentum 14; Tübingen: J. C. B. Mohr [Paul Siebeck], 1986), 115. Chester cites in agreement Paul Billerbeck (Str-B 2:316–19), Vinzenz Hamp (*Der Begriff "Wort" in den aramäischen Bibelübersetzungen. Ein exegetischer Beitrag zum Hypostasen-Frage und zur Geschichte der Logos-Spekulationen* [Munich: Neuer Fiber-Verlag, 1938], 93–97), and Domingo Muñoz-León (*Dios–Palabra. Memrá en los Targumim del Pentateuco* [Granada, 1974], 668–79). In Klein's opinion, "Muñoz León's argument for the lateness of *dibbereh* relative to *memra* is not convincing" (*Genizah Manuscripts*, 2:70).

number of opportunities to use it, and where one might expect it to be used. For example, in *Tg. Ezek.* 34:23–24; 37:24–25, "my servant David" is translated literally, whereas "David their king" in Jer 30:9 and Hos 3:5 is rendered "the Messiah, son of David, their king" in *Tg. Jon.* In Levey's view, "Merkabah Mysticism" is substituted for "Messianic activism" in *Tg. Ezek.* in order to avoid Roman persecution of Jewish nationalism. Levey ascribes this substitution to the work of Rabbi Johanan ben Zakkai.[40] The Merkabah is the divine chariot seen by Ezekiel, and it is in this context that *Dibbura* is used (the angels' wings were silent before the Word).

Since the term *Dibbura* is used only here in all of *Tg. Jon.* of the Former and Latter Prophets, it would seem reasonable to ascribe the unique use of *Dibbura* in *Tg. Ezek.* 1 also to Johanan ben Zakkai. But Johanan ben Zakkai was a contemporary of Johanan ben Zebadiah, better known as John son of Zebedee, the traditional author of the Gospel named for him. It could be, then, that *Tg. Ezek.* preserves an early usage of *Dibbura* which does not appear elsewhere in *Tg. Jon.*, and that the use of *Dibbura/Dibbera* in the *Pal. Tgs.* of the Pentateuch dates at least as far back as the first century.

For an example of *Memra* being used in the Targums where the MT refers to God, apparently to guard the transcendence of God, consider Exod 34:5. The MT reads, "The LORD came down in the cloud," whereas a marginal gloss of *Tg. Neof.* for this passage reads, "The Word of the LORD was revealed." Two devices safeguard the transcendence of God here: (1) changing the anthropomorphic "came down" to "was revealed"; (2) changing "the LORD" to "the Word of the LORD."

Anthropomorphic references to God's hand, arm, etc., were also frequently changed to "Word" in targumic translations. For instance, in the MT of Exod 33:22, God says to Moses, "I will cover you with my hand," while *Tg. Onq.* reads, "I will shield you with my Word." Such a practice could be considered an extension of the substitution of "command" for "mouth," as in *Tgs. Onq.* and *Ps.-J.* Exod 17:1, where Israel journeyed "according to the word of the LORD" (MT, "according to the mouth of the LORD"). A substitution like this may be done for the sake of idiom, not simply to remove the anthropomorphism. In such cases, *Memra* in the Targums could be understood literally as God's word, that is, command. The Word may also be used for anthropopathisms, as in *Tg. Isa.* 63:5, "By the Word of my pleasure I helped them" (MT: "my wrath sustained me").

There is some dispute about whether the Targums have avoidance of anthropomorphisms as a goal, not only because the Targums do not consistently avoid anthropomorphisms, but also because some language that has been interpreted as anti-anthropomorphic is also used of kings or people in general, meaning we may be dealing with language of respect or idiomatic renderings.[41] Still, as Andrew Chester says, "the Pentateuchal Targumim change a very great number of

---

[40] Levey, *Targum of Ezekiel*, 4.

[41] See e.g., Michael L. Klein, "The Translation of Anthropomorphisms and Anthropopathisms in the Targumim," Vetus Testamentum Supplements 32 (1979): 162–77; and "The Preposition *qdm* ('before'), a Pseudo-anti-anthropomorphism in the Targum," *Journal of Theological Studies* 30 (1979): 502–7.

expressions which bear directly upon the understanding of God, and a substantial number of which in Old Testament scholarship are generally labeled 'anthropomorphisms.'"[42] The targumists may not have been concerned so much with avoiding anthropomorphisms *per se* as with avoiding wrong impressions about God on the part of the synagogue hearers. Thus anthropomorphisms which would not mislead ordinary people could be translated literally. "The main point is their concern for the most appropriate way to speak of God in the synagogue setting."[43] Similarly, Robert Hayward notes that some anthropomorphisms remain in the Targums, but the targumist "can act quite drastically" when "anthropomorphic language of the Bible might lead to misconceptions about God," citing the example of *Tg. Jer.* 14:8–9, where Jeremiah's question to God, "Why are you like a stranger in the land . . . like a mighty man who cannot save?" is changed so that the inhabitants of Judah are strangers in the land, whom God is able to save.[44]

As for the transcendence of God, McNamara explains the "extremely frequent use" of "the Word of the LORD" to refer to God as due to "the religious mentality which produced the Targums [which] shrank from speaking of God as acting directly in the world and spoke instead of his *Memra* doing so."[45] This aspect of the targumic Word is conceptually similar to Philo's Logos. Similarly, J. Stanley McIvor writes, "The Targumist ensures that God is God and remains 'high and lifted up'"; he achieves this purpose through various means, such as "by removing God from the scene of direct action or direct contact with human beings" and "by rephrasing many expressions which might suggest that there was something human about God."[46] In Isa 57:15, the one who is "high and lifted up" says, "I dwell in a high and holy place, *yet also with the contrite and lowly of spirit.*" That is, he is both transcendent and imminent. But in the Targum, he is "high and lifted up"—period:

> For thus says the high and lofty One who *dwells in the heavens,* whose name is Holy; *in the height he dwells,* and *his Shekhinah is* holy. *He promises to deliver the broken in heart* and the humble of spirit, to *establish* the spirit of the humble, and to *help* the heart of the *broken.*[47]

At the same time, the nearness of God is rendered literally throughout some Targums, such as *Tg. Onq.* and *Tg. Ps.*

---

[42] Chester, *Divine Revelation,* 298. See all of Chester's ch. 6 for a discussion of various views on how anthropomorphisms were dealt with in the Targums, and why.

[43] Ibid., 383.

[44] Robert Hayward, *Targum Jeremiah* (ArBib 12; Collegeville, Minn.: Liturgical Press, 1987), 22–23.

[45] Martin McNamara, "*Logos* of the Fourth Gospel and *Memra* of the Palestinian Targum (Ex 12[42])," *Expository Times* 79 (1968): 115. Attributing God's actions to his Word was just one of many stratagems employed by the targumists to this end.

[46] *The Targum of Chronicles* and *The Targum of Ruth* (trans. J. Stanley McIvor (Chronicles) and D. R. G. Beattie (Ruth); ArBib 19; Collegeville, Minn.: Liturgical Press, 1994), 24–26. The second and third quotes given here are italicized in the original.

[47] Bruce D. Chilton, *The Isaiah Targum* (ArBib 11; Wilmington, Del.: Michael Glazier, 1987), 111. Italic font in The Aramaic Bible series indicates differences in meaning from (and additions to) the MT.

The targumic Word is frequently employed in passages that speak of God's interaction with his creation, including humankind (especially his people), a fact consistent with the view that such usage is meant to guard the transcendence of God. In such passages, what the MT ascribes to God the Targums often ascribe to his Word. Above, we noted Levey's description of the targumic Word: "It is everything that God is supposed to be, and its manifold activity encompasses the entire spectrum of divine endeavor."[48] Levey was not promoting any connection between the Logos of John and the targumic Word, but what he said agrees closely with what John says about the Word. "It is everything that God is supposed to be" agrees with "the Word was God" (John 1:1), or as REB translates it, "What God was, the Word was." As for the divine Word encompassing "the entire spectrum of divine endeavor," we see in John's Gospel that the Son's activities encompass the entire spectrum of divine activity in the OT. John says explicitly that creation was accomplished through the Son (1:3), but in addition John shows us that the redemption of Israel from Egypt was accomplished through the Son who came down from heaven, the law was given through the Son, Israel was led through the wilderness by the Son, as his bride, and Israel had life by believing in the Son (as shown in chs. four through eight below). The Targums employ Word in describing the works of God in all these categories.

Of course, it would be going too far to say that since the divine Word "is everything that God is supposed to be," therefore "the Son is everything that the Father is supposed to be." The Son is not the Father; the Son is in relationship to the Father, a relationship of love, trust, dependence, and submission. This relationship between the Father and the Son is not the same as that between God and his Word in the Targums, where reference to the divine Word is simply a way of speaking of God himself under certain circumstances, and sometimes "my Word" in the Targums is equivalent to "myself" in the MT.[49] In many contexts, one could view the divine Word as a projection of the transcendent God into his creation. But the Son in John and the Word in the Targums share the same relationship with God in the fact that they both speak the words of God, interact with his people, and accomplish his will in the world.

The divine Word is also associated with the divine name. The targumic paraphrase "the Word of the LORD" for YHWH in the MT is sometimes further developed as "the name of the Word of the LORD," as we can see for example in various renderings of Gen 15:6:

---

[48] Levey, *Targum of Ezekiel*, 15. Levey also said that the targumic Word was used for "safeguarding divine dignity, shielding the deity from unseemly expressions and mundane matters" (ibid.).

[49] For MT "by myself I have sworn," *Tgs. Onq.* and *Ps.-J.* Gen 22:16 and *Tg. Isa.* 45:23; *Tg. Jer.* 22:5; 49:13 have "by my Word I have sworn." In Deut 18:19, God says, "I myself will require it of him"; *Tg. Ps.-J.* says, "my Word will require it"; *Tg. Neof.* says, "I, in my Word, will require it." In Isa 44:24 God says that he is "the one who stretches out the heavens by myself"; *Tg. Isa.* has "by my Word," with obvious relevance to John 1:1. Similarly, in 1 Sam 2:35, God says he will raise up a faithful priest "who will act according to what is in my heart and soul." *Tg. 1 Sam.* has, "who will act according to my Word and according to my pleasure."

MT	Tg. Onq.	Tg. Ps.-J.	Tg. Neof.
Abram believed in the LORD.	He believed in the Word of the LORD.	He had faith in the Word of the LORD.	Abram believed in the name of the Word of the LORD.

Faith in Jesus, or faith in his name, is a key issue in John's Gospel, analogous to faith in the divine Word, or the name of the divine Word, in the Targums. This will be explored in more detail in ch. 8.

A close association between the divine Word and the divine name is also seen in *Tg. Isa.* 48:11. In the MT, God says, "For my own sake, for my own sake I will act." In the Targum, this becomes, "For the sake of my name, for the sake of my Word." Similarly, *Tg. Neof.* Num 6:27 says, "so shall they put my name, my Word, upon the sons of Israel." The association of the divine Word with the name of God is also of interest for John's Gospel, which expresses the theme that the Father's name (i.e., the Tetragrammaton, YHWH) is given to the Son and that the Son's mission is to make known or manifest the Father's name to his people (John 17:6, 11–12, 26). Similarly, John 1:18 says that while no man has seen God (the Father), the Son has explained him. "Explained" is the Greek word from which comes our word "exegesis" (ἐξηγέομαι). In light of this, it is interesting to note what Chester wrote of the targumic Word and glory of the *Shekinah* as used in the Targums of the Pentateuch: "In a sense, both these terms are used as an *exegesis* of the divine names, especially the tetragrammaton."[50]

It is my contention that understanding the Logos title of the Gospel of John is based on targumic "Word" best fits the OT background to John 1:14 and its context, can also explain at least in part the evidence put forth for the other views, and leads to the recognition of a close connection between John's Prologue and the body of his Gospel. That is, John's Gospel as a whole can be seen as showing us what it meant by the statement that "the Word [that is, YHWH the Son] became flesh and dwelt among us, and we beheld his glory." We will see that the so-called *Pal. Tgs.* to the Pentateuch are of greatest interest with respect to this subject.

Evidence from John 1

In this section, we look at various passages from John 1 that can be understood to support the view that the Logos title is based on the divine Word of the Targums. Since we are looking only at ch. 1, the case will be made only in a preliminary way. After examination of those passages, we will also be able to see, in a preliminary way, how John has adapted the divine Word of the Targums to the person of Jesus Christ.

---

[50] Chester, *Divine Revelation*, 374. "*Shekinah*" is a word used to refer to the divine presence manifested locally in some way. As discussed in ch. 2, "*Shekinah*" and "Word" are overlapping concepts.

The Word Was with God, and the Word Was God (John 1:1)

"The Word of the Lord" (or, "My Word," etc.) in the Targums is usually a translation of names and titles of God in the MT; it is a divine title. Hundreds of times, the targumic Word corresponds to the divine name or some other designation of God in the MT. The divine Word of the Targums is thus a circumlocution for God, a way of saying "God" or the Tetragrammaton. McNamara points out that such a use constitutes metonymy, that is, calling something by an attribute or feature associated with it.[51] "The Word of the Lord" can be taken literally in many cases, but often it simply means "the Lord." We can compare it to the expression "the name of the Lord" in Isa 30:27, "Behold, the name of the Lord comes from afar," where the reference is to God coming in judgment (NLT: "Look! The Lord is coming from far away").

While "the Word of the Lord" is a metonym for "the Lord," its use is not random or arbitrary (though it is inconsistent). As already noted, it tends to be used when God is interacting with his creation, so that God can be viewed as transcendent, yet still immanent. Thus, "the Word of the Lord" is metonymy used under particular circumstances, such as in the act of creation itself, as noted below. God remains transcendent over creation; his Word creates. In terms of language, the very words "his Word" imply a certain distinction between God and his Word, even though conceptually that Word is something like a projection of God himself into the creation. While this targumic relationship between God and his Word is not nearly as developed as the relationship between the Father and the Son, who are distinct persons, yet in both cases the Word is God, and yet to some extent distinct from God.

The targumic Word is explicitly called God in many passages. In Gen 17:7–8, where God says to Abraham, "I will establish my covenant . . . to be God to you," and "I will be their God," *Tg. Neof.* has "to be, in my Word, God to you" and "I will be to them in my Word a savior [*or* redeemer] God." Similar expressions are found in *Tg. Neof.* Exod 6:7; 29:45; Lev 11:45 [mg.]; 22:33; 25:38; 26:12, 45; Num 15:41 [mg.]; Deut 26:17.[52] In *Tg. Neof.* Lev 26:12, the context of the promise of the Word of the Lord being a savior God is that the Lord will make the glory of his *Shekinah* dwell among them (v. 11). For MT "I will walk among you," *Tg. Neof.* has "My Word will go among you." *Targum Pseudo-Jonathan* Lev 26:12 also refers to the divine Word as a savior God. *Targum Neofiti* Deut 26:17 is also of interest, in light of Pilate's presentation of Jesus as king in John 19: "This day you have made the Word of the Lord your God to be King over you, so that he may be for you a savior God, [promising] to walk in ways that are right before him" (also *Frg. Tg. V, CTg. AA*).

Tgs. Onq. and *Jonathan* usually render God's promises to be God to individuals or to Israel literally. However, *Tg. Onq.* Gen 28:21 has Jacob vow, "The Word

---

[51] McNamara, *Targum and Testament: Aramaic Paraphrases of the Hebrew Bible: A Light on the New Testament* (Grand Rapids: Eerdmans, 1972), 99; "*Logos* of the Fourth Gospel and *Memra* of the Palestinian Targum," 115.

[52] Listed in McNamara, *Neofiti 1: Genesis,* 141 n.16.

of the Lord will be my God," and in *Tg. Onq.* Exod 19:17 (also *Frg. Tg. P*), Moses brings the people to meet the Word of the Lord (MT: to meet God), to which we might compare the declaration of Thomas to Jesus the Word, "my Lord and my God" (John 20:28).[53] In *Tg. Onq.* Deut 4:24, Moses says, "the Lord your God, his Word, is a consuming fire, a jealous [*or* zealous] God." *Targum Pseudo-Jonathan* Deut 4:24 says, "the Lord your God, his Word is a consuming fire; the jealous God is a fire, and he avenges himself in jealousy." When Jesus cleansed the temple, the disciples were reminded of the zeal of a man, David (John 2:17; Ps 69:9). Identifying Jesus as the Word who is God points more significantly to divine zeal in the cleansing of the temple.

Creation through the Word, Who Was in the Beginning with God (John 1:1–3, 10)

Targum Onqelos and *Tg. Ps.-J.* of Gen 1 do not ascribe creation to the divine Word, but the Word of the Lord is the subject of verbs in the creation account seventeen times in *Tg. Neof.* and twenty-five times in *Frg. Tg. P.*[54] In *Frg. Tg. V*'s abbreviated account, the divine Word is the subject of the verb "create" only in v. 27, but v. 28 is quoted in Gen 35:9 of the same Targum, with the Word of the Lord as subject of "blessed" and "said" (*Tg. Neof.* [mg.] here agrees with *Frg. Tg. V*, but, interestingly, *Frg. Tg. P* Gen 35:9 has "God" as subject).

Further, where the MT of Gen 1 says "and it was so," *Tg. Neof.* and/or *Frg. Tg. P* say that it was so "according to his Word" (*Tg. Neof.* Gen 1:7, 9, 11, 15, 24, 30) or "through the decree of his Word" (*Tg. Neof.* [mg.] Gen 1:24; *Frg. Tg. P* Gen 1:7, 9, 11, 15, 24). *Targum Neofiti* Gen 1:3 says "there was light according to the decree of his Word," while *Frg. Tg. P* says "there was light through his Word."

Outside of the creation account itself, *Tg. Neof.* [mg.] Gen 3:1 says that the serpent was more clever than all the beasts of the field which "the Word of the Lord" created. In *Tg. Neof.* Gen 14:19, Melchizedek says, "Blessed is Abram before God Most High, who *by his Word* created the heavens and the earth," and Abram echoes this description of God in v. 22. Both *Tg. Neof.* Exod 20:11 and 31:17 say "In six days the Lord created the heavens and the earth," and in both passages, the gloss "and the Word of the Lord perfected" suggests an alternate text which could have read either "In six days the Word of the Lord created and perfected" etc.

---

[53] Westcott cited *Tg. Onq.* Gen 28:21 and Exod 19:17 as part of his argument for the superiority of the Targum background to Philo's Logos (*St. John*, xvi).

[54] *Tg. Neof.* Gen 1:1 (created), 3 (said), 4 (separated), 5 (called), 6 (said), 8 (called), 9 (said), 10 (called), 11 (said), 16 (created), 20 (said), 22 (blessed), 24 (said), 25 (created), 27 (created), 28 (said); 2:2 (completed). *Targum Neofiti* Gen 1:1 actually reads "the Son of the Lord," which McNamara says "is due most probably to a late, even sixteenth-century, correction. . . . The original Palestinian Targum probably read: 'From the beginning in wisdom the *Memra* of the Lord created'" (*Neofiti 1: Genesis*, 52 n.2). *Fragmentary Targum P* agrees with *Tg. Neof.* at Gen 1:3, 4, 5, 6, 8, 9, 10, 11, 16, 20, 22, 24, 25, 27, 28; 2:2 (variant). In addition, the Word of the Lord is subject in *Frg. Tg. P* Gen 1:7 (created), 14 (said), 17 (placed), 21 (created), 26 (said), 28 (blessed), 29 (said); and 2:3 (blessed and created). Of these nine, *Tg. Neof.* has "the Glory of the Lord" as subject five times (Gen 1:17, 28, 29; and 2:3 [twice]).

or "In six days the LORD created and the Word of the LORD perfected," etc. And although *Tg. Onq.* of Gen 1 does not depict creation through the divine Word, *Tg. Onq.* Deut 33:27 does, in a manner very close to John 1:10, implying that the divine Word was "with God in the beginning."

Tg. Onq. Deut 33:27	**John 1:10**
The dwelling place of God is from the beginning, (when) *through his Word* the world was made.[55]	The world *through him* (the Word) was made.

The existence of the Word from the beginning is also implied in *Tg. Neof.*, which uses the oath formula, "I live and exist in my Word forever" (*Tg. Neof.* Num 14:21; Deut 32:40; *Frg. Tg. V* Deut 32:40), and in *Tg. Neof.* and *Frg. Tg. V* Deut 32:39, which render "I am he" as "I, in my Word, am he." As God exists, so does his uncreated Word; it therefore existed "from the beginning," which in such contexts means prior to creation.

Targum Psalms 124:8 says, "Our help is in the name of the Word of the LORD, who made heaven and earth." Clearly, based on comparison to the MT, the name of the divine Word is the Tetragrammaton; this name is given to the Son according to John 17:11–12. The MT of Ps 33:6 says, "By the word of the LORD [בִּדְבַר יהוה] the heavens were made." Usually the Targums translate דְּבַר from the MT with Aramaic פִּתְגָּם (*Tg. Ps.* 33:6 uses מילה), but some MSS of *Tg. Ps.* 33:6 use *Memra*.[56]

Several passages from *Tg. Jon.* also indicate that all things were made through the divine Word:

Tg. Isa. 44:24 I am the LORD, who made all things; I stretched out the heavens *by* [or *through*] *my Word* (MT: by myself [לְבַדִּי]); I founded the earth by my might (MT: who was with me? [*ketib*; מִי אִתִּי] *or* from with me [*qere*; מֵאִתִּי] = by myself).

Tg. Isa. 45:12 *I, by my Word*, (MT: I) made the earth, and created man upon it; I, by my might (MT, my hands), stretched out the heavens.

Tg. Isa. 48:13 *By my Word* (MT: my hand) I founded the earth, by my might (MT, my right hand) I stretched out the heavens.

Tg. Jer. 27:5 I, *by my Word*, (MT: I) made the earth, the men and beasts on the face of the earth, by my great power (= MT), and by my uplifted arm (= MT).

According to these four passages, all things were made through the *Memra*, just as John says of the Logos. The question "Who was with me" (*ketib* in the MT of Isa 44:24) is of interest as well. The Targum renders it "by my might," probably to agree with *Tg. Isa.* 45:12; 48:13; and even *Tg. Jer.* 27:5, where "by my great power"

---

[55] מְדוֹר אֱלָהָא מִלְּקַדְמִין דִּבְמֵימְרֵיה אִתְעֲבֵיד עָלְמָא.

[56] For his translation of *Tg. Ps.* for The Aramaic Bible, David M. Stec consulted five MSS as well as the 1525 Bomberg's Venice printed editions (*The Targum of Psalms* [ArBib 16; Collegeville, Minn.: Liturgical Press, 2004], 22–23). Of these six sources, two use *Memra* in *Tg. Ps.* 33:6 (p. 73 n."g" of the apparatus).

agrees with the Hebrew. But if one looks at both the Hebrew and the Aramaic of Isa 44:24, as John may have done, the question in the MT, "Who was with me" (i.e., in creation; with the implied answer of "no one") is answered in the Targum, "My Word was with me." To be sure, the Word of the Targums is not another divine Person any more than God's attribute of strength is another. In fact, one could insist that in these passages *Memra* should be taken literally as God's decree, thus should not be capitalized. But that would not mean that John could not have adapted the Targum language for his own purpose, observing that the close association of God and his Word is analogous to the close association between the Father and the Son. Accordingly, to which the idea of creation through the Son, who "was in the beginning with God," does not contradict the statement that God acted "by myself" in creation.

Israel also was created: "Thus says the LORD your creator [ברא (used for the creation of man in Gen 1:27)], Jacob, and he who formed you [יצר (used for the creation of Adam in Gen 2:7)], Israel . . ." (Isa 43:1). God goes on to say "you are mine," where the Targum has דילי, "my own," which we discuss below as the Aramaic basis for "his own" of John 1:11.

Israel's creation is not unrelated to the original creation, as we discuss below when considering the Word as light, and Israel's creation is said in several places in the *Pal. Tgs.* of the Song of Moses (Deut 32) to be accomplished through the divine Word. The MT of this chapter speaks of God making Israel, sometimes using the childbirth or Father-child motif, reminiscent of Gen 1, to speak of Israel's creation through their redemption from Egypt and their wilderness experiences. Verse 10 uses the noun תֹּהוּ to describe the wilderness where God cared for Israel, and the next verse uses the verb רחף (*piel*) to compare God to an eagle hovering over its young. As Meredith G. Kline noted, the only other place in the Pentateuch where these two words appear is Gen 1:2, so it seems likely that the creation theme is being deliberately alluded to.[57] Israel's creation is described directly or indirectly in several verses: "Is he not your Father who created you [קנה; some translate *bought*]? Did he not make [עשׂה] and establish [כון] you?" (v. 6); "(Israel) forgot God who made [עשׂה] him" (v. 15); and "You forgot God who brought you to birth [*polel;* חול]" (v. 18). For v. 15, *Tgs. Ps.-J.* and *Onq.* say that Israel forsook "the fear of God who made them"; *Tg. Neof.* and *Frg. Tg. V* say that Israel forgot or forsook "the Word of God who created them" (using ברי, the Aramaic cognate of ברא). For v. 18, *Tg. Ps.-J.* joins *Tg. Neof.* and *Frg. Tg. V* in speaking of Israel forsaking "the Word of God who made them" (various verbs are used). One might object that in such expressions the antecedent of "who" is not "the Word of God" but simply "God," just as the phrase "they forsook the fear of God who made them" ascribes creation to God, not the fear of God. Grammatically this is possible, but the creation of Israel spoken of took place in the redemption of Israel from Egypt,

---

[57] "That Moses in his use of the verb *rhp* in Deuteronomy 32:11 is instituting a comparison between God's presence as Israel's divine aegis in the wilderness and God's presence over creation in Genesis 1:2b is put beyond doubt by the fact that he calls that wilderness a *tōhû*" (Meredith G. Kline, *Images of the Spirit* [Grand Rapids: Baker, 1980], 14).

in which, according to the Targums, the divine Word is often the subject or agent of redemption. Another objection might be that this creation is not that spoken of in John 1:1–3, 10, which was accomplished through the Word. Nevertheless, there is a close link between creation and redemption, redemption being brought about by a new creation, which would be one reason for John to begin his Gospel by mentioning that the original creation was through the Word, while the rest of the Gospel highlights redemption through the Word.

In any case, whether or not we include *Pal. Tgs.* Deut 32:15, 18 among the Targum passages which speak of creation through the divine Word, it is surprising that Moore claimed that the Targums do not ascribe creation to the Word of the Lord and, therefore, that the targumic Word has nothing to do with the Logos in John or Philo. "In the Targums *memra* . . . is not the creative word in the cosmogony of Genesis or reminiscences of it."[58] Moore allowed that *Tg. Isa.* 45:12 was an apparent exception, but of the kind that proves the rule (presumably meaning that *Memra* could be taken literally here; thus, there is no hypostatization). Then he pointed to another exception, *Tg. Onq.* Deut 33:27, without noting its striking similarity to John 1:10.[59] Moore considered *Tg. Onq.* and *Tg. Jon.*, not the *Pal. Tgs.*, because the former were more authoritative, apparently not wondering whether John might be more interested in the latter because of their popular nature.[60] He did, however, refer to the *Pal. Tgs.* elsewhere, saying that, unlike Philo's Logos, the *Memra* is not the agency of creation: "Consequently, the theory that derives the Logos-Word of John 1, 1–5 straight from the Palestinian *memra* is fallacious."[61] He thus overlooked cases in *Tg. Jon.* (Isa 44:24; 48:13; Jer 27:5), which we discussed above, as well as the *Frg. Tgs.* (which are earlier than *Tg. Ps.-J.*).[62] Although *Tg. Neof.* was not discovered until a few decades after Moore wrote, the other Targums were available.

The Word as Light, Shining in Darkness, in Conflict with Darkness (John 1:4–5, 9)

We have already noted *Tg. Neof.* and *Frg. Tg.* P Gen 1:3, "there was light according to the decree of his Word" and "there was light through his Word." Many have pointed to a closer identification between *Memra* and the light at the beginning of creation in the haggadah or poem of the Four Nights, which appears as an extensive addition to Exod 12:42 (where the MT refers to the Passover night of watching) in *Tg. Neof.*, *Frg. Tg.* V, CTg. FF and as an addition to Exod 15:18 (MT: "The Lord will reign") in *Frg. Tg.* P.[63] The first night corresponds to the darkness of Gen 1:2, when God gave the command "let there be light."

---

[58] Moore, "Intermediaries in Jewish Theology," 54.

[59] Ibid., 46.

[60] Ibid., 60 n.7.

[61] Ibid., 61 n.27.

[62] Ibid., 46, 54.

[63] McNamara says, "the bearing of this text of *Neofiti* on the prologue of John has been noted independently by A. Díez Macho (*Atlantida*, vol. I, no. 4, 1963, pp. 390–94) and R.

CTg. FF: The first night, when the Word of the LORD was revealed upon the world to create it, and the world was formless and void, and darkness was spread over the surface of <the>deep. And <the Word> of the LORD was <ligh>t and it shone.[64]

Tg. Neof. reads similarly, except that there it is "the LORD" (not "the Word of the LORD") who is revealed. The words for "was light and it shone" are slightly different, but glosses agree with *CTg. FF.*[65]

Fragmentary Targum V begins like *CTg. FF,* saying that "the Word of the LORD was revealed," and it ends with "and the Word of the LORD shone and gave light" (נהיר ומנהר). *Fragmentary Targum P* Exod 15:18 says that the LORD was revealed, etc., and "through his Word shone and gave light" (ובמימריה הוה נהיר ומנהיר).

The *CTg. FF* and *Tg. Neof.* are particularly close to John in saying both that the Word was "light" (using the noun) and that the Word "shone." As Robert Kysar notes, "the parallels between this targumic passage and the prologue are striking: the prevailing darkness, the word's existence at the beginning of creation, the identification of word and light, and the shining of the light in the darkness."[66]

McNamara criticizes Billerbeck because "in the course of his extensive treatment of the *Memra* in the Targums (which runs to thirty-two pages), [he] does not even once cite or refer to the text of Ex 12:42. Nowhere, in fact, in the entire four volumes of the *Kommentar* is the relevant part of the verse cited."[67] *Targum Neofiti* was not available to Billerbeck, but the *Frg. Tg.* tradition was.

Some might wonder why John would care about this extrabiblical Jewish legend of the Four Nights, or what could be viewed as mere allegory of Gen 1:1–3. One answer might be that John saw an incident in the ministry of Jesus which could be viewed as a revelation of Jesus along the lines of the appearance of the Word as light on the first night. That incident was the appearance of Jesus to his disciples over the wind-driven waters, in the darkness, recalling the pre-creation conditions of the world when, according to the poem, "the Word of the LORD was the Light, and it gave light" (John 6:16–21). This incident occurred just prior to

---

Le Déaut (*La nuit pascale,* Rome, 1963, pp. 215 f.). The latter, in fact, considers the poem on the Four Nights . . . as a type of hymn to the Word (*Memra*) of the Lord" ("*Logos,*" 116; see Roger Le Déaut, *La nuit pascale: Essai sur la signification de la Pâque juive à partir du Targum d'Exode XII 42* [AnBib 2; Rome: Biblical Institute Press, 1963]). See also McNamara, *Palestinian Judaism and the New Testament* (GNS 4; Wilmington, Del.: Michael Glazier, 1983), 237–39.

[64] Klein, *Genizah Manuscripts,* 1:220. Text in angled brackets is restored by Klein. Klein translates the last word "and illumination" (ibid.), while the CAL parses it as a verb.

[65] *Tg. Neof.* has וממריה דייי והוה נהורא ונהר, with והוה emended to הוה (which agrees with *CTg. FF*). A gloss of *Tg. Neof.* ונהר is ומנהר, which likewise agrees with *CTg. FF.* A gloss of *Tg. Neof.* נהורא is נהור; only the ר is extant in *CTg. FF,* but Klein restores the rest of the word as in the *Tg. Neof.* gloss.

[66] Robert Kysar, *The Fourth Evangelist and His Gospel: An Examination of Contemporary Scholarship* (Minneapolis: Augsburg, 1975), 109. Kysar mistakenly locates the text in *Tg. Neof.* at Exod 15:18 (where *Frg. Tg. P* has it). This statement is also found in Kysar's *Voyages with John: Charting the Fourth Gospel* (Waco, Tex.: Baylor University Press, 2005), 83.

[67] McNamara, *Targum and Testament,* 102 n.7. I would add that nowhere in those thirty-two pages does Billerbeck discuss a single verse from John's Gospel.

the Passover, when the hymn of the Four Nights would presumably be recited (6:4). One could also view the incident as a somewhat literalistic picture of John 1:12, with Jesus coming to a remnant of his own and this remnant receiving him. "They were willing *to receive him* into the boat" (John 6:21, which uses λαμβάνω for "receive" as in John 1:12). We will discuss this passage further in ch. 8 in connection with the "I am he" saying of John 6:20, where we will see that *Tg. Isa.* 43 will help us complete the picture.

Another case where the divine Word is associated with shining light is *Tg. Neof.* Exod 13:21–22, which says that "the Word of the LORD led on before them during the daytime in a pillar of cloud to lead them on the way, and by night in a pillar of fiery cloud to give them light. . . . The pillar of cloud did not cease during the daytime, nor the pillar of fire by night, leading and standing in readiness and *shining before the people*" (similarly *Frg. Tg. P* for v. 21). The divine Word in the pillar of fire leading the Israelites can also be seen as background to John 8:12, where Jesus is the light of the world, so that his followers should not remain in darkness (more on this in ch. 8).

After saying that the light shines in the darkness, John goes on to say that the darkness did not overtake it (1:5), which suggests conflict between light and darkness, a theme also found in the body of the Gospel (3:19). "Overtake" is καταλαμβάνω, which some versions (including the Vulgate) translate as "understand." Yet a *prima facie* case for the translation "overtake" can be made from John 12:35, which has so much in common with 1:5: "Jesus said to them, 'For a little while longer *the Light* is among you. Walk while you have *the Light,* so that *darkness will not overtake you.*"

"I will overtake . . . my hand will destroy them" was Pharaoh's boast as he set out after the Israelites (Exod 15:9). Pharaoh was thwarted, however, because the pillar of cloud came between the Israelites and the Egyptians, and when darkness came, the cloud remained to keep the Egyptians in darkness, while the night for the Israelites was illuminated.[68] Thus darkness (identified with the Egyptians) did not overcome light (identified with the Israelites). Again, according to *Tg. Neof.* Exod 13:21–22, the divine Word was in the pillar of cloud and fire, even though this statement is not repeated in Exod 14 in connection with the pillar of fire. For "I will overtake" (Exod 15:9), the LXX uses καταλαμβάνω (middle voice).

In an acrostic poem to Exod 14:30 in *CTg. T,* the Red Sea is depicted as refusing to part for the Israelites, but then "The voice of the Holy Spirit called out to Moses and the Word [*Dibbera*] began speaking to him. . . . The sea heard the Word speaking to Moses <from the midst of the fire>. The sea repented with all its might, and the tribes of Jacob passed through it." The bracketed text is supplied by Klein

---

[68] The NIV of Exod 14:20 ("Throughout the night the cloud brought darkness to the one side and light to the other side") follows the Syriac, which agrees with the interpretation found in *Tg. Onq.* and the *Pal. Tgs.* It is also supported by Josh 24:7: "He put darkness between you and the Egyptians." The MT is obscure and often deemed corrupt. See discussion in John L. Ronning, "The Curse on the Serpent: Genesis 3:15 in Biblical Theology and Hermeneutics" (PhD diss., Westminster Theological Seminary, Glenside, Pa., 1997), 215–18.

from a parallel (although in any event it may be assumed from the context that the voice of the Word would come from the pillar of fire).[69] If Kline's emendation is correct, then the text depicts the Word speaking to Moses from the pillar of fire at the shores of the Red Sea, giving us another association of the divine Word (this time *Dibbera*) with light in the pillar of fire which led Israel through the sea.

Thus *Pal. Tg.* texts describing the appearance of light at creation as well as light in the pillar of fire associate the divine Word closely with this light. We should observe that even apart from the Targums, there is more than light that binds these two texts together. The division of light and darkness at the Red Sea may be part of a reenactment of the first three days of creation (most obviously with the third day corresponding to the drying up of the Red Sea, and dry land appearing).[70] Light is thus connected with redemption, conceived of as symbolic of a new creation. Again, recognizing redemption as a new creation allows us to see a link between John's Prologue, where John identifies the divine Word as the agent of creation, and the body of the Gospel, which deals not with creation but with redemption, which was also accomplished through the divine Word according to the Targums (more on this in chs. four through seven). The targumic divine Word is associated both with light shining in the darkness at creation and with the redemption of Israel, when light is in victorious conflict with darkness.

Some MSS of *Tg. Ps. 27:1* say "The Word of the LORD is my light and my redemption."[71] We can compare "my light" to "the light of men," John 1:4. The context of Ps 27:1 is one of danger from evildoers who, when they approach, stumble and fall. This could be figuratively connected with John 1:5, which says that the darkness did not overcome the light. The stumbling and falling of those who came to arrest Jesus (John 18:6) could similarly serve as a sign that though the forces of darkness appear to succeed, they are actually in the category of those who perish.

A variant reading of *Tos. Tg. Zech. 2:10* is quite striking in its association of the divine Word with light. In the MT, the LORD says, "Sing for joy and be glad, O daughter of Zion; for behold I am coming and I will dwell in your midst." The *Tos. Tg.* reads, "Rejoice and be glad, assembly of Zion, for the glory {Word} of the Lord will be revealed, and he shall illumine the world from the brilliance of his glory, in that he said (i.e., promised) to make his *Shekinah* dwell in your midst. And it is not before him to act falsely, and he will not turn from what he says. Behold, like the light {splendor} of morning which goes forth and prevails [*or* increases, becomes strong; תקיף] and increases his light to all the world more than all."

The text with the variant "Word" (*Memra*) is like the poem of the Four Nights in associating light with the divine Word, but here the light happens not at creation but on the occasion when the LORD comes to dwell with his people. He illumines all the world with his light, and his light prevails over darkness. Thus

---

[69] Klein, *Genizah Fragments,* 1:238–39 (slightly adapted). *CTg. X* Exod 14:30 (an acrostic poem thereto) says (letter *Shin*), "The sea heard the voice of the Holy Spirit, that was spea[king] with Moses from the midst of the fire" (ibid., 236–37).

[70] See Ronning, "Curse on the Serpent," 215–18; Kline, *Images of the Spirit,* 14–16.

[71] The same two MSS that use *Memra* in *Tg. Ps. 33:6* (see above, n. 56) do so here as well (Stec, *Targum of Psalms,* 65 n."a" of the apparatus).

this text adds two parallels to the Word as light in John 1 that are not in the poem of the Four Nights: "The true light which enlightens every man" (1:9) agrees with "increases his light to all the world," and "the darkness did not overcome it" (1:5) agrees with the *Tos. Tg.* description of the light as prevailing from morning (thus prevailing over darkness). Judges 5:31 (where the wording is similar to *Tos. Tg. Zech.* 2:10) speaks of the sun going forth in its strength as a simile for the righteous, in contrast to the LORD's enemies, who perish.

A further parallel between *Tos. Tg. Zech.* 2:10 and John's Prologue pertains to John 1:14, which we discuss below. Rimon Kasher compares the character of the *Tos. Tgs.* of the Prophets to *Tg. Jon.*, noting that they tend to be more like *Tg. Ps.-J.* than *Jonathan*, that they arose in the synagogue rather than the academy, and that they are later than *Jonathan* in their final form but "obviously . . . may also contain traces of ancient traditions."[72]

Receiving/Not Receiving the Divine Word; Believing in His Name (John 1:11–12)

In these verses, John indicates that the Word came to those who were "his own" and contrasts his own, who did not receive (παραλαμβάνω) him, with those who did receive (λαμβάνω) him, those who believed in his name. In the Targums, the idea of receiving or not receiving the Word of the LORD is very common, where the MT speaks of listening to God himself (or his voice) or coming to him, etc.

It has been suggested that "his own" from v. 11 reflects an underlying Aramaic דִּילֵיהּ.[73] Moses says to Israel in *Tg. Onq.* Deut 32:6, "You (Israel) are his (God's) own." "My own" (דִּילִי) is what God calls Israel in *Tgs Ps.-J.* and *Onq.* Lev 25:55 and *Tg. Isa.* 43:1. In *Tg. Isa.* 46:3 (and many other places), he urges them (whom he has called "my own") to "receive my Word" (for MT "listen to me"). "My own" is also what God calls "the ages of the ages" in conjunction with some of the "I am he" declarations in Isaiah (*Tg. Isa.* 41:4; 43:10; 48:12). Indeed, Isa 43:10 is echoed by Jesus in John 13:19 and alluded to in other places (see chs. eight and nine below).

Concerning the expression "those who believed in his name," Anthony Tyrell Hanson comments, "in the context this must refer to the name of the Logos."[74] The expression "the name of the Word of the LORD" is common in the *Pal. Tgs.* of the Pentateuch and is found also in other Targums, except for the "official" Targums, *Tg. Onq.* (the Pentateuch) and *Tg. Jon.* (the Former and Latter Prophets).

Both the idea of believing in the name of the Word of the LORD and the idea of not receiving the Word of the LORD are found in *Tg. Ps.* 106. Psalm 106:12 says

---

[72] Rimon Kasher, "Eschatological Ideas in the Toseftot Targum to the Prophets," *Journal for the Aramaic Bible* 2 (2000): 58–59. The text published by Kasher is available on the CAL website and in BibleWorks 7 (under the FTT database). The English translation given here is mine.

[73] Charles F. Burney, *The Aramaic Origin of the Fourth Gospel* (Oxford: Clarendon, 1922), 33, 41; this agrees with Peshitta and Old Syriac. Cf. Hebrew שֶׁלּוֹ.

[74] Anthony Tyrell Hanson, *The Prophetic Gospel: A Study of John and the Old Testament* (Edinburgh: T&T Clark, 1991), 24.

that after Israel passed through the Red Sea and witnessed the destruction of the Egyptians, "they believed his words." This probably refers to Exod 14:31, which says they "believed in the LORD and in his servant Moses." *Palestinian Targums* Exod 14:31 speaks of believing in the name of the Word of the LORD, language also used to interpret Ps 106:12. The following shows how plausible it is to associate John's language with that of the Targums:

MT of Exod 14:31	The people . . . *believed in the* LORD.
Tg. Ps.-J., Tg. Neof., Frg. Tg. P, and *CTg. J* Exod 14:31	The people . . . *believed in the name of the Word of the* LORD.
MT of Ps 106:12	They believed *his words.*
Tg. Ps. 106:12	They *believed in the name of his Word.*
John 1:12	He gave the right to become children of God to those who *believed in his (the Word's) name.*

We can carry out a similar analysis of *Tg. Ps.* 106:25 to show how the "receive/ not receive" language of John 1:11–12 likewise can be related to a frequent use of the targumic Word. The reference is to the great rebellion of Num 14, when Israel refused to enter the promised land:

MT of Ps 106:25	They did not *listen to the voice of the Lord.*
Tg. Ps. 106:25	They did not *receive the Word of the Lord.*[75]
MT of Num 14:22	All the men . . . who have not *listened to my voice.*
Tg. Onq. and *Tg. Ps.-J.* Num 14:22	The men who . . . have not *received my Word.*

We can also relate *Tg. Onq.* and *Tg. Ps.-J.* Num 14:22 to John 1:14 and 2:11, 23:

> The men who have seen my glory and my signs which I have done . . . and have not received my Word.

> John 1:11, 14: His own *did not receive him* (the Word). . . . The Word became flesh and . . . *we beheld his glory.*

> John 2:11: He manifested *his glory.*

> John 2:23: Many believed in his name, beholding *his signs which he was doing.*

John could easily see biblical history repeating itself in his own generation; some believed, most did not.

A few verses earlier in Numbers (14:11), the LORD asks, "How long will they not believe in me," which in *Tg. Neof.* becomes, "How long will they not believe

---

[75] לא קבילו במימרא דיהוה

in the name of my Word?" Numbers 14:11 seems to be paraphrased in John 12:37 and applied to Jesus.[76] The corresponding passage in *Tg. Neof.* makes it natural to suppose that John has taken the Logos title from the Targums:

John 12:37	Though he had performed so many *signs* before them, they were *not believing in him.*
Num 14:11 (MT)	How long will they not believe *in me*, in spite of all the *signs* which I have performed in their midst?
Tg. Neof. **Num 14:11**	How long will they not *believe in the name of my Word* (*Tgs. Onq.* and *Ps.-J.*: believe in my Word), in spite of all the *signs of my miracles* which I have performed among them?

The targumic expression "the name of the Word of the LORD" cannot be taken literally. The LORD's Word has no name of its own, and phrases such as "the name of the Word of the LORD" and "the name of my Word" occur in the Targums where the MT has the Tetragrammaton, or in contexts such as *Tg. Ps.* 106:12 (mentioned above) where, though the MT does not have the Tetragrammaton, it is clear that the Tetragrammaton is meant (in this case because the language depends on another passage [Exod 14:31] where the Tetragrammaton is used). We are thus forced again to the conclusion that "the Word of the LORD" is metonymy for "the LORD"; thus, "the name of the Word of the LORD" is "the name of the LORD," i.e., the Tetragrammaton. Further confirmation that "his name" should be interpreted in light of the Targums as the Tetragrammaton is found in John 2:23 and 3:18, which also speak of people believing in his name, and in other passages which speak of belief or disbelief in Jesus (John 5:46; 12:37; 14:1). The context of all these passages suggests a connection between this theme in John and a Targum passage that speaks of belief/disbelief in the name of the Word of the LORD, which stands for the Tetragrammaton (see ch. 8 for further discussion and demonstration of this conclusion).

Most commonly, "listening" (Heb) to the LORD or to the voice of the LORD in the MT is rendered as "receiving" in the Targums. "Receiving" is used to render other expressions as well, such as turning to the LORD and coming to the LORD. If John was thinking of the Aramaic קביל, he could have expressed it in Greek with ἀκούω (just as modern English translations of Targums use "heed," "listen to," "attend to," etc.). Likewise, ἀκούω in various Gospel passages could reflect an originally spoken Aramaic קביל, but John's use of the literal translation παραλαμβάνω/λαμβάνω in 1:11–12 helps us make the connection to קביל of the Targums.

The expression "the name of the Word [*Memra*] of the LORD" (or variants such as "the name of my Word") is used differently in *Tgs. Neof.* and *Ps.-J.*[77] For

---

[76] Reim, *Alttestamentlichen Hintergrund,* 139 n.61.

[77] See *Tg. Neof.* Gen 4:26; 8:20; 12:7–8; 13:4, 18; 15:6; 16:13; 21:33; 22:14, 16; 24:3; 26:25; 35:1; Exod 4:31; 5:23; 14:31; 17:15; 23:21 [mg.]; 32:13; 34:5; Lev 16:8–9; Num 14:11; 18:9; 20:12; 21:5; Deut 1:32; 4:4 [mg.]; 9:23; 10:8; 11:22; 13:5; 18:5, 7, 19–20, 22; 21:5; 32:51; and *Tg. Ps.-J.* Gen 4:26; 5:2; 18:5; 21:33; 24:3; 35:9; Exod 14:31; 20:7; 26:28; 33:19; 34:5; 36:33;

example, the language of believing/not believing in "the name of the Word of the LORD" is found in *Tg. Neof.,* but in these passages *Tg. Ps.-J.* usually agrees with *Tg. Onq.,* which speaks of believing or disbelieving in "the Word of the LORD."[78] We can illustrate this with Deut 9:23, where Moses speaks of the refusal of Israel to enter the promised land. As we saw for *Tg. Ps.* 106, so we see in the various Targums of Deut 9:23 both the "receive" language and the "believe in his name" language of John 1:11–12:

MT	You rebelled against the mouth of the LORD your God and *did not believe him* or *listen to his voice.*
Tg. Neof.	You rebelled against the decree of the Word of the LORD your God, and you did not *believe in the holy name of the Word of the LORD,* and you did not *listen to the voice of his Word.*
Tgs. Onq. and Ps.-J.	You rebelled against the Word of the LORD your God and did not believe him and *did not receive his Word.*

To summarize:

	MT	*Tg. Neof.*	*Tgs. Onq., Ps.-J.*
you did not:	believe him	believe in the holy name of the Word of the LORD	believe him
you did not:	listen to his voice	listen to the voice of his Word	receive his Word

Targum Joshua 5:6 likewise says that the wilderness generation perished because it did not receive the Word of the LORD. Likewise, the exile of Israel and Judah took place because of a failure to receive the Word of the Lord (*Tg. 2 Kgs.* 18:12; *Tg. Jer.* 40:3). Such passages are significant to John's Gospel not only because of the similarity in wording to John 1:11–12, but also because of the Gospel's modeling of the generation that rejected Jesus after the wilderness generation (as we will discuss in ch. 8, and because John is writing from a post-exilic perspective,

---

Lev 5:21; Num 6:2; 21:8–9; Deut 4:7; 5:11; 6:13; 18:7; 32:6, 9; 33:29. *Frg. Tgs.*, where extant, agree with *Tg. Neof.* According to Robert Hayward, "the name of the *Memra* of the LORD" is the Tetragrammaton properly pronounced, as it was in the ceremonies associated with the Day of Atonement in the temple (*Divine Name and Presence,* 100–11). He cites *m. Yoma* 4:2; *Soṭah* 7:6; *Tamid* 7:2 in connection with *Tg. Neof.* Lev 16:8–9, which mentions the "lot for the name of the Word of the LORD" where MT has "lot for the LORD" (Martin McNamara, *Targum Neofiti 1: Leviticus* [introduction and notes by Robert Hayward]; Michael Maher, *Targum Pseudo-Jonathan: Leviticus* [ArBib 3; Collegeville, Minn.: Liturgical Press, 1994], 62 n.6).

[78] Generally, where the MT speaks of someone believing/not believing in the LORD, *Tg. Onq.* and *Tg. Ps.-J.* speak of believing/not believing in the Word (*Memra*) of the LORD, *Tg. Neof.* speaks of believing/not believing in the name of the Word of the LORD (Gen 15:6; Num 14:11; 20:12; Deut 1:32; 9:23). In Exod 14:31, however, all of the *Pal. Tgs.* (including *Frg. Tg. P*) say that Israel believed in the name of the Word of the LORD (MT says simply "the people believed . . . in the LORD").

which might naturally be compared to earlier exiles and give rise to identical explanations). Further, John's identification of Jesus as the Word would suggest a reason for Jerusalem's destruction in C.E. 70 that could make sense to Aramaic-speaking Jews who contemplated that catastrophe in relation to the covenant curses: "If in this you do not receive my Word . . . you shall eat the flesh of your sons and the flesh of your daughters . . . and I will destroy your cities and make desolate your sanctuaries" (*Tg. Onq.* Lev 26:27–31).

In Ezek 3:7, God says to Ezekiel, "The house of Israel will not be willing to listen to you, for they are not willing to listen to me." In *Tg. Ezek.*, he says, "they will not be willing to receive from you because they will not be willing to receive my Word" [לְקַבָּלָא לְמֵימְרִי]. Jesus the Word uses similar language in speaking of those whom he sends: "Whoever receives [λαμβάνω] the one I send receives me (the Word), and whoever receives me receives him who sent me" (John 13:20; similarly Matt 10:40, which uses δέχομαι for "receive").

Finally, we note that John's connection between receiving the Word and being given the right to become children of God (1:12) can be seen as based on the reading of *Tgs. Onq.* and *Ps.-J.* Exod 19:5–6: "If you will diligently receive my Word, . . . you shall be before me . . . a holy people." This passage is cited in Jer 7:23, where *Tg. Jer.* reads, "Receive my Word, and I will be your God and you shall be a people before me." The equation of the holy people of God and the children of God is made in Deut 14:1–2: "You are children (*Tg. Ps.-J.*: beloved children; cf. Eph 5:1) of the LORD your God. . . . You are a holy people."

We should also take note of the doctrinal implications of understanding the word "receive" in John 1:11–12 according to the Aramaic background. To "receive the Word of the LORD" has connotations of obedience, and is thus not accurately explained as analogous to merely receiving a gift.

Word, Glory, Shekinah (John 1:14)

"The Word became flesh and dwelt among us, and we beheld his glory." In ch. 2 we explore the idea of God dwelling among his people and manifesting his glory as an important OT theme (e.g., Exod 40:34–35). "Glory" could be directly related to OT references to God's glory when he dwells among his people. Further, in John's word "dwelt" we have the rare situation where a Greek word (σκηνόω) is related to a Semitic word, namely, the Hebrew verb used for God dwelling among his people, שָׁכֵן as well as the noun מִשְׁכָּן used for the tabernacle (translated in Greek as σκηνή). Σκηνόω can also be related to the Aramaic word שְׁכִינְתָּא, the *Shekinah*, the manifest presence of God. This word is used commonly in the Targums with the word "glory," and the two are commonly also found with *Memra*. Charles F. Burney suggested, therefore, that "so far from owing his λόγος-doctrine to an Alexandrian source, [John] is soaked through and through with the Palestinian Jewish thought which is represented by the Targums."[79] For proof Burney noted that

---

[79] Burney, *Aramaic Origin*, 38–39. Burney credits this observation to Gustaf Dalman, *The Words of Jesus Considered in the Light of Post-biblical Jewish Writings and the Aramaic Language* (Edinburgh: T&T Clark, 1902), 231. R. D. Middleton cites Burney approvingly:

John 12:40–41 says that Isaiah saw Christ's glory, which depends on Isa 6:1, where *Tg. Isa.* reads, "I saw the glory [יְקָרָא] of the LORD resting on a throne," and v. 5 says, "my eyes have seen the glory of the *Shekinah* of the King of the ages."

It should however be noted that the use of "glory" in John 12:41 does not prove influence from *Tg. Isa.* 6:1, since the LXX of that verse interprets "the train of his robe" as "his glory" (similarly, *Tg. Isa.:* "the brilliance of his glory"). That is, "Isaiah saw his glory" could be influenced by LXX Isa 6:1 "I saw the Lord . . . and the temple was full of his glory." On the other hand, a connection between John 12:41 and *Tg. Isa.* 6:1 seems likely if one has already accepted a targumic background of the Logos title, since *Tg. Isa.* 6:8 says Isaiah heard the voice of the Word of the Lord speaking to him. In *Tg. Isa.* 6:5, Isaiah pronounces woe upon himself, because, he says, "my eyes have seen the glory of the *Shekinah* of the eternal King." Thus in these two verses from Isaiah's commissioning we have the three key targumic words that have been connected to John 1:14. Further, *Tg. Ps.-J.* Deut 4:7 borrows a phrase from Isa 6:1 with a significant variation from *Tg. Isa.:* "The Word of the LORD sits on his throne, high and lifted up." We may infer that the now-lost "Palestinian" Targum of Isa 6:1 might have read something like, "I saw the Word of the LORD sitting on his throne, high and lifted up, . . . and the temple was filled with the brilliance of his glory." If such a reading existed in John's day, the connection to John 12:41 would be even more obvious.

Tg. Ps.-J. Deut 5:24 also associates these three key words:

Deut 5:24 (MT)	*Tg. Ps.-J.* **Deut 5:24**
And you said, "Behold, the LORD our God has shown us his glory and his greatness, and we have heard his voice from the midst of the fire."	And you said, "Behold, *the Word of the LORD* our God has shown us *the Shekinah of his glory* and the greatness of his praise, and we have heard *the voice of his Word* from the midst of the fire."

Deuteronomy 5:24 looks back to God's revelation on Mt. Sinai to all the people. As we shall see in ch. 2, John 1:14 also has echoes of God's revelation on Sinai, but primarily of the private revelation to Moses in Exod 34.

We also noted above that one variant of *Tos. Tg. Zech.* 2:10, besides associating the divine Word with light which illumines the whole world, also speaks of his glory and making his *Shekinah* dwell among his people. Below is a comparison of John 1:14, MT, *Tg. Zech.*, and *Tos. Tg. Zech.* 2:10:

"Thus the three terms are used together to describe the mystery of the incarnation" ("Logos and *Shekinah* in the Fourth Gospel," *Jewish Quarterly Review* 29 [1938–1939]: 130). Similarly George R. Beasley-Murray, "The language used of the incarnation of the Logos is reminiscent of the dwelling of the *Shekinah* among the people of God in the wilderness" (*John* [Word Biblical Commentary 36; Dallas: Word, 1987], lix). McNamara also connected the three targumic terms *Word, glory,* and *Shekinah* to John 1:14 (*Palestinian Judaism,* 238). More recently Mary L. Coloe said, "These terms from the Targums used in the Jewish synagogue worship may have provided the Johannine author with the theological tools to express the divinity they saw, heard, and experienced in Jesus" (*God Dwells With Us: Temple Symbolism in the Fourth Gospel* [Collegeville, Minn.: Liturgical Press, 2001], 61).

MT	"Sing for joy and be glad, O daughter of Zion; for behold *I am coming* and *I will dwell* (LXX: κατασκηνόω) *in your midst*," declares the LORD.
Tg. Zech.	Rejoice and be glad, O congregation of Zion, for behold, *I will reveal myself* and *I will make my Shekinah dwell in your midst*, says the LORD.
Tos. Tg. Zech.	Rejoice and be glad, assembly of Zion, for the Word {glory} of the LORD will be revealed, and he shall illumine the world from the brilliance of his glory, in that he said to make his Shekinah dwell in your midst.
John 1:14	*The Word* became flesh and *dwelt among us*, and we beheld *his glory*.

Whether *Tos. Tg. Zech.* 2:10 existed in a similar form to that above in John's day we cannot be sure, but the conceptual similarities between the two passages could be used to argue that this targumic way of speaking is early. John of course would have to have transformed the idea of the divine Word being revealed into the idea of the Word becoming flesh, which, we can be sure, was not in the mind of the targumist.

Burney's observation about the relationship between the Word, glory, and *Shekinah* in the Targums implies that in assessing the likelihood of a targumic background to the Logos title, we are interested not only in potential Johannine allusions to the targumic Word, but also in possible allusions to the *Shekinah*, the glory of the *Shekinah*, etc. It is often the case that in a particular passage both "Word" and "*Shekinah*" (or "glory" or "glory of the *Shekinah*") are used, or that one Targum might use "Word" where another uses "*Shekinah*." In the case of *Tg. Neof.*, this variation often occurs between the main text and marginal readings.

One important place where the divine Word, glory, and *Shekinah* occur together is in the revelation of the glory of God to Moses on Mt. Sinai after the golden calf incident (Exod 33–34). In *Tg. Neof.* Exod 33:23, for example, God says to Moses, "You shall see the Word of the glory of my *Shekinah*" (mg.: "I make you see the Word of glory"). *Dibbura* occurs in both the main text and the marginal reading. This passage is especially significant because John 1:14–18 arguably has this revelation of the glory of God to Moses as its background, with "full of grace and truth" being John's translation of "abounding in kindness and truth" of Exod 34:6 (רַב חֶסֶד וֶאֱמֶת). The OT background of John 1:14–18 is explored in more detail in ch. 2.

Jesus Identified as the Word and the Messiah in His Baptism (John 1:32–34)

John 1:32–34 twice mentions the Spirit descending and remaining on Jesus, thereby identifying him as the Son of God. The association of the Spirit with the Messiah in OT prophecy is well known (Isa 11:2; 42:1; 61:1) and can be seen in continuity with the Spirit of God coming upon David when he was anointed to be king (1 Sam 16:13). The Spirit "remaining [μένω] on him" especially agrees with Isa 11:2: "the Spirit of the LORD will rest [וְנָחָה] upon him (a Branch from the roots of Jesse)." John's testimony about Jesus that he is "the Son of God" could be understood in a purely human sense, in connection with Isa 11:2, since the concept of sonship expressed in the metaphor "I will be a Father to him, and he will be to me a son" (2 Sam 7:14//1 Chr 17:13) originally applied to Solomon, a man from the roots of Jesse. But John's testimony also strikingly resembles *Tg. Ps.-J.* Num 7:89, noted above for its use of *Dibbera,* and the verbs "descending" and "remaining" used by John can be related to the Messiah of the MT of Isa 11:2 ("resting") and to the Word of the LORD from this Targum passage ("descending"):

Tg. Ps.-J. **Num 7:89**	When Moses entered the tent of meeting to speak with him [YHWH], he heard the voice of the Spirit who was speaking with him, *as he descended from the heaven of heavens* over the mercy seat which was upon the ark of the testimony, from between the two cherubim. And from there was the Word [*Dibbera*] speaking with him.[80]
Isa 11:1-2	A branch from (Jesse's) roots shall bear fruit. The Spirit of the LORD will *rest* upon him.
John 1:32-33	I have seen the Spirit *descending* as a dove *out of heaven*, and he *remained* upon him. And I did not recognize him, but he who sent me to baptize in water said to me, "He upon whom you see the Spirit *descending* and *remaining* upon him, this is the One who baptizes in the Holy Spirit."

Targum Isaiah 11:2 uses the verb שׁרי for "rest." This verb (or the causative) is also used in the Targums for the dwelling of the *Shekinah*. For example, it appears in *Tg. Song* 3:10, which is reminiscent of Num 7:89: "Between the cherubim over the mercy seat dwelt [שׁרי] the *Shekinah* of the LORD, who made his name dwell [שׁכן] in Jerusalem." Thus the *Shekinah* dwells, and the Word speaks, from between the cherubim. One might add that *Tg. Isa.* 6:1–8, noted above, conveys the same idea, since in that passage Isaiah sees the heavenly reality represented by the situation in the holy of holies (i.e., he sees the glory of the Lord's *Shekinah* in the temple, with angels, and hears the voice of the Lord's Word speak to him).

The two verbs "descending" (agreeing with *Tg. Ps.-J.* Num 7:89) and "remaining" (agreeing with the MT of Isa 11:2) support the idea that "the Word (who used to speak to Moses from between the cherubim) has become flesh (from the root of David)." This connection further implies that "Son of God" in John the Baptist's testimony (John 1:34) is not a merely human title connected to 2 Sam 7:14, but corresponds to the targumic divine "Word of the LORD," now become a man. We also see that the initiative for this identification is from the Father, who chose this means to identify his Son to the Jews through John's testimony.

---

[80] Westcott noted the use of *Dibbera* in *Tg. Ps.-J.* Num 7:89 in arguing for a targumic background for the Logos title but did not relate that passage to John 1:32–34 (*St. John*, xvi). McNamara also noted this passage but focused on the mention of the Spirit as possibly illuminating 2 Cor 3:17, "the Lord is the Spirit," i.e. the Spirit of Jesus, who spoke to Moses (*Palestinian Judaism*, 230–31). *Tg. Ps.-J.* Num 7:89 can be compared to *Midrash Numbers Naso* 14:19: "A voice would then descend from heaven, as though through a kind of tube of fire, to between the two cherubim, and Moses would hear the voice speaking to him from within" (Judah Slotki, *Midrash Rabbah Numbers II* [London: Soncino, 1951], 632–33).

It also may be observed that in this linking of "the Word of the LORD" with the Messiah on whom the Spirit rests, there is a clear difference from the usage of the *Memra/Dibbera* of the Targums, where the Word represents God, but not the Messiah. For example, *Tg. Isa.* 42:1 says, "Behold, my servant, . . . my chosen in whom my *Memra* (MT: my soul) is pleased. I will put my Holy Spirit upon him." That God's *Memra* is pleased with the Messiah obviously demonstrates that John's usage of the Logos title (if targumic) represents an adaptation, not a simple reproduction. The targumists did not think of the Word of the LORD as the Son of God in any NT sense. When the Targum says "the Word spoke to Moses," it is a way of saying "YHWH spoke to Moses."

Could this connection between the Targums and the Spirit's descent upon Jesus be mere coincidence? Is there any other reason to see John's report of the baptism of Jesus as connected to *Ps.-J.* Num 7:89? In answer I would point to what might be called the Moses–Elijah–John the Baptist typology.[81] A comparison of Exod 34 to 1 Kgs 19 (Moses and Elijah seeing God on Mt. Sinai) would seem to establish Elijah as a "new Moses." That John the Baptist is considered a "new Elijah" is further evident in the Synoptic Gospels (Matt 3:4 and Mark 1:6 compared to 2 Kgs 1:8; also Matt 11:14; 17:12; Mark 9:13; Luke 1:17). Viewing the Gospel of John's experience of the Spirit's descent upon Jesus in the light of the OT experience of Moses in the holy of holies as described in *Tg. Ps.-J.* Num 7:89 provides another way in which John the Baptist could be considered a new Moses (though there are differences, such as Moses hearing the Spirit speak, John seeing the dove representing the Spirit, and John hearing the Father speak). Perhaps John has also pointed in this direction in that the first three people mentioned by name in his gospel (besides Jesus) are John the Baptist (1: 6, 15, 19), Moses (v. 17), and Elijah (vv. 21, 25).

Moses died outside the promised land for his episode of unbelief, and was succeeded by Joshua, who brought Israel into the promised land. In this sense, Joshua is one greater than Moses, and God began to exalt Joshua at the miraculous crossing of the Jordan (Josh 3:7). One sees the same pattern in Elijah and Elisha (2 Kgs 2:14), the new Moses/Joshua pair. Elijah crosses over to the east side of the Jordan before being taken up by the whirlwind, and God begins to exalt the successor Elisha in the miracle of crossing the Jordan. Then Elisha follows Joshua's path into the promised land, where he fulfills Elijah's unfinished mandate. Like-

---

[81] In Rom 5:14 Paul describes Adam as "a type of the coming one" (i.e. Jesus). In his discussion of Adam and Jesus it is evident that for Paul there is significance both in the similarities and differences between the two. The criteria for what makes for a "type" have been much discussed, and opinions have ranged from one extreme (someone can only be called a "type" if designated so in the NT) to the other (a type can be found almost literally under every rock). A middle ground should, I believe, recognize that there are rather clear examples of types and historical foreshadowings that are not mentioned by NT writers (but may be presumed by them). Further, types may be designated as such by other means than the use of the word "type" or "figure," etc., as e.g. when the Messiah is called "David" in OT prophecy (Jer 30:5; Ezek 34:23; 37:24–25; Hos 3:5) and when John the Baptist is called "Elijah" (Mark 9:13). Here we are describing *historical* typology, in which a person living in one historical period, and the events with which he was involved, somehow relate to a later period in which history is to some extent repeated.

wise, John the Baptist speaks of his successor as one who is greater than him (John 1:15, 27), and the Father begins to exalt Jesus at his baptism in the Jordan. John died at Herod's palace (Matt 14:10; Mark 6:27), which according to Josephus at least was Machaerus, on the east side of the Jordan (*Ant.* 18.119). That John was aware of this typology is further evident from the fact that he added to the Synoptic material, since the activities of Jesus at the Jordan in John 1 are reminiscent of those of Joshua at the Jordan before Israel crossed, as we will see below in ch. 5.

This combination of OT and targumic backgrounds to Jesus' baptism therefore sheds light on the phrase "the Word became flesh" not only by reference to prophecy (Isa 11:2), but also by typological connections to Israel's history. The Word has become "flesh"—a man like Joshua (his human namesake) and Elisha (a name with the same meaning as Joshua). Since the Synoptic Gospels also describe the Spirit descending upon Jesus, they too could convey the message "the Word has become flesh" to those familiar with the reading of *Tg. Ps.-J.* Num 7:89 (see ch. 11).

While it is true that there is no direct proof that the reading in *Tg. Ps.-J.* Num 7:89 was current in the first century, interpreters must account for John's emphasis on the Spirit "descending" and "remaining" on Jesus. The interpretation offered above does so in a way that agrees with a stated theme of John's Gospel, namely, the Word became flesh. We will see this theme brought out over and over as we examine John's Gospel from the Targum background. Therefore, one can turn the tables and suggest that John 1:32–34 can be considered evidence that *Tg. Ps.-J.* Num 7:89 preserves a pre-Christian tradition. It would hardly be the only case where *Tg. Ps.-J.,* alone of the Targums, preserves a passage of interest to NT studies.

The Word Speaks to Jacob and Nathanael (John 1:43–51)

As many interpreters recognize, the Lord's words to Nathanael, "you [pl.] shall see heaven opened, and the angels of God ascending and descending upon the Son of Man," draw in some way upon Gen 28:12, Jacob's dream of a ladder extending from earth to heaven:

Gen 28:12	John 1:51
(Jacob) had a dream, and behold, a ladder was set on the earth with its top reaching to heaven; and behold, *the angels of God were ascending and descending* upon it.	And he said to (Nathanael), "Truly, truly, I say to you [pl.], you [pl.] will see heaven opened, and *the angels of God ascending and descending* on the Son of Man.

This comparison can be analyzed from at least three perspectives:

1. In a verbal comparison of John 1:51 to the LXX of Gen 28:12, "the Son of Man" takes the place of the ladder:

Gen 28:12	John 1:51
καὶ οἱ ἄγγελοι τοῦ θεοῦ ἀνέβαινον καὶ κατέβαινον ἐπ᾽ αὐτῆς	καὶ τοὺς ἀγγέλους τοῦ θεοῦ ἀναβαίνοντας καὶ καταβαίνοντας ἐπὶ τὸν υἱὸν τοῦ ἀνθρώπου

Noting this similarity, Burkett suggests that substituting Jesus for the ladder symbolizes that Jesus is the way to heaven, much as Jesus says in calling himself the way to the Father (14:6).[82]

2. To state the obvious, John 1:51 portrays Jesus as a man—the Son of Man. As we shall argue in ch. 4, the Son of Man title depends in part on the depiction of Jacob in the OT as a new Adam.

3. Jesus' dialogue with Nathanael has several features that correspond to the LORD speaking to Jacob in Gen 28: (a) Jesus calls Nathanael "an Israelite indeed, in whom is no deceit" (John 1:47). Jacob was at Bethel, fleeing for his life, precisely because of his deceit in Gen 27 ("Your brother came in deceit"; v. 35). His deceit consisted in lying about his identity (v. 32). "Israel" was the name given to Jacob when he had lost his deceit, answering truthfully when asked, "What is your name?" (Gen 32:27–28). Nathanael is thus like Jacob after he was renamed Israel. (b) What Jesus claims Nathanael (and/or others) will see is similar to what Jacob did see (the angels of God ascending and descending). (c) Nathanael's astonishment and change of mind at the revelation of Jesus recall Jacob's at Bethel (Gen 28:16–17).[83]

Interpreters tend to focus on and pick one or at most two of these three perspectives—Jesus as the ladder, Jesus as the new Jacob, or the pre-incarnate Jesus as the one who appeared to Jacob. But there is no reason not to combine them: "All three interpretations of the Son of Man are conclusions an ancient reader well versed in the Scriptures and in the on-going tradition of their interpretation might reach after pondering John's Gospel."[84]

---

[82] Burkett, *Son of the Man in the Gospel of John*, 117–18. Cf. Alan R. Kerr, *The Temple of Jesus' Body: The Temple Theme in the Gospel of John* (JSNTSup 220; New York: Sheffield Academic Press, 2002), 164: "This suggests that Jesus as Son of Man is a mediator between heaven and earth."

[83] "We are led to conclude that the text apparently sees the disciples of Jesus in the position of Jacob, promising them that they will see a vision just as Jacob did. The Gospel does not state explicitly that Jacob saw the heavenly Jesus, but that is a safe inference both from the examples of Abraham [8:58] and Isaiah [12:41] and from the argument in the text that *no one* (Jacob included) has ever seen God" (Jerome H. Neyrey, "The Jacob Allusions in John 1:51," *CBQ* 44 [1982]: 591). But Neyrey somewhat incongruously says, "Jesus is not making himself identical with Yahweh but identifying himself as the appearing God of OT theophanies" (ibid.).

[84] Jennifer K. Berenson Maclean, "A Tale of Two Weddings: The Divine Trickster in John" (paper presented at the annual meeting of the SBL, Boston, Mass., November 21, 1999), n.p. (accessed December 11, 2007; no longer available). http://www.roanoke.edu/religion/Maclean/SBL/DivineTrickster.htm.

Anthony Tyrell Hanson combined two of the three perspectives: "In this piece of elaborate typology Jesus corresponds to 'the Lord' in the Bethel vision, the Lord who stood at the top of the ladder: but he also corresponds to the ladder itself, since the point of the midrash [John 1:51] is to emphasize that Jesus is now the place where God is to be found, both in heaven and on earth. . . . The conclusion is of course, that according to John he whom Jacob saw in his vision at Bethel was the pre-existent Logos, just as Moses saw him on Sinai" (*Prophetic Gospel*, 37).

Turning to the *Pal. Tgs.*, we note that all of them (including both traditions of the *Frg. Tgs.*) have a lengthy addition at Gen 28:10 describing a legend of five miracles that "were done for our father Jacob when he went forth from Beersheba to go to Haran." The first miracle was that "the hours of the day were shortened, and the sun set before its time, because the Word [*Dibbera* or *Dibbura*] desired to speak to him." (This desire led to the LORD's appearance to Jacob in his dream.)[85]

A number of parallels are evident between the LORD speaking to Jacob (in the MT) and Jesus speaking to Nathanael. In the *Pal. Tgs.* the parallel is with *the Word* speaking to Jacob. Three perspectives on John 1:51 and its OT and targumic contexts show us (1) Jesus as the ladder from earth to heaven; (2) Jesus as a man; and (3) Jesus as the divine Word who spoke to Jacob and now speaks to Nathanael. In combination, they suggest that the invisible Word (who spoke to Jacob) has become flesh (a person like Jacob but without sin) so as to provide for lost people (not for angels) a way to heaven. In ch. 9 we will see that the "I am he" (ἐγώ εἰμι) sayings of Jesus in John can be placed into these same three categories.

Recalling Burney's suggestion that in John 1:14 not just "the Word" but "dwelt" and "his glory" reflect targumic concepts (the *Shekinah* and the glory, or the glory of the *Shekinah*), we note that these latter two are combined in *Tg. Neof.* and *Tg. Ps.-J.* Gen 28:16. For MT "surely the LORD is in this place," they say "truly the glory of the *Shekinah* of the LORD dwells in this place." *Targum Onqelos* reads similarly but omits "the *Shekinah* of." Elsewhere John connects the revelation of the glory of Jesus to the evidence of the supernatural in his working of miracles (John 2:11). Here likewise Jesus gives evidence of the supernatural in his knowledge of Nathanael's circumstances when Philip called him (1:48). Nathanael's experience could thus be described, even without referring to the Targums, as seeing the glory of the Word who became flesh and dwelt amongst us. Turning to the *Pal. Tgs.*, we find much the same language describing Jacob's experience at Bethel before the Word became flesh.

We can also see in the rest of John's Gospel various elements of the Word's promises to Jacob and Jacob's vow at Bethel as rendered in the Targums, if we understand them as fulfilled in Jesus the Word. The common divine promise to be with someone is often rendered in the Targums with the idea that God will be with someone in his Word (always *Memra*) or that the Word of the LORD will be with them or that his Word will be for their help. For MT "I am with you" *Tgs. Ps.-J.* and *Onq.* Gen 28:15 read "My Word is for your help" (similarly v. 20, and *Tg. Neof.* [mg.] v. 20). In *Tg. Neof.* this phrase is rendered "I, in my Word, am with you." In John 13:33, Jesus the Word says he will be with the disciples a little while longer. In 14:16, he says, "I will ask the Father and he will give you *another Helper,* that he might be with you forever," which means that until then Jesus (the Word) has been their helper (similarly, 1 John 2:1).[86] Genesis 28:15 also says, "I will not leave you

---

[85] In arguing for a targumic background for the Logos title, Westcott noted the use of *Dibbera* in *Tg. Ps.-J.* Gen 28:10 but did not relate that passage to John 1:51 (*St. John*, xvi).

[86] "For your help" is בסעדך. For סעד McNamara uses "aid," Maher "assistance." I translate this term as "help" to illustrate the possible Targum background to the term Paraclete,

until I have done what I have promised," which in *Tg. Neof.* is "*My Word will not leave you . . .*" (*Tgs. Onq.* and *Ps.-J.*: "I will not leave you"). Jesus the Word likewise says in connection with the promise of another helper, "*I will not leave you* as orphans, I will come to you" (John 14:18).

For MT "the LORD will be my God," *Tg. Onq.* Gen 28:21 reads, "the Word of the LORD shall be my God." *Tg. Neof.* [mg.] and *CTg. E* read, "(if) the Word of the LORD is for my help as a redeemer God."

At the same time, this journey on which Jacob is embarking can also be seen to provide a paradigm for the mission of Jesus Christ during the "little while" that he is with Israel. Jacob left his father's house on a two-fold mission. The first was to save his life from his brother Esau, whom he had wronged (Gen 27:41–45). The second was to find a wife (Gen 28:1–2). Likewise Jesus has left his Father's house and will return (John 14:12, 28) when his mission is complete. Based on the idea of the church being the bride of Christ (which we explore in chapter six as we look at John 4 in part from a background of Jacob meeting his bride Rachel at a well in Gen 29), we can relate this second mission of Jacob to the mission of Jesus. But since the bride of Christ is gained by saving her (eternal) life, this mission of Jesus also relates to the first mission of Jacob: Jesus left his Father's house because of the wrong Jacob did, and to save Jacob's life (the same may be said of all of God's people), not just for "a few days" (Gen 27:44), but forever. Seeing the twofold mission of Jacob as a paradigm of Christ's mission is consistent with the fact that in Isa 49:3–5 the Servant of the Lord is named "Israel," and this same mission is described in different words, "to bring Jacob back" to God.

One might dismiss the foregoing interpretation based on *Pal. Tgs.* Gen 28:10 by saying that the addition of the five legends is late (it is not in *Tg. Onq.*) and of no interest to NT studies. Against this, it is of interest that another of these five miracles is apparently alluded to in John 4:14, a fact which makes it more plausible that the first legend was also known at the time, and thus that something like the present reading of *Pal. Tgs.* Gen 28:10 was extant in the first century. The fifth miracle (the fourth in *Tg. Ps.-J.*) was that when Jacob removed the stone from the mouth of the well (Gen 29:10), the water surged up and overflowed for twenty years, the time that Jacob lived in Haran. Similarly, in response to the Samaritan woman's question, "You are not greater than our father Jacob are you?" Jesus replies that for anyone who drinks "the water that I shall give," that water "shall become in him a well of water springing up to eternal life." "Our father Jacob" or "Jacob our father" occurs six to seven times in the *Pal. Tg.* legend (except that it

---

which is rendered as "Helper" in some NT translations. The verbal and nominal forms from root עזר in MT are often rendered in the Targums with verbal and nominal forms from root סעד (see, e.g., Targums at Exod 18:4; Ps 20:2; 35:2; 60:11; 70:5; 71:12; 108:13; 119:86; 121:1, 2; 146:5). We could also note that when the targumists made such changes they liked to have precedent elsewhere in Scripture. Such precedent could come from Exod 18:4, "The other [son of Moses] was named Eliezer, for, 'the God of my father was my help, and delivered me from the sword of Pharaoh.'" Such wording could easily be interpreted as equivalent to "the God of my father was with me." For "my help" (בעזרי), all of the Targums have בסעדי, the same word used when the Targums render "I am with you" as "my word is your help."

does not occur at all in *Tg. Ps.-J.*). Thus even if the legend were true, what was believed about Jacob is insignificant when compared with the work of Jesus in giving the waters of eternal life to his people. While we might be tempted to ignore the embellishments of the Targums as distracting inventions designed to cast the spotlight on humans (Jacob in this case), it is plain that familiarity with them can add to our understanding of the Gospel of John. It follows that it is the task of the interpreter to discover and bring this information out to educate those who read the Gospel without knowledge of this background.

How John Has Adapted the Divine Word
of the Targums as a Title for Jesus

One might observe first of all that the examples discussed above seem to justify including *Dibbera/Dibbura* along with *Memra* in examining the possibility of a targumic background to the Logos title. Although *Dibbera/Dibbura* appears in a small number of cases compared to *Memra*, it figures prominently in possible Targum passages illuminating portions of John 1. Of the seven passages from John 1 that we looked at in the previous section, *Dibbera/Dibbura* figures in the last three (John 1:14–18, 32–34, and 43–51). These results reinforce the suggestion that John's terminology of "the Word" fits targumic usage, since *Dibbera/Dibbura* is used in this absolute sense, while *Memra* is not (or at least, its absolute usage is rare enough to be considered anomalous when it does occur). Adding to this conclusion is the fact that though John 1:32–34 is the fourth of the passages discussed above, chronologically it would be the first identification of Jesus as the Word in the ministry of Jesus, coming after his baptism, which, again, recalls *Pal. Tgs.* Num 7:89, "from there the Word [*Dibbera*] spoke to him."

John Lightfoot wrote in 1859 that almost all then-recent commentaries took note of targumic *Memra* and that this expression "may something (i.e., somewhat) enlighten the matter now before us." Lightfoot was noncommittal, however, noting, for example, that for "by my Spirit" of Zech 7:12 the Targum has "by my Word," which would not fit John's purpose.[87] We have already noted that the Word is clearly not the Messiah in the Targums (see above on *Tg. Isa.* 42:1, where God's Word delights in the Servant of the Lord; the MT says "my Soul delights in him"). For another example, on the fourth night of the haggadah of the Four Nights mentioned above, the Messiah and Moses return, with the Word of the Lord leading them. *Targum Pseudo-Jonathan* Deut 30:4 says that the divine Word will gather Israel through the mediation of Elijah and the Messiah.

Clearly, then, if the divine Word of the Targums lies behind John's Logos title, some modification of the concept would be required in the process of appropriation. Does that fact constitute evidence against the Targum background of

---

[87] John Lightfoot, *A Commentary on the New Testament from the Talmud and Hebraica; Matthew–I Corinthians* (Oxford: Oxford: University Press, 1859; repr., Grand Rapids: Baker, 1979), 238.

the Logos title? Not when one recognizes that all proposals regarding the origin of the Logos title require some modification of the source concept. For instance, neither the OT word of the LORD, nor Wisdom, nor Philo's Logos is identified with the Messiah. Reasons that scholars have rejected targumic *Memra/Dibbera* as the background for the Logos title will be explored more in ch. 12. For now we can say that a substantial number of passages in John 1 make good sense when seen against a targumic background for the Logos title, and that these connections reinforce John's opening statement that "the Word was God." In particular, the Targums support that idea that the divine Word was the God of Moses (John 1:14 compared to *Pal. Tgs.* Exod 33–34, to be examined in more detail in ch. 2; and John 1:32–33 compared to *Pal. Tgs.* Num 7:89) and the God of Jacob (John 1:51 compared to *Pal. Tgs.* Gen 28:10). These results suggest that McNamara was correct in his proposal that John used the Logos title because in the Targums the Word of the LORD is a metonym for God. While we can't claim that the divine Word of the Targums refers explicitly to the second person of the Godhead, the fact that the divine Word is employed especially in contexts where God interacts with the creation to accomplish his will in the world (especially the redemption of his people) makes it a suitable term to apply specifically to the Son. While *Memra* and *Dibbera* in the Targums are used to refer to God under certain circumstances, and *Memra* implies the name of God, the Tetragrammaton, John uses Logos specifically and exclusively of the Son. Thus the Targums make clear that by "the Word," John means, in NT terms, "YHWH the Son."

JOHN'S MOTIVES FOR THE LOGOS TITLE

Although at this point there is much more to be said in favor of the Targums as forming the background for the Word of John's Gospel, from what has already been seen we can suggest John's motivation for identifying Jesus as the targumic Word who has become flesh. I would put John's motives in two categories: *Christology* and *apologetics*.

Christology

If it is correct to say that the Logos title has a Targum background based on the fact that the Word of the LORD implies the Tetragrammaton and refers to God through metonymy, especially as he interacts with his creation, then presumably John has a christological motive for identifying Jesus as the Word. Jesus is YHWH the Son. John is unique in calling Jesus the Word, but is he unique in identifying him as YHWH? We discuss this question in ch. 11, but the short answer for now is no. In terms of Christology, then, the question becomes, why does John use this particular way of saying that Jesus is YHWH?

I suggested above that the symbolism of the Spirit descending as a dove at the baptism of Jesus points to a Targum reading of Num 7:89 that would identify Jesus as the Word who spoke to Moses from between the cherubim. My reader might have taken note of the fact that, although the reports of the baptism of Jesus in the Synoptic Gospels do not stress "descending" and "remaining," corresponding to Jesus as "Word" and as "Messiah," nevertheless the Synoptics point just as readily to *Tg. Ps.-J.* Num 7:89 as does John, since they also describe the Spirit descending on Jesus. They too could have said "the Word has become flesh." In ch. 11, we will note a number of other synoptic texts where the same conclusion comes out. Why, then, does only John explicitly identify Jesus as the Word?

My suggestion is that in terms of Christology, identifying Jesus as the Word is only a means to an end. That end is to identify Jesus as both fully God and fully human. The goal is not simply to identify Jesus as the divine Word of the Targums; rather, identifying Jesus as the Word is a means to identifying him as YHWH the God of Israel, a name he shares with the Father (as we discuss in more detail in ch. 3). For Aramaic-speaking Jews, accustomed to hearing the Scriptures read in the synagogue, the Aramaic Scriptures help make a connection between what John says about Jesus, or what Jesus says about himself, and what the OT says about God, or what in the OT God says about himself.

Again we can note how John 12:37 seems to depend on Num 14:11:

John 12:37	MT of Num 14:11
Though he had performed so many *signs* before them, they were *not believing in him*.	How long will they *not believe in me*, in spite of all the *signs* which I have performed in their midst?

Is the similarity a coincidence? Does John just happen to use the terminology of Num 14:11 without intending that we see a parallel? Or are we to understand that history is repeating itself such that the unbelief of the Jews in Jesus parallels the unbelief of the OT Israelites in YHWH their redeemer? When we read this passage in conjunction with the Prologue of John's gospel, where Jesus is referred to as the Word who is God, and in light of the Targums of Num 14:11, we see that in John 12:37 the Gospel writer clearly intends to portray Jesus as YHWH, the God of Israel, now come in the flesh:

Tg. Neof. Num 14:11	*Tgs. Onq.* and *Ps.-J.*
How long will they not *believe in the name of my Word*, in spite of all the *signs of my miracles* which I have performed among them?	How long will they not *believe in my Word* . . .

In short, identifying Jesus as the Word helps readers make the proper connection between John 12:37 and Num 14:11 and draw the appropriate christological conclusion. Jesus says to Philip in the upper room, "Have I been with you so long, and you have not come to know me?" (John 14:9). But this is the same Philip who was not slow to recognize Jesus as the Messiah: "We have found him of whom Moses in the Law, and the Prophets wrote—Jesus of Nazareth, the son of Joseph"

(1:45). Perhaps John observed many in the church in its second and third generations who, like Philip, acknowledged and believed in Jesus as the Messiah, but did not fully comprehend his divine nature. This, it seems to me, is John's great christological burden as he writes.

Apologetics

I believe there is a second reason that John identifies Jesus as the Word. John might have seen the incorporation of the *Memra* theology into the Targums as a providential preparation for the coming of the Son into the world. Beyond the passages which are of christological significance, there are many texts that over time could be looked back upon as something like the "prophecy" of Caiaphas (John 11:49–52). John says that Caiaphas prophesied that Jesus would die for the nation. What John takes from this statement is quite different from what Caiaphas meant. Similarly, there are many texts in the Targums that speak of the divine Word with no explicit intention to refer to the Messiah, but which, when "Son" is substituted for "Word," can be taken as "unwitting prophecies" in the same sense.

We will look at the phenomenon of unwitting targumic prophecies with reference to the divine Word of the Targums in ch. 10. I suggest that John identifies Jesus as the Word as a way of appealing to his fellow Aramaic-speaking Jews who have survived the destruction of Jerusalem by the Romans in c.e. 70. Ezekiel 39:23 says that as a consequence of the exile to Babylon, "The nations will know that the house of Israel went into exile for their iniquity, because they *acted unfaithfully against me,* and *I hid my face from them,* so I gave them into the hand of their adversaries, and they fell by the sword, all of them." The changes made in *Tg. Ezek.* are quite suggestive of the first-century c.e. exile, once Jesus of Nazareth is identified as the divine Word, especially in light of the Jewish tradition that the miracles indicating the presence of the *Shekinah* in Israel ceased forty years prior to the destruction of the temple by the Romans:[88]

> The nations will know that the house of Israel went into exile because of their sins, because *they dealt falsely with my Word,* so that *I removed my Shekinah from them,* and delivered them into the hand of their enemies, and they were slain by the sword, all of them.

If the tradition of the cessation of the miracles indicating the presence of the *Shekinah* in Israel was current when John wrote, then combining this tradition

---

[88] According to the Mishnah and Talmud, the westernmost light of the lamp in the temple never went out, which "was taken as a sign that the *Shechinah* rested over Israel" (*b. Yoma* 39a; pp. 184–85 n.7 of the Soncino edition). The rabbis also believed that a crimson thread that was tied to the sanctuary door turned white when the scapegoat reached the wilderness on the day of atonement: "Our Rabbis taught: During the last forty years before the destruction of the Temple the lot ['For the Lord'] did not come up in the right hand; nor did the crimson-coloured strap become white; nor did the westernmost light shine; and the doors of the *Hekal* would open by themselves, until R Joḥanan b. Zakkai rebuked them" (*b. Yoma* 39b; see also *m. Yoma* 6:8; *b. Shabbath* 22b; *b. Menahot* 86b).

with *Tg. Ezek.* 39:23 would lead naturally to the question, "How did the LORD's people deal falsely with his Word forty years prior to the destruction of Jerusalem?" John provides a compelling answer by identifying Jesus as this divine Word.

CONCLUSION

We have now seen in a preliminary way that a Targum background to the Logos title makes good sense and that there is a good deal of evidence for it just from the first chapter of John, both in the Prologue and beyond. In the next chapter, we will go into more detail on the OT background of John 1:14–18, reinforcing what has been said so far. The third chapter examines the overall mission of Jesus as revealing the Father's name, and what that means in the light of the Targums. In subsequent chapters, we will see that Jesus as a human speaks and acts as people of God did in OT times, yet without their sinful failures. At the same time, he speaks and acts on earth as the LORD did when he "came down" from heaven in OT times. These two features are explained by John's assertion that "the Word [i.e., YHWH, the Son] became flesh, and dwelt among us." In both features we will see continuity with the OT as well as change due to the incarnation. Thus, much of John's Gospel can be seen as a commentary on this introductory statement. In the synagogue readings in Palestine, the Jews would hear the Scriptures read in Hebrew, then in an Aramaic translation. Those who knew both languages would hear first of the person and works of the LORD as recorded in the MT. Then they would very often hear in Aramaic of the person and works of the Word of the LORD. John shows his readers that this progression of thought was not just a curiosity of the Aramaic translations recited in the synagogues every Sabbath, but pointed to a deeper reality in the history of redemption, in the transition from the old covenant to the new, from the pre-incarnate Word to the incarnate Word.

2

The Old Testament Background
to John 1:14–18

INTRODUCTION

In this chapter, we look at the OT background of John 1:14 both with and
without reference to the Targums, again with a view to answering the question of
which of the four views of the Logos title is supported by the OT background to
John 1:14 itself. First we look at the theme of God dwelling among his people and
manifesting his glory, without reference to the Targums, to see what conclusions
can be drawn in terms of the meaning of the Logos title. Next we look at Targum
texts that combine references to the Word and the *Shekinah* or glory of the *Shekinah,* or Targum texts referring to the Word that have alternate readings (or Targum texts) referring to the *Shekinah,* to see if they provide support for the idea that
John is employing terminology from the Targums. Finally, we look at a commonly
proposed OT background to John 1:14–18, namely, the revelation of the glory of
the LORD to Moses in Exod 34. Each of these studies supports the view that John
derived the Logos title from the Targums.

THE MANIFESTATION OF THE GLORY OF THE LORD
IN THE TABERNACLE AND THE TEMPLE

Part of the argument outlined in ch. 1 for a targumic background for the Logos
title rested on the view that John uses or alludes to three terms that are important
in how the Targums render OT texts dealing with revelation: Word (*Memra* and
Dibbera), glory, and *Shekinah*. Of course, "glory" is important in the Hebrew text
of the OT itself, though it does not occur there as often as in the Targums. Similarly, while the term *Shekinah* does not occur in the Hebrew MT, the related verb
שָׁכֵן ("dwell") and noun מִשְׁכָּן ("tabernacle") do occur, allowing the possibility that
"dwelt" in John 1:14 alludes to these terms rather than directly to the *Shekinah*. One
could argue therefore that the Targums are not necessary to explain John's terminology, and we would be left wondering whether the Logos title comes from the

idea of the OT word of the LORD, from personified Wisdom, or from Philo's Logos. In this section, we essentially look at "_____ dwelt among us, and we beheld his glory" from an OT perspective, in order to try to fill in the conceptual blank.[1]

Our main problem in filling in the blank is that there are no explicit passages that use any of the OT words for "word" that would be suitable for this purpose. If we therefore allow for the possibility that John's "Word" is really "Wisdom," we can find a parallel to "dwelt among us," although the parallel is with intertestamental Wisdom literature, not the OT (see ch. 1, in the subsection, Three Plausible Proposals: Wisdom in the Wisdom Literature).[2] Even if we grant that for John (or whoever wrote the Prologue or the hymn, poem, etc. upon which the Prologue is based) such literature was part of Scripture or at least expressed ideas suitable for his purposes, there would still be no parallel in the Wisdom literature to John's statement that "we saw his glory." Advocates of Philo's Logos have not found a close parallel to this phrase either.

If we keep our focus on the OT, however, we see the LORD dwelling among his people in the tabernacle and the temple, and manifesting his glory to his people. As noted above, the Hebrew verb for "dwell" is שָׁכַן, and the word for "tabernacle" is מִשְׁכָּן, both of which can be related to the verb σκηνόω, "dwell," used in John 1:14. In the LXX, the related noun σκηνή, "tent," is used for the tabernacle. For the Pentateuch, the LXX often avoids translating שָׁכַן (when God is the subject) with a verb that means "dwell." For example, in the LXX the phrase "that I might dwell among them" (Exod 29:46) is "to be called upon by them." However, one time in the Pentateuch (Num 35:34), and often outside of the Pentateuch, the LXX uses κατασκηνόω to translate verbal forms of שׁכן where the subject is God, his tabernacle, his name, or his glory.[3] In Rev 21:3, σκηνόω is used much as κατασκηνόω is in the LXX, in a way that also reminds us of John 1:14: "the tabernacle [σκηνή] of God is with men, and he will dwell [σκηνόω] with them, and they shall be his people; and God himself will be with them." This can be compared to Exod 29:45: "I will dwell in the midst of the Israelites, and I will be their God." In the LXX, σκηνόω is used only in three verses, always with human subjects (Gen 13:12; Judg 5:17; 8:11).

The tabernacle was built so that the LORD, after delivering his people from Egypt, might dwell among them and be their God (Exod 25:8; 29:45–46). When the tabernacle was built, the glory of the LORD filled it in an evident way, consecrating it and indicating that this purpose was accomplished (40:34–35). Instructions for the construction of the tabernacle, its anointing, the priestly garments,

---

[1] I leave out the phrase "became flesh" because scholars agree that in all views as to why John calls Jesus the Word, this part is unique to John and has no counterpart in any of the proposed source materials for the Logos title.

[2] Bar 3:37 (NRSV), "Afterward she appeared on earth and lived [συναναστρέφω] with humankind" (when the law was given); Sir 24:8 (NRSV), "Then the Creator of all things gave me [Wisdom] a command, and my Creator chose the place for my tent [σκηνή]. He said, 'Make your dwelling [κατασκηνόω] in Jacob, and in Israel receive your inheritance.'"

[3] Josh 22:19; 1 Chr 23:25; 2 Chr 6:1–2; Neh 1:9; Ps 68:18; 74:2; 78:60; 85:9; Jer 7:12; Ezek 43:7, 9; Joel 3:17, 21; Zech 2:10; 8:3. In Ezra 6:12; 7:15, κατασκηνόω is used for Aramaic שׁכן (pael; make dwell) and מִשְׁכַּן (dwelling).

and priestly ordination and consecration offerings take up chs. 25 through 31 of the book of Exodus. After the sin with the golden calf, the threatened destruction of the nation, the intercession of Moses, and the partial judgment of the people (Exod 32), Moses set up the tent of meeting "outside the camp, far off from the camp," and "everyone who sought the LORD would go out to the tent of meeting, which was outside the camp" (33:7). This "tent of meeting" (אֹהֶל מוֹעֵד) predates the tabernacle, but this term was used often for the tabernacle (starting at 27:21) when the instructions for its construction were given, as well as after it was built. The fact that Moses set up this tent of meeting "outside the camp," in contrast to the tabernacle, which would be erected in the midst of the camp with the tribes around it (Num 2) so that "I might dwell in their midst" (Exod 29:46), would seem to support the rabbinical interpretation of Exod 33:7 that the LORD had in effect excommunicated the nation and that the Israelites who wanted to seek the LORD must go outside the camp to do so (*Exodus Rabbah* 45.3; this interpretation will be discussed in connection with John 7:34 and 12:26 in ch. 8).[4] After the LORD shows his glory to Moses and Moses returns from the mountain with the second giving of the Ten Commandments (Exod 34), the instructions given in chs 25–31 are carried out. The tabernacle is erected on New Year's Day (40:2, 17), and then,

> The cloud covered the tent of meeting, and the glory of the LORD filled the tabernacle. And Moses was not able to enter the tent of meeting because the cloud had settled [שָׁכַן] on it, and the glory of the LORD filled the tabernacle. (40:34–35)

All of this suggests that anyone familiar with these events who looked at John's expression "_____ dwelt among us, and we beheld his glory," would naturally infer that the name of God was to be inserted in the blank. This supposition would be based on understanding John 1:14 in light of an important theme developed over sixteen chapters in the law of Moses, as opposed to two verses in intertestamental Wisdom literature which only support "dwelt among us," not "and we saw his glory" (see ch. 1, in the subsection, Three Plausible Proposals: Wisdom in the Wisdom Literature), and which are in any case arguably dependent on this dominant theme of Exodus.

The theme continues when the time comes to build a temple. We see both continuity with Israel's past as well as change from it, in keeping with the fact that there has also been a change in Israel's government with the establishment of the monarchy and David's dynasty, with Jerusalem as the permanent capital city. In terms of change, or discontinuity, we can point to the permanence and fixed location of the temple (a reflection of the peace and increased security provided to Israel by David's victories), its greater grandeur (i.e., "glory" in the physical sense), and the fact that its fate is not connected to the obedience to the covenant of the Israelites in general, but to the obedience of the house of David (1 Kgs 9:1–9).

---

[4]S. M. Lehrman, *Midrash Rabbah: Exodus* (London: Soncino, 1939), 520 n.5: "The excommunicated was cut off entirely from the camp; here, Moses removes himself afar off from those excommunicated by God."

In terms of continuity, the temple has the same general arrangement as the tabernacle, and the same ark is housed in the holy of holies, containing the terms of the covenant, the Ten Commandments. Most importantly, the temple serves the same purpose as the tabernacle: "I will dwell [וְשָׁכַנְתִּי] among the sons of Israel" (1 Kgs 6:13), the fulfillment of which is indicated again by the visible manifestation of the glory of God at the temple's dedication, much as in the tabernacle in the wilderness:

> It happened that when the priests came from the holy place, the cloud filled the house of the LORD, so that the priests could not stand to minister because of the cloud, for the glory of the LORD filled the house of the LORD. (1 Kgs 8:13–14; similarly, 2 Chr 5:13–14; 7:1–3)

Again, with this history in mind, in our "fill in the blank" exercise we would posit that "the Word" in John 1:14 refers to the name of God. Again we note that the source material covers numerous chapters of the OT (1 Kgs 6–8, paralleled and supplemented in 1 Chr 28, 29; 2 Chr 2–7), in contrast to a couple of verses from the Wisdom literature that parallel only the first half of the sentence for which we are filling in the blank.

An alert interpreter, then, not knowing anything of Philo or the Targums, might suppose that "the Word" is a circumlocution for the name of God, which was no longer pronounced, similar to "the Name," which John uses elsewhere (3 John 7). Or if we had Philo but not the Targums, one might suppose that John was using "the Word" for "the name of God," as did Philo (and perhaps other contemporaries who are unknown to us today). This is basically the conclusion that John C. Meagher came to:

> From the first verse of the Gospel of John, we are confronted with the Logos—a concept which Philo considers identical with the Name—precisely as divine. It is therefore perfectly reasonable that exegetes have taken vs. 14 as an allusion to the temple, even though it speaks of the Logos rather than of the Name.[5]

For OT support one could point to passages where God's name is said to dwell among his people.[6]

In its sad history, Israel later sees the destruction of the temple "for the sins of Manasseh," son of David (2 Kgs 24:3; 25:9), but not before the glory of the LORD has departed from the temple, as seen in Ezekiel's vision (Ezek 10:18–19; 11:23). When the second temple is built after the return of the Jews from exile, there is again continuity in that the temple itself is built on the same site as the first. There

---

[5] John C. Meagher, "John 1 14 and the New Temple," *JBL* 88 (1969): 57. Meagher cites Philo's *On the Confusion of Tongues* 146, where the firstborn Word is called "the name of God, and His Word, and the Man after His image" (Colson, LCL). Meagher also pointed for support to John 17:11–12, where Jesus says that the Father's name is given to him (ibid., 57 n.1).

[6] E.g., in Deut 12–26 (often); Ezra 6:12; Neh 1:9; Ps 69:36; 74:7; Jer 7:12. In Ezek 43:7, where MT says, "I shall dwell among the Israelites forever," LXX says, "My name shall dwell among the Israelites forever."

is also discontinuity, in that the ark is no more, the temple seems insignificant compared with its former glory (Hag 2:3), and there is no statement "the glory of the Lord filled the temple." Instead, there is a promise for the future in light of the present, apparent relative insignificance of the temple:

> "I will shake all the nations; and they will come [with] the wealth of all the nations; and I will fill this house with glory," says the Lord of hosts. . . . "The latter glory of this house will be greater than the former," says the Lord of hosts, "and in this place I shall give peace," declares the Lord of hosts. (Hag 2:7, 9)

For John, the incarnation and earthly ministry of YHWH the Son represents the next phase of this theme, again involving both discontinuity and continuity. John expresses the continuity, if we allow that "the Word" implies the Tetragrammaton: "YHWH [the Son] . . . tabernacled among us, and we saw his glory." As Leon Morris put it:

> John is saying to his readers, then, that the glory that had been manifested in one way or another in the wilderness wanderings and later, as at the dedication of Solomon's temple . . . was manifested in its fullness in the life of Jesus of Nazareth.[7]

Change is seen in that instead of an inanimate tent, or a temple whose fate is connected to the obedience of the house of David, this dwelling place is flesh—the perfectly obedient son of David. The Ten Commandments are not in an ark inside this tabernacle as tablets of stone but are expressed in his lifelong perfect obedience to the law.[8]

Solomon's temple was destroyed for the sins of the house of David, but the life of Jesus, also from the house of David, is one of perfect obedience. This temple will be destroyed for the sins of others, that is, his people, then raised again (rebuilt) on the third day (2:19).

Without even considering the Targums, then, we have seen that through a careful examination of John 1:14 in light of the significant OT theme of God dwelling among his people and manifesting his glory, one could arrive at the same conclusion as that which I proposed in ch. 1 based on the Targums, namely, that "the Word" stands for the Tetragrammaton. "The Word" means "YHWH the Son."

Word, Glory, and *Shekinah* in the Targums

In this section we expand on the argument from ch. 1 that John 1:14 takes its vocabulary from these three important targumic terms. We noted there how all three are found in *Tg. Isa.* 6:1–8, and even in the single verse, *Tg. Ps.-J.* Deut 5:24. We further noted that both of these passages are also significant because they can be related to John's Gospel: John tells us that Isaiah saw Christ's glory, and John

---

[7] Leon Morris, *The Word Was Made Flesh: John 1–5* (vol. 1 of *Reflections on the Gospel of John*; 4 vols.; Grand Rapids: Baker, 1986), 20. See also Carson, *John,* 127–28.

[8] Cf. the adaptation of Ps 40:8 in Heb 10:5–10.

1:14 goes beyond the mere employment of targumic terms in its similarity to *Tg. Ps.-J.* Deut 5:24 ("the Word of the LORD our God has shown us the Shekinah of his glory . . . and the voice of the Word we have heard"). Moreover, both John 1:14 and Deut 5:24 look back at the revelation of God's glory on Mt. Sinai (we explore this further in the next section).

Our procedure will be to list passages in canonical order where there is some kind of combination of the targumic Word with *Shekinah*, glory, or the glory of the *Shekinah*. The "combination" could be of several kinds. A single Targum might employ all the relevant terms, as in the examples given above. Where there is more than one Targum for a passage, one might use Word, another might use glory and/or *Shekinah*. This kind of example will come from the Pentateuch, where we have not only *Tgs. Onq., Ps.-J.,* and *Neof.,* but sometimes in addition also marginal readings in *Tg. Neof.,* two *Frg. Tg.* traditions, and fragments of *Pal. Tgs.* of the Pentateuch from the Cairo Genizah. And sometimes where there is only one Targum of a passage (e.g., the *Tg. Ps.* and *Tg. Jon.* of the Prophets), different manuscripts of that Targum differ in their use of these terms.

Although we should still keep in mind that all the extant Targums postdate the first century, the sheer number of examples that can be listed, and the fact that so many of them can be related to various passages in John's Gospel, seems to indicate that the extant Targums reflect an earlier interpretive tradition. Thus it would be foolish simply to ignore them *a priori* based on the late date of the extant manuscripts.

Assuming that the Targums do indeed preserve earlier readings of the Hebrew Bible, an Aramaic-speaking Jew, having heard the Targums recited in the synagogue weekly and on feast/fast days, could easily be led to think in these terms when he or she read John 1:14 thoughtfully, even though it is written in Greek. I also intend to show that a large proportion of these examples deal with contexts that I discussed in the preceding section where I deliberately left the Targums out of the discussion (i.e., passages concerning the construction of the tabernacle and temple).

Targum Passages

Genesis

1. In ch. 1, we noted that the Word of the LORD is frequently the subject of verbs in the creation account in *Tg. Neof.* and *Frg. Tg. P.* But in *Tg. Neof.,* "the glory of the LORD" is used as the subject of these verbs five times (Gen 1:17, 28, 29; 2:3 [2x]), with no discernable difference in use or meaning. In all five cases, *Frg. Tg. P* reads "the Word of the LORD," as does 1:28 as quoted in *Frg. Tg. V* Gen 35:9 as well as *Tg. Neof.* [mg.] for 1:29 and both cases of 2:3.

2. In Gen 3:8, 10 Adam and Eve heard the sound of the Word of the LORD walking in the garden (*Tgs. Onq.* v. 10, and in a variant of v. 8, *Neof., Ps.-J., Frg. Tg. P,* and *Tg. Neof.* [mg.] v. 10; *Dibbura* is used in v. 10 in *Tg. Neof.* [mg.], *Frg. Tg. P;* otherwise, *Memra*). They hid from before the Word of the LORD in *Tg. Neof.* [mg.], *Frg. Tg. P* Gen 3:8. The Word of the LORD called out to Adam in the garden in *Tg. Neof.* [mg.], *Frg. Tgs. P, V* Gen 3:9. God made the glory of the *Shekinah* dwell

between the cherubim (as in the holy of holies) in the garden (*Tg. Ps.-J.* Gen 3:24), above the garden (*Frg. Tg. P*), or to the east of the garden (*Tg. Neof., Frg. Tg. V*).

3. In *Tg. Ps.-J.* Gen 16:13, Hagar gave thanks "before the Lord whose Word had spoken to her," in the course of which she said, "behold, here indeed the glory of the *Shekinah* of the Lord was revealed." In *Tg. Neof., Frg. Tgs. P, V,* she "prayed in the name of the Word of the Lord who was revealed to her."

4. *Targum Neofiti* Gen 17:1 says that "the Word of the Lord" was revealed to Abraham and spoke to him (also in vv. 3, 9 [mg.], 15 [mg.], "the Word of the Lord" spoke with him). *Targum Neofiti* v. 22 says that "when he finished speaking with him, the glory of the *Shekinah* of the Lord (*Tgs. Ps.-J.* and *Onq.*: "the glory of the Lord") went up from him."

5. *Targum Neofiti* and *Frg. Tgs. P, V* Gen 18:1 say that "the Word of the Lord" was revealed to Abraham (likewise in *Frg. Tg. V* Gen 35:9 which looks back on this incident), while *Tg. Ps.-J.* Gen 18:1 says "the glory of the Lord" was revealed to him. In *Tgs. Neof.* and *Ps.-J.* 18:3, Abraham implored, "Do not let the glory of your *Shekinah* go up from your servant." In 18:17 of both of these Targums (and *Frg. Tgs. P, V*), the Lord said to Abraham in (or through) his Word, "Shall I hide . . . ," and in both, "the glory of the *Shekinah* of the Lord went up from him" (v. 33); *Tg. Onq.* has "the glory of the Lord."

6. *Targum Neofiti* and *Frg. Tgs. P, V* Gen 22:14 say that on Mt. Moriah "the glory of the *Shekinah* of the Lord was revealed" to Abraham (*Tg. Ps.-J.*: "the *Shekinah* of the Lord"), for mt "on the mount of the Lord it will be provided" (which could also be rendered, "he will be seen"). This happened in the course of "the Word of the Lord" testing Abraham (*Tgs. Neof.* [mg.] and *Ps.-J.* Gen 22:1).

7. Jacob stopped at Bethel on his way to Haran due to the miraculous shortening of the day, which happened because "the Word [*Dibbera/Dibbura*] desired to speak with him" (*Tgs. Neof., Ps.-J., Frg. Tgs. P, V* Gen 28:10). The speaking occurred in his dream that night, after which Jacob said, "Truly the glory of the *Shekinah* of the Lord dwells in this place" (*Tgs. Neof.* and *Ps.-J.* Gen 28:16; *Tg. Onq.* reads "the glory of the Lord"). *Targum Pseudo-Jonathan* and *Tg. Onq.* Gen 28:13 say that "the glory of the Lord" stood above him and spoke to him (in the dream).

8. When Jacob returned to Bethel more than twenty years later, "the Word of the Lord was revealed to him" (*Tg. Neof.* [mg.], *Frg. Tg. V,* and *CTg. C* Gen 35:9), and "the glory of the *Shekinah* of the Lord went up from him" (*Tg. Neof., Tg. Ps.-J.,* and *CTg. C* Gen 35:13; *Tg. Onq.* reads "the glory of the Lord"). Jacob named the place where the Word of the Lord spoke to him "Bethel" (*Tg. Neof.* [mg.] Gen 35:15). He also called it "El who made his *Shekinah* dwell in Bethel" (*Tg. Ps.-J.* Gen 35:7). *Tg. Neof.* [mg.] Gen 35:7 says Jacob "worshiped and prayed there in the name of the Word of the Lord, the God who was revealed to him in Bethel, for the glory of the *Shekinah* of the Lord was revealed to him there when he fled from before Esau."

Exodus

9. "The Word of the Lord" was revealed to Moses at the burning bush (*Tg. Neof.* Exod 3:8; 4:1 [mg.]); "the Word of the Lord" called out and spoke to Moses

(*Tg. Neof.* Exod 3:4, 14 [mg.]; 4:2 [mg.], 6 [mg.], 11 [mg.], 21 [mg.]; *Frg. Tgs. P, V* Exod 3:14), and Moses hid his face because he was afraid to look at "the glory of the LORD's *Shekinah*" (*Tgs. Neof.* and *Ps.-J.* Exod 3:6; *Tg. Onq.* reads, "the glory of the LORD").

10. In *Tg. Neof.* Exod 8:22, the LORD said to Pharaoh that he will perform miracles in Egypt "so that you may know that I am he, the LORD, whose Word dwells [mg.: "the glory of whose *Shekinah* dwells"] within the land."

11. On Passover night, "the Word of the LORD" (*CTg. AA* Exod 12:12, 23; *Tg. Neof.* Exod 11:4; 12:12 + [mg.]; 12:23 [mg.]) or "the glory of the LORD" (*Tg. Ps.-J.* Exod 12:23) or "the glory of his *Shekinah*" (*Tg. Neof.* Exod 12:23) or "the *Shekinah* of his glory" (*Tg. Ps.-J.* Exod 12:12) passed through (or was revealed in) the land of Egypt; "the Word of the LORD" struck down the Egyptian firstborn (*Tg. Neof.* [mg.], *Tg. Ps.-J.* and *CTg. AA* Exod 12:29) and saw the blood (*CTg. AA* Exod 12:13) and defended the Israelites (*Tg. Neof.* Exod 12:13 (+ [mg.]), 23; *Tg. Ps.-J.* 12:23).

12. As the Israelites left Egypt, they were led by "the Word of the LORD" (*Tg. Neof.* and *Frg. Tg. P* Exod 13:21) or "the glory of the LORD's *Shekinah*" (*Tg. Ps.-J.* Exod 13:21) in the pillar of fire and cloud.

13. At the Red Sea, Moses encouraged the people by telling them that "the glory of the LORD's *Shekinah*" gains Israel's battle victories for them (*Tg. Neof.* [mg.] and *Frg. Tg. V* Exod 14:13–14; cf. *Frg. Tg. V* Exod 15:3) and that "the Word of the LORD will wage war for you" (*Frg. Tg. P* Exod 14:14). Subsequently, "the Word of the LORD" looked down upon the Egyptians (*Tg. Neof.* [mg.] and *Frg. Tg. V* Exod 14:24) and drowned them in the sea (*Tg. Neof.* [mg.] and *Frg. Tg. P* Exod 14:27) after the Egyptians acknowledged that "this is the Word of the LORD who fought for them in Egypt" (*Tg. Ps.-J.* Exod 14:25).

14. At Massah the Israelites tested the LORD, asking, "Is the glory of the *Shekinah* of the LORD dwelling among us or not?" (*Tgs. Neof.* and *Ps.-J.* Exod 17:7; *Tg. Onq.* reads, "Is the *Shekinah* of the LORD among us?"). At this place the LORD said, "My Word will stand in readiness on the rock at Horeb, and you shall strike the rock" (*Tg. Neof.* 17:6).

15. For the clause "I will come to you in a thick cloud" (Exod 19:9), *Tg. Neof.* and *Frg. Tgs. P, V* have "My Word will be revealed to you"; *Tg. Ps.-J.* has "I will be revealed to you in the thickness of the cloud of glory." For the giving of the Ten Commandments on Mt. Sinai, "the glory of the *Shekinah* of the LORD" (*Tg. Neof.* Exod 19:11) or "the Word of the LORD" (*Tg. Neof.* [mg.], *Frg. Tgs. P, V*) were to be revealed on the third day.

16. On the third day Moses brought the people to meet "the Word of the LORD" (*Tg. Onq.* and *Frg. Tg. P* Exod 19:17) or "the *Shekinah* of the LORD" (*Tg. Ps.-J.*) or "the glory of the *Shekinah* of the LORD" (*Tg. Neof., Frg. Tg. V,* and *CTg. F*).

17. For "The LORD came down on Mt. Sinai . . . and the LORD called to Moses" (Exod 19:20), *Tg. Neof.* and *CTg. F* say "the glory of the *Shekinah* of the LORD was revealed." *Targum Neofiti* [mg.] and *Frg. Tgs. P, V* say "the Word of the LORD was revealed." *Targum Neofiti* says "the Word (*Memra*) of the LORD called to him." *Fragmentary Targums P, V* say "the Word (*Dibbera*) of the LORD called to him."

18. The LORD promised that after the tabernacle was constructed, he would meet with the Israelites at the doorway of the tent of meeting, which would be consecrated by his glory, and he would dwell among them and be their God, and "they shall know that I am the LORD their God, who brought them out of the land of Egypt, that I might dwell (MT, שָׁכַן) among them; I am the LORD their God" (Exod 29:43, 45–46). *Targum Neofiti, Tg. Ps.-J.* and *Tg. Onq.* 29:43 read, "I will appoint my Word to be there for the sons of Israel." Verse 45 of the same Targums have "I will make my *Shekinah* (*Tg. Neof.* [int.]: "the glory of my *Shekinah*)" dwell in the midst of the sons of Israel," and *Tg. Neof.* continues "my Word will be for them a redeeming God." For MT "that I might dwell among them" (v. 46), *Tg. Neof.* says "so that the glory of my *Shekinah* might dwell among them;" *Tg. Ps.-J.* and *Tg. Onq.* read "my *Shekinah*" instead of "the glory of my *Shekinah*."

19. After the golden calf incident, the LORD told Moses, "I will not go up (to the promised land) in your midst . . . lest I destroy you on your way" (Exod 33:3); and in v. 5 Moses is told to inform the people of this. *Targum Neofiti* and *Tg. Ps.-J.* of these two verses speak of the glory of the LORD's *Shekinah* not going up among them, but *Tg. Neof.* [mg.] 33:3 says, "My Word will not go up before you." In *Tg. Neof.* [mg.] 33:1, 5, it is the Word of the LORD who was speaking to Moses about the glory of his *Shekinah* in vv. 3, 5. *Targum Pseudo-Jonathan* adds to v. 3, "My glory will not dwell where you reside in your camps." Similarly, in *Tg. Onq.* 33:3, 5 God said he will cause "his *Shekinah*" not to go up in their midst.[9]

20. In response to Moses' request, "Show me your glory" (Exod 33:18), the LORD says that when "the glory of my *Shekinah*" passes by, "You will see the Word (*Dibbera*) of the glory of [my] *Shekinah*, but it is not possible for you to see the face of the glory of my *Shekinah*" (*Tg. Neof.* Exod 33:22–23; *Frg. Tg. V* 33:23 is like *Tg. Neof.*). According to *Tg. Neof.* [mg.] 33:21, this was spoken by "the Word of the LORD." *Targum Neofiti* [mg.] 33:23 says, "I will make [you] see the Word (*Dibbura*) of glory." In *Frg. Tg. P* 33:23, God tells Moses he will see the "Word (*Dibbura*) of the LORD," but it is impossible for him to see "the glory of my *Shekinah*." *Targum Onqelos* 33:20 and *Tg. Ps.-J.* 33:23 say Moses will not be able to see "the face of the glory of my *Shekinah*." *Targum Onqelos* 33:22–23 says, "When my glory passes by, I will . . . shield you with my Word (MT: "hand") until I have passed by."

21. Exodus 34:5 says that the LORD came down in the cloud and stood by Moses. In the Targums, this is rendered, "the glory of the *Shekinah* of the LORD was revealed" (*Tg. Neof.*), "the Word of the LORD was revealed" (*Tg. Neof.* [mg.]), and "the LORD revealed himself in the clouds of the glory of his *Shekinah*" (*Tg. Ps.-J.*). All the Targums of 34:6 (including both *Frg. Tg.* traditions) have "the *Shekinah* of the LORD" or "the glory of his *Shekinah*" pass before Moses.

---

[9] Some interpret these passages to say that God will not remove his presence from his people. See discussion in Bernard Grossfeld, *The Targum Onqelos to Exodus* (ArBib 7; Collegeville, Minn.: Liturgical Press, 1988), 92 n.3, and Michael Maher in the combined Aramaic Bible volume on Exodus (Martin McNamara, *Targum Neofiti 1: Exodus;* Michael Maher, *Targum Pseudo-Jonathan: Exodus* [ArBib 2; Collegeville, Minn.: Liturgical Press, 1994], 255 and n. 5).

Leviticus

22. In Lev 9:4, at the consecration of Aaron and his sons, Moses tells the people to take certain sacrifices and offerings, "for today the LORD shall appear to you." *Targum Neofiti* has "today the Word of the LORD will be revealed to you"; *Tg. Ps.-J.* has "today the glory of the *Shekinah* of the LORD will be revealed to you"; and *Tg. Onq.* has "the glory of the LORD will be revealed to you." In place of the MT of 9:6, "so that the glory of the LORD may appear to you," *Tgs. Neof.* [+ mg.] and *Ps.-J.* both say "the glory of the *Shekinah* of the LORD will be revealed." *Targum Onqelos* renders as in v. 4 (= MT of v. 6). The Targums translate v. 23, "the glory of the LORD appeared to all the people," consistently with v. 6. In *Ps.-J.*, the *Shekinah* is not immediately revealed after Aaron's sacrifice, causing Aaron to wonder whether "the Word of the LORD was not pleased with the work of my hands." Then he and Moses blessed the people, saying, "May the Word of the LORD receive with favor your offerings, and may he remit and forgive your sins," at which point "the glory of the LORD's *Shekinah*" was revealed.

23. After the death of Aaron's two sons, the LORD told Moses to warn Aaron that he may not enter at any time into the holy of holies, lest he die, "for I will appear in the cloud over the mercy seat" (Lev 16:2). In *Tg. Neof.*, "the Word of the LORD" and "the *Shekinah* of his glory" are equated: "In my cloud, the glory of my *Shekinah*, my Word, is revealed over the mercy seat." In *Tg. Ps.-J.*, he spoke, "My *Shekinah* is revealed in the clouds of my glory over the mercy seat." *Targum Onqelos* has, "I will be revealed" for "I will appear."

24. In Lev 26:11–12, the LORD promised that if Israel is obedient, (1) "I will put my dwelling [מִשְׁכָּנִי my *mishkan*] among you," (2) "and my soul will not reject you." (3) "I will also walk among you" (4) "and be your God." These promises are rendered as follows in the Targums: for (1), *Tg. Onq.* translates literally; *Tg. Neof.* has "I will make the glory of my *Shekinah* dwell among you," and *Tg. Ps.-J.* has "I will put the *Shekinah* of my glory among you." For (2), *Tg. Neof.* translates literally; *Tgs. Ps.-J.* and *Onq.* read, "my Word will not reject you." For (3), *Tg. Neof.* says, "My Word will go among you"; *Tg. Onq.* has "I will make my *Shekinah* dwell among you"; *Tg. Ps.-J.* is like *Tg. Onq.* but with "the glory of my *Shekinah*." For (4), *Tg. Onq.* translates literally, and *Tgs. Neof.* and *Ps.-J.* say, "my Word will be to you a redeeming God."

Numbers

25. Whenever the people set out with the ark of the covenant, Moses would pray, "Rise up, O Word of the LORD" (*Frg. Tg. V* and *Tg. Neof.* [mg.] Num 10:35), or "Let the Word of the LORD be revealed in the power of your anger" (*Tg. Ps.-J.*). Whenever the ark rested, Moses would pray, "Turn, O Word of the LORD, from your mighty wrath" (*Tg. Neof.* [mg.]; *Frg. Tg. V* 10:36), or, according to *Tg. Ps.-J.* Num 10:36, "Return, O Word of the LORD . . . and let the glory of your *Shekinah* dwell among them" (similarly the second part in *Tg. Neof.*). *Targum Onqelos* Num 10:36 has "Return, O Word of the LORD . . . and dwell in your glory."

26. According to Num 11:20, Israel's dissatisfaction with the manna provided by God and their demand for meat indicated that "you have rejected the LORD

who is among you." *Targum Onqelos* says "You have despised (or, rejected) the Word of the LORD, whose Shekinah dwells among you;" similarly *Tg. Ps.-J.* which says "the glory of whose *Shekinah* dwells among you." *Targum Neofiti* says "You rebelled against what is according to the decree of the Word of the LORD, the glory of whose *Shekinah* dwells among you." In v. 17, the LORD promised Moses "I will come down and speak with you," and v. 25 says, "The LORD came down in the cloud." In v. 17, *Tg. Neof.* has "I will be revealed in my Word," and in v. 25 it has "The glory of the *Shekinah* of the LORD was revealed in the cloud." *Targum Pseudo-Jonathan* has "the glory of the *Shekinah*" in both passages, and *Tg. Onq.* says "I will be revealed" (v. 17) and "the LORD was revealed" (v. 25).

27. In Num 12:5, "The LORD came down in a pillar of cloud and stood at the doorway of the tent." In *Tg. Onq.*, he "revealed himself." In *Tg. Ps.-J.*, "The glory of the LORD was revealed in the pillar of the cloud of glory." In *Tg. Neof.*, "The glory of the *Shekinah* of the LORD was revealed in the pillar of cloud." *Targum Neofiti* [mg.] has "the Word of the LORD."[10]

28. In Num 14:9, Joshua and Caleb told the people not to rebel against the LORD by refusing to go into the promised land. In the Targums they say, "do not rebel against the Word of the LORD" (*Tg. Onq.*), or "against the name of the Word of the LORD" (*Tg. Neof.* [mg.]), or "against the glory of the *Shekinah* of the LORD" (*Tg. Neof.*).

29. In Num 14:14, Moses says in his prayer that the nations have heard "that you, O LORD, are in the midst of this people, and that eye to eye you are seen, O LORD, and your cloud stands over them." For "you are in the midst of this people" *Tg. Neof.* says "you are he, the glory of whose *Shekinah* is in the midst of this people," while *Tgs. Onq.* and *Ps.-J.* say "your *Shekinah* dwells in the midst of this people." For "eye to eye you are seen," *Tg. Neof.* says "appearance to appearance you have been revealed in your Word," while *Tgs. Onq.* and *Ps.-J.* say "with their eyes they saw the *Shekinah* of your glory." For "your cloud," *Tg. Neof.* says "the cloud of the glory of your *Shekinah*," while *Tgs. Onq.* and *Ps.-J.* translate literally.

30. In Num 14:41, Moses asks the Israelites, "Why are you transgressing the mouth of the LORD?" *Tgs. Onq.* and *Ps.-J.* say "against the decree of the Word of the LORD," *Tg. Neof.* "against what is according to the decree of the LORD." In v. 42 Moses warns them not to go up and fight, lest they be defeated, "for the LORD is not in your midst," for which *Tg. Onq.* says "the *Shekinah* of the Lord is not in your midst." *Tg. Ps.-J.* says "the *Shekinah* of the LORD does not dwell in your midst, . . . and the cloud of glory will not go with you." *Tg. Neof.* says "the glory of the *Shekinah* of the Lord does not dwell over you." In v. 43, Moses says, (1) they will be defeated "because you have turned back from (following) after the LORD," and (2) "the LORD will not be with you." For (1) *Tgs. Onq.* and *Ps.-J.* say "you have turned back from the worship of the LORD," *Tg. Neof.* says "you have turned back from (following) after the Word of the LORD." For (2), *Tgs. Onq.* and *Ps.-J.* say "the Word

---

[10]The marginal reading "Word of the LORD" of *Tg. Neof.* v. 5 was not indicated by Martin McNamara (*Targum Neofiti 1: Numbers*; Ernest G. Clark, *Targum Pseudo-Jonathan: Numbers* [ArBib 4; Collegeville, Minn.: Liturgical Press, 1995], 77).

of the LORD will not be for your help," as does *Tg. Neof.* [mg.] (*Neof.* main text, "the LORD will not be with you").

31 & 32. During the rebellion of Korah, "the glory of the *Shekinah* of the LORD was revealed" to the people (*Tg. Neof.* Num 16:19; *Tgs. Onq.* and *Ps.-J.*: "the glory of the LORD"), and "the Word of the LORD spoke with Moses and Aaron" (*Tg. Neof.* [mg.] 16:20]). One finds the same situation in the Targums of Num 20:6–7, except that *Tg. Ps.-J.* agrees with *Tg. Neof.* in the use of *Shekinah* (v. 6).

33. Num 21:5 says that the hungry and thirsty Israelites "spoke against God and against Moses." For "God," *Tgs. Neof., Ps.-J.,* and *Onq.* say "the Word of the LORD" (*Tg. Onq.* has a variant, they complained "before the LORD"). In v. 7, after the snakes were sent among them, they confessed they had spoken against the LORD. For "the LORD," *Tg. Ps.-J.* says "the glory of the *Shekinah* of the LORD," *Tg. Onq.* says "before the LORD," and *Tg. Neof.* says "the Word of the LORD" (mg. adds "name of the").[11]

34. In *Tg. Onq.* Num 23:21, Balaam prophesied, "The Word of the LORD their God is their helper, and the *Shekinah* of their King is among them." The *Frg. Tgs. P, V* are similar but have "glory" instead of "*Shekinah*." The *Tgs. Ps.-J.* and *Neof.* are similar to *Tg. Onq.* in their use of "the Word" (*Tg. Neof.* has "the Word of the LORD is with them"), but do not refer to "the *Shekinah*."

Deuteronomy

35. In Deut 1:30, Moses recorded his attempt to persuade the Israelites not to be dismayed by the report of the ten spies (Num 13–14). He assured them, "The LORD your God who goes before you will fight for you." In *Tg. Onq.*, the LORD will go before them and "his Word will fight for you." In *Tg. Ps.-J.*, it is "the Word of the LORD your God" who will go before them and fight for them; *Tg. Neof.* reads, "In the glory of his *Shekinah* he will lead before you."

36. In Deut 5:24, Moses quoted the people's response to hearing the Ten Commandments from Mt. Sinai: "Behold the LORD our God has shown us his glory and his greatness, and we have heard his voice from the midst of the fire." In *Tg. Ps.-J.*, this is rendered, "Behold, the Word of the LORD our God has shown us the *Shekinah* of his glory . . . and the voice of his Word we have heard from the midst of the fire." *Targum Neofiti* is similar but has "his glory" instead of "the *Shekinah* of his glory," and adds another reference to the divine Word: "this day we have seen that the Word of the LORD speaks with man (lit., the son of man) and he lives." *Targum Onqelos* also says "we heard the voice of his Word." The *CTg. D* says, "The LORD our God has shown us his glory and might, and the voice of his Word [*Dibbera*] we have heard. . . . His Word speaks."

37. In *Tg. Ps.-J.* Deut 9:3, Moses assured Israel, "the LORD your God, the *Shekinah* of his glory goes before you, his Word is a consuming fire." *Targum Neofiti* is similar to the first part ("the glory of his *Shekinah* leads before you";

---

[11] In Martin McNamara's translation for The Aramaic Bible, part of v. 7 was omitted due to homoioteleuton: "We have sinned, for we have *murmured* against you" (*Targum Neofiti 1: Numbers*, 116).

mg.: "the *Shekinah* of his glory), *Tg. Onq.* resembles the second part ("his Word is a consuming fire").

38. In Deut 12:5, Moses told Israel to seek the Lord at the place which (1) "the Lord your God shall choose from all your tribes," (2) "to put his name there." In *Tg. Ps.-J.* Deut 12:5, (1) "the Word of the Lord your God" chooses the place (2) "to cause his *Shekinah* to dwell" (similarly v. 11). In *Tgs. Onq.* and *Neof.* (1) is translated literally (but in *Tg. Neof.* 12:14 "the Word of the Lord" chooses); for (2), *Tg. Onq.* agrees with *Tg. Ps.-J.*, and *Tg. Neof.* has "the glory of his *Shekinah*."

39. In Deut 23:14, Moses said, (1) "The Lord your God walks in the midst of your camp to deliver you and defeat your enemies before you; therefore your camp must be holy..." (2) "lest he turn away from you." For (1), *Tgs. Onq.* and *Ps.-J.* have "the Lord your God, his *Shekinah*"; *Tg. Neof.* has "the Lord your God, the glory of his *Shekinah*." For (2), *Tg. Neof.* has "that the glory of his *Shekinah* not turn back"; *Tg. Ps.-J.* has "that his *Shekinah* not go up"; and *Tg. Onq.* has "lest his Word turn away from doing good to you."

40. In Deut 31:3–8, Moses again assured Israel that the Lord will cross over before the Israelites, go with them, go ahead of them, and fight for them. The Lord's *Shekinah*, the glory of his *Shekinah*, and his Word are used in various ways in the Targums of this passage:

Tg. Onq. **Deut 31:6,** **8**	[6]The Lord your God, *his Word* will lead before you; he will not forsake you. ...[8]The Lord, he will lead before you, *his Word* will be for your help; he will not forsake you.
Tg. Ps.-J. **Deut 31:3,** **5, 6, 8**	[3]The Lord your God, even *his Shekinah* shall cross before you.... [5]*The Word* of the Lord will hand them (the Canaanites) over before you.... [6]The Lord your God, *his Shekinah* leads before you.... [8]*The Word* of the Lord, *his Shekinah*, is leading before you and *his Word* will be for your help.
Tg. Neof. **Deut 31:3,** **4, 6, 8**	[3]The Lord your God, the glory of whose *Shekinah* leads before you.... [4]*The Word* of the Lord will do to them (the Canaanites) as he did to Sihon. ...[6]The Lord your God, *the glory of whose Shekinah* leads before you ... [8]*the Word* of the Lord, *the glory of whose Shekinah* is leading before you, shall be for your help.

41. Deuteronomy 31:15 reads, "The Lord appeared in the tent in a pillar of cloud," which *Tg. Onq.* translates literally (except for using "was revealed" for "appeared"). In *Tg. Neof.*, "the Word of the Lord was revealed," and in *Tg. Ps.-J.* "the glory of the *Shekinah* of the Lord was revealed."

42. In Deut 31:17–18, Moses anticipated that the Israelites will ask, in time of calamity, "Is it not because our God is not among us that these evils have come upon us?" and God responded, "I will surely hide my face from them." In *Tg. Neof.*, they will ask, "Is it not because the glory of the *Shekinah* of the Lord is not dwelling among us?" and God said, "I in my Word will surely hide the face of my good pleasure." In *Tgs. Onq.* and *Ps.-J.*, they said, "Is it not because the *Shekinah* of my God no longer is / dwells in my midst?" and God will say, "I will surely make my *Shekinah* go up from them."

The Former Prophets

43. In *Tg. Josh.* 22:31, Phinehas said to the tribes on the east side of the Jordan, "This day we know that the *Shekinah* of the LORD dwells among us (MT: "the LORD is among us"), that you have not acted deceitfully against the Word of the LORD (MT: "have not rebelled against the LORD")."

44. In *Tg. Judg.* 6:12, the angel of the LORD said to Gideon, "The Word of the LORD is for your help," to which Gideon responded in v. 13, "If the *Shekinah* of the LORD is for our help. . . ." A variant of v. 13 has, "If the Word of the LORD is for our help. . . ."

45. In *Tg. 1 Sam.* 4:4, the Israelites sent to Shiloh to take possession of the ark of the covenant of the LORD, "whose *Shekinah* dwells above the cherubim." It seems from the similar phrase in 2 Sam 6:2 that the figures of the cherubim on the ark are meant: "whose *Shekinah* dwells above the cherubim upon it" (i.e., upon the ark). When the ark above which the *Shekinah* dwells was taken into battle, the Philistines asked, "Who will save us from the hand of the Word of the LORD?" (*Tg. 1 Sam.* 4:8).

46. *Targum 2 Samuel* 6:2 is noted in the paragraph above; at v. 7 it says that "the Word of the LORD" struck down Uzzah.

The Latter Prophets

47. *Targum Isaiah* 6:1–8. In his call to the prophetic office (Isa 6), Isaiah saw something of the reality modeled by the ark and the cherubim in the holy of holies. He said, "I saw the Lord, sitting on a throne, high and lifted up, and the train of his robe filled the temple" (v. 1). In *Tg. Isa.*, this reads, "I saw the glory of the LORD . . . and the temple was filled with the brilliance of his glory" (the LXX also says "his glory filled the temple"). In *Tg. Isa.* 6:5, the prophet said, "My eyes have seen the glory of the *Shekinah* of the eternal king." Verse 6 refers to "him whose *Shekinah* is upon the throne of glory in the heavens," and in v. 8 Isaiah said, "I heard the voice of the Word of the LORD." Also note again *Tg. Ps.-J.* Deut 4:7, perhaps giving us a "Palestinian" version of *Tg. Isa.* 6:1: "The Word of the LORD sits upon his throne, high and lifted up, and hears our prayer."

In connection with Isa 6, we can also note the promise of *Tg. Isa.* 30:20, "Your eyes will see the *Shekinah* in the sanctuary," for MT "Your eyes will see your Teacher." So in the Targum, this is a prediction that in the future Israel in general will see the *Shekinah* in the temple as Isaiah himself did. Aramaic-speaking Jewish Christians might naturally have seen this as being fulfilled when Jesus taught in the temple.

48. *Targum Ezekiel* 39:23 says, "The nations will know that the house of Israel were exiled because of their sins, because they have dealt falsely with my Word (MT: acted unfaithfully against me), so that I removed my *Shekinah* (MT: hid my face) from them."

49. In *Tg. Ezek.* 43:7, 9, the LORD promised to make his *Shekinah* dwell in the temple described to Ezekiel. Verse 8 recalls how the Israelites had defiled the temple by placing idolatrous buildings "beside my temple court, with only a wall of my holy temple between my Word and them" (indicating the presence of the Word of the LORD in the temple).

50. *Targum Hos.* 5:6–7 says, "He has withdrawn his *Shekinah* from them; against the Word of the LORD they have dealt falsely." Similarly, v. 15: "I will withdraw my *Shekinah*; I will return to my holy dwelling in heaven."

51. In *Tg. Zech.* 2:5, the LORD promised concerning Jerusalem, "My Word (MT: I) will be to her . . . like a wall of fire encircling her round about, and in glory I will make my *Shekinah* dwell in her midst (MT: I will be the glory in her midst)."

52. *Tosefta Targum Zechariah* 2:10 says, "Rejoice and be glad, assembly of Zion, for the glory {Word} of the LORD will be revealed, and he shall illumine the world from the brilliance of his glory, in that he said to make his *Shekinah* dwell in your midst."

Psalms

53. In *Tg. Ps.* 16:8, David says, "I have placed the LORD {the Word of the LORD} before me continually; because his *Shekinah* rests at my right hand, I shall not be moved."

54. In *Tg. Ps.* 44, Israel's victories in battle are accomplished "through your Word" (v. 5; MT: "through you"), while defeat is due to "the *Shekinah*" not dwelling with their armies (v. 9; MT: "You do not go out with our armies"), or "the *Shekinah* of God's glory" having withdrawn (v. 24; MT: "He hides his face"). In v. 5, "your Word" is in parallel with "your name."

55. *Targum Psalms* 46 says that "the LORD's *Shekinah*" is in the midst of Jerusalem (v. 5), and "the Word of the LORD" is for the help of his people (vv. 7, 11).

56. In *Tg. Ps.* 57:1, David says that he trusts "in your Word" (MT: "in you") and "in the shadow of your *Shekinah*" (MT: "of your wings").

57. *Targum Psalms* 68:16 says, "Behold, the Word of the LORD has desired Mt. Sinai, that is humble, to cause his *Shekinah* to dwell upon it" (for the giving of the law).

58. *Targum Psalms* 125:2 says, "The Word of the LORD is round about his people." A variant reads "the *Shekinah* of the LORD."

Chronicles

59. In *Tg. 1 Chr* 23:25 David says "the Word of the LORD God of Israel has given rest to his people and caused his *Shekinah* to dwell in Jerusalem forever."

60 & 61. In *Tg. 2 Chr.* 6:1 Solomon says "the Lord was pleased to make his Shekinah dwell in the city of Jerusalem, in the temple that I built for the name of his Word" (similarly Jehoshaphat in 20:8–9).

62. In *Tg. 2 Chr.* 19:6, Jehoshaphat says to the judges he had appointed and sent out, "you are judging before the Word of the LORD and his *Shekinah* dwells with you in the passing of judgment."

63. In *Tg. 2 Chr.* 30:7–9, Hezekiah invites the survivors in the northern kingdom to come and celebrate the Passover in Jerusalem. Speaking of the captives, he says, "If you return to the fear of the LORD, your brethren and your sons, . . . he will return in his Word to restore them to this land. . . . He will not take up his *Shekinah* from you."

Discussion

(1) A considerable number of the passages cited above deal with the same theme we dealt with in the previous section—the LORD's dwelling among his people and manifesting his glory. Passages cited in no. 18 speak of the tabernacle as a place where God's Word would meet Israel (think of how much of John's Gospel has Israel meeting the Word in the temple), of his Word being for them a savior God, and of the glory of his *Shekinah* dwelling there. The passages cited in nos. 22, 23, 25, 27, 31, 32, 41, 45, and 46 speak of the fulfillment of these purposes in the tabernacle or in relation to the ark when Israel is on the move.

The passages in nos. 60 and 61 say that the temple was built for the name of God's Word (the Tetragrammaton), and the *Shekinah* dwells there, as Isaiah saw in no. 47. Forty-nine speaks of this purpose being fulfilled in a future temple.

Other passages deal with the issue of the LORD dwelling among or revealing himself to his people, leading his people through the wilderness, etc., without explicitly mentioning the ark or the tabernacle or the temple (nos. 12, 14, 19, 24, 26, 28–30, 35, 37, 39, 40, 42, 43, 51, 54, 58, 59). Finally, 52 is unique in promising a future revelation of the Word in glory (reading the variant *Memra*) when the *Shekinah* dwells in the midst of the LORD's people.

(2) More than half of the passages listed above (thirty-nine of sixty-three) have the LORD's Word in the same context, setting, scene, etc., as his *Shekinah* or the glory of his *Shekinah,* as opposed to the other twenty-four passages where Word is an alternative for God's glory or the glory of his *Shekinah.* In one case (no. 23), which could perhaps be the result of conflating two readings, the terms are equated. Typically, the *Shekinah* of the LORD manifests the presence of God among his people, often visibly, while his Word speaks or interacts with his people in other ways. From these results one might ask, if both "glory" and the idea of being visible tend to be associated with the *Shekinah* more than the Word, why does John call Jesus the Word rather than the *Shekinah*?

One answer is that the targumic Word is more comprehensive than *Shekinah* in describing divine activity. The targumic Word is said to be God, and connected with the name of God, while the *Shekinah* is not. While *Shekinah* may be used in the Targums for "name" in the MT in passages which speak of God's name dwelling in a particular place (Deut 12:5, etc.), the Targums themselves do not speak of the name of the *Shekinah* as they do of the name of the Word. We saw above in nos. 18, 33, 60, and 61 that the *Memra* is explicitly identified as God (the Tetragrammaton), and examples can be multiplied in other passages where we have Word but not glory and/or *Shekinah*, such as the common expression mentioned in ch. 1, "the name of the Word of the LORD."

Additionally, the fact that there are so many passages where Word is an alternate for God's glory or the glory of his *Shekinah* is evidence of considerable overlap in usage of the terms; they are not kept strictly to distinct spheres of usage. Thus we do have passages that speak of the glory of God's Word (no. 20) or associate the Word of the LORD and the glory of his *Shekinah* (nos. 19, 26, 36, 38, 40, 57), which is understandable since in the Targums, as in John 1:1, "the Word was

God." Number 20 is of special interest because it deals with the revelation of the glory of God to Moses on Mt. Sinai (as do 19 and 21), which many scholars see as an important background to John 1:14–18. We will discuss this in the next section.

Other passages speak of the LORD's Word rather than (or as an alternate reading to) his *Shekinah* dwelling among Israel, or going among or before Israel (10, 12, 24), or of Israel (or Moses by himself) meeting and/or seeing his Word (16, 18, 20, 23, 29). Such passages fit nicely with the terminology of John 1:14.

(3) A considerable number of these passages can be related to specific passages in John and/or to categories of divine activity which the Gospel ascribes to the person of Jesus. We will discuss these in subsequent chapters of this book. We have already examined nos. 7, 36, and 47 in ch. 1. Number 10 is of interest because God says (in *Tg. Neof.*) not only that his Word dwells in the land, but also that Pharaoh should know this because of the miracles God does. Similarly, the first instance in which Jesus' disciples "beheld his (the Word's) glory" is at Cana, where Jesus changes the water into wine. This "beginning of signs" is like the beginning of signs in Egypt, when water in the Nile was turned blood red (for further discussion, see ch. 8).

The passages in nos. 24 and 25 can both be related to John 14. Number 24 is similar to John 14:23, as we see below in ch. 7 (the theme of Jesus as divine lawgiver), while no. 25 can be related to John 14:1–6, and is discussed in ch. 5 (the theme of Jesus as divine warrior). Numbers 15, 16, 17, 36, and 57 above are also connected with the theme of the divine lawgiver, while 11, 13, 40, 45, 46, and 54 also relate to the theme of the divine warrior. The passages in nos. 18, 19, 30, 42, 50, and 63 can be related to the theme of the withdrawal of the *Shekinah,* which we discuss in ch. 8, relating that theme to John 7:34 and 12:26.

In short, examination of targumic passages where Word, glory, and *Shekinah* are either synonymous alternatives or occur together in the same context supports the conclusion that John intended 1:14 to bring these terms to the mind of his Aramaic-speaking Jewish readers. Contemporary readers, as well as John's original Greek-speaking readers, can profit by being educated in the terminology of the Aramaic translations of the OT Scriptures. While it is likely that there was some degree of textual change between the first century Targums and those now extant, the similarities that do exist should convince us of the likelihood that if we had the first-century Targums, we would probably see an even longer list of passages relevant to John. Indeed, the above list of sixty-three passages would have been shorter by about a fourth before the discovery of *Tg. Neof.*, convincing us that the discovery of additional targumic evidence has tended to confirm the observation of Gustaf Dalman and Charles Burney that John is using or alluding to Targum terminology in John 1:14.

JOHN 1:14–18 AND EXODUS 33:18–34:7

The dependence of John 1:14–18 on the account of the manifestation of the glory of the LORD to Moses on Mt. Sinai after the golden calf incident is evident enough when we look at this account in the Hebrew text, or a literal translation of it. It is even more evident when we look at this account in the *Pal. Tgs.* of the Pentateuch, where the revelation to Moses is a revelation of the divine Word, adding more evidence for the view that the Logos title is based on the Targums.

"Full of Grace and Truth" and Exodus 34:6

Hanson wrote in 1976 that "by far the largest number of scholars whom I have consulted" saw a dependence of "full of grace and truth" (πλήρης χάριτος καὶ ἀληθείας) in John 1:14 on God's self description in Exod 34:6, רַב־חֶסֶד וֶאֱמֶת "abounding in lovingkindness and truth" (NASB); "abounding in love and faithfulness" (NIV).[12] The case for relating these phrases further is strengthened by "the accumulation of allusions to Exod 33–34 in John 1:14–18," which "leaves little doubt that John's phrase is a conscious allusion to the occurrence in that context."[13]

A second group of scholars mentioned by Hanson acknowledges a dependence of "grace and truth" on the common Hebrew word pair חֶסֶד וֶאֱמֶת but doubts a specific connection to Exod 34:6. In considering this possibility, it should be noted that although חֶסֶד וֶאֱמֶת is common in the OT, רַב־חֶסֶד וֶאֱמֶת occurs only in Exod 34:6 and Ps 86:15, both of which describe God, and Ps 86:15 is clearly a quote from Exod 34:6. Thus although "grace and truth" from John 1:17 might theoretically be related to any of the two dozen or so OT passages where חֶסֶד and אֱמֶת are associated, and which might speak of God or men, "full of grace and truth" from John 1:14 must be related to one of these two passages that describes God, unless one denies any connection at all between the two phrases (the position of the third group mentioned by Hanson, "a very small group indeed").[14]

So if we just had "grace and truth" in John 1:14 (as in v. 17), we might see a messianic implication from Ps 40:10, where David says, "I have not hidden your kindness and your truth from the great congregation." The author of Hebrews takes this Psalm as a pattern for the work of Christ (Heb 10:5–10), and John might have done the same thing—"grace and truth came by Jesus Christ" (v. 17) being meant to indicate that Jesus did (in a greater way, to be sure) what David did. But "full of grace and truth" from v. 14 can only be referred to descriptions of God in the OT. Of course, the statement that "the Word became flesh" could account for why one use of "grace and truth" could be related to David or some other person (v. 17) while the other (v. 14) refers to God.

A shortened version of this OT phrase, רַב־חֶסֶד "abounding in kindness," occurs in Num 14:18; Neh 9:17; Ps 86:5; 103:8; Joel 2:13; and Jonah 4:2 (it is probably also behind Paul's expression "rich in mercy," Eph 2:4). This phrase, too, is used only of God and is always dependent on Exod 34:6. In Num 14:18, Moses is quoting from the revelation he received in Exod 34, as part of his petition that the LORD

---

[12] Anthony Tyrell Hanson, "John I. 14–18 and Exodus XXXIV," *New Testament Studies* 23 (1976): 90.

[13] Keener, *John,* 417.

[14] Hanson, "John I. 14–18 and Exodus XXXIV," 90.

forgive Israel for choosing to go back to Egypt rather than to enter the promised land. The LORD grants his request, but says,

> [22]Surely all the men who have seen my glory and my signs, which I performed in Egypt and in the wilderness, yet have put me to the test these ten times, and have not listened to my voice (*Tgs. Onq.* and *Ps.-J.*: have not received my Word), [23]shall by no means see the land which I swore to their fathers . . . [24]but my servant Caleb, because he had a different spirit and has followed me fully (*Tg. Neof.*: has followed my Word fully), I will bring into the land.

Thus John's phrase "full of grace and truth" likely reflects not only the original context in Exod 34:6, but also the secondary one in Num 14, where there are important connections to John's Gospel, including the Prologue and the idea of receiving the Word. We also noted in ch. 1 the similarity between John 12:37 and Num 14:11.

In the other occurrences of רַב חֶסֶד (Neh 9:17; Ps 86:5; 103:8; Joel 2:13; Jonah 4:2), only Ps 86:5 does not indicate in its immediate context its dependence on Exod 34:6 directly or indirectly via Num 14:18. Yet here there can be no doubt because the fuller expression, as noted above, is used ten verses later, and there the dependence on Exod 34:6 is obvious. In Joel 2:13 and Jonah 4:2, the phrase "relenting concerning harm" (וְנִחָם עַל הָרָעָה) is added after "abounding in kindness." This phrase is likely taken from Exod 32:12, 14, where Moses asks the LORD to relent from wiping out the nation after the sin of the golden calf. *Targum Jonathan* of Joel 2:13 and Jonah 4:2 says that God draws back his Word from inflicting evil.

The Glory of the Word Seen by Moses and John

The manifestation of the glory of the LORD to Moses in Exod 34 is in response to his request, "Show me your glory" in Exod 33:18. Similarly, John says, "We saw his glory" (John 1:14). John tells us, "No man has seen God at any time" (v. 18), which means that Moses, whom John mentions in v. 17, did not see him either. Therefore,

> On those occasions in Israel's history when God is described as being seen, it was not in fact God [the Father] who was seen, but the Logos. John says this *totidem verbis* in xii. 41, where he describes Isaiah's vision in the Temple as Isaiah having seen Jesus' glory; in other words, Jahweh Sabaoth is the Logos.[15]

John also says that the one and only God, who is in the bosom of the Father, he has explained him, which agrees with Exod 34:5–7 where the manifestation of the LORD's glory is accomplished by proclamation of the divine name, and an explanation of the divine person, which includes the description "full of grace and truth." Craig Evans sees the description of the eternal Son "who is in the bosom of the Father" as a contrast "with Moses' fleeting glimpse of God's 'back' (Exod. 33.23)."[16]

---

[15] Hanson, "John I. 14–18 and Exodus XXXIV," 96.
[16] Evans, *Word and Glory*, 80–81.

In the previous section, we noted the use of glory, *Shekinah,* and Word in the Targums of this portion of Exodus. Since the dependence of John 1:14–18 on Exod 33 and 34 is generally acknowledged by scholars apart from any reference to the Targums, the fact that in some of these Targums Moses sees the glory of the Word, or the Word of glory, should be considered strong evidence in favor of a targumic background for the Logos title.

Again we note the context: Moses has set up the tent of meeting outside the camp, and there "the LORD used to speak to Moses face to face, just as a man speaks to his friend" (Exod 33:11). According to *Tg. Neof.* [mg.], it was "the Word of the LORD" who spoke with him there. According to *Tg. Ps.-J.* of the same verse, "He would hear the voice of the Word [*Dibbura*], but he would not see the splendor of his face . . . and when the voice of the Word [*Dibbura*] had gone up, he would return to the camp." Thus outside the camp, Moses heard the voice of the Word, as Israel had from Mt. Sinai and as Moses would later hear from the holy of holies. In v. 13, he says, "Let me know your ways, that I may know you, so that I might find favor in your sight." The LORD responds in v. 14:

MT	*My presence* [lit.: face] will go with you, and I will give you rest.
Tg. Onq.	*My Shekinah* will go, and I will give you rest.
Tg. Neof.	*The glory of my Shekinah* will lead among you, and I will prepare a resting place for you.
Tg. Neof. [mg.]	*The face of my good pleasure* will lead you and give you rest.
Tg. Ps.-J.	Wait until *the face of my anger has passed,* and afterwards I will give you rest.

Moses responds, vv. 15–16:

MT	*If your presence does not go,* do not lead us up from here. For by what can it be known that I have found favor in your sight, I and your people? *Is it not by your going with us,* so that we may be distinguished, I and your people, from all the people on the face of the earth?
Tg. Onq.	*If your Shekinah does not go* among us . . . Is it not by your *Shekinah* going with us . . . ?
Tg. Neof.	If the glory of your Shekinah is not among us . . . If not by the glory of your Shekinah leading [mg.: speaking] with us, and signs and wonders shall be performed with us. . . .
Tg. Ps.-J.	*If your presence* [lit.: face] *does not go* among us . . . *unless your Shekinah speaks with us and wonders are performed for us.* . . .

In *Tgs. Ps.-J.* and *Neof.* [mg.], the *Shekinah* speaks, evidencing the overlap of *Shekinah* and Word, and the miraculous is mentioned as evidence that the *Shekinah* is among his people, just as John sees the miracles as evidence that the Word "dwelt among us." In making this addition, the targumists may have taken a cue from the verb "distinguished" (*niphal* of פלה), which was used (in the *hiphil*) in the course of narrating the miracles in Egypt. These miracles both distinguished Israel from Egypt (Exod 8:22; 9:4; 11:7) and demonstrated that the LORD dwelt in the midst of the land (8:22; listed on p. 53, no. 10 of this chapter). *Targum Pseudo-Jonathan, Tg. Neof.* Exod 8:22, and *Tg. Ps.-J.* Exod 9:4 interpret this verb as being from the root פלא, to do miracles:

MT of Exod 8:22	On that day I will set apart the land of Goshen, where my people live, . . . so that you might know that I, the Lord, am in the midst of the land.
Tg. Neof.	I will do signs and miracles on that day with the land of Goshen, upon which my people dwell . . . so that you may know that I am he, the Lord, whose Word dwells [mg.: the glory of whose Shekinah dwells] within the land.

In Exod 33:17–18, the LORD grants the request of Moses, and Moses makes the further request, "Show me your glory." The LORD says that he will make all his goodness pass before Moses, and,

MT	[19]I will proclaim the name of the Lord before you. . . . [20]You cannot see my face, for no man can see me and live. . . . [22]And it shall be that while my glory is passing by, I will put you in the cleft of the rock and cover you with my hand until I have passed by. [23]Then I will take my hand away and you shall see my back, but my face shall not be seen.
Tg. Onq.	[19]I will proclaim the name of the LORD before you. . . . [20]You cannot see the face of my Shekinah {my glory}, for no man can see me and survive. . . . [22]When my glory passes by . . . I will cover you by my Word until I have passed by, [23]and I will take away the _____[17] of my glory, and you will see that which is after me, but that which is before me shall not be seen.
Tg. Neof.	[this portion of v. 19 is omitted in *Neofiti*] [20]You cannot see my face, for it is not possible that a son of man see my face and live. . . . [22]When the glory of my *Shekinah* passes by . . . I shall spread my palm over you until the groups of angels, which you shall see, pass by. [23]And I will make the groups of angels pass by, and they will stand and serve before me, and you will see the Word [Dibbera] of the glory of my *Shekinah*, but it is not possible that you see the face of the glory of my *Shekinah*.
Tg. Neof. [mg.]	[21]The Word of the LORD (said . . .), [23]"And I will make (you) see the Word [Dibbura] of glory."

---

[17] Aramaic הברת, which Etheridge and Grossfeld apparently took as a corruption of *Dibbera*: "Then I will remove the Word of My Glory" (Grossfeld, *Targum Onqelos Exodus*, 94; see discussion n. 18, p. 95) Similarly Etheridge, "word (*dibberath*) of My Glory" (*Targums Onqelos and Jonathan on the Pentateuch*, 424). This would be the only occurrence of *Dibbera* in *Tg. Onqelos*. I. Drazin translates "I will remove the guidance of My glory," citing the explanation that *Tg. Onq.* "does not substitute '*Memra*' here because it is inappropriate to state that God removes His word" (*Targum Onkelos to Exodus: An English Translation of the Text with Analysis and Commentary, Based on A. Sperber's Edition* (New York: Ktav, 1990), 310, and 311, n. 52).

Frg. Tg. **P**	[23]I will remove the groups of angels who stand and serve before me, and you will see the Word [*Dibbura*] of the LORD, but the glory of my *Shekinah* it is not possible for you to see.
Frg. Tg. **V**	[19]I will proclaim the good name of the LORD before you. . . . [23]I will remove the groups of angels who stand and serve before me, and you will see the Word [*Dibbera*] of the glory of my *Shekinah*, but <the face of the glory of my *Shekinah*> it is impossible for you to see.[18]
Tg. Ps.-J.	[19]I will proclaim the name of the Word of the LORD before you. . . . [20]It is not possible for you to see my face, for man may not see me and survive. . . . [22]And when the glory of my *Shekinah* passes by . . . I will protect you with my Word until the time I pass by. [23]And I will make the groups of angels who stand and serve before me pass by, and you will see the knot _____ of the phylacteries of the glory of my *Shekinah*, but the face of the glory of my *Shekinah* it is not possible for you to see.[19]

Observations

1. In *Tg. Ps.-J.*, the LORD says, "I will proclaim the name of the Word of the LORD before you." This proclamation of the name of the Word of the LORD in v. 6 of the next chapter (34:6) includes the description, "full of grace and truth," with obvious implications for associating the Logos with *Memra/Dibbera*.

2. Although there is considerable variety in how the various Targums handle the contrast "You will see my back but my face will not be seen," *Tg. Neof.* (and mg.) and both *Frg. Tg.* traditions all say that Moses will be allowed to see only the Word. In all of these, *Dibbura/Dibbera* is used for Word. Recall that this term can stand alone, "the Word," as does the Logos in John. That is, it is not used with personal pronouns and need not be followed by "of the LORD." It is also interesting that the other two Targums have obscure words that could be a corruption of *Dibbera* (*Tg. Onq.*) or due to conflation (*Tg. Ps.-J.*). In any case, interpreters have already seen a fit between this passage and John without looking at the Targums, and the case gets stronger when we look at the Targums, especially *Pal. Tgs.* which speak of Moses seeing "the Word of the glory of my *Shekinah*" (*Tg. Neof.*; *Frg. Tg. V*), "the Word of glory" (*Tg. Neof.* [mg.]), or "the Word of the LORD" (*Frg. Tg. P*).

The revelation of the LORD's glory occurs in 34:5–7. Again the various Targum readings are of interest:

---

[18]Text in angled brackets supplied by Klein from *Tgs. Neof.* and *Ps.-J.*

[19]The word after "knot" is either דבירא or דבידא. The former could be translated "which is on the hand." Maher takes it as the latter and leaves it untranslated, as a conflation of other *Palestinian Targum* readings of *Dibbera* (spelled variously). Maher notes that *b. Berakot* 7a says that God "showed Moses the knot of the tefillin" (*Pseudo-Jonathan Exodus*, 258, n. 37).

MT	⁵The Lord came down in the cloud and stood with him there as he called on the name of the Lord. ⁶The Lord passed by before him and proclaimed, "The Lord, the Lord God, compassionate and gracious, slow to anger, and abounding in kindness and truth. . . ."
Tg. Onq.	⁵The Lord was revealed in the cloud. . . . ⁶And the Lord made his *Shekinah* pass before him. . . .
Tg. Neof.	⁵The glory of the *Shekinah* of the Lord was revealed in the cloud, and he stood beside him there, and he prayed there in the name of the Word of the Lord. ⁶And the glory of the *Shekinah* of the Lord passed by, and Moses prayed and said, "O Lord, O Lord, gracious and merciful God, patient, far from anger and near to mercy and abounding to do kindness and truth. . . ."
Tg. Neof. [mg.]	⁵The Word of the Lord was revealed.
Frg. Tg. P	⁶The glory of the *Shekinah* of the Lord passed before him, and Moses prayed, and he said, "O Lord God. . . ."
Frg. Tg. V	⁶And the glory of the *Shekinah* of the Lord passed before him, and Moses prayed and said, "O Lord, O Lord, merciful and gracious God, patient, far from anger and near to mercy and abounding to do kindness and truth. . . ."
Tg. Ps.-J.	⁵The Lord was revealed in the clouds of the glory of his *Shekinah*. And Moses stationed himself there with him, and Moses proclaimed the name of the Word of the Lord. ⁶The Lord made his *Shekinah* pass before him and he called out, "The Lord, the Lord God, merciful and gracious, patient and bringing mercy near, and abounding to do kindness and truth. . . ."

Again we note the association in *Tg. Ps.-J.* of "abounding to do kindness and truth" (which I have related to "full of grace and truth," John 1:14) with the proclamation of "the name of the Word of the Lord" (which I have related to "his [the Word's] name," John 1:12). This observation provides a convenient conclusion as we go to the next chapter, where we study the mission of Jesus as the revealer of the divine name; that is, the name of the Father, which has also been given to the Son. We will also see in subsequent chapters more evidence of the importance of Exod 34 in John's Gospel. Reflecting on the language of the Targums, John shows his readers in the person and work of Christ an extended revelation of the glory of God such as was seen briefly by Moses on Mt. Sinai.

Conclusions

Several different lines of evidence have now been considered that point to the conclusion that John's Logos—"the Word"—is a divine title taken from the Targums: (1) "Word," "glory," and "*Shekinah*" are three key expressions used in the Targums to describe God manifesting his presence among, and interacting with, his people. They seem to form the background for three words John uses in John 1:14, namely, "Word," "dwelt," and "glory." Even without consulting the Targums, we can appreciate that 1:14 alludes to the OT pattern of God dwelling among his people and manifesting his glory, which entails the conclusion that "the Word" must be a divine title or allude to the name of God. (2) These three targumic terms are frequently collocated in the Targums, and many passages where this occurs have a direct bearing on John's Gospel. (3) The OT background of John 1:14–18 points especially to the revelation of God to Moses in Exod 33–34, where the corresponding Targum passages make abundant use of the concept of the divine Word in order to convey the idea that Moses saw the glory of the divine Word, but did not see the face of God.

3

The Name of the Father and the Mission of Jesus

INTRODUCTION

There are four references to the name of the Father in John 17. In two of them Jesus says he has manifested or made known the Father's name to the disciples, and in the other two Jesus says that the Father's name is given to the Son. These references to the Father's name can be grouped as follows:

> I *manifested* [ἐφανέρωσα] *your name* to the men whom you gave to me (v. 6).
>> Keep them in *your name which you have given me* (v. 11).
>> I was keeping them in *your name which you have given me* (v. 12).
> I have *made known* [ἐγνώρισα] *your name* to them, and *will make it known* (v. 26).

Jesus' prayer makes it clear that the manifestation of, or making known, the name of the Father to the disciples—that name which is also given to the Son—is central to the mission of Jesus. In this chapter, we ask what is the Father's name, what is the meaning of that name, and how did Jesus fulfill the mission of making that name known? The last question is again taken up in chs. four through eight.

As we saw in ch. 2, John 1:14–18 recalls the manifestation of the glory of the LORD (or in the language of the *Pal. Tgs.*, the glory of the Word) to Moses in Exod 34. The revelation of the glory of God involved a proclamation of the divine name before Moses, including the LORD's description of himself as "full of grace and truth" (34:6). The words and deeds of Jesus before the disciples can likewise be seen (and I believe John intended them to be seen) as an exposition of the divine name, as one would expect based on Jesus' words in John 17:6, 26. As noted in ch. 1, often in the *Pal. Tgs.*, including *Tg. Ps.-J.* Exod 34:6, the divine name is "the name of the Word of the LORD." This means that if we see the background of the Logos title as being this targumic Word, there is a "fit" with the Gospel, where the Father's name, YHWH, is also the name of the Son ("your name which you have given me"), whom John has called "the Word." The targumic "Word" seems to be closely related to the divine name also in *Tg. Isa.* 48:12, where the MT's "For my own sake, for my own sake," is rendered "For the sake of my name, for the sake of my Word." Some parallel between "Word" and "name" also seems to be presumed in *Tg. Isa.* 26:13, where MT "Through you alone we commemorate your name" becomes "We trust in your Word, we praise your name." More often, MT "name" is in the Targums "*Shekinah*," in contexts where God speaks of causing his name to dwell (*Tgs. Onq., Ps.-J.,* and *Neof.* Deut 12:11, 21; 14:23; 16:2, 6, 11; 26:2; *Tg. 1 Kgs.* 11:36; *Tg. 2 Kgs.* 21:4, 7; *Tg. 2 Chr.* 6:20; 12:13; 33:7; *Tg. Jer.* 7:12). Again we note that such passages are of interest because of the conceptual overlap between "Word" and "*Shekinah*."

THE NAME OF THE FATHER

The following considerations suggest that the name of the Father in John 17 is the Tetragrammaton.

1. Jesus said to the Jews, "I have come in my Father's name, and you do not receive me" (5:43), which can be compared to "Blessed is he who comes in the name of the Lord" (12:13), a citation of Ps 118:26, where "Lord" stands for the Tetragrammaton. Further, the phrase "you do not receive me" parallels an earlier portion of Ps 118: "The stone that the builders rejected" (v. 22), strengthening the connection between John 5:43 and 12:13. Thus the implication for John 17:11–12 of John 12:13 is that, as Burkett states, "the Son has been given the Father's name, i.e., 'Yahweh.'"[1]

2. Jesus' statement in John 17:6, 26 that he made known the Father's name to the disciples can be related to 4:26, because in that verse Jesus uses the language of Isa 52:6, where the LORD promises that there will be a day when his people know his name. The connection between Isa 52:6 and John 4:26 is not evident in translation, unless one translates more literally than is usually done:

Isa 52:6	Isa 52:6 (LXX)	John 4:26
Therefore my people shall know my name. Therefore, in that day (they shall know) that I am he, the one who is speaking, here am I. ['אֲנִי הוּא הַמְדַבֵּר הִנֵּנִי]	I am he, the one speaking; I am here. ['Ἐγώ εἰμι ὁ λαλῶν, πάρειμι]	I am he, the one who is speaking to you. ['Ἐγώ εἰμι ὁ λαλῶν σοι]

The translation of John 4:26 is not entirely literal, but it reflects the fact that Hebrew אֲנִי־הוּא ("I [am] he") is usually translated in the LXX, including at Isa 52:6, idiomatically by ἐγώ εἰμι (lit.: "I, I am").

Arguably, "my name" in Isa 52:6 refers to the Tetragrammaton. The ἐγώ εἰμι sayings of Jesus in John are examined in more detail in chs. eight and nine, but for now we can see how John 4:26 can be read along the same lines as John 17:6,

---

[1] Burkett, *Son of the Man in the Gospel of John*, 128.

26, that the mission of Jesus was to reveal the name of the Father (YHWH) to his people, and in agreement with John 17:11–12, which says that this name is also given to the Son, since the Son says "I am he" in a manner that seems to be based on God's "I am he" in Isa 52:6. In ch. 6 we will show how the Samaritan woman does in fact symbolize the people of God once we properly understand the OT background to John 4, so that Jesus is fulfilling the promise: "my people will know my name."

THE MEANING OF THE TETRAGRAMMATON

Most would agree that Exod 3:14 has something to do with explaining the meaning of the divine name. The Hebrew אֶהְיֶה אֲשֶׁר אֶהְיֶה is often translated "I am who I am." Alviero Niccacci notes, however, that this translation is problematic since clause-initial אֶהְיֶה would be expected to express volition (a promise, etc.).[2] Taking the first אֶהְיֶה as volitional would lead to the possibility of "I will be who I will be," which would not seem to be much of an explanation. Niccacci argues that the second אֶהְיֶה is not future, but a past habitual, "I will be who I have been," and that such an interpretation suits the context, in which God is stressing that he is the God of the fathers. That is, he is the God of the fathers, who made promises to the fathers, and he will be the God of Israel and keep the promises he made concerning Israel to the fathers (most obviously, to bring them from Egypt and make them his people in the promised land). One could use the perfect tense to express the idea of being in the past, as, for example, in such expressions as "Just as I was [הָיִיתִי] with Moses, so I will be with you" (Josh 1:5), but the imperfect could be used as well. Niccacci cites the use of אֶהְיֶה in 2 Sam 15:34, where David suggests that Hushai the Archite pledge loyalty to Absalom with the preface, "I used to be [אֶהְיֶה] your father's servant."

Niccacci notes that this seems to be the interpretation of *Tg. Ps.-J.* Exod 3:14, since the expansion of "I am he" in *Tg. Ps.-J.* Deut 32:39 ("I am he who is, and was, and I am he who will be") is similar to *Tg. Ps.-J.* Exod 3:14 ("I am he who is and who will be"), which follows a description of God as "he who said, and the world was." That is, God is described in terms of continuity in the past, present, and future. *Targum Neofiti* and *Frg. Tg. P* Exod 3:14 refer to the past and future when rendering the text, as noted below.

---

[2] Alviero Niccacci, "Esodo 3,14a 'lo sarò quello che ero' e un parallelo egiziano," *Liber annuus Studii biblici franciscani* 35 (1985): 7–26. For an example where the verb "to be" is clause initial and volitional, we can take note of the divine promise, "My name shall be there" (וְהָיָה שְׁמִי שָׁם;1 Kgs 8:29; 2 Kgs 23:27), which is also of interest because of a possible word play between the name of God and the verb "to be," consistent with Exod 3:14. For his English summary, see Niccacci, e-mail to Biblical Greek mailing list, April 5, 1997. Online: http://www.ibiblio.org/bgreek/test-archives/html4/1997-04/18095.html (accessed: June 26, 2009). He suggests translating 2 Sam 15:34 as "As for your servant, I, O king—I used to be a servant of your father—and I was it since long time—and now, I am your servant."

In Rev 1:4, 8; 4:8, we find something very similar to *Tg. Ps.-J.* Deut 32:39:

Tg. Ps.-J. Deut 32:39	I am he who is, and was, and I am he who will be.
Rev 1:4	Grace and peace to you, from him who is, who was, and who is to come.[3]
Rev 1:8	I am he ['Εγώ εἰμι], the Alpha and the Omega, says the Lord God, who is [ὁ ὤν], and who was, and who is to come, the Almighty.
Rev 4:8	Holy, holy, holy is the Lord God Almighty, who was, and who is, and who is to come.

Revelation 1:8, besides being similar to the Targum text, also contains the LXX of Exod 3:14, ἐγώ εἰμι ὁ ὤν (I am he who is), though split up.[4] In Rev 1:4, following the preposition "from" (ἀπό), one would expect "him who is . . ." to be in the genitive case, but it is in the nominative, making the phrase (including the definite articles) look like non-declining Hebrew names taken over from the OT, which would be the case if it stands for the Tetragrammaton.[5] Also of potential interest for the possibility that *Tg. Ps.-J.* Deut 32:39 is expounding the divine name, in Deut 32:3 Moses says "I will proclaim the name of the LORD," so that "the overall scope and purpose of the song is presented as a proclamation of the name of the Lord" (though *Tg. Ps.-J.* as well as *Tg. Neof.* and *Frg. Tgs.* P, V change "proclaim [קרא] the name" to "pray [צלי] in the name").[6]

---

[3]ἀπὸ ὁ ὤν καὶ ὁ ἦν καὶ ὁ ἐρχόμενος. In Rev 4:8 the first two terms are switched: ὁ ἦν καὶ ὁ ὤν καὶ ὁ ἐρχόμενος.

[4]This point is made by Robert M. Bowman Jr. and J. Ed Komoszewski, *Putting Jesus in His Place* (Grand Rapids: Kregel, 2007), 181.

[5]Cf. ἀπὸ 'Αβραάμ and ἀπὸ Δαυίδ in Matt 1:17. The circumlocution is "a quaint and deliberate violation of grammar . . . in order to preserve the immutability and absoluteness of the divine name from declension. . . . The divine title is a paraphrase probably suggested by rabbinic language (e.g., Targum [Pseudo-] Jonathan apud Deut. xxxii. 39 . . .)" (James Moffatt, "The Revelation of St. John the Divine," in *Expositor's Greek Testament* [ed. W. R. Nicoll; 5 vols.; Grand Rapids: Eerdmans, 1956], 5:337). One could try to reproduce the effect in English by using capital letters, appropriate to a name, and by translating "Grace and peace *from He* Who Is. . . ." McNamara made the case for dependence on *Tg. Ps.-J.* Deut 32:39 in *The NT and the Palestinian Targum to the Pentateuch*, 97–117. He followed the suggestion of A. Debrunner that the definite articles in the title were not declined because they actually are meant to represent the Aramaic relative pronoun ד. as used in *Tg. Ps.-J.* Deut 32:39, for example, which also explains the anomalous ὁ ἦν. Thus ὁ ὤν from Rev 1:4, etc. agrees with Aramaic דהווי in *Tg. Ps.-J.* Deut 32:39 (ibid., 110; source for Debrunner is *Göttingische gelehrte Anzeigen* 188 [1926]: 148). He also suggests that ὁ ἐρχόμενος is a Christian adaptation of the title (ὁ ἐσόμενος would be expected) due to the emphasis in Revelation on the coming of Christ and his kingdom; he attributes the two forms without ὁ ἐρχόμενος (Rev 11:17; 16:5, discussed below) to the fact that in these two contexts the kingdom has already come (ibid., 101; see Rev 11:15).

[6]Thomas A. Keiser, "The Song of Moses: A Basis for Isaiah's Prophecy" (*VT* 55 [2005]), 487.

As Niccacci suggests, we can also compare *Tg. Ps.-J.* Deut 32:39 with *Tg. Ps.-J.* Exod 3:14, and it is instructive to compare *Tg. Ps.-J.* Exod 3:14 with the other *Pal. Tg.* readings of that verse, and then to a shorter paraphrase of the divine name also found in Revelation:

Tg. Ps.-J. **Exod 3:14**	"He who said, and the world was, who said, and everything was." And the LORD said to Moses, "Thus you shall say to the children of Israel, 'I am he [אנא הוא] who is and who will be has sent me to you.'"
Tg. Neof. **Exod 3:14**	(after reproducing the Hebrew אֶהְיֶה אֲשֶׁר אֶהְיֶה) He who said, and the world was from the beginning, and is to say to it again: "Be!", and it will be.
Frg. Tg. P	(similar to *Tg. Neof.* [mg. 1]) The one who said to the world in the beginning, "Be!", and it was, and who will say to it in the future, "Be!", and it will be (spoken by the Word of the LORD).
Tg. Neof. **[mg. 2]**	"I was before the world was created and I was after the world was created. I am he [אנא הוא] who was for your help in the captivity of the Egyptians, and I am he [אנא הוא] who is yet to be for your help in every generation." And he said, "Thus you shall say to the children of Israel, 'אהיה has sent me to you."
Rev 11:17	We give you thanks, Lord God Almighty, the one who is, and who was.
Rev 16:5	Righteous are you, the one who is, and who was.

These descriptions of God in Revelation use present and past tenses of the verb "to be." In *Tg. Neof.* and *Frg. Tg. P*, it is past and future; *Tg. Ps.-J.* has present and future (*Tg. Ps.-J.* also refers to the past, by describing God's creation in the past, rather than saying that he existed in the past).

There is good reason to think, therefore, that *Tg. Ps.-J.* Deut 32:39 reflects an interpretation of the meaning of the divine name given in Exod 3:14 as "I will be who I have been," that is, "I am the same, past, present, future." Some of the *Pal. Tgs.* of Exod 3:14 use "I am he" (אנא הוא) to expound the divine name, as noted above (*Tgs. Ps.-J.* and *Neof.*). Obviously, this expression could have been taken from Deut 32:39 itself, but there could also be some influence from the repeated use of "I am he" by God in Isaiah. These sayings occur with respect to God's activity in the past, present, and future; this fact, along with their combination with "I am the first and the last," might have influenced or reinforced the interpretation of Exod 3:14 given above. These sayings occur as follows:

Isa 41:4: Who has performed and accomplished it, calling forth the generations from the beginning? I, the LORD, am the first, and with the last. I am he (LXX: ἐγώ εἰμι).

Targum Isaiah does not use אנא הוא here and paraphrases considerably: "I, the LORD, created the world from the beginning, even the ages of ages are mine, and besides me there is no God."

Isa 43:10: You are my witnesses, declares the LORD, and my servant whom I have chosen, so that you may know and believe me, and understand that I am he (LXX: ἐγώ εἰμι). Before me there was no God formed, and there will be none after me.

Here *Tg. Isa.* does use אנא הוא for MT אני הוא, and in addition it adds another "I am he" saying. For the second sentence quoted above, *Tg. Isa.* has "I am he who is from the beginning [אנא הוא דמלקדמין], even the ages of ages are mine, and there is no God besides me."

> Isa 43:13: Even from eternity I am he [גַּם מִיוֹם אֲנִי הוּא], and there is no one who can deliver out of my hand; I act and who can reverse it?

Besides having "I am he" in common with Deut 32:39, the saying "there is no one who can deliver out of my hand" also agrees with that verse. Here the LXX omits "I am he" but translates מִיּוֹם as "from the beginning" (ἀπ' ἀρχῆς), joined to the previous verse, "I am the Lord God from the beginning." *Targum Isaiah* translates this phrase as "from eternity I am he" (מעלמא אנא הוא). Modern translations disagree as to whether מִיּוֹם refers to the beginning of time ("before there was day") or to the future ("from now on"), as if it were from מֵהַיּוֹם, "from today." The LXX and *Tg. Isa.*, at least, take it as referring to the beginning.

> Isa 43:25: I, even I, am he [אָנֹכִי אָנֹכִי הוּא; *Tg.:* אֲנָא אֲנָא הוּא] who wipes out your transgressions for my own sake (*Tg.:* who forgives your sins for my name's sake).

The LXX translates the beginning of this verse with a double ἐγώ εἰμι, which has led some interpreters to think that already in the LXX ἐγώ εἰμι is used as a surrogate for the Tetragrammaton: "I am 'I am he.'" The Targum could be taken the same way, or as the MT is translated above. The Targum paraphrase of God's self-description in this verse bears a strinking resemblance to 1 John 2:12: "I write to you, children, because your sins are forgiven you for his name's sake." In the Johannine context, "his name" is Christ's name, which, if based on *Tg. Isa.* 43:25, must be the Tetragrammaton. That *Tg. Isa.* 43:25 is the source of John's language is further suggested by the fact that John goes on to utilize a Targum paraphrase of another "I am he" saying from the same chapter of Isaiah: "I write to you, fathers, because you know *him who is from the beginning*" (τὸν ἀπ' ἀρχῆς, vv. 13–14; see Isa 43:10 above). While it is true that the LXX of Isa 43:13 uses ἀπ' ἀρχῆς, as noted above, John 2:12 clearly agrees with *Tg. Isa.* 43:25, not the LXX of this verse, which is rendered literally; this makes it likely that John derived his language from the Targum rather than from the LXX. Further, as we see below, "I am he who is from the beginning" is used twice more in the Targum of this section of Isaiah, and in ch. 8 we will see that the "I am he" saying of Isa 43:10 is quite important for interpreting a number of the ἐγώ εἰμι sayings of Jesus in John's Gospel.

> Isa 44:6: Thus says the LORD, the King of Israel, and his Redeemer, the Lord of hosts: "I am the first and I am the last, and there is no God besides me."

Neither the MT nor the LXX uses "I am he" here, but the *Isaiah Targum* reads identically to *Tg. Isa.* 43:10, to give us a double "I am he": "I am he; I am he who is from the beginning; even the ages of ages are mine. Besides me there is no God." In this case, "I am he who is from the beginning" paraphrases MT "I am the first," and another "I am he" is added at the beginning. Likely the motivation for this addition is to make this verse identical to *Tg. Isa.* 48:12 where "I am he" and "I am the first and the last" are together in the MT, and "I am the first" is paraphrased as in *Tg. Isa.* 44:6 (see Isa 48:12 below).

> Isa 46:4: Even to (your) old age, I am he (LXX: ἐγώ εἰμι), and even to (your) time of gray hair, I [אֲנִי LXX: ἐγώ εἰμι] will bear (you). I have acted, and I will carry (you); and I will bear, and I will deliver.

Targum Isaiah reads here, "Even to eternity, I am he, and to the age of ages my Word endures." The association of the divine Word with "I am he" is not quite so close as in *Tg. Neof.* Deut 32:39, "I, I in my Word, am he."

> Isa 48:12: Listen to me, O Jacob, even Israel whom I called; I am he, I am the first, indeed I am the last.

The LXX has ἐγώ εἰμι πρῶτος καὶ ἐγώ εἰμι εἰς τὸν αἰῶνα, essentially combining "I am he" with "I am the first" and "I am the last." As noted above, *Tg. Isa.* reads as in *Tg. Isa.* 43:10 and 44:6: "I am he. I am he who is from the beginning. Even the ages of ages are mine, and besides me there is no God." *Targum Isaiah* 48:12 begins by saying, "Receive my Word, O those of the house of Jacob" (see ch. 1 on the language of John 1:11–12), and v. 13 says, "By my Word I founded the earth" (again, see ch. 1, on the targumic background of John 1:1–3, 10).

> Isa 51:12: I, even I, am he [אָנֹכִי אָנֹכִי הוּא; *Tg.*: אֲנָא אֲנָא הוּא] who comforts you. Who are you that you are afraid of man who dies? And of the son of man who is made like grass?

Here again, as in Isa 43:25, the LXX translates with a double ἐγώ εἰμι, which might be understood, "I am 'I am he.'"

> Isa 52:6: Therefore my people shall know my name; therefore in that day (they shall know) that I am he (LXX: ἐγώ εἰμι), the one who is speaking; here I am.

Targum Isaiah paraphrases in such a way that the promise is not of God's people knowing his name, but of the other nations: "Therefore my name shall be exalted among the peoples; therefore in that time you shall know that it is I who speak, and my Word endures." It is of interest that the Targums render the future divine "Here I am" as "My Word endures," in light of the dependence of John 4:26 on Isa 52:6, which we noted above. Isaiah 52:6 is the last in a series of nine OT "I am he" sayings (counting Deut 32:39, but not counting Isa 44:6 where "I am he" is not in the MT); John 4:26 is the first in a series of twenty-two "I am he" sayings of Jesus in John. As the first of these in John is based on the last of them in Isaiah, Jesus the divine Word is basically picking up where he left off in Isaiah, saying that the promised time of revelation of the divine name has come.

The use of "I am he" in Isaiah can be seen as supporting the interpretation of the meaning of the divine name in Exod 3:14 given above, since (1) the "I am he" sayings refer to God's constancy in the past (Isa 43:13), present (Isa 41:4; 43:10, 25; 48:12; 51:12), and future (46:4; 52:6), and (2) they occur along with the "I am the first and the last" sayings (Isa 41:4; 44:6; 48:12), which point to the whole spectrum of time. These sayings assure the LORD's people that the LORD is the one true God, the same past, present, and future, in contrast with the gods of pagans, many of whom follow a changing career path, often starting out as mere mortals.

THE NAME OF THE FATHER IS GIVEN TO THE SON

As noted above, twice in John 17:11–12 Jesus says that the Father's name has been given to him. As we have seen, this name refers to the Tetragrammaton. This passage is among the clearest indications of the deity of Jesus Christ in the NT, since there can be no clearer indication of deity than possession of the name YHWH. Unfortunately, the value of John 17:11–12 in refuting Arianism is reduced by the fact that in each case there is a variant reading of the text stating that it was the disciples rather than the Father's name that had been given to the Son. The KJV, which translates "those whom thou hast given me" (v. 11) and "those that thou gavest me" (v. 12), is based on these variants. However, the variants were rejected by the committee that produced the UBS (United Bible Societies) text because, as Bruce Metzger explained in commenting on both variants, "The reading that best accounts for the origin of the others [i.e., the reading that states that it was the Father's name that had been given to the son] has also the strongest attestation."[7] The UBS text is also preferable on the grounds that it is the more difficult text. Any scribes who were unaware that the Father's name referred to the Tetragrammaton might have mistakenly understood "Father" as the name being referred to. To avoid the perceived heresy of modalism—the implication that Jesus is the Father, they made a slight change in the text. Modern translators also seem confused about the meaning and importance of the Father's name in John 17. Of the four references to "your name" in John 17, the NIV retains only one (v. 11; a footnote gives the correct reading for vv. 6, 26). In 17:12 "your name" is changed to "the name," which could be interpreted as the name Jesus. NLT does not use the word "name" at all in its translation of these verses.

Elsewhere in the NT we see that the divine name is given to the Son. Just as the LORD says in Isaiah, so too Jesus says in Revelation, "I am he" (1:17; 2:23; 21:6; 22:16) and "I am the first and the last" (1:17; 2:8; 22:13). The two sayings are together in Rev 1:17, just as in Isa 41:4. In both Isaiah and Revelation, "I am he, the first and the last" is the first "I am he" saying in the series. In Rev 2:23 ("all the churches will know that I am he who searches the minds and hearts"), which follows closely Jer 17:10 ("I, the LORD, search the heart . . ."), ἐγώ εἰμι stands for LXX ἐγὼ κύριος.

Further, after saying "I am the first and the last" in Rev 1:17, Jesus says "I am the Living One, and I was dead, and behold, I am alive forever and ever" (v. 18), which could be viewed as an incarnational adaptation of Deut 32:39–40, both by reference to MT/LXX/*Tg. Onq.* ("I kill and make alive . . . I live forever"), and to the

---

[7] Bruce Metzger, *A Textual Commentary on the Greek New Testament* (2d ed., Stuttgart: German Bible Society, 1994), 213.

Pal. Tgs. The present (the Living One), past (I was dead), and future (I am alive forever) of Rev 1:18 reminds us of *Tg. Ps.-J.* Deut 32:39 (I am he who is and was and I am he who will be), and "I am alive forever," spoken by the divine Word, can be related to *Tg. Neof.* and *Frg. Tg. V* Deut 32:40, "I live and exist in my Word forever." Similarly, in Rev 2:8, Jesus is "the first and the last, who died, and has come to life."

We also find in the book of Hebrews a title of Jesus that is similar to *Tg. Ps.-J.* Deut 32:39: "Jesus Christ the same, yesterday, today, and forever" (Heb 13:18). There is good reason to think that this is an allusion to the Tetragrammaton, similar to "I am he who is and was, and I am he who will be" of *Tg. Ps.-J.* Deut 32:39. In Heb 1:4, the author says that the Son has inherited a more excellent name than the angels. The word for "more excellent" (the comparative of διάφορος) could also be translated "more distinguished."

The Tetragrammaton is referred to as "the distinguished name" (שמא מפרשא with slight variations of spelling) or "the great and distinguished name" in *Tg. Neof.* Exod 32:25; *Tgs. Neof.* and *Ps.-J.* Exod 33:6; and *Tg. Ps.-J.* Num 20:8. In these three passages, Targum references to the Name occur in additions to the text (i.e., the MT has no reference to the name of God). But in *Tg. Ps.-J.* Lev 24:11, "the great and glorious name of distinction" (שמא רבא ויקירא דמתפרש) translates "the Name" that was blasphemed, which in context must mean YHWH. In Judg 13:18, the angel of the LORD asks Manoah, "Why do you ask my name, since it is Wonderful?" *Targum Judges* 13:18 uses the word מְפָרַשׁ for "Wonderful": "Why do you ask my name, (seeing) it is Ineffable?" (meaning that it is the name of God).[8]

Not only is the title "Wonderful" from Judg 13 used in the promise of the divine child in Isa 9:6, but the wording of the promise "Behold, you will become pregnant and bear a son" (Judg 13:5, 7) is used in Isa 7:14, slightly adapted, in the prediction of the birth of Immanuel. The root פלא from which "Wonderful" comes, is used also in connection with the miraculous conception of Isaac (Gen 18:14): "Is anything too difficult for the LORD?" (הֲיִפָּלֵא מֵיהוה דָּבָר). Thus the use of "Wonderful" in Isa 9:6, pointing back to Judg 13:18, where it can be taken as a reference to the name of God, and whose context (Judg 13:5, 7) in turn points to Isa 7:14, could be the basis for the writer's statement that the Son has "a more distinguished name" than the angels (implying that the angel of the LORD in Judg 13 is a manifestation of the LORD himself, rather than a created angelic being). That is, the "more distinguished name" of the Son is not "Son" but YHWH.

But the author of Hebrews makes his point, not by referring to the messianic prophecies of Isa 7:14 and 9:6, but by citing Ps 102:25–27: "You, Lord, in the beginning laid the foundation of the earth. . . . You are the same, and your years will

---

[8] As translated by Willem F. Smelik, *The Targum of Judges* (Leiden: Brill, 1995), 566. Smelik comments, "It comes as a surprise to find מפרש applied to the name of the angel. Even though the exact meaning of שם המפורש is not beyond doubt, it always represents the tetragrammaton." Smelik suggests an early date for this exegetical tradition (ibid., 565–67). In contrast, Daniel J. Harrington and Anthony J. Saldarini translate the Targum of the angel's question as "Why are you asking for my name? And it is *interpreter*" (*Targum Jonathan of the Former Prophets* [ArBib 10; Collegeville, Minn.: Liturgical Press, 1987], 86).

not come to an end." The author quotes this passage in a series of OT passages that refer to the Son, meaning therefore that "You, Lord" addressed by the psalmist is the Son (the psalm itself makes no reference to the Messiah as a human). In addressing God, the psalmist is addressing the Son, who bears the name of God, no less so than the Father. Interpreters who try to make Ps 102 a "messianic psalm" miss the point: the Messiah bears the divine name; therefore he is present before the incarnation so that when the psalmist addresses YHWH, he is addressing the Son, whether he knows it or not.[9] The author of Hebrews, like John in his Prologue, takes the work of the Son back to creation, by identifying Jesus with the Lord who in the beginning founded the earth, just as in 1:2 the author of Hebrews said that the world was made through the Son.

Now if the author of Hebrews simply wanted to apply the divine name to the Son, identifying Jesus as the God of Israel, he could have picked any of hundreds of OT texts that, like Ps 102, speak of God but not of a future Messiah. Why would he pick Ps 102? The reason may be that "You are the same" (ὁ αὐτός) from Ps 102:27 translates the Hebrew "You are he" (also reflected in the *Tg.*) the second person equivalent of the divine "I am he" so important in Deut 32:39 and Isaiah. The LXX translator possibly picked up on the significance of "I am he" in Deut 32:39 and Isaiah, namely, as an affirmation that the meaning of the divine name is that God is the same, past, present, and future, and thus renders the second person equivalent "you are he" as "you are the same." A number of English translations translate Ps 102:27 as did the LXX. Interestingly, NASB translates "I am he" in Isa 46:4 as "I will be the same." I am suggesting, then, that the more distinguished name of the Son is the Tetragrammaton, and that the author of Hebrews chooses Ps 102:27 to convey that fact because the phrase "you are the same" expresses the meaning of the divine name. Confirmation of this interpretation can be inferred from Heb 13:8, where "the same" is applied explicitly to Jesus as part of what could be interpreted as a paraphrase of the divine name along the lines of *Tg. Ps.-J.* Deut 32:39:

Ps 102:27; Heb 1:12	Heb 13:8	*Tg. Ps.-J.* Deut 32:39
You are the same [ὁ αὐτός; for MT "You are he"], and your years shall not fail.	Jesus Christ, the same [ὁ αὐτός] yesterday, today, and forever.	I am he who is and was, and I am he who will be.

Hebrews thus agrees with John 17 in saying that the Tetragrammaton, the Father's name, the distinguished name, is given to the Son. Paul makes the same point in Phil 2:9, where he says that the name above all names is given to Jesus; Paul's reference in v. 10 to Isa 45:23 ("every knee will bow to me") shows that the "name" in question is the Tetragrammaton.

---

[9] Similarly, "this psalm . . . is correctly sung to Jesus on the grounds that Jesus, while fully human, is fully God and worthy of divine praise" (Tremper Longman III, *How to Read the Psalms* [Downers Grove: InterVarsity, 1988], 69).

THE MISSION OF JESUS: EXPLAINING THE DIVINE NAME

If the mission of Jesus is to reveal the name of God, and if the meaning of that name is that the LORD is the one true God, and that he does not change, then we can see a motivation for John's use of the targumic Word as a title for Jesus. Recall from ch. 1 some of the things that scholars have said in describing the targumic Word: Levine stated that this title "conveys the *being* and *doing* of *YHWH*, across the entire spectrum." Levey wrote that the targumic Word "is everything that God is supposed to be, and its manifold activity encompasses the entire spectrum of divine endeavor." Chester noted that Word and *Shekinah* "are used as an *exegesis* of the divine names, especially the tetragrammaton." None of these scholars, incidentally, is an advocate of a Targum background of the Logos title.

What I intend to show in chs. four through eight is that in the person and work of Jesus Christ, John shows us a comprehensive continuation of the divine person and work from the old covenant. That is, as the meaning of the name of God suggests, he does not change, even in that most decisive event of human history, the incarnation. The statement, "I will be in the future who I have been in the past" finds its fulfillment in the person and work of Christ. Of course, one of the first things John tells us is that Jesus was "full of grace and truth," applying to Jesus that phrase from God's self-disclosure to Moses (Exod 34:6), a phrase that is used exclusively for God in the OT, which God spoke to Moses in proclaiming his name before him and showing him his glory. Even though he has taken on human nature, he is still "the same" as when Moses saw him in his glory.

The conception that the LORD is the one who comes down from heaven to reveal his name is another theme from Exod 34 (v. 5) that John applies to Jesus (see ch. 4). In 34:11, the LORD promises to fight for his people, as does Jesus (see ch. 5). In 34:12–16, the LORD warns Israel that he is a jealous God, that Israel must not intermarry with Canaanites, who would cause their sons to commit spiritual immorality with Canaanite deities. Likewise John shows us Jesus as the bridegroom of his people (see ch. 6). In 34:7, the LORD quotes from the second commandment, speaking as Israel's lawgiver, as does Jesus (see ch. 7). Thus in John we see that the Word who became flesh does indeed convey "the *being* and *doing* of *YHWH*, across the entire spectrum." As REB translates John 1:1, "What God was, the Word was."

We have, then, several explanations of the divine name. In Exod 3:14, he is the one who does not change. In 34:6–7, there is a moral explanation of the divine attributes which (according to 3:14) do not change: "full of grace and truth." Then in 34:10–16, we might say we have an experiential explanation of the divine name, as his attributes are revealed in how he deals with his people according to these various categories of "being and doing."

It would seem, then, that John viewed the ministry of Jesus as analogous to the revelation of God to Moses in Exod 34, which was in response to the petition of Moses, "Show me your glory" (33:18). This revelation by Jesus can be described in the same terms as those given to Moses: "I will make all my goodness pass before you, and will proclaim the name of the LORD before you" (33:19). In the case of Jesus, this revelation lasted not just a few moments, but several years. Jesus himself paraphrased Exod 34:10 in his upper room discourse:

Exod 34:10	John 15:24
Before all your people I will do *wonders which have not been done* in all the earth, or among all the nations.	If I had not done works among them which no other has done . . .

We will note, however, that along with this comprehensive continuity from OT to NT, there is change due to the incarnation (a change of works, not a change of person). We often see that in addition to the parallels between the words and deeds of Jesus in John and the words and deeds of God in the OT, there are also similarities to the words and deeds of various OT men of God. This dual parallelism comports with the NT's teaching that the divine Word has taken on human flesh, revealed to us as both God and human.

There is another facet of *Tg. Ps.-J.* Deut 32:39 that interests us in connection with the revelation of the divine name. So far, we have focused on the "I am he" saying itself: "I am he who is and was, and I am he who shall be." But in the Targum this saying has a future context. The full verse is given below, along with the MT and *Tg. Neof.* for comparison (*Frg. Tg. V* is substantially the same as *Tg. Neof.*):

MT	*Tg. Ps.-J.*	*Tg. Neof.*
	When the Word of the LORD shall be revealed to redeem his people, he shall say to all the peoples,	
See now that *I, I am he*, and there is no God besides me.	"See now that *I am he* who is and was, and *I am he* who will be in the future, and there is no other God besides me."	See now that *I, I in my Word am he*, and there is no other God besides me.
I put to death and bring to life;	I by my Word put to death and bring to life.	*I am he* who causes the living to die in this world and who brings to life the dead in the world to come.
I have wounded, and I will heal,	I struck the people of the house of Israel, and I will heal them at the end of days,	*I am he* who strikes and *I am he* who heals,
and there is no one who delivers from my hand.	and there is no one who delivers from my hand;	and there is no one who delivers from my hands.

If we have understood the "I am he" saying of *Tg. Ps.-J.* Deut 32:39 correctly, it is an exposition of the divine name. This explanation is to take place "When the Word of the LORD is revealed to redeem his people," which raises two questions: (1) What is meant by the targumist? (2) Could John have viewed this text, having identified Jesus as the divine Word, as being fulfilled by Jesus in a manner similar to the unwitting "prophecy" of Caiaphas, as discussed in ch. 1?

As for what the targumist meant, we can be certain that for him the Word of the LORD is not the Messiah and that this is not meant to predict what the Messiah will do when he comes or "is revealed." But what occasion might be anticipated in the statement, "when the Word of the LORD shall be revealed to redeem his people"? In the next chapter we take note that MT language about God "coming down" may be rendered in the Targums as "the Word of the LORD (or the glory of his *Shekinah*) was revealed" and that God's "coming down" may be associated with a revelation of the meaning of the divine name, such as at the burning bush to Moses or on Mt. Sinai (Exod 34, again to Moses). *Targum Pseudo-Jonathan* Deut 32:39, therefore, looks forward to a new exodus ("When the Word of the LORD shall be revealed" = MT "When the LORD comes down") and a making known of God's name to the peoples. Such an event is prayed for in Isa 64:1–2: "Oh that you would rend the heavens and *come down . . . to make your name known* to your adversaries." *Targum Pseudo-Jonathan* Deut 32:39 looks toward its fulfillment.

As for the second question, John does not record Jesus as saying "I am he who is and was, and I am he who will be in the future," but, as we have already seen, the first ἐγώ εἰμι saying of Jesus in John (4:26) depends on the last "I am he" saying in Isaiah (52:6), which is in fact connected to a promise from God that his people will know his name. Jesus says ἐγώ εἰμι twenty-two times in John's Gospel, each of which might represent a spoken Aramaic אנא הוא, which means that John quite possibly gives us twenty-two "I am he" sayings of Jesus. The number twenty-two could be of significance as the number of letters in the Hebrew and Aramaic alphabet. Recall that "I am the first and the last" occurs three times in Revelation, as in Isaiah, where it accompanies the "I am he" declarations. "I am the Alpha and Omega" is also found three times in Revelation. In 22:13, "I am the first and the last" is paralleled with "I am the Alpha and Omega." In Rev 1:8, "I am . . . the one who is and who was, and who is coming" agrees with *Tg. Ps.-J.* Deut 32:39. "I am" in Rev 1:8 is also Ἐγώ εἰμι, as also in some MSS of 21:6. Thus John, by including twenty-two ἐγώ εἰμι sayings of Jesus, may be bringing out the idea of Rev 22:13, "I am the Alpha and the Omega, the first and the last."

As in Isaiah, most of the ἐγώ εἰμι sayings in John pertain to the present (4:26; 6:20, 35, 41, 48, 51; 8:12, 18, 24; 10:7, 9, 11, 14; 11:25; 14:6; 15:1, 5; 18:5, 8), but 8:28 and 13:19 pertain to the future and 8:58 pertains to the past. In fact, it is tempting to see the threefold "I am he" of John 8:24, 28, 58, spoken in the temple on the last day of the Feast of Booths ("pre-eminently the Feast for foreign pilgrims"),[10] a feast for which "I am he" seems to have been used liturgically as a way of saying the divine name,[11] as an indication that the promise of the divine Word making known the divine name to all the nations is being fulfilled:

---

[10] Alfred Edersheim, *The Life and Times of Jesus the Messiah* (3d ed.; 2 vols.; 1886; repr., London: Longmans, Green & Co., 1901), 2:148.

[11] *M. Sukkah* 4:5 says, "Each day they went in procession a single time around the Altar, saying, *Save now, we beseech thee, O Lord! We beseech thee, O Lord, send now prosperity.* R.

I am he who is (present)	Unless you believe that *I am he*, you will die in your sins. (v. 24)
and was (past)	Before Abraham existed, *I am he*. (v. 58)
and I am he who will be (future)	When you lift up the Son of Man, then you will know that *I am he*. (v. 28)

Or one could look first at John 8:24, 28 in comparison with *Tg. Ps.-J.* Exod 3:14 ("I am he who is and who will be"), and then at John 8:24, 28, 58 in comparison with *Tg. Ps.-J.* Deut 32:39.

Not only is *Tg. Ps.-J.* Deut 32:39 of interest, the version in *Frg. Tg. V* and *Tg. Neof.* is of interest as well: "I *in my Word* am he." Taken together, the twenty-two ἐγώ εἰμι sayings might be taken as a comprehensive exposition of the divine name which the Son bears, and whose meaning he reveals to the world as the Word who has become flesh. More on this in the following chapters, especially ch. 9, which looks at all twenty-two of these sayings.

Judah says: '*Ani waho!* save us we pray! *Ani waho!* save us we pray!' But on that day [the last], they went in procession seven times around the Altar." R. Judah's expression was apparently suggested by the Hebrew particles of entreaty used in Ps 118:25, אָנָּא יהוה הוֹשִׁיעָה נָּא ("O Lord, save we pray"), and אָנָּא יהוה הַצְלִיחָה נָּא ("O Lord, send prosperity"). "To avoid pronouncing the sacred name Yahweh . . . the priests modified the opening words of the verse, *'anna' YHWH*, to *'ani wehu'*" (Phillip B. Harner, *The "I Am" of the Fourth Gospel: A Study in Johannine Usage and Thought* [Facet Books, Biblical Series 26; Philadelphia: Fortress, 1970], 20). Thus, "Having celebrated the feast and hearing the daily recitation of *ani hu*, Jesus' use of the phrase 'I Am' as a term of self-designation would be both striking and offensive to his opponents" (Mary L. Coloe, "Like Father–Like Son: The Role of Abraham in Tabernacles—Jn 8:31–59," *Pacifica* 12 [February 1999]: 8. Cited 5 Nov 2007. Online: http://www.cecs.acu.edu.au/coloe/Pacifica_Abraham_word.pdf).

4

The Son of Man Came Down from Heaven

Introduction

In John 6:38, Jesus says, "I have come down from heaven." Morris notes concerning John 6, "The thought of His coming down from heaven is repeated seven times in this chapter (vv. 33, 38, 41, 42, 50, 51, 58)."[1] In context the obvious OT background is the manna coming down in the wilderness. But Jesus also told Nicodemus that he had come down from heaven (John 3:13), where there is no mention of manna in the context (though there is a reference to the bronze serpent made by Moses as a remedy to the bite of the poisonous snakes sent to punish the Israelites who had complained about the manna; Num 21:4–9). He also speaks of ascending to heaven in these two contexts where he speaks of descending from heaven, something which obviously does not have anything to do with the manna.

This raises the question, is there also another OT background to this language, namely, that the OT often refers to the LORD coming down for other purposes? This chapter answers that question in the affirmative. As we explore the theme of divine descents in the OT, we will again see that recognition of a targumic background to the Logos title helps us to make the proper OT connections, and thus interpretations, of the language of Jesus.

The Divine Descents in the OT

One of the ways used to speak of divine intervention in the OT is to say that the LORD came down, or will come down.

- The first case is in connection with the Tower of Babel, where "the LORD came down to see the city and the tower which the sons of men had built" (Gen 11:5), and then the LORD said (presumably to the angels), "Come, let us go down and there confuse their language" (v. 7).[2] This intervention

---

[1] Leon Morris, *The Gospel according to John* (rev. ed.; NICNT; Grand Rapids: Eerdmans, 1995), 368.

[2] According to *Pirqe R. El.* 14, this was not the first but the second of ten descents, the first being in the Garden of Eden, where a descent is inferred by the LORD's presence in the garden (but one could instead suppose that the LORD's presence in the garden was an ordi-

is clearly judgmental and intended to limit the humans' ability to carry out their rebellious intentions.

- A similar divine inspection and judgment is indicated in Gen 18:21, where the LORD said to Abraham, "*I will go down* now (to Sodom and Gomorrah), and see if they have done entirely according to its outcry which has come to me; and if not, I will know."

- From the burning bush the LORD said to Moses, "*I have come down* to deliver them from the power of the Egyptians, and to bring them up from that land" (Exod 3:8). After this deliverance, the LORD came down on Mt. Sinai to speak the Ten Commandments to Israel (19:20) and to show his glory to Moses (34:5).

- Isaiah promises deliverance from the Assyrians during the reign of Hezekiah by saying, "The LORD of Hosts *will come down* and wage war on Mt. Zion" (Isa 31:4). In ch. 5 we will see how this relates to the work of Jesus.

- One might petition for divine intervention by asking the LORD to part, or tear, the heavens and come down (Ps 144:5; Isa 64:1), as he had in the past (Ps 18:9).[3]

The LORD "comes down," that is, intervenes, to judge, to reveal (his law, his name, his glory), and to deliver his people, to dwell among them and be their God. Certainly the ultimate divine intervention was the incarnation, which Jesus describes with this same kind of language, "I have come down from heaven," and which leads to the accomplishment of these same purposes seen in the OT.

We note especially that in several of these passages that speak of the LORD coming down, revelation of the divine name is also involved. This observation provides the logical connection between the present and previous chapters. The scene of the burning bush contains a grammatical explanation of the divine name, as noted in ch. 3 ("I will be who I have been"). In Exod 34, Moses is given a moral description of the divine name—the LORD is "full of grace and truth," etc. The meaning of the divine name is also revealed through God's works in history. Thus Isaiah's petition that the LORD would "rend the heavens and come down" (Isa 64:1) is in order "to make known your name to your adversaries, that the nations may tremble at your presence" (v. 2). One might say that this is a petition for the LORD to bring about a new exodus—to intervene, to come down, as he had done before (vv. 2, 3), to make his name known. In continuity with the OT pattern, then, John presents Jesus as coming down from heaven to make known the divine name.

---

nary occurrence, not a descent from heaven). Genesis 11 is the first case where the language of descent is actually used.

[3] Psalm 144:5, יְהוָה הַט־שָׁמֶיךָ וְתֵרֵד; Isa 64:1, לוּא־קָרַעְתָּ שָׁמַיִם יָרַדְתָּ.

Targumic Language Used to Speak of the Divine Descents

Generally, the Targums use the language of revelation (אִיתְגְּלִי; cf. Heb. נִגְלָה) where the MT speaks of the LORD coming down. Isaiah 40:5 in the MT is typical of the change of language found in the Targums: "The glory of the LORD will be revealed" (וְנִגְלָה כְּבוֹד יהוה; Tg.: וְיִתְגְּלֵי יְקָרָא דֵיוֹי). As we have seen, revelation is one of the purposes for the LORD's coming down. The Tgs. Onq. and Ps.-J. of Gen 11:5 say, "The LORD was revealed to punish," in place of MT "The LORD came down to see." Targum Pseudo-Jonathan Gen 11:7 is surprisingly (and uniquely) literal ("Let us go down"), presumably because in this Targum the LORD is addressing "the seventy angels who stood before him." The Pal. Tgs. of the Pentateuch usually speak either of the glory of the LORD's Shekinah or of the Word of the LORD being revealed, as we saw already in ch. 2 (pp. 54–56, nos. 9, 17, 21), except that this is another case where Tg. Ps.-J. is often adapted in the direction of the language of Tg. Onq. Again we will note the readings for Exod 3:8 and 34:5, beginning with the former:

MT	I have come down to deliver them.
Tg. Onq.	I have been revealed to deliver them.
Tg. Ps.-J.	I have been revealed to you today that *by my Word* they might be delivered.
Tg. Neof.	I have been revealed *in my Word* to deliver them.

We saw in ch. 3 that Tg. Ps.-J. Deut 32:39 ("I am he who is and was, and I am he who will be") likely refers back to the scene of the burning bush, since Tg. Ps.-J. Exod 3:14 has a similar paraphrase of the divine name ("I am he who is and who will be"). One might expect, then, that the phrase "when the Word of the LORD shall be revealed to redeem his people" (from Tg. Ps.-J. Deut 32:39) should have its counterpart in Tg. Ps.-J. Exod 3:8 as "My Word has been revealed to you," or something like Tg. Neof. Presumably, the reason it does not is that Tg. Ps.-J. Exod 3:8 has been adapted towards the reading of Tg. Onq. In other words, Tg. Ps.-J. is inconsistent. A more consistent Pal. Tg. at Exod 3:8 would speak of the revelation of the Word of the LORD, or the glory of his Shekinah.

Below are the readings for Exod 34:5:

MT	The LORD came down in the cloud.
Tg. Onq.	The LORD was revealed in the cloud.
Tg. Ps.-J.	The LORD was revealed in the clouds of the glory of his Shekinah.
Tg. Neof.	The glory of the Shekinah of the LORD was revealed in the cloud.
Tg. Neof. [mg.]	The Word of the LORD was revealed.

With these Targum readings in mind, it is interesting to compare the words of Jesus, which agree with the MT language, with the words of John in John 1:14, that describes the same event using what sounds like the language of the targumic Word:

John 6:38   I have come down from heaven (Jesus echoing the language of the MT).

John 1:14   The Word became flesh (John adapting targumic language to describe the same event).

The adaptation consists of changing the targumic "was revealed" to "became flesh," the exact parallel of which is obviously not to be found in the Targums, where Word is reasonably understood to be a way of avoiding anthropomorphic language. The idea that the Word could become flesh highlights the clear difference in John's use of the targumic Word. Yet elsewhere John does use the language of revelation: "The Son of God was revealed" (1 John 3:8). But if John had said in his Prologue "the Word was revealed" instead of "the Word became flesh," it would not be clear that he was speaking of the incarnation. The public revelation of Jesus as the divine Word was a progressive revelation, beginning with his baptism (see ch. 1 on John 1:32–33). The incarnation was when he "came down."

In ch. 3 I suggested that *Tg. Ps.-J.* Deut 32:39 ("When the Word of the LORD shall be revealed to redeem his people . . .") should be interpreted to mean that when the LORD brings about a new exodus (i.e., *comes down* to redeem), he will do what he did at the first exodus: he will make known his name as he did to Moses at the burning bush; he will reveal his glory as he did to Moses in Exod 34; he will make known his name to his adversaries, as petitioned in Isa 64:2. Recall that the holy of holies in the tabernacle served as a model of the heavenly throne room, with curtains serving as a wall separating this room from the rest of the tabernacle. From here, according to the *Pal. Tgs.* of the Pentateuch, the Word spoke to Moses. If we interpret the psalmist's petition to "part the heavens" (144:5) according to this tabernacle symbolism, it is in effect a petition that the LORD would draw back the curtain of the holy of holies and intervene to save his servants. Or, speaking in terms of the *Pal. Tgs.* of the Pentateuch, it would be a petition that the Word who spoke from the holy of holies would be revealed in the world. John is telling us that this petition has been answered by the invisible Word, who spoke to Moses from between the cherubim, becoming a servant, "the Son of Man."

"I Have Come Down from Heaven" as Divine Language

In the previous section, we saw the plausibility of relating John 6:38 to OT language which speaks of the LORD coming down to judge, save, reveal, etc. In this section, we see further evidence that this is the proper OT background to this language of Jesus.

In connection with John 6:38, we can take note that the emphasis Jesus places on his having come down from heaven is mixed with other clearly divine language. While speaking of himself as the bread from heaven upon whom people must feed to have eternal life, Jesus makes multiple references to the idea of people coming to him (6:35, 37 [2x], 44, 45, 65). There are good reasons to relate this language to the divine invitation "come to me" in Isa 55:3, and discuss this in more detail in ch. 8.

For now we can note the evident dependence of John 5:40 and 7:37, which frame the instances of "come to me" in ch. 6, on Isa 55:1–3:

Isa 55:1–3   Ho! *Everyone who thirsts*, come to the waters. . . . Incline your ear and *come to me*; listen, *that your soul may live.*

John 5:40   You are unwilling to *come to me, that you may have life.*

John 7:37   If any man is thirsty, let him *come to me* and drink.

Along with the language of descent and coming to Jesus, the divine language in John 6 includes the fourfold "I am he" (ἐγώ εἰμι) of vv. 35 (lit., "I am he, the bread of life"), 41 ("I am he, the bread that came down from heaven"), 48 (as v. 35), and 51 ("I am he, the living bread that came down from heaven"). We defer a discussion of these until ch. 9, when all twenty-two of them are discussed together. I will point out there that even though many ἐγώ εἰμι sayings do not seem to be divine sayings (e.g., "I am he, the bread of life" does not seem to be a divine saying), all of them occur in contexts of divine speech by Jesus. For now we can again note that the "I am he" language of *Tg. Ps.-J.* Deut 32:39 is expected to be used in conjunction with the revelation of the divine Word, and that the language "When he is revealed" is arguably based on MT language from elsewhere, namely, "When he comes down." Those familiar with both the Hebrew and the Aramaic Scriptures could have put together "I have come down from heaven" (v. 38) with "I am he" (vv. 35, 41, 48, 51) as divine language, since "When the Word of the LORD shall be revealed" in *Tg. Ps.-J.* Deut 32:39 implies a Hebrew scriptural equivalent, "When the LORD comes down," even though those words are not in the Hebrew of Deut 32:39.

Further, the emphasis of these sayings on Jesus both as living and as source of life fits the theme of Deut 32:39 and its context in both the MT and *Pal. Tgs.* From the MT, we have the divine oath, "as I live forever," in the next verse, which in *Tg. Neof.* is rendered, "as I live and endure in my Word forever." The briefer "As I endure" of *Tg. Ps.-J.* could be interpreted as being part of what is spoken by the divine Word (a continuation of v. 39, what the divine Word says when he is revealed). As for source of life, the MT of Deut 32:39 makes the point, "I put to death, and I bring to life," which in *Tg. Ps.-J.* is "By my Word I put to death and bring to life," and in *Tg. Neof.* is "I, in my Word, am he . . . who causes the living to die in this world, and brings to life the dead in the world to come" (similarly *Frg. Tg. V*). This fits the context of John 6 where life beyond this present one is obviously in view.[4]

Further evidence that "I have come down from heaven" is divine speech comes from consideration of John 3:13: "No one has ascended into heaven, except he who descended from heaven, the Son of Man." The statement seems to imply that Jesus has already ascended into heaven. Scribes and translators who

---

[4]Klein translates *Frg. Tg. V* in part, "It is I Who puts to death and gives life in this world" (*Fragment Targums*, 2:186), which, however, does not agree with the Aramaic text he provides (ibid., 1:229), which is similar to *Tg. Neof.* He apparently took the adjective חיין ("living") as a *haphel* participle.

did not understand this as divine speech have resorted to various means to remove what seemed to them to be a problem: Jesus has not yet ascended to heaven; his only ascent was after the resurrection. The scribal addition to the verse, "who is in heaven," seems to be a device to alleviate the difficulty by making the whole verse a parenthetical remark by John made after the ascension of Jesus, rather than the words of Jesus. In other words, it is impossible to consider v. 13 as the words of Jesus if it reads as in KJV, "No one has ascended into heaven except . . . the Son of Man who is in heaven." A modern translator could reflect this solution By using parentheses (No one has ascended into heaven except . . . the Son of Man, who is in heaven).

Another way of avoiding the difficulty is to interpret the ascent language spiritually rather than physically: "No one has ever gone into heaven except the one who came from heaven" (NIV). The spiritual interpretation could also accommodate the scribal addition at the end of the verse. Godet comments: "The primary reference of the words may well be spiritual rather than physical. 'No one has *entered into* communion with God and possesses thereby an intuitive knowledge of divine things, in order to reveal them to others, except He to whom heaven was opened and who dwells there at this very moment.'"[5]

But the spiritual interpretation does not actually resolve the problem. If one grants that Jesus could speak appropriately of his dwelling in heaven at the same time that he walks the earth, the fact remains that he said he has ascended there in the past, which is not the same as saying "I always am in heaven." When did this ascent take place? If one ignores what John says about Jesus in his Prologue when interpreting the words of Jesus in John's Gospel, then one considers only the time between the birth of Jesus and the time he speaks to Nicodemus: "John knows a tradition which claims that Jesus, in comparison with or contrast to Moses, has at some point *in the course of his life* ascended into heaven and returned."[6] Yet what is "in the course of his life" supposed to mean with respect to the one who *in the beginning* was with God, through whom all things were made, in whom was life, and the life was the light of men?

However, if we take seriously what John says about Jesus in his Prologue, and understand the descent language as divine language, we have a ready solution to the problem. If the LORD "descended" on many occasions in the OT, then it may be inferred that he also ascended, and in fact it is explicitly stated in the Targums on a number of occasions that the Word did so: "And when he finished talking with him, God (*Tgs. Ps.-J., Onq.*: the glory of the LORD) *went up* from Abraham" (Gen 17:22). As noted in ch. 2, *Tg. Neof.* says, "the glory of the *Shekinah* of the LORD went up from him," while the chapter begins, "the Word of the LORD was revealed

---

[5] F. Godet, *Commentary on the Gospel of St. John* (3 vols; Edinburgh: T&T Clark, 1899), 2:62, quoted in Morris, *John*, 223 n.50.

[6] James F. McGrath, *John's Apologetic Christology: Legitimation and Development in Johannine Christology* (SNTSMS 111; Cambridge: Cambridge University Press, 2001), 162. John Ashton makes the same assumption (*Understanding the Fourth Gospel* [Oxford: Clarendon, 1991], 354), contending that Jesus (the one through whom the world was made) ascended to receive revelation.

to him," and v. 3 says, "the Word of the LORD spoke with him" (also *Tg. Neof.* [mg.] 17:9, 15). Similarly, "God *went up* from (Jacob) in the place where he had spoken with him" (Gen 35:13). *Targum Neofiti* here is as in Gen 17:22 (also *Ps.-J.*), and it follows the statement that "the Word of the LORD" spoke to him, according to the marginal gloss of v. 11.

An "ascent" to heaven could also be interpreted as a reversal of the exodus "descent" because of apostasy. Such an ascent could be inferred from Hos 5:6, 15: "They shall go to seek the LORD but will not find him; he has withdrawn [חָלַץ] from them. . . . 'I will go and return to my place.'" In ch. 8 I connect this passage with John 7:34 ("You will seek me but you will not find me") and to the theme of the withdrawal of the *Shekinah* mentioned in some Targum passages, such as the Targum of the passage just quoted (cited also in ch. 2, p. 61, no. 50): "He has *withdrawn his Shekinah* from them; *against the Word of the* LORD they have dealt falsely." "*I will withdraw my Shekinah;* I will return to my holy dwelling in heaven, until they acknowledge their sin."

We could also take note that the angel of the LORD, when he had finished speaking to the parents of Samson in Judg 13, "went up in the flame of the altar" (v. 20). This is the angel who said his name was "Wonderful" and who announced the miraculous birth of Samson with wording similar to that used later for the miraculous birth of Immanuel (Judg 13:5, 7; Isa 7:14), Immanuel being traditionally identified with the child named "Wonderful" (Isa 9:6), who would sit on David's throne forever.

If the LORD "came down" for the purpose of warfare in delivering his people, as in Exod 3:8, then it would also make sense to speak of his ascension as a consequence of victory. We see such language in Ps 47: "He subdues peoples under us, and nations under our feet" (v. 3). "God has ascended with a shout; the LORD, with the sound of a trumpet" (v. 5). "God reigns over the nations, God sits on his holy throne" (v. 8). One can see this pattern repeated in the work of Jesus of Nazareth; he came down from heaven to defeat Satan (the subject of the next chapter), he ascended in victory, and he sits at the right hand of the Father. When, in the course of his discussion with Nicodemus, Jesus says that he has ascended into heaven, he is indicating that he is the one who has done it before, as described in passages like Ps 47.

Paul takes the same interpretation in Eph 4:8–10, where he quotes Ps 68:18, another passage speaking of God's ascent in victory in OT times, and applies it to Christ. From the ascent language, Paul infers a prior descent "to the lower parts of the earth" (v. 9). In Ps 139:15 a similar expression, "the depths of the earth," is a metaphor for the womb of David's mother. Thus Paul, too, may have interpreted Christ's entrance into the womb of a woman as a divine descent in continuity with the OT divine descents. At the same time, while Paul describes Christ's descent in continuity with the OT theme, he also expresses an expanded meaning: In OT times, the LORD came down on Mt. Sinai, at the burning bush, etc.; in the incarnation he came down as a human being, "the Son of Man." The meaning of this title will be discussed in the next section.

As many commentators have noted, "No man has ascended into heaven" could be considered a refutation of the view, of which Nicodemus was presumably aware, and may even have shared, that Moses had ascended into heaven. One place this view is found is in *Tg. Ps.* 68:18, where, contrary to Paul's interpretation, "You ascended on high" is taken as Moses going up to the sky to receive the law. Of special interest is the view that Moses ascended into heaven because of the withdrawal of the *Shekinah* after the apostasy of the golden calf (Exod 32):

> The assembly of Israel said, "Moses and Aaron and the Levites, who keep watch over the Word [*Memra*] of the LORD in the Tent of Meeting and who go around it, found me, and I asked them about the *Shekinah* glory of the LORD which had been removed from me. Moses, the great Scribe of Israel, answered and this is what he said, 'I will ascend to heaven on high and pray before the LORD. Perhaps he will forgive your sins and make his *Shekinah* dwell among you as before.'" (*Tg. Song* 3:3)

This is of special interest because it brings us again to the revelation of Exod 34 (the Targum interprets Moses' ascent up the mountain in Exod 34 as an ascent into heaven), of such obvious importance to John, and to the theme of the withdrawal of the *Shekinah*, which helps us understand John 7:34.

Besides the LORD "coming down" to reveal his name and to wage war to redeem his people, he also came down to give the law. Exodus 19:11 says, "on the third day the LORD will come down on Mt. Sinai in the sight of all the people," and v. 20 says, "the LORD came down on Mt. Sinai, to the top of the mountain." Some of the Targum renderings of these verses were given in ch. 2 (pp. 54–55, nos. 15, 17). *Targum Onqelos* and *Tg. Ps.-J.* speak of the LORD being revealed (or revealing himself), while *Tg. Neof.* and the *Frg. Tgs.* speak of the revelation of the Word of the LORD or the revelation of the glory of his *Shekinah*. As we will discuss further in ch. 7, Jesus speaks as the divine lawgiver, with the upper room as a "new Sinai," so in the work of Jesus there is continuity with the LORD's descent on Mt. Sinai to give the law; or in targumic terms, continuity with the revelation of the Word on Mt. Sinai in the giving of the law.

Continuity from OT to NT can also be observed in the Lord coming down (*Tg. Neof.*, "being revealed in his Word") to give the Holy Spirit. In place of "I will come down . . . and take some of the Spirit who is upon you, and put [him] upon them (the seventy elders)" (Num 11:17), *Tg. Neof.* says, "I will be revealed in my Word . . . and increase some of the Holy Spirit who is upon you, and put [him] upon them." Similarly, when the Word of the Lord was revealed in the flesh, "he breathed on them and said to them, 'receive the Holy Spirit'" (John 20:22). Instead of "the Lord came down in the cloud," *Tg. Onq.* Num 11:25 says "the Lord was revealed in the cloud;" *Tg. Ps.-J.* says "the Lord was revealed in the cloud of glory of the *Shekinah*; *Tg. Neof.* says "the glory of the *Shekinah* of the Lord was revealed in the cloud."

The obvious discontinuity from OT to NT is that when the Word becomes flesh, "he who descended from heaven [is] the Son of Man" (John 3:13). In the incarnation, he comes down as a human, "the Son of Man." And he comes down as a servant: "I have come down from heaven, not to do my own will, but the will of him who sent me" (John 6:38).

Why Jesus Called Himself "the Son of Man"

Issues Concerning the Son of Man Title

In his historical survey and evaluation of the various issues involved in "the Son of Man debate," Burkett noted that at the end of the twentieth century these issues were still unresolved.[7] Burkett listed about eight hundred bibliographic references, including sixty-four survey works. Although I cannot interact with all the scholarship on these issues, nonetheless, the solution I offer is, I think, fairly straightforward and convincing.[8] I suggest that the Son of Man title used by Jesus is based on three interrelated OT texts: Ps 8:4; 80:17; and Dan 7:13. This solution is not a new one (Burkett traces it back at least to the seventeenth century), although some of the evidence presented for it here may be.[9] There is no need to resort to extrabiblical texts, although some assistance is provided by the Targums.

Any plausible solution to the question of why Jesus called himself the Son of Man must account for at least the following factors:

1. It seems that the Jews in general did not understand the title as messianic and were not even sure Jesus was talking about himself when he used it. For example, in John 12:34 the people tell Jesus that what he says about the Son of Man does not fit with what they have heard about the Messiah. This prompts them to ask, "Who is this 'Son of Man'?" When asked by Jesus, "Who do people say the Son of Man is" (Matt 16:13), Peter answers with the term more familiar to Jews: "You are the Christ" (i.e., the Messiah).

2. There seems to be an obvious relationship between some of the sayings and Dan 7:13.

3. Paul never uses the expression to speak of Jesus in all of his writings.

4. Hebrews 2:6–9 applies Ps 8:4–6, which speaks of dominion given to man/the son of man at creation, to Jesus. Does Ps 8 have anything to do with the Son of Man title? If so, there could be a link to the Son of Man title in Paul's understanding of Jesus as the "last Adam" (1 Cor 15:45; cf. Rom 5:14), which could be Paul's equivalent title for Jesus. But if the Son of Man title depends in part on Ps 8:4, why do the Gospels not bring that point out more clearly?

---

[7] Delbert Burkett, *The Son of Man Debate: A History and Evaluation* (SNTSMS 107; Cambridge: Cambridge University Press, 2000), 122. Burkett put the bulk of nonmarginal interpretations in two camps: (1) "the Son of Man" is not a title at all but an Aramaic idiom, a circumlocution for "I"; (2) the expression is a messianic title (the view taken here).

[8] Much of the argument here is condensed from portions of my doctoral dissertation. See Ronning, " Curse on the Serpent," 144–78, 184–210, 308–19, 332–48.

[9] Burkett (*Son of Man Debate,* 60) noted that Jacques Cappel proposed that all three of these passages made up the background to the title (*Observationes in novum testamentum. Una cum eiusdem Ludovici Cappelli Spicilegio* [Amsterdam: Elzevir, 1657], at Matt 8:20 and John 5:27).

Dependence of the Son of Man Title on Daniel 7:13 and Psalm 8:4

The connection between the Son of Man title and Dan 7:13 is clear in the synoptic accounts of the Olivet discourse and the trial of Jesus:

Dan 7:13	I kept looking in the night visions, and behold, with *the clouds of heaven one like a Son of Man was coming.*
Matt 24:30	And then the sign of the Son of Man will appear in the sky, and then all the tribes of the earth will mourn, and they will see *the Son of Man coming on the clouds of the sky* with power and great glory. (cf. Mark 13:26; Luke 21:27)
Matt 26:64	Jesus said to him, "You have said so; however I tell you, hereafter you will see *the Son of Man* sitting at the right hand of the Power, and *coming on the clouds of heaven.*" (cf. Mark 14:62)

One usage of the title in John could also depend on Dan 7:13: "He gave him authority to execute judgment, because he is the Son of Man" (John 5:27). Revelation 1:7 ("Behold, he is coming with the clouds") also applies Dan 7:13 to Jesus, but without using the Son of Man title. It would be tempting, then, to say that "the" Son of Man is simply the one seen by Daniel in his vision, but that would leave some of the questions above unanswered. So, although "perhaps the widest measure of agreement attaches to the view that the titular use of 'Son of Man' originated in a christological interpretation of Daniel 7.13,"[10] some important questions are left unanswered.

Ps 8:4 and Matt 8:20/Luke 9:58

Speaking of suggestions that the title depends on Ps 8:4 and/or Ps 80:17, Burkett notes that "the major critique of such theories has been that no allusion to Psalm 8.4 or 80.17 appears in the Son of Man sayings."[11] Burkett seems to have overlooked that in one of the articles listed in his bibliography (the *ABD* article, "Son of Man"), a connection was indeed made between Ps 8:4 and the Son of Man title in the Gospels. Matthew 8:20 is the first place where this title occurs in the canonical order of the NT (the saying is also found at Luke 9:58), and its dependence on Ps 8:4 can be readily seen:

Ps 8:4–8	What is man . . . or *the son of man*, that you care for him? . . . You have put all things under his feet (i.e., you gave him dominion over the whole creation, including) . . . *the beasts of the field, the birds of the sky.*
Matt 8:20/Luke 9:58	The *foxes* (beasts of the field) have holes, and *the birds of the sky* have nests, but *the Son of Man* has nowhere to lay his head.

George Nickelsburg explains, "Ironically, the son of man, who has been given glory and honor as well as dominion over the beasts of the field and the birds of

---

[10] Burkett, *Son of Man Debate*, 122.
[11] Ibid., 61.

the air, does not have the shelter they possess."[12] A further irony is that Matt 8:20, whose dependence on Ps 8:4–8 does not seem evident, has been cited to argue against any connection between the Son of Man title and Ps 8:

> The predicates of sovereignty which Jesus adopts as the Son of Man are totally different than those which Ps 8 would have provided, as also the lowliness of man so highly honored according to the psalm can by no means be confused with the totally heterogeneous self-denial and humble renunciation of the Son of Man as it is expressed in the saying (Matt. 8.20).[13]

As we shall see, the difficulty felt in deriving the Son of Man title from Ps 8:4 is alleviated by the fact that the Psalm is adapted, not simply taken over, when applied to Jesus. Such adaptation is already indicated in Dan 7:13 itself, as shown below.

In Matthew, then, the first use of the title is dependent on Ps 8:4, while the last is dependent on Dan 7:13, which is appropriate since Ps 8:4 looks back to creation, and Dan 7:13 looks forward to the end.

Ps 8:4 and John 1:51

Similarly, the first use of the Son of Man title in John can be related to Ps 8:4. The saying of Jesus in John 1:51 brings to mind a picture of the Son of Man as being "lower than the angels":

John 1:51   You shall see . . . the angels of God ascending and descending upon the Son of Man.

Ps 8:4–5   What is . . . the son of man, that you care for him? You have made him a little lower than the heavenly beings (MT: *elohim;* LXX, *Tg. Ps.: angels*).

The Hebrew (and Greek and Aramaic) verb for "make lower" in Ps 8:5 does not normally imply spatial movement; more broadly, the *qal* form of חסר means "to lack, be less than, or subside"; the verb in Ps 8:5 is the *piel:* "to make less than." In a suitable context, however, it can refer to something going lower spatially, as in the case of the level of the flood waters (Gen 8:3, 5). Likewise, in Ps 8:5 "lower" can be inferred from the comparison between humans (on earth) and heavenly beings.

The more obvious allusion of John 1:51 is to Jacob at Bethel, since there Jacob saw in a dream the angels of God ascending and descending (Gen 28:12). Interestingly, the Son of Man saying of Matt 8:20/Luke 9:58 can also be related to this same context. Genesis 28:11 tells us that when Jacob arrived at Bethel, "he took one of the stones of the place and *put it under his head, and lay down* in that place." That is, like Jesus, Jacob on his journey in Gen 28 "had nowhere to lay his head."

---

[12] George W. E. Nickelsburg, "Son of Man," *ABD* 6:143. I also noted this connection independently (Ronning, "Curse on the Serpent," 357).

[13] Johann Martin Usteri, "Die Selbstbezeichnung Jesu als des Menschen Sohn," *Theologische Zeitschrift aus der Schweiz* 3 (1886): 4, quoted (and presumably translated) by Burkett, *Son of Man Debate,* 61.

Thus, the first occurrence of the title in both Matthew and John can be taken as an allusion to "the son of man" of Ps 8:4 and its context is associated with Jacob in Gen 28. This raises the question as to whether that title itself has some specific connection with Jacob. As we shall see below, the OT development of the theme of the new Adam does in fact involve Jacob as one who seems to be spoken to by God as if he is a new Adam, an idea related to the Son of Man title.

We may further note that John 3:13 ("the Son of Man has come down from heaven") combined with 6:62 ("the Son of Man will ascend to heaven") speak of the temporary descent (he has descended and is going to ascend) of the Son of Man to this position where he is "lower than the angels" (1:51). The expression "a little while longer, I am with you" (7:33; cf. 12:35; 13:33; 14:19; 16:16 [2*x*], 17 [2*x*], 18, 19) could be seen as based in part on an adaptation of מְעַט from Ps 8:5, "a little lower in degree," to another meaning, "lower for a little *while*." The last three times "the Son of Man" occurs in John (12:23, 34; 13:31) are in contexts where "a little while" is mentioned. Adam and Eve were created *a little* lower (in degree) than the angels; Jesus descended (in the incarnation) *for a little while* lower than the angels.

The "Son of Man" in Psalm 8 and Daniel 7

If some of the sayings in the Gospels where Jesus calls himself "the Son of Man" can be related to Ps 8:4, while others are obviously derived from Dan 7:13, the question arises as to whether there is any connection between these two OT texts that could explain why both of them serve as background for the Son of Man title. Again, Nickelsburg suggested a possibility. The contrast between Jesus and the animals made in Matt 8:20/Luke 9:58, though pointing to Ps 8, "could imply the contrast evident in Dan 7:3, 13 and, thus, also Jesus' future status as son of man."[14] In both Ps 8 and Dan 7, the theme of dominion of a "son of man" over animals is in view. In Ps 8, it is the animal kingdom over which Adam and Eve were given dominion when they were created. In Dan 7, one like a son of man is given dominion over the kingdoms of men, which are portrayed as beings with an unnatural combination of animal characteristics.[15] The kingdoms of men, over whom one like a son of man is given dominion, are portrayed as "beasts of the field" and "birds of the air," to use the terminology of Ps 8. The first son of man has dominion over the literal animals at creation; the second son of man has dominion over opposing kingdoms at the end of their history, portrayed prophetically as animals. Perhaps Matthew has reflected this chronology with the first use of Son of Man

---

[14] Nickelsburg, "Son of Man," 6:143.

[15] Arguing for the importance of Dan 7:13 for the Son of Man title, William Manson wrote, "the fact that he [one like a son of man] is deliberately contrasted in his human *likeness* with the bestial forms which symbolize the world-empires throws on the human element in the picture a greater fulness of ethical meaning than belonged to any mythological 'First Man' after whose image the Danielic concept is sometimes supposed to have been fashioned" (*Jesus the Messiah: The Synoptic Tradition of the Revelation of God in Christ: With Special Reference to Form-Criticism* [London: Hodder & Stoughton, 1943], 118).

alluding to Ps 8, which in turn looks back to creation, and the last use alluding to Dan 7:13, which points forward to the last things.

The description in Dan 7 of the first of these "animals" is particularly noteworthy: "The first was like a lion but it had wings of an eagle. I kept watching until its wings were plucked off and it was lifted up from the ground and set upon its feet *like a man,* and the *heart of a man* was given to it" (7:4). The transformation of the first beast is often related to the transformation of Nebuchadnezzar described in Dan 4. In Nebuchadnezzar's dream, he was a great tree (vv. 10, 22) under which the wild animals (the beasts of the field of Ps 8?) found shelter, and in whose branches the "birds of the sky" nested (Dan 4:12). The king was then sentenced to have "the mind of an animal" for seven "times," until he recognizes that the Most High is ruler over the kingdom of men (vv. 16–17). When the sentence was executed, the king was given a combination of characteristics of "beasts of the field" and "birds of the sky" referred to in Ps 8:7–8; he ate grass like cattle, his hair grew like eagles' feathers, and his nails like birds' claws (Dan 4:33). But when he recognized the rule of God, he in effect became a "man" (v. 34).

The first beast is the only one in Dan 7 which has such a transformation. The fourth beast "trampled the remainder with its feet" (v. 7; cf. vv. 19, 23), whereas at creation, God "put all things (including animals) under his (Adam's) feet" (Ps 8:6).

Thus more than just the phrase "son of man" binds these two texts; the son of man in Dan 7:13 can be viewed as an eschatologization of the first son of man mentioned in Ps 8:4. Likewise one can speak of these two sons of men as representative of their respective people. Few interpreters would think that in Ps 8 David is merely musing on the mandate given to Adam for its own sake, with only Adam in view, and not also on its application to his day as well. The phrase "son of man" in Ps 8:4 is בֶּן אָדָם, "son of Adam," which does not apply literally to Adam. Adam received dominion on behalf of the whole human race, and it could not be fulfilled apart from his offspring filling the earth to subdue it.

Likewise, the one like a son of man in Dan 7:13 receives dominion not merely for himself, but also for "the saints of the Most High" who "take possession of the kingdom" (v. 22). To be sure, many would like to say that because of v. 22 the one like a son of man in v. 13 is not an individual.[16] This is hardly a necessary interpretation, however, any more than taking "son of man" in Ps 8:4 generically (because it applies to men generally) would mean that it did not apply first to Adam as an individual.

The rule of the four beasts in Dan 7 portrays a situation where the purpose of creation as described in Ps 8 has not yet been fulfilled. Powerful and fearsome "animals" (unregenerate men) are ruling over the earth, including over the people of God (Daniel writes as a captive of the first beast). But with the coming of "one like a son of man," the situation is restored to that envisioned at creation. With his coming (Dan 7:14, 18, 22, 27), God restores to the people of God the dominion,

---

[16]E.g., note Dan 7:27: "their [the saints'] kingdom shall be an everlasting kingdom," rather than "his [God's] kingdom." The NRSV and ESV take the singular "his" to refer to the collective people, reflecting the view that "one like a son of man" refers to the people who will receive the kingdom.

glory, and honor given to the first son of man before the fall into sin (Ps 8:5–6). Such a person could then naturally be referred to as the last Adam, but could also be referred to more cryptically as "the Son of Man."

Psalm 8:6 and Psalm 110:1

Matthew 26:64 (Mark 14:62) was cited above to show the dependence of the Son of Man title on Dan 7:13. This statement by Jesus at his trial also equates the Son of Man with David's Lord in Ps 110:1 (whom Jesus had earlier identified as the Messiah; Matt 22:42–44; Mark 12:35–36; Luke 20:41–43). Psalm 110:1 ("Sit at my right hand, until I make your enemies a footstool for your feet") is much like Dan 7:13–14 in its promise of eschatological victory, and is sufficient to account for the Jesus' putting the two texts together. Yet Ps 110:1 is also like Dan 7:13 in that it can be viewed as an eschatologized version of Ps 8:6:

Ps 8:6   You have put all things under his feet.

Ps 110:1   Sit at my right hand, until I make your enemies a footstool for your feet.

Paul brings these two texts together twice, citing Ps 110:1 first in both cases and applying both to Jesus (1 Cor 15:25, 27; Eph 1:20, 22). Similarly, before the discussion of Ps 8 in Heb 2, the author quotes Ps 110:1 in the previous chapter (Heb 1:13; also see v. 3). It is possible then that in this last Son of Man saying in the Synoptic Gospels, Jesus brings together these two texts upon which the Son of Man title is based. That is, Jesus quotes from Dan 7:13 but also refers indirectly to Ps 8:6 because of its similarity to Ps 110:1, which he quotes along with Dan 7:13.

Is the order of quotation (Ps 110:1 followed by Ps 8:6 in three different passages) significant?[17] I suggested above that there is significance in the fact that in Matthew the first Son of Man saying depends on Ps 8:4, which points back to creation, while the last saying depends on Dan 7:13, which points ahead to the eschaton. But Paul and the writer of Hebrews reverse the order (with Ps 110:1 substituting for Dan 7:13). This may be related to the order of fulfillment of these two Psalms. Yes, Ps 8 looks back to creation, but the entry of sin into the world affected how the glorious commission given to Adam and Eve would be fulfilled. To make this point clear, it will be helpful to relate Ps 8:6 and Ps 110:1 to two similar early texts in Genesis.

Psalm 8:6 and Genesis 1:28; Psalm 110:1 and Genesis 3:15

Genesis 1:26–28 tells us that Adam and Eve were created in the image of God and given a twofold mandate: (1) to be fruitful and multiply; (2) to exercise

---

[17] I thank Brad Mellon for drawing this usage to my attention; it is also mentioned in his "The 'Son of Man' in Hebrews 2:1–10" (Master's Thesis, Biblical Theological Seminary, Hatfield, Pa., 1985), 40.

dominion over the earth and its creatures. Franz Delitzsch noted that Ps 8:6 alludes to the second part of this mandate. "The words 'put under his feet' sound like a paraphrase of the רְדָה in Gen 1:26, 28,"[18] since "rule" (*qal* of רדה) as well as "subdue" (*qal* of כבש) have the literal meaning "to step on, tread upon."[19] This literal meaning of כבש is possibly seen in Mic 7:19,[20] as well as in the noun כֶּבֶשׁ, footstool (2 Chr 9:18). For רדה as "tread," see Joel 3:13.

The last part of the curse on the serpent, "He shall strike you on the head; you shall strike him on the heel," brings to the reader's mind a picture of a person stepping on the head of a snake. This picture is similar to what would be evoked by Gen 1:28, because of the literal meaning of the verbs "rule" and "subdue" mentioned above. Karl Friedrich Keil made a similar point when he wrote that since 1:28 already presumes the triumph of humans over the animals, 3:15 points to a higher, spiritual enemy; thus if a mere reptile were the object of the curse in Gen 3:15, it would be a repetition of Gen 1:28.[21]

That Gen 3:15 does not deal with a mere reptile is also evident from the following chapter, which records the murder of Abel by Cain. In this incident we find the first fulfillment of the enmity between the woman's seed and the serpent's seed that was predicted in the curse. In Gen 4, however, the two seeds are identified not literally as snakes and humans, but as the wicked and the righteous among humanity. Cain is appropriately called the offspring of the serpent since he is morally like him (a liar and a murderer; 4:8–9), and like him is cursed (4:11). Righteous Abel must then exemplify the offspring of the woman. Genesis 3:15 thus contains a promise of victory (the striking of the serpent's head) for the righteous over the wicked.

Further, the fact that the outcome of the enmity in Gen 4 seems to be the opposite of what was predicted in the curse, since Abel is killed whereas Cain's life is protected, forces us to an eschatological interpretation of the curse and its cure. The victory promised must be something beyond our present earthly circumstances; otherwise the promise is without value, and the righteous like Abel are punished, not rewarded, for their righteousness, while the curse is to no effect, since the wicked, like Cain, are rewarded for their wickedness rather than being punished. There must be an eschatological, "crushing of the head" victory of the righteous over the wicked.

These considerations lead us to see an interesting correlation between the verses in Genesis and those in the Psalms: Gen 3:15 is related to Gen 1:28 as Ps

[18] Franz Delitzsch, *Psalms* (vol. 5 of *Commentary on the Old Testament*; London, Hodder and Stoughton, 1887; repr., Grand Rapids: Eerdmans, 1986), 155. Nickelsburg ("Son of Man," 6:137) proposed that Ps 8:4 combines Gen 1:26–28 with Ezek 28:12–18. The latter, in his view, places a king in the garden of Eden as the first man, which "makes it particularly apt to be conflated, in Christian tradition, with Dan 7:13–14."

[19] J. N. Oswalt, "כָּבַשׁ" *TWOT* 430; W. White, "רָדָה" *TWOT* 833.

[20] Micah 7:19: "He will subdue [tread under foot] our iniquities" (יִכְבֹּשׁ עֲוֹנֹתֵינוּ). Some also translate כָּבַשׁ in Zech 9:15 as "tread down": "They shall tread down the stone slingers," or "the stones of slingers."

[21] Karl Friedrich Keil, *The Pentateuch* (vol. 1 of *Biblical Commentary on the Old Testament*; Grand Rapids: Eerdmans, 1949), 100.

110:1 (like Dan 7:13) is related to Ps 8:6. Victory over human moral enemies is the theme of Gen 3:15 and Ps 110:1–2 (and Dan 7:13–14); dominion over the good creation is the theme of Gen 1:28 and Ps 8:6. These passages from Genesis and Psalms all express the idea of dominion or victory as putting under foot. Psalm 110:6 also uses the language of Gen 3:15 about crushing the head,[22] although "head" is usually interpreted as "leaders" in Ps 110:6 (equivalent to the kings of v. 5).

Genesis 1:28, to which Ps 8:6 points, pertains to a world in which there are no moral enemies. Once sin enters the world, the only way the situation of Gen 1:28 can prevail is if those enemies are defeated. In other words, Gen 1:28 cannot be fulfilled until Gen 3:15 has been accomplished. I would suggest that this explains why when NT writers jointly quote Ps 8:6 and Ps 110:1, the latter is always put first: human enemies must be put under foot before the victorious righteous can have dominion over the creation.

This sequence of events can be seen in the OT reigns of David and Solomon. David is the man of blood who carries out extensive warfare against surrounding enemies. Solomon uses language like Ps 110:1 to describe David's victories: "You know that David my father was unable to build a house for the name of the LORD his God because of the wars which surrounded him, until the LORD put them under the soles of his feet" (1 Kgs 5:3). With victory over human moral enemies secured (albeit only temporarily), Solomon could express his dominion as Adam was commanded to do before the Fall (Gen 1:28)—by exercising dominion over the creation: "He spoke of trees, from the cedar that is in Lebanon even to the hyssop that grows on the wall; he spoke also of animals and birds and creeping things and fish" (1 Kgs 4:33).

The Call and Fall of the New Adam in the OT

Noah, Abraham, and Jacob as "new Adam"

The reason for an eschatologization of Gen 1:28 (i.e., Gen 3:15) was that Adam and Eve sinned. Had they not fallen into sin, their offspring would have inherited their unfallen nature and Gen 1:28 would have been fulfilled naturally as inherently righteous humanity filled and subdued the earth. Adam and Eve would have brought "many sons to glory" (Heb 2:10) naturally, through procreation. But since sin entered the world, when the earth was filled with people, it was also filled with corruption (Gen 6:5, 11–13). Adam cannot be seen as the progenitor of the righteous people of God, as he would have been if sin had not entered the world. But in the book of Genesis, a number of individuals seem to be presented to the reader as "new Adams" in the sense that the two aspects of the original creation mandate of fruitfulness and dominion are given again to them as a blessing, in wording that is reminiscent of the mandate given to Adam and Eve:

---

[22] מָחַץ רֹאשׁ עַל־אֶרֶץ רַבָּה.

Noah	Abraham	Jacob
(Gen 9:1, 7)	(Gen 17:2, 4, 5, 6)	(Gen 35:11)
And God blessed Noah and his sons and said to them, "Be fruitful and multiply, and fill the earth. . . . ⁷As for you, be fruitful and multiply; populate the earth abundantly and rule over it."²³	I will multiply you greatly. . . . You will be the father of many nations. . . . I will make you the father of many nations. I will make you exceedingly fruitful. I will make you nations; kings shall come forth from you.	Be fruitful and multiply. A nation, and a company of nations, shall come from you; kings shall come forth from your loins.

One might infer from Exod 6:3 that Isaac received a similar blessing, since there God says he appeared to all three patriarchs as El Shaddai, whereas Genesis records only the appearances to Abraham and Jacob (Gen 17 and 35).

The disqualification of the new Adam

If God spoke to an individual as if he were a new Adam, one might expect that individual to be able to fulfill the purpose for which the first Adam was disqualified. One might expect to see him as completely blameless before God, unlike Adam. One might expect to see him as the progenitor only of the righteous seed, with no "Cain" among his offspring. But reality does not meet up with these expectations. In reality, these various new Adam figures are much like the old Adam. Scripture does not simply show them as sinners, but it highlights their sin in such a way that we can see similarities to the first Adam's sin. Moreover, we see among their offspring not just righteous children, but the same two seeds at enmity that were evident in Adam's children. These two disqualifiers may be conveniently summarized as *sins* and *sons*.²⁴

Noah's sins

Noah's drunkenness, described in Gen 9:21, recalls the fall of Adam most obviously in the fact that Noah's nakedness was revealed, bringing shame. When Noah awoke (and thus opened his eyes), "he knew what his youngest son had done to him" (v. 24); this can be compared to Gen 3:7, "the eyes of both of them were opened, and they knew that they were naked." There may also be a reminder of the eating of the forbidden fruit in the overconsumption of the fruit of the vine.

Noah's sons

The two seeds among Noah's sons are manifested in this same incident. This is the second disqualifier mentioned above. Ham brings shame to his father, thus showing himself to be the offspring of the serpent who brought shame to Adam and Eve. He resembles the serpent morally, though he is physically the son of the

---

²³Reading וּרְדוּ for the redundant וּרְבוּ; see *BHS*.

²⁴The following analysis is condensed from Ronning, "Curse on the Serpent," 179–211.

(apparent) new Adam. Righteous Shem and Japheth, however, imitate God's action in Gen 3:21 of covering their father's shame.

Abraham's sins

Three incidents in Abraham's life may be analyzed similarly. In the two cases where he passed off his wife as his sister (Gen 12:10–20; 20:1–18), he violated an ordinance given in the garden of Eden, as Adam did (though not the same ordinance). The rebuke of the king in each of these incidents (12:18: "What is this you have done to me?"; 20:9: "What have you done to us?") is reminiscent of the LORD's words to Eve, "What is this you have done?" (3:13).[25] Abraham's sin in taking Hagar as a surrogate wife is also subtly similar to the sin of Adam, as a comparison of the language of Gen 3:6, 17 with 16:2–3 demonstrates:[26]

Gen 3:17, 6	Gen 16:2–3
[17] To Adam he said, "Because you *listened to the voice of your wife . . .*" [6] . . . And *she took* from its fruit and she ate, *and she gave also to her husband*, and he ate.	[2] . . . Abram *listened to the voice of Sarai.* [3] . . . *Sarai* the wife of Abram *took* Hagar the Egyptian servant girl *and gave* her *to Abram her husband* as his wife.

Besides the verbal allusion, there is a thematic similarity to Gen 3 in this sin, in that it is motivated by dissatisfaction with God's providence—the attitude that God is withholding something good from people, so they must take action on their own.

Abraham's sons

The two seeds at enmity appear among the children of Abraham, despite the fact that Abraham is portrayed as the new Adam in Gen 17. We see this in Ishmael's mocking of Isaac at the feast on the occasion of Isaac's weaning. The redundant manner in which Abraham is said to be Isaac's father in 21:2–7 (8 times in 6 verses, including 3 times in v. 3: "Abraham called the name of *his son* who was born *to him*, whom Sarah bore *to him*, Isaac" may have been in response to an accusation of Isaac's illegitimacy, particularly in light of the fact that Sarah had just returned from spending some time in the house of Abimelech (Gen 20).[27] The enmity

---

[25] Werner Berg, "Nochmals: Ein Sündenfall Abrahams—der erste—in Gen 12, 10–20," *BN* 21 (1983): 7–15.

[26] Werner Berg, "Der Sündenfall Abrahams und Saras nach Gen 16, 1–6," *BN* 19 (1982): 7–14.

[27] Noted in John L. Ronning, "The Naming of Isaac: The Role of the Wife/Sister Episodes in the Redaction of Genesis," *WTJ* 53 (1991): 17. Menachem M. Kasher quotes Rabbi Obadiah Sforno (d. 1550), "He [Ishmael] derided the whole business, suggesting that Isaac was not Abraham's child at all, but Abimelech's" (*Genesis* [vol. 3 of *Encyclopedia of Biblical Interpretation: A Millennial Anthology;* New York: American Biblical Encyclopedia Society, 1957], 111). See also Rashi on Gen 25:19: "The cynics of that time were saying that Sarah conceived from Abimelech" (Chaim Pearl, *RASHI, Commentaries on the Pentateuch* [New York: W. W. Norton & Co., 1970], 52); and Ronning, "Curse on the Serpent," 187–88.

culminates in Ishmael's expulsion (21:10-14). If Abraham—the new Adam—is the father of the righteous, how is it that not all of his children are righteous?

Isaac and Jacob

One sees the same two disqualifiers (*sins* and *sons*) in the next two genera-tions of patriarchs as well. In Gen 26:1–11, Isaac lies about Rebekah being his wife, repeating the twice-committed sin of Abraham. Jacob takes two more wives because of a perceived lack of children, again as Abraham had done by taking a surrogate wife in Gen 16.

Likewise, the enmity between the two seeds is seen among the sons of Isaac (Esau towards Jacob) and of Jacob (Jacob's ten oldest sons against Joseph). In both cases, this enmity is much like that of Cain towards Abel, though it did not result in actual murder. In the case of Jacob's sons, there is also a surprising outcome of reconciliation rather than disinheritance and exclusion from the covenant as in the previous two generations.

David as new Adam

Although the language is not so close to Gen 1:26–28 as we saw in the case of Noah and the patriarchs, the two aspects of the creation mandate (fruitfulness and dominion) are discernable in Nathan's oracle given to David (2 Sam 7; 1 Chr 17). The LORD promises David that he will build him a house, a perpetual dy-nasty: "Your house and your kingdom will endure forever before me" (2 Sam 7:16). Since the dominion aspect of the neo-Adamic commission to the patriarchs was expressed as a promise of kings, and since David's dynasty was to be perpetual, it seems apparent that he has now become heir of the promise of the new Adam given to the patriarchs. One can read 2 Sam 7:19 (and 1 Chr 17:17) as David's rec-ognition of this fact, as he exclaims, "and this is the law of mankind, O LORD God" (with תּוֹרַת־הָאָדָם referring to the creation mandate of Gen 1:28).[28]

David's meditation on the creation mandate in Ps 8 could have been inspired by Nathan's oracle, which involves David in the fulfillment of that mandate. Con-versely, David's prior meditation on the creation mandate as expressed in Ps 8 could have been the basis for his quick recognition of the significance of Nathan's oracle concerning that mandate when Nathan issued it. In any case, one can see a number of connections between these two passages:

1. David's response in marveling at the LORD's promise parallels his marvel at the commission given to the first Adam:

Who am I, O Lord GOD, and *what is my house*, that you have brought me thus far? (2 Sam 7:18//1 Chr 17:16)

What is man, that you are mindful of him; *the son of man*, that you care for him? (Ps 8:4)

---

[28]Ronning, "Curse on the Serpent," 309–12.

2. The "glorification" of David can be compared to the glorification of the first Adam:

What more can David add (i.e., say) to you for honoring [לְכָבוֹד should possibly be read as לְכַבֵּד; see *BHS*] your servant? (1 Chr 17:18)

With glory [וְכָבוֹד] and honor you crowned him. (Ps 8:5)

3. Finally, David speaks of the LORD's great name in both Ps 8:1, 9 and 2 Sam 7:22–23//1 Chr 17:20–24.

We also observe that David makes a statement about himself in Ps 21:5 that is very similar to what he said about Adam in Ps 8:5:

Ps 21:3, 5	Ps 8:5
You set a crown of fine gold upon his head [תָּשִׁית לְרֹאשׁוֹ עֲטֶרֶת פָּז].... Splendor and honor you bestow upon him [הוֹד וְהָדָר תְּשַׁוֶּה עָלָיו].	With glory and honor you crowned him [וְכָבוֹד וְהָדָר תְּעַטְּרֵהוּ].

The son of man in Ps 80:17 and John 15

Israel is personified as a vine in Ps 80:8, 14, referred to as "root and son" in v. 15. Verse 17 contains the petition, "Let your hand rest on the man of your right hand, the son of man whom you strengthened for yourself." Interpreters differ as to whether Israel is still being personified here, or if the psalmist has moved from petitioning for the nation to petitioning for the current Davidic king. The latter seems preferable, since "man"/"son of man" applied to Israel would be unique, while a reference to David as being at or benefitting from the LORD's "right hand" is common (Ps 16:11; 18:35; 20:6; 63:8; 138:7; 139:10; cf. Ps 110:1). If this is the case, "whom you strengthened for yourself" could refer back to Nathan's oracle establishing the Davidic dynasty, and the "man"/"son of man" parallel used here could depend on the connection we have suggested above between Ps 8 and Nathan's oracle. That is, Ps 80:17 could be evidence that David was regarded, on the basis of Nathan's oracle, to be heir to the creation mandate given to the first Adam as described in Ps 8.

If "man of your right hand" and "the son of man whom you have strengthened for yourself" are understood as referring to the Davidic king, then this designation is especially applicable to Jesus. Commentators often place Ps 80 first in their lists of OT passages that supply a background to the vine and branches discourse of John 15. As in John 15, *Tg. Ps.* also interprets the branches as disciples (v. 11), spreading out from the academies of Jerusalem. Besides the vine/branches connection, with the image of burning branches as judgment, both passages address the issue of unanswered prayer (Ps 80:4, 18; John 15:7), and Jesus speaks so that the disciples' joy might be full, that is, so that they do not have to lament over unanswered prayer as in Ps 80.[29]

---

[29] Despite this fact, Keener comments that "it is nowhere clear that John 15 has Ps 80 ... in view" (*John*, 990–91).

While Jesus claims to be the true vine (or the true "son of man" of Ps 80:17) in comparison to Israel, the "vine" that was brought out of Egypt (Ps 80:8), the antitype of what Jesus represents appears in another passage. The Davidic king Zedekiah is compared to a false vine in a parable of Ezek 17. Zedekiah violates his oath before God given to Nebuchadnezzar, breaks his covenant, sends out branches (envoys) to Egypt, and receives God's judgement as a result. The fate of Zedekiah, then, is an example of a judgment similar to what Ps 80 is lamenting. The true son of man of Ps 80:17 remedies the false vine, Zedekiah. In an indirect way, then, by claiming to be the true vine in light of Ps 80 and Ezek 17, Jesus is claiming to be the true man/son of man, the true Davidic king, even though the Son of Man title is not used in John 15.

The disqualification of David

Examining David's *sins* and *sons* yields results very similar to those we saw from Genesis. His great sin with Bathsheba is an aggravated version of Abraham's sin in Gen 20.[30] There Abraham was the foreigner who feared that someone might kill him in order to take Sarah from him (20:11). A pagan king took Sarah in the integrity of his heart and innocence of his hands (20:5). In contrast, in 2 Sam 11 we see that David took Bathsheba, knowing that she was married, and killed the foreigner Uriah, so that what happened to Uriah at the hand of David is what Abraham feared for himself in a land in which he thought, "there is no fear of God in this place" (Gen 20:11).

We also see the two seeds of Gen 3:15 among David's descendants. David's firstborn son Amnon comes across as worse than the Canaanite Shechem (comparing Gen 34 with 2 Sam 13, and particularly Gen 34:7 with 2 Sam 13:12). Absalom is next in line to the throne, and he dishonored his father in a far worse way than Ham did Noah (2 Sam 15–17). Adonijah exalted himself to the throne in opposition to his brother Solomon and David's, disregarding the LORD's decree that Solomon would become king.

Thus if Noah and the patriarchs are disqualified from being the new Adam, surely David is as well, and more so! "David" is one of the many names given to the Messiah before he comes into the world (Isa 55:3; Jer 30:9; Ezek 34:23–24; 37:25). In view of the first David's disqualifications, the name "David" given to the Messiah may suggest that he is the "true David," which in turn, because of David's connection to the idea of the new Adam (via Nathan's oracle), could be taken to indicate that the Messiah is the true eschatological Adam, the true son of man.

---

[30] Peter D. Miscall, "Literary Unity in Old Testament Narrative," *Semeia* 15 (1979): 27–44; Ronning, "Curse on the Serpent," 312. Warren Austin Gage also noted David's flight to the east in judgment (2 Sam 15) and the sword that would never depart from his house as analogous to Gen 3 (*The Gospel of Genesis: Studies in Protology and Eschatology* [Winona Lake, Ind.: Carpenter Books, 1984], 68).

JESUS OF NAZARETH, THE SON OF MAN

Jesus as the True Adam

Here we analyze the person and works of Jesus of Nazareth in light of the two disqualifying factors of the various putative new Adams in the OT. First, with respect to "sins," we note that Jesus was tempted in every way as believers are, yet without sin (Heb 4:15). Specifically, Paul's description of the self-humiliation of Jesus (Phil 2:5–8) appears to be worded to bring out the contrast between the attitude of Jesus and the attitude urged upon Eve by the tempter (Gen 3:5). The tempter promised Eve that she and Adam could become like God (or, as gods); the tempter urged Eve to seize this equality with God for herself, thereby expressing discontent with the high status in which the first pair was created ("a little lower than the angels"). In contrast, Jesus gave up equality with God in order to become not just a man like Adam, put in charge of creation, but a servant, for the purpose of enabling his followers to truly gain the godlikeness lost in Adam.

The sin of Abraham and Isaac in passing off their wives as their sisters in order to save their own lives forms an apt contrast to the work of Jesus, once we recognize that the church is his bride (cf. ch. 6 below). Isaac lied about his wife, subjecting her to potential defilement, "because I thought, 'lest I die on account of her'" (Gen 26:9). Jesus, in sharp contrast, gave up his life for his bride to make her holy (Eph 5:25–26).[31]

With respect to "sons," we may note first the indications in messianic prophecy that the Messiah has "offspring," though not in the ordinary way. One of his titles is "Everlasting Father" (Isa 9:6). Isaiah 53:10 notes that after suffering to the point of death, he will see offspring and prolong his days. In Isa 52:14, he is said not even to look human as a result of his suffering; his form is marred "more than the sons of man," contrasting with the son of man that Daniel saw in Dan 7:13. One of the Son of Man sayings in the Gospels indicates that, unlike the OT new Adams, the Messiah does not have both types of seeds among his offspring: "He who sows the good seed is the Son of Man," and the good seed represents "the children of the kingdom," whereas the tares are "the sons of the evil one" (Matt 13:37–38). Unlike the new Adams of the OT, all his children are righteous, because he is the true progenitor of the righteous seed.

Finally, we can see the appropriateness of Jesus' alluding to Jacob's dream of a ladder (Gen 28) in the Son of Man sayings in Matt 8:20//Luke 9:58 and John 1:51, particularly if that title depends on the OT development of the idea of the new Adam, since Jacob is one of the OT putative "new Adams" or "sons of man." Further, though we cannot find any analogy in the OT for a human coming down from heaven, the twofold mission on which Jacob went in Gen 28 can be seen as a paradigm for the mission of Jesus when he came down from heaven. Jacob left his father's house (1) to save his life from Esau and (2) to find a wife and then return to his father. Jesus left his Father's house (1) to give his life, or, put another way, to

---

[31] I noted this in "Naming of Isaac," 23.

save Jacob's life (and ours), eternally, and (2) to gain his bride, the church, and then return to his Father. In the case of Jesus, this twofold mission is actually one since saving the (eternal) life of Jacob (who stands for the people of God) is the same as gaining his bride, the church.

Adam in the Targums

In addition to the Hebrew OT background to the Son of Man title and the idea of the Messiah as the new, true Adam, it is potentially relevant that *Tg. Neof.* on a number of occasions refers to Adam as "the son of man" (בר נשא *Tg. Neof.* Gen 1:27; 2:18, 23; 9:6 [mg.]; and possibly Exod 4:11). בר נשא (or בר נשה) is also used for Hebrew אָדָם when used for humankind or generically of humans (*Tg. Neof.* Gen 6:7; 8:21 [mg.]; 9:5; 40:23; 49:22; Lev 18:5; Deut 8:3). In *Tg. Neof.* Exod 4:11 ("Who gave the son of man a mouth"), "son of man" might be used generically, but since *Tg. Ps.-J.* at that verse employs another expression for Adam (which we discuss below), "son of man" may in fact refer to Adam. *Targum Neofiti* Gen 1:27 forms an interesting comparison to John 1:14, especially if we understand John's "Word" from a Targum background:

Tg. Neof. Gen 1:27	John 1:14
The Word of the LORD created the son of man in his likeness.	The Word became flesh (i.e., the Son of Man, that we might become the children of God, that his likeness might be created in us).

If "the son of man" was a contemporary Targum rendering of "Adam," then Jesus could also call himself "the Son of Man" from a Targum background with the same implication that this title had from the Hebrew OT; namely, that he is the true Adam.

"The Son of Man," then, is the promised Messiah. The term Messiah ("Anointed One") is not used frequently in the OT itself to refer to the one who was to come. But during the intertestamental period it seems to have become a catchall term to refer to the promised person who would come to save his people. Thus in the Targums, "Messiah" is used frequently, appearing for other messianic titles such as Branch (*Tg. Isa.* 11:1; *Tg. Jer.* 23:5, etc.) or even when no title is used at all. "Messiah means "anointed one," and this reminds us of David, "the anointed of the God of Jacob" (2 Sam 23:1); indeed, the Messiah is explicitly called "David" (e.g., Jer 30:9; Ezek 34:23, 24; 37:24; Hos 3:5). There is no Targum of Daniel, even of the Hebrew portions, and Dan 7:13 is in Aramaic. But if Daniel were entirely in Hebrew, a Targum might have substituted the title "the Messiah" for "one like a son of man" in Dan 7:13, just as it was substituted for "Branch," etc.

The Jews could have selected a different catchall term, such as "the Son of Man," to refer to the one who would come. As we have seen, "the Son of Man" would remind the biblically literate of David as well as Adam, Noah, Abraham, and Jacob, and was used (without the article) of the coming one in Dan 7:13. It points to the important OT theme of the new Adam, which harks back to creation, unlike the title Messiah, which harks back only to the Davidic monarchy.

The simple solution to the question of the meaning of "Son of Man," then, is that Jesus took the title the Son of Man as a catchall term in the same way that the Jews had taken Messiah. "The title thus appears to function as a general title for Jesus as the Christian Messiah."[32] It was a way for Jesus to identify himself as the Messiah without using that term. Thus it served to obscure his public claim to be the Messiah, as we see he was concerned to do from passages such as Matt 16:20: "He warned his disciples that they should tell no one that he was the Christ." "Jesus might have deliberately chosen a title which was little known and vaguely understood."[33] "No term was more fitted both to conceal, yet at the same time to reveal to those who had ears to hear, the Son of Man's real identity."[34] It should be obvious from the obscurity of the title that the early church would have no reason for inventing a mysterious title equivalent to "Christ" and applying it to Jesus in place of the well-understood title used in the epistles.

The Son of Man and the Last Adam in Paul

The reason that Paul does not call Jesus "the Son of Man," then, becomes obvious: the claim that Jesus is the Messiah is no longer to be obscured. Paul does, however, teach that Jesus is the new Adam, which is what the title "Son of Man" was meant to point to. As in the Gospels, he uses Ps 8 to do so, but instead of pairing Ps 8:4–8 with Dan 7:13 as in the Gospels, he pairs Ps 8:6 with Ps 110:1, as noted above.

Paul's primary exposition of Jesus as the new Adam (or as he puts it, the last Adam) is in 1 Cor 15:21–49, in the course of which he says, "He must reign until he has put all his enemies under his feet" (v. 25, from Ps 110:1), and "He has put all things in subjection under his feet" (v. 27, from Ps 8:6). Chrys C. Caragounis deduces from Paul's use of Ps 8:6 here and elsewhere that Paul "was clearly acquainted with the [Son of Man] title but refrained from using it."[35]

In 1 Cor 15:45, Paul quotes Gen 2:7 in making an analogy between Adam and Jesus: "The first man, Adam, became a living soul. The last Adam, a life-giving spirit." Clearly, Paul's understanding of Jesus as the last Adam in the sense that he is the one who gives life to his people agrees with what I suggested above as the significance of the theme of the new Adam as it is developed in the book of Genesis itself.

---

[32] Burkett, *Son of Man Debate*, 122.

[33] Frederick Houk Borsch, *The Son of Man in Myth and History* (New Testament Library; London: SCM, 1967), 47. Borsch himself does not endorse this view; he is describing the rationale for the view that the title is derived from the single passage Dan 7:13.

[34] Matthew Black, *An Aramaic Approach to the Gospels and Acts* (3d ed.; Oxford: Clarendon, 1967), 329.

[35] Chrys C. Caragounis, *The Son of Man: Vision and Interpretation* (WUNT 38; Tübingen: J. C. B. Mohr, 1986), 164.

Paul's expression, "the first man, Adam," may be influenced by how the Targums describe Adam. In English this expression looks like a conflation of two different ways that translators of The Aramaic Bible series render the Aramaic expression אדם קדמיא, used for Adam.[36] In favor of the translation "first Adam," it may be argued that אדם in Aramaic is the proper name Adam, not a common noun for a human or humankind in general.[37] In favor of "the first man," it may be argued that at least some Aramaic speakers who knew some Hebrew might know that in Hebrew the word can mean "human." Paul's expression, "the first man, Adam," gives both translation possibilities at the same time. Such double translation is, in fact, typical of the Targums themselves.

בר נשא (the son of man) is used for Adam only in *Tg. Neof.*, while אדם קדמיא (the first man/Adam) is used for Adam in *Tg. Neof.* and a number of other Targums, as noted above. *Targum Neofiti* in fact calls Adam אדם קדמיא in the verse following the one quoted by Paul ("there he put the first man/Adam whom he had created"). A first-century *Pal. Tg.* might have used that term at Gen 2:7.

So, while it is true that Paul does not call Jesus "the Son of Man," and that this is understandable because the messiahship of Jesus is no longer to be obscured, Paul does apply to Jesus the title "the last Adam," which can be viewed as an adaptation of a targumic term אדם קדמיא ("first man/Adam"), which (in *Tg. Neof.* at least) is the targumic equivalent of "the son of man."[38] It is also a term that reveals the meaning (especially for non-Aramaic speakers) of the title "the Son of Man" with which the Corinthians would presumably be familiar through the apostolic teaching, even if none of the Synoptics had yet been written. Paul is in effect telling the Corinthians the meaning of the title "the Son of Man."

Frederick Houk Borsch endorses the view that Paul uses "the *second* Man" and "the *last* Adam" as phrases equivalent to "the Son of Man," and he argues that Paul does this because "the phrase 'the Son of Man' was as much a barbarism in Greek as it is in English. Taken out of its Semitic context it would cease to have the same meaning."[39] This explanation overlooks the fact that this "barbarism" (without the definite article) was already present in the LXX at Ps 8:4 (quoted in Heb 2:6), 80:17, and Dan 7:13. "Son of Man" may not represent smooth Greek or English,

---

[36] *Tg. Neof.* Gen 2:8; 3:22; 48:22; Deut 4:32; *Tg. Ps.-J.* Gen 27:15; Exod 4:11; *Frg. Tg. P, V* and *CTg. Z* Gen 48:22; *Tg. Ps.* 49:2; 69:31; 92:1; 94:10; *1st Tg. Esth.* 3:7; *2nd Tg. Esth.* 1:2. McNamara translates אדם קדמיא in *Tg. Neof.* as "first Adam," pointing, in a note at Gen 2:8 to 1 Cor 15:45 (*Neofiti 1: Genesis,* 57 n.16). Maher translates the expression as "the first man" in *Tg. Ps.-J.* In *Targum of Psalms* (ArBib), David Stec translates the expression as "first Adam" in Ps 49:2, but as "first human" or "first human being" in 69:31; 92:1; and 94:10. In his online translation "Psalms Targum," Edward M. Cook translates the expression in the Psalms passages consistently as "first Adam."

[37] For the same reason, in *Tg. Ezek.,* where the Hebrew phrase "son of man," (בֶּן אָדָם) is rendered in Aramaic as בַּר אָדָם, the Aramaic is always translated by Levey as "son of Adam" (*Targum of Ezekiel,* 6–7).

[38] As noted above, *Tg. Neof.* Exod 4:11 has "the son of man" while *Tg. Ps.-J.* of the same verse has "the first man/Adam" in rendering the MT of "Who made man's mouth?"

[39] Borsch, *Son of Man,* 241.

but without a literal translation it is impossible to understand the significance of the title used by Jesus.

Borsch quotes others in support of the view that Paul is explaining the Son of Man title. On the citation of Ps 8:6 in 1 Cor 15:27, Borsch writes, "William Manson contended that 'If the Apostle was not thinking of Christ as the Son of Man, it would not have occurred to him to base Christ's universal sovereignty on this text.' 'The title Son of Man trembles on Paul's lips,' writes A. M. Hunter."[40]

Galatians 3:16 and the two seeds of Genesis 3:15[41]

The idea of Jesus as the new Adam, the progenitor of the righteous seed, as it is developed from Genesis, may also be the key to explaining Paul's often misunderstood statement in Gal 3:16:

> The promises were spoken to Abraham and to his seed. The Scripture does not say "and to seeds," meaning many people, but "and to your seed," meaning one person, who is Christ. (NIV)

The NIV, adopting the standard interpretation of Paul's words, takes Paul to mean that the promises to Abraham's "seed" are given to only one individual (Christ), implying that if the promises were meant for "many people," God would have said to Abraham, "and to your seeds." Advocates of the standard interpretation explain that Paul is here engaging in rabbinical midrash—that he is unpacking the meaning of "seed" in the patriarchal promises.

There are, however, several reasons for doubting this standard interpretation: (1) Jewish interpretations that focus on whether a word in Scripture is singular or plural deal with words that sometimes are found in the singular, sometimes in the plural. The word "seed," however, when used to refer to a descendent or descendant(s), is always singular;[42] (2) rabbinical tradition consistently takes "to their seed" to mean "to their sons";[43] and (3) it is doubtful that one can find any Jewish rabbi or other practitioner of midrash in history who had anything but scorn for Paul's assumed reasoning, which makes it highly unlikely that he is emulating rabbinic interpretation.[44]

---

[40] Borsch, *Son of Man*, 243, quoting from Manson, *Jesus the Messiah*, 187–88; and A. M. Hunter, *Paul and His Predecessors* (London: SCM, 1961), 86.

[41] Most of this section is condensed from Ronning, "Curse on the Serpent," 335–48.

[42] E.g., *m. Shabbat* 9:2 on זַרְעֶיהָ in Isa 61:11; *m. Sanhedrin* 4:5 (and *Gen. Rab.* 22) on דְּמֵי in Gen 4:10 (interpreted as the blood of Abel and of his posterity).

[43] *Sifre Deut.* 8.2 on Deut 1:8. The Targums use the word "sons" in translating "and to your seed" spoken to the patriarchs.

[44] As Earl Ellis wrote, "If this is Paul's argument, then it must be confessed that its baseless caprice out-rabbis the rabbis; only Akiba could applaud it and even he would substitute something more intricate" (*Paul's Use of the Old Testament* [Grand Rapids: Baker, 1981], 71). John Calvin said of the rabbis of his day: "Having, as they imagine, detected the fallacy of [Paul's] argument, they treat us with haughty triumph" (*Commentaries on the Epistles of Paul: Galatians and Ephesians, Philippians* [Grand Rapids: Eerdmans, 1957], 94).

Following, however, from the fact that Paul recognizes Jesus as the last Adam, the progenitor of the righteous seed, we would expect him to be arguing not that the seed is Christ, but that the seed is *Christ's*. And, actually, that is what he seems to say just a few verses later: "If you are Christ's, then you are 'Abraham's seed,' heirs according to promise" (v. 29). In other words, if Gentiles with no relationship to Abraham believe in Christ, they are counted as "Abraham's seed" because it is actually Christ's seed.

Can Gal 3:16 be understood in this way? Yes it can. Consider first the Greek text:

τῷ δὲ Ἀβραὰμ ἐρρέθησαν αἱ ἐπαγγελίαι καὶ τῷ σπέρματι αὐτοῦ. οὐ λέγει, Καὶ τοῖς σπέρμασιν, ὡς ἐπὶ πολλῶν ἀλλ' ὡς ἐφ' ἑνός, Καὶ τῷ σπέρματί σου, ὅς ἐστιν Χριστός.

I propose that: (1) "many" in "as of many" (ὡς ἐπὶ πολλῶν) does not refer to "many people," but "many seeds," where "many" has the grammatical meaning of "plural," as it does in Semitic languages like Akkadian and modern Hebrew.[45] (2) Paul is referring to what I have described above as the second disqualifying factor that shows that Abraham cannot be the true new Adam, though he seems to be spoken to as if he is in Gen 17 (one of three places where the precise words quoted by Paul occur in LXX).[46] "It does not say 'and to seeds.'" What is the point? The point is a significant historical observation, not a bizarre grammatical one: Abraham had more than one seed, namely, both righteous and wicked offspring (Isaac and Ishmael), and the promise applies to only one of these seeds.

Justin Martyr made the same point in his *Dialogue with Trypho* (135). In the LXX of Isa 65:9, God says, "I will lead forth offspring ("seed") from Jacob and Judah." Justin says, "it is necessary for us here to observe that *there are two seeds of Judah,* and two races, as there are two houses of Jacob: the one begotten by blood and flesh, the other by faith and the Spirit."[47] Justin says Jesus Christ is the "Israel" and "Jacob," just as I am suggesting here that Paul is saying in Gal 3 that Jesus Christ is the "Abraham"—the true, spiritual progenitor. "So we," Justin continues, "who have been quarried out from the bowels of Christ, are the true Israelite race."[48]

It is this historical fact of Abraham's "seeds" that disqualifies him from the position of new Adam and points towards the one who truly is the new Adam, the progenitor of the righteous seed.

---

[45] According to *CAD* 10:13, the Akkadian word "many" is used in lexical texts to indicate the plural suffixes of Sumerian words. Reuben Alcalay gives שֶׁל רַבִּים, "that of many" (which agrees nicely with Paul's ἐπὶ πολλῶν), as the modern Hebrew adjective "plural" (*The Complete English—Hebrew Dictionary* [Hartford, Conn.: Prayer Book, 1965], 2795). In fact, a number of translations use the word "plural" in their translation of Gal 3:16; e.g., William F. Beck, James Moffatt, New Berkley, New English, New Jerusalem, J. B. Phillips, and Charles B. Williams.

[46] "And to your seed" (καὶ τῷ σπέρματί σου), spoken to Abraham, occurs in the LXX of Gen 13:18; 17:8; and 24:7.

[47] *Ante-Nicene Fathers* 1.267.

[48] Ibid.

(3) The antecedent of ὅς ("which") is not σπέρματί ("seed") but σου ("you"). Following the word order of the Greek (which uses the pronoun "you" in the genitive to indicate possession instead of an adjective like English "your"), it reads "'and to the seed of *you*,' who is Christ."[49] That is, when the LORD said to Abraham, "your seed," it referred only to the righteous seed, which is in reality the seed of the true Adam, the Son of Man, Jesus Christ. Ishmael is Abraham's (other) seed, but he is not Christ's seed, and thus he is not an heir of the promise. Paul's point is that Jewish unbelievers are like Ishmael, of the seed of Abraham but not of the seed of promise, while Jewish and Gentile believers are like Isaac, of the seed of promise because they are Christ's (seed) (Gal 3:29). Abraham is a figurehead for the true progenitor of the righteous seed (Christ), as the snake in Gen 3:15 is a figurehead for Satan, the progenitor of the unrighteous seed. If Justin Martyr were as laconic as Paul, he might have said that Isa 65:9 "does not say 'seeds,' in the plural, but in the singular, 'seed from Jacob,' who is in reality Christ" (i.e., "Jacob" in the text is really "Christ"). That is, Christ is not the singular seed, he is the progenitor of that seed; agreeing with Isa 53:10, not to mention Gal 3:29, that seed is his seed.

Grammatically, there can be no objection to the foregoing. Σου is a pronoun, which, by definition, stands in place of a noun, and thus can serve as antecedent to ὅς. The reason this solution has not been proposed in the past (by the Greek fathers, for example) is not because of ignorance of Greek grammar, but because the church lost sight of the significance of the idea of Christ as the true Adam, the obvious evidence for this being that the significance of the Son of Man title, just as the significance of the Logos title, was quickly forgotten in the process of the hellenization of the early church.

If we begin with the proposition, "the church is the offspring of Christ," which is consistent with Gal 3:29 and the idea of Jesus as the true Adam, then it is interesting that in Aramaic, "the offspring of Christ" could be expressed זַרְעֵיהּ דִּי מְשִׁיחָא which, translated literally, is "the offspring of him who [is] the Christ." This is quite similar to what we have at the end of Gal 3:16, except that there we have a shift from second person ("the seed of you," when Genesis is being quoted) to third person (for Paul's comment on it, "who is Christ").[50] Interestingly, in Gal 4:27 Paul quotes Isa 54:1, which in the Hebrew shifts from second person to third person within direct address: "Rejoice, O barren one—she has not borne, break forth with a shout and cry out—she has not labored."[51]

---

[49] The reason for the change from second person ("you") to third person ("is") is that the quoted words end with "you," and what follows is Paul's comment, essentially saying, "the word 'you' in the quote refers actually to Christ (not Abraham)." I mention this to forestall the objection that if my interpretation were correct, Paul would have to say, "you who are Christ."

[50] ὅς ἐστιν stands for דִּי; σπέρματί σου stands for זַרְעֵיהּ, but in the second person, since it is in a quote from Genesis.

[51] S. R. Driver cited this example as well as 2 Kgs 9:31 ("Is it peace, O Zimri, slayer of *his* master?"); Isa 22:16 ("What right do *you* have here . . . who hews out a grave for *himself*," etc.); and 47:8 ("Hear this, O sensual one . . . who says in *her* heart"); 48:1 ("Hear this, O house of Jacob, called by the name Israel, from the loins of Judah *they* came forth"); 54:11 ("O afflicted one, storm tossed, *she* is not comforted"); Mic 1:2 ("Listen, O peoples,

This interpretation has the advantage that it views Gal 3:16 not only as the product of a sane mind and rational thought, but also as consistent with what Paul says elsewhere, not only in Gal 3:29, but also in Rom 9:6–13. "Nor are they all children (of the promise, or of God) because they are Abraham's seed" (v. 7). Here Paul clearly takes "seed" (singular) as "many people." He goes on, "but, 'Through Isaac seed will be called yours.' That is, it is not the children of the flesh who are the children of God, but the children of promise." Obviously, Paul takes the singular seed as a collective, just as everyone else does, as referring to "many people," the children of promise, who are children of God. The only difference between this passage and Gal 3:16 is that in the latter, Paul more specifically identifies the divine progenitor as the Messiah, who is both a man, like the figurehead Abraham, and God.

Against all of the above one might insist from Gal 3:19 that Paul is thinking at least in that passage of Christ as the singular seed who was to come: the law was ordained "until the seed should come to whom the promise was given." This seed is future in relation to OT times and thus cannot mean believers in general because there was such a seed in OT times. But the context actually supports the view that this seed to come is the church. Paul says that the law "shut up all men to sin" (v. 22), and "*before faith came,* we were kept in custody under the law, being shut up to the faith which was later to be revealed . . . but *now that faith has come,* we are no longer under a tutor. For you are all sons of God through faith in Christ Jesus" (vv. 23–26). Yes, there was a believing seed prior to the coming of Christ, just as there was faith prior to the coming of Christ. Yet Paul speaks of both faith and the seed as things that were to come, with the coming of Christ; they were both "fundamentally alike in kind" with the OT faith and seed, yet "specifically different."[52]

Hebrews 2:5–10

Hebrews 2:5–10 shows us how the words of David about the first Adam in Ps 8 may be adapted to speak of the last Adam. When David says in Ps 8:5, "You made him a little lower than the angels, and crowned him with glory and honor,"

---

all of *them*" [= 1 Kgs 22:28]); 3:9 ("Hear this, heads of the house of Jacob . . . *they* twist everything straight"); Zeph 2:12 ("You also, O Cushites, *they* [will be] slain by my sword"); Mal 3:9 ("You are robbing me, the whole nation, all of *it*"). *Treatise on the Use of the Tenses in Hebrew and Some Other Syntactical Questions* (3rd ed.; Oxford: Clarendon Press, 1892), 268 (§198).

[52] Ernest Burton uses these descriptions for "faith" of v. 23, but I think they are equally applicable to "seed" understood as the NT church compared to the OT church. The full quote is, "By τὴν πίστιν is meant not faith qualitatively; the article excludes this; not generically; Paul could not speak of this as having recently come, since, as he has maintained, it was at least as old as Abraham; nor the faith in the sense 'that which is believed' . . . ; but the faith in Christ just spoken of in v. 22. That this was, in the apostle's view, fundamentally alike in kind with the faith of Abraham is clear. . . . That it was specifically different is indicated by the use of the definite article, the frequent addition of Ἰησοῦ Χριστοῦ, and by the assertion of this verse that faith came at the end of the reign of the law" (*A Critical and Exegetical Commentary on the Epistle to the Galatians* [ICC; Edinburgh: T&T Clark, 1921], 198).

both clauses refer to the high status which our first parents were given when they were created. In Heb 2, these clauses are adapted to refer to two different events with respect to Jesus. As we saw above in relation to John 1:51; 3:13; 6:62, the first clause applies to the incarnation and temporary humiliation of the Son of Man, made "for a little while lower than the angels." While Heb 2:7 retains the LXX word βραχύ, which can mean either "a little bit" or "a little while," the "little while" sayings in John are unambiguous.

The author of Hebrews adapted the second clause of Ps 8:5 to refer to the glorification of Jesus in his suffering. This is not clear in the NIV rendering of Heb 2:9, which changes the order of glorification and suffering to the point of death; the Greek is quite clear that Jesus is glorified *in order that* he might taste death for every person (ὅπως . . . γεύσηται θανάτου).[53] We will also see this viewpoint confirmed in the Son of Man sayings in John.

Hebrews 2:8 notes that we do not presently see all things under his (Adam's) feet. Indeed, the author of Hebrews writes under the conditions described in Dan 7:7, when "all things" were trampled under the feet of Rome, a condition which will be remedied by the coming of the heavenly Son of Man of Dan 7:13. For the present, however, "we do see Jesus," who, after being made for a little while lower than the angels, has been glorified in his suffering (Heb 2:9).

Further, the work of the new Adam is to be the progenitor of the righteous seed, which the author describes as "bringing many sons to glory" (Heb 2:10). If Adam and Eve had not sinned, they would themselves have brought many sons to glory (children born in an uncorrupted image of God) naturally through procreation. The last Adam, the firstborn over creation and true image of the invisible God (Col 1:15), makes people children of God by his own glorification in suffering.

The Son of Man in the Gospel of John

There are twelve "Son of Man" sayings by Jesus in John,[54] all of which can be related to Ps 8 as it seems to be adapted to Jesus in Heb 2. Even a thirteenth, the crowd's question, "Who is this 'Son of Man'" (John 12:34), can be related to Ps 8 in one of the ways that John gives us the answer.

We have already noted that John 1:51, 3:13, and 6:62 together speak of the temporary descent of the Son of Man, or in the words of the psalm, "a little while lower than the angels." Five more sayings speak of the Son of Man being "glorified" or "lifted up," clearly referring to the crucifixion or his suffering in general (3:14;

---

[53] So Marcus Dods: "The construction of the sentence is much debated. But it must be admitted that any construction which makes the coronation subsequent to the tasting death for every person is unnatural; the ὅπως depends upon ἐστεφανωμένον" ("The Epistle to the Hebrews," in *The Expositor's Greek Testament* [ed. W. Robertson Nicoll; 5 vols.; New York: Hodder and Stoughton, 1912; repr. Grand Rapids: Eerdmans, 1983], 4:263.

[54] John 1:51; 3:13, 14; 5:27; 6:27, 53, 62; 8:28; 9:35; 12:23, 34; 13:31.

8:28; 12:23, 34; 13:31). The "lifted up" language clearly alludes to Isa 52:13. "Glorified" could also refer to that verse if it interprets "lifted up" or alludes to the LXX of that verse, which uses δοξάζω as in John.[55] Yet it could also be a way of tying the Suffering Servant of Isa 53 to the figure of the new Adam. As we have already seen, Isa 53:10 speaks of the Servant's offspring. The first Adam was "crowned with glory and honor" at his creation, the last Adam is crowned when he is "lifted up and glorified" (52:13) in his suffering.

Three more Son of Man sayings in John can be related to the idea of "bringing many sons to glory." In John 9:35, the Son of Man is the proper object of the believer's faith, which John tells us in 1:12 results in the believer becoming a child of God. In 6:27 and 53, the Son of Man gives himself as food that leads to eternal life for those who believe; again, as 1:12 indicates, this means that they become children of God. The first Adam brought forth children to corruption, the last Adam brings forth children to glory.

One last saying is John 5:27: "He gave him authority to execute judgment, because he is the Son of Man." Here, "the Son of Man" lacks the definite article, either simply because it precedes the verb (in which case it can be translated with the definite article),[56] or because it is saying that Jesus is given authority because he is (i.e., became) a human being, in which case this is not necessarily a "Son of Man" saying. We noted above that this saying could be related to Dan 7:13, where it also lacks the definite article (i.e., it is not in the emphatic state); it lacks the definite article in Ps 8:4 as well, but this is probably because it is poetry, in which the definite article may be omitted.

For our purposes, we will simply note that if it is used as a title here, it can be related to Ps 8:6, because it expresses the idea of authority being given to the Son of Man. One might prefer to make the primary reference to Dan 7:13, since the authority Jesus speaks of goes beyond that of which Ps 8 speaks.

Finally, the crowd asks, "Who is this 'Son of Man'?" (John 12:34), a question which Jesus does not answer directly. However, we can see the irony of God himself answering the crowd's question through the mouth of Pontius Pilate as he brings Jesus out to the crowd, "crowned with glory and honor," and says "Behold the man!" Thus between the question in 12:34 ("Who is this 'Son of Man'?") and the answer in 19:5 ("Behold the man!") we see the man/son of man parallelism of Ps 8:4. "Behold the man" is also commonly related to Zech 6:12, spoken to Joshua the high priest, who has been given an ornate crown: "Behold a man whose name is Branch" (in *Tg. Zech.* it is, "Behold the man whose name is Messiah"). We discuss this passage in more detail in ch. 5.

---

[55] Nickelsburg noted the use of "lifted up" and "glorified" of the Servant of the LORD in the LXX of Isaiah, noting that John 13:31 uses "glorify" four times "in a way that parallels the servant passages in Isa 53:12 [*sic;* 52:13?] and 49:3" ("Son of Man," 6:146–47).

[56] "There is no reason why the phrase in John 5:27 should not mean *the* Son of man, in accordance with the rule that definite predicate nouns preceding a verb usually lack the article, just as θεοῦ υἱός in Matt 27:54 may actually mean '*the* Son of God'" (A. J. B. Higgins, *Jesus and the Son of Man* [London: Lutterworth, 1964], 166).

SUMMARY

In this chapter, I have begun to expound the theme of "the Word became flesh" as an understanding that in the theology of John's Gospel, what God did in OT times from heaven, the Son now does as a person, in submission to the Father. We looked specifically at the "descent" language of Jesus in John 3:13; 6:38, 42, arguing that it expresses a continuation of the OT idea that God "comes down," that is, intervenes in human affairs, to judge, to redeem, to reveal his name and his will, and ultimately, to dwell among his people and be their God. The Targums almost always avoid the anthropomorphic language of God coming down and instead speak of the Word of the LORD being revealed or the glory of his *Shekinah* being revealed. While Jesus uses the language found in the MT (comparing, e.g., John 6:38, "I have come down from heaven," to Exod 3:8, "I have come down to deliver them"), John uses language adapted from the Targums to describe the descent of Jesus: "The Word became flesh."

At the same time, John's adaptation highlights a change from OT times. Jesus has come down as the Son of Man, the last Adam, a real person, the head of a new redeemed race. I have attempted to confirm one particular understanding of the question of why Jesus called himself the Son of Man, explaining the title as a catchall term substituted for the currently prevalent catchall term "Messiah" and dependent on the phrase "son of man" used in Ps 8:4; 80:17; and Dan 7:13. Jesus used this title as a way of obscuring his messianic claim, and his usage has confounded Bible scholars of all subsequent generations. In his reported usage of the title, John seems particularly concerned to bring out its dependence on Ps 8, since all of its uses in this gospel can be related to the type of adaptation of Ps 8 found in Heb 2:5–10.

In subsequent chapters, we will see that as Jesus fulfills various OT divine roles (warrior, bridegroom, lawgiver), there are both human and divine precedents or paradigms in the OT for what Jesus does, in keeping with the idea that he is both divine and human, that is, that the Word has become flesh. Furthermore, we will see how the language of the Targums sheds light on how these themes are reflected in the Gospel of John.

5

Jesus of Nazareth, Man of War

INTRODUCTION

In the last chapter, we saw that Jesus' claim to have come down from heaven was to be understood in continuity with OT texts that say that the LORD came down or will come down. The incarnation is the ultimate coming down. But what did the Lord come down to do? He came down for several reasons, but the most immediate purpose was to wage war. We see this in the scene of the burning bush: "I have come down to deliver them from the hand of the Egyptians" (Exod 3:8). Similarly, in predicting the defeat of Sennacherib, Isaiah says, "the LORD of Hosts [צְבָאוֹת] will come down to wage war [לִצְבֹּא] on Mt. Zion" (Isa 31:4). Likewise, Jesus came down from heaven to wage war, to defeat Satan, to save his people in a way he could not save them without the incarnation—to save them eternally.

After crossing through the Red Sea and seeing the Egyptian army that pursued them destroyed by the outstretched hand of the LORD, the Israelites praised him as a warrior: "The LORD is a man of war; the LORD is his name" (Exod 15:3). If the mission of Jesus was to make that name known not just by describing God, as a prophet would do, but by his own works, then we might expect to see Jesus engaged in warfare against the enemies of his people, which are also his enemies. In the book *God Is a Warrior*, Daniel G. Reid showed how the Synoptic Gospels portray Jesus as the divine warrior.[1] The present chapter explores the targumic background for this theme as it is reflected in the Gospel of John.

The LORD showed himself as warrior not only in the events of the exodus, but also in the conquest and at various other times in Israel's history, such as the deliverance of Jerusalem from Sennacherib and the Assyrians in the time of Hezekiah. Scripture also speaks of "his strange work, his unusual task" (Isa 28:21)—his rising up in battle against his own people who have not obeyed him. Frequently the Targums employ the divine title, "the Word of the LORD," in describing his victorious warfare.

In John we see Jesus the Word as the victorious divine warrior over the ultimate enemy, Satan, and Jesus wins his victory at the cross. As comparison of his words to certain OT texts will make clear, when Jesus speaks of going to the cross,

---

[1] Tremper Longman III and Daniel G. Reid, *God Is a Warrior* (Grand Rapids: Zondervan, 1995), 91–135.

he speaks as YHWH the divine warrior. Or, to use targumic terms, he speaks as the Word of the Lord. Christ's victory on the first night of the Passover feast can be seen as analogous to the defeat of Sennacherib, which at some point in Jewish tradition was also thought to have taken place at Passover (*Tg. 2 Chr.* 32:21). The basis for such a tradition may be the Lord's promise to deliver and "pass over" (פָּסַח) Jerusalem (Isa 31:5), a choice of words that seems to invite comparison between the impending deliverance from Sennacherib and the first Passover in Egypt, when the firstborn among the Egyptians also perished by "a sword not of man" (Isa 31:8). *Fragmentary Targum P* Exod 12:2 seems to anticipate a future repetition of such a deliverance, saying through Moses that Nisan would be the first month of the year "because in it the Lord redeemed his people, the sons of Israel, and in it *he will eventually redeem them.*"

The Lord also went before his people as a warrior when the Israelites left Mt. Sinai on their way to the promised land, as seen in Moses' prayer, "Rise up, O Lord, and let your enemies be scattered, and let those who hate you flee before you" (Num 10:35). We will see that Jesus spoke as the one who is going to answer this petition, as the one who would rise and defeat the great enemy of his people, the devil himself.

In addition to following an OT model for divine warfare, Jesus also follows a human OT model, in keeping with the idea that the Word has become flesh. As we will see, Jesus follows in the footsteps of the great OT human warriors Joshua (at the beginning of his ministry) and David (at the end of his ministry).

Some General Statements of Warfare and Victory

John 5:43

In John 5:43, Jesus says, "I have come in my Father's name, and you do not receive me." We noted in ch. 3 that this echoes two verses from Ps 118: "I have come in my Father's name" relates to v. 26, "Blessed is he who comes in the name of the Lord," recited in John 12:13. "You do not receive me" relates to Ps 118:22, "The stone which the builders rejected has become the chief cornerstone."

Although this psalm has no superscription indicating the author, and few interpreters think of it as Davidic, the situation described in the psalm fits David's life well. To begin with, David was like a stone that was rejected by builders, for he was rejected not only by Saul and his servants, but also by the Ziphites, the people of Keilah, and Nabal (all of Judah), who would not risk helping David while Saul was king. The interpretation of the stone as David is found in the *Tg. Ps.* of this verse, where a play on the word "stone" (Heb. *'eben*) as "son (Heb. *ben*) of Jesse" is made.

Further, "Blessed is he who comes in the name of the Lord" calls to mind the words of David when he came to fight Goliath: "You come to me with a sword, a spear, and a javelin, but I come to you in the name of the Lord of Hosts, the God of the armies of Israel, whom you have reproached" (1 Sam 17:25).

Finally, Ps 118:10–14 makes better sense as referring to the conquests of David over the surrounding nations than it does connected to any other period of Israel's history: "All nations surrounded me; in the name of the LORD I will surely cut them off," etc. One could conclude, then, that Jesus' statement, "I have come in my Father's name," suggests, given the background to that claim in Ps 118 and 1 Sam 17, that Jesus has come to wage war.

John 16:33

In the upper room, before going to the cross, Jesus says to the disciples, "In the world you have tribulation, but take courage, I have conquered the world." In this statement, Jesus indicates that what looks to all the world like a climactic, humiliating defeat—death by crucifixion—is in fact the greatest of victories.

JESUS IN THE FOOTSTEPS OF JOSHUA AND DAVID

John 1:35–42 and Joshua 3–4

It is clear by comparison with the Synoptic Gospels that Jesus' calling of the twelve disciples took place before the baptism of Jesus and his return to the Jordan following his forty-day temptation in the wilderness. These disciples have been followers of John the Baptist and they leave John to follow Jesus to the place where he is going to stay that night. Simon, one of the disciples, comes the next day and Jesus names him Kephas, an Aramaic word meaning "rock" (from which comes "Peter" in Greek). We can compare these events to Josh 3 and 4, where Israel crosses the Jordan under Joshua's leadership.

In broader terms, when John 1:35–42 is viewed together with material in the Synoptics, we can see how the history of Israel is being recapitulated in the steps of Jesus.

Israel in the OT	Jesus
Israel crossed through the Red Sea.	Jesus was baptized in the Jordan.
Israel was tested for forty years in the wilderness.	Jesus was tested for forty days in the wilderness.
Israel came to the Jordan under Joshua, and crossed into the promised land.	Jesus returned to the Jordan, then crossed into the promised land.

The crossing of the Jordan is similar enough to the crossing of the Red Sea that the Jordan serves to recapitulate the crossing of the Red Sea. Indeed, the two events are explicitly compared in Josh 4:23 as similar miracles, with dry ground being brought out of the water in both cases. The word "heap" (נֵד), used in Exod 15:8 and Ps 78:13 to describe the piling up of the waters of the Red Sea, is used also for the backing up of the Jordan's waters (Josh 3:13, 16).

John 1:28 tells us that the place Jesus came to when he returned to the Jordan was "Bethany beyond the Jordan," that is, on the east side of the Jordan. A good case has recently been made that this place was across from Jericho and therefore was likely very close to the place where Israel crossed the Jordan after camping there following Moses' death (Num 22:1; Josh 3:16).[2] By coming to this place, Jesus may be intentionally following in the footsteps of his namesake Joshua, who led Israel across the Jordan. As Reid noted, John did not go to Jerusalem to baptize, but rather to the Jordan, because of its historical importance. "A prophetic figure [John] readies God's people for the approach of the divine warrior by immersing the faithful penitents in the very waters that parted for Israel's original entry into the land."[3]

Several details of the events of John 1:35–42 can also be seen as recapitulating the actions of Joshua when he crossed the river. Notice the following:

(1) The LORD told Joshua to take twelve stones from the river, carried by twelve men, a man from each tribe, and to set them up as a monument, as a witness to the mighty deeds that the LORD had done (Josh 4:1–8; 20–24). Likewise, Jesus begins at the Jordan River to gather twelve disciples as witnesses of the great deeds that the LORD is going to accomplish. Rather than twelve men carrying stones, the disciples are the stones themselves, i.e., witnesses.

(2) The twelve stones were taken from the Jordan River. These disciples (though not yet numbering twelve), being John's disciples, would also have been taken from the Jordan River, where they had been baptized. Jesus even names one of them, who is going to be their leader, "Rock."

While this understanding of the significance of Peter's name is chronologically earlier than Matt 16:18, it is consistent with it, since there Simon is called Peter because of his witness, "You are the Christ, the Son of the living God." Someone might object that if Jesus names Peter after the stones of the monument that Joshua erected, Peter should be called "stone," not "rock," since the Targum uses Aramaic אֶבֶן (not כֵּיף) for Hebrew אֶבֶן in translating Josh 4. However, in Aramaic, just as in English, one could easily use the word "rock" in making a play on the use of the word "stone." Furthermore, in the Syriac translation of Josh 4 (Syriac being an Aramaic dialect), the word כֵּיף is in fact used to translate the Hebrew word for stone. The disciples may have been familiar with such a translation, and indeed, a first-century Targum may have read differently than *Tg. Josh*. We might add that if one does not accept this typological association between John 1:35–42 and Josh 4, then there is no explanation in the context for why Simon is now named Kephas (Peter) at the Jordan. Finally, since on this analogy all the disciples, not just Peter, are "stones," witnesses to the works of the LORD, "rock" could be used to indicate that Peter was going to be the leader of the other witnesses.

(3) Just as Joshua set up a monument at the place where he was going to stay that night (Gilgal), so the disciples follow Jesus to the place where he is staying.

---

[2] Rami Khouri, "Where John Baptized," *Biblical Archaeology Review* 31, no. 1 (January/February 2005): 34–43.

[3] Longman and Reid, *God Is a Warrior*, 93.

So a number of parallels indicate that Jesus at the beginning of his ministry may be been consciously following in the footsteps of Joshua, that great OT warrior. Although neither the events of Joshua or John seem particularly warlike, we should take note of the fact that Gilgal was Joshua's war camp, where he prepared for war and to which he returned after battle. Likewise, Jesus is preparing for ministry in the promised land. As Reid has shown, the Synoptics contain a number of other parallels with events in Joshua, such as the "driving out" of demons, where the evangelists use the same Greek word that the LXX uses to translate the Hebrew word for "driving out" the Canaanites.[4]

John 18:1 and 2 Samuel 15

This verse says that after leaving the upper room, Jesus crossed over the Kidron to a garden, where he was later arrested by those led by his betrayer, Judas. The Synoptics say that he went to the Mount of Olives (Matt 26:30; Mark 14:26; Luke 22:39), which would also tell the reader familiar with the geography of Jerusalem that he must have crossed the Kidron valley.

Jesus had predicted his betrayal by saying that what happened to David was going to happen to him (John 13:18, quoting Ps 41:9). At this place the prediction comes true. The most memorable betrayal experienced by David was that of his son Absalom and his trusted counselor Ahithophel, recorded in 2 Sam 15. Although the betrayal spoken of in Ps 41 does not seem to be that of 2 Sam 15 (Ps 41:3 implies David is vulnerable due to some sickness), the words of Ps 41:9 were appropriate to the situation in the upper room: "He who eats my bread has lifted up his heel against me."

The path that Jesus takes after his betrayal parallels that taken by David when he fled Jerusalem before his son Absalom. Second Samuel 15:13 says that a messenger told David, "the hearts of the men of Israel are with Absalom." Unlike Jesus, who predicted his betrayal, David was taken by surprise and fled. Verse 23 tells us that the king passed over the brook Kidron, as did Jesus (John 18:1), and v. 30 says that David went up the ascent of the Mount of Olives, as did Jesus (Matt 26:30; Mark 14:26; Luke 22:39).

It appears, then, that Jesus followed in the footsteps of Joshua in the beginning of his ministry, and Jesus followed in the footsteps of another great OT warrior, David, at the end of his ministry.

Israel from the Time of Joshua, to David, to Jesus

The book of Joshua represents the high point in the obedience of Israel during OT times; never again did the nation so consistently follow the law of Moses and submit to their God-appointed leader. Although Israel reached a relatively high

---

[4]Longman and Reid, *God Is a Warrior*, 108 n.41. The Hebrew גֵּרֵשׁ is translated by ἐκβάλλω. Reid cites Exod 23:28–31, Deut 33:27, and Josh 24:12, 18.

point of obedience during the reign of David, the man after the LORD's own heart, the rebellion of Absalom points to a downward trajectory. Absalom' rebellion took place as a judgment of God upon David's sin.

Perhaps symbolic of this downward trajectory, the rebellion of Absalom caused David and those faithful to him (and to the LORD) to flee across the Jordan River to the east, the opposite direction to Israel's crossing under Joshua. After the rebellion was put down, David then crossed back, now in the same direction as did Joshua years before. Yet David's crossing, stands in stark contrast to that of Joshua. Under Joshua, Israel was completely united, with no tribal rivalry, and a death sentence was pronounced upon any who would not obey Joshua (Josh 1:18). But when David crosses the Jordan, a foolish argument develops between the tribe of Judah (which had been in the forefront of the treachery against David) and the other tribes about who should have the honor of bringing David back. Another brief civil war breaks out as a result (2 Sam 19:41–20:22).

The downward trajectory continues into the NT. Jesus is attested as the LORD's leader, appointed as such in his baptism at the Jordan, just as the LORD began to magnify Joshua at the crossing of the Jordan (Josh 3:7; 4:14). Unlike in the case of David, there was no sin in Jesus that could serve as a pretext for rebellion against him. When David fled, at least the high priest Zadok and the Levites were loyal to him (and to the LORD) and came with him (2 Sam 15:24). But in the arrest, trial, and execution of Jesus, the high priest Caiaphas, a Sadducee (a party name derived from the name Zadok), and the Pharisees, who were teachers of the Law (as the Levites were supposed to be according to Deut 33:9–10), were the instigators and perpetrators.

My examination of John 1 and 18 in light of Josh 4 and 2 Sam 15 has intentionally left out the most important similarity. In this chapter, I am presenting to the reader material in the order in which I have discovered it myself in studying and teaching over a number of years. It is a good example of how it is easy to see the humanity of Jesus, and to see OT human "types" of Jesus, but to overlook the more important "divine typology," which does not involve a mere similarity of persons, but rather a similarity of deeds done by the same divine person. My meaning should become clear in the remaining sections of this chapter.

JESUS OF NAZARETH, DIVINE MAN OF WAR

John 12:31–32; the Defeat of Sennacherib and the Defeat of Satan

Jerusalem's Deliverance from Sennacherib

One of the greatest examples of divine warfare and victory in the OT is the LORD's defeat of Sennacherib in the time of Hezekiah. The historical accounts appear in 2 Kgs 18:13–19:37 (largely reproduced in Isa 36–37) and 2 Chr 32:1–23. Other material from Isaiah is helpful, as we shall see.

Israel was strategically located between Egypt and Mesopotamia, which gave it an opportunity to be a blessing to all the nations around. More often, however,

Israel disobeyed and was an example of God's judgment. Assyria was the dominant superpower in the time of Hezekiah, who would have been alive when the Assyrians conquered Samaria and made Israel an Assyrian province. The Assyrian king was a "great king" (Isa 36:4, 13), that is, a suzerain who has other kings (vassals) under his authority. In his apostasy, Hezekiah's father Ahaz made himself a vassal of the Assyrian king Tiglath–pileser III with the words, "I am your servant and your son" (2 Kgs 16:7). Yet he was supposed to be servant and son to the LORD (2 Sam 7:5, 8, 14, 20, 26).

Judah was still a vassal to the Assyrians when Hezekiah became king. Sennacherib became king of Assyria in about 704 B.C.E., and often when a new king came to the throne, his inexperience and the fact that he may have to deal with domestic rivals, made successful rebellion by the vassal states more likely than at other times. Under Hezekiah, Judah joined a coalition of vassal states (including Babylon) in rebelling against Sennacherib. Egypt encouraged the rebellion, no doubt desirous of regaining the glory days when that nation was the dominant power in the region.

Second Kings 18:7 says that the LORD was with Hezekiah, and he rebelled against the king of Assyria. Did he do so in faith? The context would seem to suggest that he did, as his rebellion is listed among his successful works of reformation. Such faith would have been grounded in predictions of divine deliverance from the Assyrians, made through Isaiah since the time of Ahaz. Subsequent events, however, were to show the limitations of his faith.

Sennacherib set out to deal with the rebels, and they were, one by one, beginning with Babylon, forced to submit. Hezekiah held out as he saw his allies successively defeated, and as the help of Egypt against Assyria proved useless. As Sennacherib turned his armies towards Judah, Hezekiah had to decide whether to continue what looked by now like a hopeless cause or to quit and try to come to the best possible terms with Sennacherib. He continued to hold out, and Sennacherib conquered "all the fortified cities of Judah" (2 Kgs 18:13; the number of fortified cities was forty-six according to the Assyrian annals), with Jerusalem alone left.

If Hezekiah had rebelled in faith, trusting in the LORD for his salvation, he should have continued in faith after his little human allies were defeated. Eventually, Hezekiah capitulated, saying to Sennacherib, "I have sinned; whatever penalty you impose on me I will bear" (2 Kgs 18:14). He paid Sennacherib thirty talents of gold and three hundred talents of silver in order to get Sennacherib to leave him alone.

Because 2 Kgs goes on to describe Sennacherib attacking Jerusalem instead of withdrawing as he agreed to do, some have supposed that there were actually two invasions of Judah by Sennacherib and that 2 Kgs 18:17 describes a second invasion some years later. A more plausible explanation is indicated in Isa 33, the sixth and last woe of Isa 28–35. The first five woes are pronounced against Israel and Judah, but the sixth is pronounced on "you destroyer, who was not destroyed; he who dealt treacherously, though others did not deal treacherously against him" (33:1). This treacherous destroyer is Sennacherib. His treachery is that he agreed to withdraw from Judah for the price Hezekiah paid, but after getting the money, he went on to demand the unconditional surrender of Jerusalem, after which he would take the rebels into exile (Isa 36:17; 2 Kgs 18:32) and probably tear down the walls of Jerusalem in order to prevent future rebellions. Thus Isa 33:8 says, "he [Sennacherib] has broken the agreement"—that is, the agreement to leave Jerusalem alone and Hezekiah's kingdom standing.

At this point, Hezekiah apparently realizes that his wavering and attempt at appeasement have made things worse. No doubt the same advisers who were so insistent that their hope of salvation lay in Egypt turned and told him he had no choice but to pay off Sennacherib; it was the only way to ensure "peace for our time." When appeasement failed, Hezekiah reverted to trusting in the promise of the Lord through Isaiah that Judah would be delivered from the Assyrians, and thus refused the demand of unconditional surrender.

It is ironic that Sennacherib's "prophet" Rabshakeh called on Hezekiah to surrender from the same spot that the Lord's prophet Isaiah had called upon Hezekiah's father Ahaz to surrender to the Lord some thirty years earlier (Isa 7:3; 36:2; 2 Kgs 18:17). Isaiah's message to Ahaz at that time was that he must not turn to Assyria for help against his enemies Aram and Israel. He should instead trust in the Lord.

For those without faith, the situation was hopeless: "Their brave men cry in the streets; the envoys of peace weep bitterly" (Isa 33:7). The "brave men" would be those charged with fighting the undefeated and exceptionally cruel Assyrians. The "envoys of peace" were no doubt those who trusted that their appeasement of Sennacherib would succeed. Jerusalem's best human hope now would be that their walls would hold and their water supply would not fail, so that after a while they would die of starvation! "Both 'hawks' . . . and 'doves' . . . were equally at their wits end."[5]

In the midst of this hopeless situation the Lord says that the long-promised deliverance will be accomplished:

Now I will arise, says the Lord, now I will be exalted, now I will be lifted up. (Isa 33:10)

This threefold "now" comes about thirty years after Isaiah began predicting deliverance from the Assyrians. Isaiah 8 predicts that Assyria will sweep through Immanuel's land like a flood, reaching the neck, but the Assyrians will then be shattered, because "God is with us" (Heb.: *Immanu El*). Thirty years later that point was reached; Jerusalem was the head out of water, the body submerged in the military "deluge" from Assyria. But with your head out of water, you will survive the flood. In Isa 10:24–25, the Lord says, "My people who live in Zion, do not be afraid of the Assyrians who strike you with the rod. . . . In a very short time my indignation against you will end, and my anger will be to their destruction."

Isaiah 18 contains a remarkable message to some ambassadors from Cush, "a nation tall and smooth, a people feared far and wide." No doubt they came to Jerusalem to discuss the great issue of the day, "Are we strong enough together to rebel

---

[5] Alec Motyer, *The Prophecy of Isaiah* (Leicester: InterVarsity, 1993), 264.

against Assyria?" The LORD's message to them through Isaiah, using the analogy of a farmer waiting for the proper time to harvest, is that the LORD is watching and waiting until the right time, and then he will "harvest" the Assyrian army and leave them for vultures and wild animals (vv. 4–6). "At that time a gift of homage will be brought to the LORD of Hosts from a people tall and smooth, from a people feared far and wide, a powerful and oppressive nation, whose land the rivers divide, to the place of the name of the LORD of Hosts, Mt. Zion" (v. 7). The "now" in Isa 33:10 means the time of harvest has come.

Likewise victory over the Assyrians is predicted in the verse cited in the introduction to this chapter, "The LORD will come down and wage war on Mt. Zion" (Isa 31:4), and "The Assyrian will fall by a sword that is not of man" (v. 8; similarly Hos 1:7). The "now . . . now . . . now" of Isa 33:10 means this long awaited time has come.

Additionally, the point is not just that this deliverance was predicted a long time previously, so that when it happened, Judah could recognize it as a fulfillment of prophecy. "Now" also means that Judah has come to the point where it is completely helpless, and the situation is completely hopeless. Sennacherib had destroyed the great powers of the day, and he had almost completely overrun Judah. His taunting boasts were quite accurate. Hezekiah's allies have been defeated, and all his treasures are gone in a vain bid to send Sennacherib away. All human wisdom and human means have failed. They can go through the motions of preparation in fortifying the walls of Jerusalem and securing a reliable water supply. Indeed, "Hezekiah's Tunnel" was a remarkable engineering achievement to bring in such a supply from outside the walls. But again, such efforts only secured an eventual death by starvation. Thus "now" means that in such a situation, all will recognize that this salvation is a work of God, not of a human.

In Isa 33:10, the LORD says, "I will arise." The idea of the LORD arising goes back to Num 10, when Israel departed from Mt. Sinai after receiving the law and building the tabernacle. The Israelites began their journey to the promised land with the ark of the LORD's covenant going before them. Numbers 10:35–36 declares:

> When the ark set out, Moses said, "Arise O LORD! Let your enemies be scattered, and let those who hate you flee from before you." And when it came to rest, he said, "Return, O LORD, to the myriad thousands of Israel."

Similar petitions for God to arise are found in the Psalms. Psalm 68:1 says, "Let God arise, and let his enemies be scattered." Psalm 7:6 uses two of the verbs used in Isa 33:10, "*Arise O* LORD in your anger. *Lift yourself up* against the rage of my enemies." It is easy to see Isa 33:10 as a response to such petitions.

The result of the LORD rising up in this situation is described very briefly. "The angel of the LORD went forth and struck down 185,000 in the camp of the Assyrians" (Isa 37:36; 2 Kgs 19:35). Second Chronicles 32:21 says that the angel destroyed every mighty warrior, commander, and officer.

In Isa 33:13, the LORD calls on those near (Jerusalem) and far away (nations such as Cush, to which this victory was prophesied years earlier by Isaiah) to take notice of his power and what he has done. Isaiah's prophecy came true as "many were bringing gifts to the LORD at Jerusalem, and choice presents to Hezekiah king of Judah, so that he was exalted in the sight of all the nations thereafter" (2 Chr 32:23).

Isaiah 33:14 says that "the sinners in Zion are terrified; trembling seizes the godless." Why were they terrified after such great deliverance? No doubt because all the time Isaiah has been predicting deliverance they have been mocking him. Further, they recognize that not only has Sennacherib put himself in disfavor with God, but they have as well. Isaiah 33 is the sixth woe of this section of Isaiah (chs. 28–35), but the first five have been pronounced against them. What had been their response to Isaiah? "Get out of the way, turn aside from the path. Stop confronting us with 'the Holy One of Israel'" (30:11). Now they know that what Isaiah has been saying is true, and that they face the same judgment as Sennacherib's horde. Isaiah goes on to tell them the terms for living in security with the LORD on Mt. Zion (vv. 14b–16).

Of the three verbs used of the LORD's attack against Sennacherib, two have been used together of the LORD previously in Isaiah, and they are found together two more times in the rest of the book as well. In Isaiah's prophetic call, he says he "saw the Lord, seated on a throne, high and lifted up" (6:1). "Lifted up" is the *niphal* participle of נשא corresponding to "I will be lifted up" of 33:10, the *niphal* imperfect of the same root. "High" in 6:1 is the *qal* participle of רום corresponding to the second verb of 33:10, the *hithpolel* imperfect of the same root. In these two passages, the use of the "high and lifted up" language with reference to the LORD contrasts with the negative use of these two verbs in describing idolatrous and proud men in Isa 2: Isaiah 2:12 announces the day of the LORD against everyone who is high and lifted up; v. 13 condemns men using the figure of cedars of Lebanon that are high and lifted up; v. 14 speaks of the mountains that are high and lifted up. Finally, vv. 17–18 conclude: "The pride of men will be brought low, and the loftiness of men will be abased, and the LORD alone will be exalted in that day, and the idols will completely vanish."

In light of the fact that this "high and lifted up" language used about men implies that they are proud and idolatrous, and in light of the LORD's determination that he alone should be exalted, it is most instructive that the next time this word pair occurs, it is used in a very positive sense to describe the Servant of the LORD in Isa 52:13: "Behold my servant will act wisely; he will be high [*qal* imperfect of רום], he will be lifted up [*niphal* waw consecutive imperfect of נשא], he will be greatly exalted." In this context, the servant is shown to be a victorious warrior: "Therefore I will allot him a portion with the great; he will divide the spoil with the strong, because he poured out his soul to death" (53:12).

The Defeat of Sennacherib as a Picture of Christ's Victory

Given the parallels we have just noted, it would not be surprising if the LORD's defeat of Sennacherib were taken up by NT writers as a picture of salvation through Christ in the gospel. The "near and far" language of Isa 33:13 is used again in 57:19, which Paul quotes in Eph 2:17, applying it to the invitation to the gospel to both Jew and Gentile, just as both Jew and Gentile were invited to see what the LORD had done in defeating Sennacherib. Paul also described the deliverance brought about through Christ in terms that closely parallel the situation in Jerusalem around 700 B.C.E.: "While we were still helpless, at the right time, Christ died for the ungodly" (Rom 5:6). Jerusalem at the time of Isa 33 was completely helpless; all human means had failed (Hezekiah's allies, his army, his treasure). In the same way, all human means of eternal salvation and all human-devised religion has failed. As in the deliverance of Jerusalem in the time of Hezekiah, "at the right time," that is, at the last possible moment, God provides salvation.

For these reasons, in the course of teaching the book of Isaiah, I taught for several years that the deliverance of Jerusalem from Sennacherib was a picture of the gospel, but all the while I was unaware that Jesus himself pointed in this direction. The relevant text is John 12:31–32:

> *Now* judgment is upon this world; *now* the ruler of this world shall be cast out. And I, if *I be lifted up* from the earth, will draw all men to myself.

"Now . . . now" can be related to the threefold "now" of Isa 33:10. Isaiah, who predicted deliverance from the Assyrians for some thirty years, also predicted the lifting up of the Servant of the LORD seven hundred years before it came to pass. A third "now" occurs in John 13:31: "Now is the Son of Man glorified." "Glorified" and "lifted up" occur together in the LXX of Isa 33:10, where the two Greek verbs (δοξάζω and ὑψόω) translate verbs from the roots רום and נשׂא. They also occur together in Isa 52:13, where they translate the three Hebrew verbs "he will be high, he will be lifted up, he will be greatly exalted."

In John's Gospel, "the ruler of this world" is Satan, not Sennacherib, but we should note how suitable a picture Sennacherib was of the devil, or the antichrist. As a mere person, he presumed to make the same promises for submission, and threats for rebellion, that the LORD himself made to his people in the Law and the Prophets. Sennacherib threatened famine in siege for those who would not surrender (Isa 36:12; cf. Deut 28:53). He promised that if Jerusalem submitted, he would take them away to a fair land (as the LORD promised Israel when they were in Egypt), where each would sit under his own vine and fig tree (which is what the LORD promised his people through Micah and Zechariah; Isa 36:16; Mic 4:4; Zech 3:10).

The phrase, "I will draw all men to myself" in John 12:32 parallels the invitation to those near and far in Isaiah's day to "see what I have done" (Isa 33:13). The context mentions Greeks who wish to see Jesus (John 12:20–21).

The words, "If I be lifted up," refer to the crucifixion. However, when seen in light of the background of Isa 33:10, they imply that Jesus is going into battle; he is going to wage war against the devil. His going to the cross is an act of war. The *via dolorosa*, the way of sorrow, the way to the cross, is the divine warpath, and the victory Christ won there was a far greater deliverance than the striking down of 185,000 soldiers of the Assyrian army, which merely prolonged the earthly life of the people of Judah.

A chronological note is relevant here. As noted, Isa 33:10 is part of the sixth woe of this section of Isaiah (28–35), the first five being pronounced against the LORD's people, especially the leaders of Israel (before its demise) and Judah. In Matt 23:13–36, Jesus repeats this pattern during the passion week by pronouncing seven woes against the hypocritical scribes and Pharisees, drawing on terminology from the first five woes pronounced by Isaiah. Generally, he condemns their blindness (vv. 16, 17, 19, 24, 26), as in Isa 29:9 (cf. 29:18; 32:3; 35:5). Jesus' description of the whitewashed tombs of Matt 23:27 is similar to the first woe, which begins with a condemnation of the outward beauty of Samaria (Isa 28:1, 4). Isa 28:1, which speaks of "the proud crown of the drunkards of Ephraim," compares with Matt 23:11–12 (the greatest shall be servant, he who humbles himself shall be exalted). More specifically, Jesus speaks of "dill and cumin" (v. 23), which is used in a parable in Isa 28:23–29. Jesus then completes the series of parallels in John 12:31–32 by announcing, in effect, the sixth woe, not against Sennacherib, but against "the ruler of this world," the devil himself.

"High and Lifted Up" in Isaiah and "Lifted Up" in John

To confirm that Jesus' statement, "If I be lifted up," should be understood in light of Isa 33:10, we can note that there are a number of connections between the various "high and lifted up" passages in Isaiah and the various passages in John where Jesus speaks of himself being lifted up. We have already seen that this language is used in Isa 6:1; 33:10; and 52:13. A fourth occasion is 57:15: "Thus says the one who is high and lifted up, who dwells forever, whose name is holy; 'I dwell in a high and holy place, yet also with him who is contrite and lowly in spirit, to revive the spirit of the lowly, and to revive the heart of the contrite.'" In four places in John's Gospel, Jesus speaks of his being "lifted up." Since each of these refers to the same event, the crucifixion, one might conclude that each of them is based on the "lifted up" of Isa 52:13. The fact is, however, that each of the four "lifted up" passages of John can be related to a different "high and lifted up" passage in Isaiah with which it shares verbal and contextual associations.

John 3:14 and Isa 52:13

The first "lifted up" passage in John is 3:14, where Jesus says to Nicodemus, "As Moses lifted up the serpent in the wilderness, so must the Son of Man be lifted up." This statement can most obviously be related to Isa 52:13, since the fourth Servant Song portrays the servant in several ways as one who is suffering under the curse of God, like the serpent (Gen 3:15).

Isa 53:5 says he was "pierced through for our transgressions." "Pierced through" is a *poal* participle from חלל. We find a *poel* participle of the same root used in Isa 51:9, "Awake, awake, put on strength, O arm of the LORD; awake, as in days of old. Was it not you who cut Rahab in pieces, who pierced the dragon?" The next verse makes it clear that the crossing of the Red Sea is in view: "Was it not you who dried up the sea, the waters of the great deep; who made the depths of the sea a pathway for the redeemed to cross over?"

"Rahab" can be a nickname for Egypt (e.g., Isa 30:7) but is also a name of the devil. This is clearest in Job 26:12–13: "By his power he stilled the sea, and by his understanding he shattered Rahab. By his breath the heavens were cleared; his hand pierced the evil serpent." "Pierced" is again from the root חלל (here a *poel* perfect verb). The adjective "evil" does not appear in any translation of which I am aware, but this meaning, suggested first by Cyrus Gordon, was confirmed more than twenty years ago in the ancient Eblaite language, and a Janus parallelism was noticed that uses a verb from the same root (ברח) in Job 9:25. A Janus parallelism exists when a word has two meanings and a parallel is drawn to each of them. The two meanings of the verb evident in Job 9:25 are "flee" (the well-known meaning) and "to be evil": "My days are swifter than a runner. They flee away/they are evil; they see no good." The meaning "flee" points back to "swifter," while the meaning "are evil" points forward to "they see no good."[6]

What Isa 51:9 refers to, then, is the defeat of Satan, which is involved in the defeat of his spiritual offspring (cf. Gen 3:15), the Egyptians, at the Red Sea. This was an example of the "arm of the LORD" in action. But now the arm of the LORD (Isa 53:1) is directed at piercing his servant, who is thus treated like the devil, under the curse of God.

Similarly, Isa 53:5 says the servant was "crushed" for our iniquities, and v. 10 says it pleased the LORD to crush him (using the same Hebrew word). This verb (*piel/pual* of דכא) is also used for what the LORD did to Satan at the Red Sea: "You yourself crushed Rahab like one slain; with your strong arm you scattered your enemies" (Ps 89:10). *Tg. Ps.* 89:10 uses the Aramaic verb שפי, which Marcus Jastrow related to the rare Hebrew verb used in Gen 3:15 (שוף), "He will strike you on the head, and you will strike him on the heel."[7]

Another way in which the servant is shown to be suffering as one cursed is in Isa 52:14, "Just as many were astonished at you (Israel), so his appearance was marred more than any man." That the nations would be astonished at the LORD's judgment on Israel (i.e., exile and all that went with it) was predicted in the covenant curses (Lev 26:32), and here we read that people are likewise astonished at what happens to Isaiah's servant; he appears to be suffering under the same kind of judgment.

John 8:28 and Isa 6:1

"When you lift up the Son of Man, then you will know that I am he" (John 8:28). Again, since Jesus is referring to his crucifixion, there is an obvious connec-

---

[6] The meaning "evil" for the adjective בָּרַח was suggested by Cyrus H. Gordon based on Arabic ("Near East Seals in Princeton and Philadelphia," *Orientalia* 22 [1953]: 243–44). The Eblaite/Sumerian confirmation was brought out by Alfonso Archi, "Les textes lexicaux bilingues d'Ebla," *Studi Eblaiti* 2 (1980): 81–89. The Janus parallelism was noted by Eduardo Zurro, "Disemia de *brh* y paralelismo bifronte en Job 9,25," *Biblica* 62 (1981): 546–47. See Ronning, "Curse on the Serpent," 137–38. My external reader Gary Rendsburg drew my attention to this material.

[7] Marcus Jastrow, *A Dictionary of the Targumim, the Talmud Bibli, and Yerushalmi, and the Midrashic Literature* (New York: Putnam, 1903), 1614.

tion to Isa 52:13 here. In addition, however, we can relate this saying specifically to Isa 6:1. There Isaiah says, "I saw the Lord, sitting on a throne, high and lifted up, with the train of his robe filling the temple." John 8:28 is also spoken in the temple, where Jesus is identifying himself as the LORD with his multiple "I am he" sayings. We have already examined these sayings (ch. 3), and we explore them in more detail in ch. 9, where it is confirmed that "the style of the sentence is that of Divine proclamations."[8]

We can also see a contextual similarity between the two texts. Isaiah is commissioned in ch. 6 to a ministry met primarily with unbelief and apostasy. In John 8:28, Jesus is likewise predicting an act of apostasy—"when you lift up the Son of Man."

John 12:32 and Isa 33:10

The connections between these two texts have been noted above.

John 12:34 and Isa 57:15

The crowd then answered him, "We have heard out of the Law that the Christ is to remain forever; and how can you say, 'The Son of Man must be lifted up'? Who is this 'Son of Man'?" (John 12:34). Possibly they were thinking of Isa 9:6–7, which speaks of one who will sit on the throne of David forever. One of his names is "Eternal Father" (אֲבִי עַד). However, a fourth "high and lifted up" text in Isaiah also speaks of one who "remains forever": "Thus says the one who is high and lifted up, who dwells forever, whose name is Holy, 'I dwell on a high and holy place, yet also with the contrite and lowly of spirit, to revive the spirit of the lowly, and to revive the heart of the contrite" (Isa 57:15). The phrase, "dwells forever," is from the Hebrew שֹׁכֵן עַד, which can be compared to "Eternal Father" of Isa 9:6. "High and lifted up" in 57:15 is identical to the phrase in 6:1, and "whose name is Holy" seems to be a clear reference to 6:3.

In this case, it is not only the words of Jesus themselves that point to the relevant text in Isaiah, since the words quoted by the crowd are virtually identical to those of John 3:14, but rather the context of the crowd's question as well. The answer to the question comes from Isa 57:15, which says that the one who is "lifted up" also "dwells forever"; there is no contradiction between the two ideas.

Not only are two of the four "high and lifted up" texts of Isaiah alluded to in the space of a few verses in John 12, but John goes on to refer to the context of the other two "high and lifted up" passages, which he ties together by another common theme, that of unbelief. In the first (12:38), John quotes Isa 53:1 ("Lord, who has believed our report?") to show that the majority's unbelief in Jesus, far from being an indication that Jesus is not the real Christ, is a fulfillment of prophecy. Isaiah 53:1, of course, is just three verses after "My servant will prosper; he will be high and lifted up, and greatly exalted." John then goes on to explain the unbelief

---

[8] J. H. Bernard, *A Critical and Exegetical Commentary on the Gospel according to St. John* (2 vols.; ICC; New York: Charles Scribner's Sons, 1929), 2:303.

of the majority on the basis of Isa 6:10, spoken to Isaiah when he saw the Lord high and lifted up in the temple. John comments that Isaiah said these things "because he saw his (Christ's) glory," confirming that the one seen by Isaiah high and lifted up in the temple is the one seen by the Jews in the temple and predicting that he would be lifted up (John 8:28).

Seen against these parallels in Isaiah, we are warranted in understanding John 12:31–32 as the divine warrior's announcement that he is again going to war on behalf of his people, not to deliver them from a temporal foe like Sennacherib or to secure a temporal salvation, but to deliver them eternally from the power of the devil. John shows Jesus' followers that in the work of Christ there is a deeper fulfillment of Isa 31:4, "The Lord of Hosts will come down and wage war on Mt. Zion." He "came down" in the incarnation (John 6:38), and waged war as a servant, in his suffering.

The Word of the Lord and the Defeat of Sennacherib

Though John's dependence on warrior themes in Isaiah is clear enough in its own right, the Targum of Isaiah makes these parallels even more explicit by attributing the actions of the divine warrior to the Word of the Lord. *Targum Isaiah 33:11* ascribes the victory to the Word of the Lord: "Because of your evil deeds, my Word, as the whirlwind the chaff, will destroy you" (MT: "Your breath, a fire will consume you"). It is not evident in the Targum that this chapter is directed against the Assyrians, however ("you" in v. 11 refers to the Gentiles).

Targum Isaiah 33:10 does not speak of the Word of the Lord arising, being lifted up, etc. It is not hard to imagine a "Palestinian" Targum of Isa 33:10 that might have said something like "Now I, in my Word, shall arise; now I, in my Word, will be exalted; now I, in my Word, will be lifted up," though one would not need such a Targum to relate John 12:31–32 to Isa 33:10, as the link is clear enough in a literal translation of the two passages. We will see in the next section that another saying of Jesus can be related to the first biblical text that speaks of the Lord arising (Num 10:35, mentioned above), and some *Pal. Tgs.* do indeed speak of the Word of the Lord arising (or being revealed). One could also imagine a "Palestinian" version of Isa 31:4 reading, "So will the Word of the Lord of Hosts be revealed, and he will wage war on Mt. Zion." Elsewhere John uses similar language: "The Son of God was revealed, . . . to destroy the works of the devil" (1 John 3:8). Our extant *Tg. Isa.* 31:4 says "the kingdom of the Lord will be revealed to settle upon Mt. Zion and upon its hill."

In other Targum passages, the defeat of Sennacherib or the Assyrians is ascribed to the divine Word. *Targum Isaiah 10:17*, speaking of the defeat of the king of Assyria (mentioned in v. 16), says, "The master of the light of Israel and his Holy One, his Word, will be strong as the fire, and his words as the flame, and he will kill and destroy his rulers and his tyrants in one day" (MT: "The light of Israel will become a fire, and his Holy One a flame, and it will burn and devour his thorns and his briars in a single day"). *Targum Isaiah 30:31* says, "At the voice of the Word of the Lord (MT: "At the voice of the Lord") the Assyrian will be broken." In *Tg.*

Isa. 36:7, Rabshakeh says, "If you say to me, 'We trust in the Word of the LORD our God (for protection from the Assyrians)'"; v. 15 and *Tg. 2 Kgs.* 18:22, 30 are similar.

Targum Second Kings 18:5 says that Hezekiah trusted in the Word of the LORD; this was the reason for his success and his motivation for rebelling against Assyria. In *Tg. 2 Kgs.* 19:28, the LORD's message to Sennacherib is that "you have provoked my Word," and he therefore will be turned back. In v. 31, the promise of recovery from the Assyrian campaign is to be accomplished "by the Word of the LORD of Hosts" (MT: "the zeal of the LORD of Hosts").

Targum Second Chronicles 32:1 says that the LORD decided in (or through) his Word to bring Sennacherib to Israel so that he might destroy him. In *Tg. 2 Chr.* 32:8, Hezekiah encourages his people by saying that Sennacherib has the support only of the strength of flesh, "but for our help is the Word of the LORD, to help us and to wage our wars." In *Tg. 2 Chr.* 32:16, Sennacherib's servants "spoke rebellion against the Word of the LORD God" (MT: "spoke against the LORD God"). Verse 21 says that the Word of the LORD sent Gabriel on Passover night to destroy the Assyrians. So it is possible that many of the Jews listening to Jesus in John 12, having come to Jerusalem for the Passover, were also remembering and speaking about what the LORD did in defeating Sennacherib, which was believed to have happened at Passover. As mentioned above, Hos 1:7 promises deliverance for Judah in terms similar to Isa 31:8, not by human means of warfare, "but by the LORD their God," or, in the Targum, "by the Word of the LORD their God." For John, when the Word became flesh, he promised an even greater deliverance.

I mentioned above the promise of deliverance from Assyria in Isa 8:8–10. According to Isaiah, Assyria will sweep like a flood into Immanuel's land (v. 8), but they will be shattered "because God is with us" (v. 10). Those who lived at that time might have expected that this Immanuel would have something to do with the deliverance of Jerusalem. We can see from Mic 5:2 that they would be correct. This passage promises a future savior who will come forth from Bethlehem, but "whose goings forth are from of old, from ancient times" (or, "from days of eternity").

Some modern translations render the word "goings forth" as "origins," so that the verse is not speaking of the preexistence of the Messiah, but of his genealogical origins in David and Bethlehem. Of course, to state that someone's genealogical origins were ancient would merely state the obvious. Such is true of all people, and Israelites kept track of their ancient origins. Even to say that one's origins go back to David would be saying very little; after two hundred years of royal polygamy it is likely that many people in Judah could trace some branch of their ancestry back to David. In terms of qualifications, it would be much more significant to trace one's ancestry to the current reigning Davidic king.

The word in question (מוֹצָאֹתָיו) occurs only here in the OT, so its meaning cannot be firmly established. It is of interest, however, that the LXX translates it with the word "exodus," "going forth," which is used for the LORD going forth to war in Judg 5:4. This meaning fits well with what we see in John 12:31–32, where Jesus speaks as one who has done it before. In fact, this may be the meaning of John 12:28, where Jesus says, "Father, glorify your name," and a voice from heaven answers, "I both have glorified it (e.g., in the deliverance of Hezekiah) and will glorify it again (in Jesus' going to the cross)." Hezekiah was delivered, in targumic terms, by the Word of the LORD, in a temporal salvation. Now the Word of the LORD has become flesh, for the believer's (and Hezekiah's) eternal salvation.

John 14:2–3; Jesus Prepares a Place for His People

In John 14:2–3, Jesus says to the disciples, "I go to prepare a place for you," and promises that he will return. As in the case of John 12:31–32, the military nature of this statement is not obvious unless we see the connection to the relevant OT passage, which is Num 10:35–36. We get to this passage via Deut 1:32–33, which shares with John 14 the theme of faith and the idea of preparing a place:

John 14:1–3, 6	Believe in God, believe also in me. . . . I go to prepare a place for you. . . . I am the way.
Deut 1:32–33	You did not believe in the LORD your God, who goes before you on your way, *to search out* a place for you to camp.[9]
***Tg. Neof.* Deut 1:32–33**	You did not believe in the name of the Word of the LORD your God, who led before you in the way *to prepare* for you a place for your encampment. (*Tgs. Ps.-J.* and *Onq.* read similarly, except that they omit "the name of.")

The change of "to *search out* a place for you" to "to *prepare* for you a place" is in keeping with the slightly different situation in which Jesus is making the promise. But it also agrees with the change made by the targumists in Deut 1:33, presumably to avoid the anthropomorphism of God searching.[10] As is often the case, the targumic substitute is not chosen arbitrarily but is taken from elsewhere in Scripture, in this case most likely from Exod 23:20: "I am sending my angel before you to guard you along the way, and to bring you into the place which I have prepared" (Heb.: הֲכִנֹתִי; LXX: ἑτοιμάζω, as in John 14:2). None of the Targums of Exod 23:20 involve the divine Word in preparing the promised land for God's people, but Deut 11:12 expresses a similar idea as Exod 23:20, describing the promised land as "a land which the LORD your God inquires after," to which *Tg. Ps.-J.* adds, "by his Word."

Moses is speaking in Deut 1:32–33 of the rebellion of Num 14, but the language about the LORD going before the Israelites to search out a place for them goes back to Israel's original departure from Mt. Sinai. Numbers 10:33 says that they set out from the mountain of the LORD on a three days' journey, with the ark of the covenant going before them *to search out* a resting place for them. All the Targums change "search out" to "prepare."

---

[9] Raymond E. Brown, *The Gospel According to John: Introduction, Translation, and Notes* (Anchor Bible 29A [xiii–xxii]; Garden City: Doubleday, 1970), 625.

[10] McNamara pointed out the connection between the Targums and John 14:2 (with respect to the change from "search" to "prepare") and noted that the same change is found in the Peshitta (*Palestinian Judaism*, 239–40).

Verses 35–36 record Moses' petitions whenever the ark set out and came to rest, and it is instructive to compare these petitions, especially as rendered in the *Pal. Tgs.*, with the situation in John 14.

> MT: [35]When the ark set out, Moses said, "Rise up, O LORD, and let your enemies be scattered. Let those who hate you flee before you." [36]And when it came to rest, he would say, "Return, O LORD, to the myriad thousands of Israel" (Num 10:35–36).

> *Tg. Neof.:* [35]When the ark set out, Moses spoke and prayed, and he said, "Arise please, O LORD, and let your enemies be scattered, and let those who hate you flee from before you." [36]And when it came to rest, Moses would pray, saying, "Turn, please, O LORD, from the might of your anger, and return to us in your good mercies, and make the glory of your *Shekinah* dwell in the midst of the thousands and myriads, and bless the thousands of the sons of Israel."

> *Tg. Neof.* [mg.]: [35]When the ark used to set out, Moses would raise his hands in prayer, and say, "Arise please, his Word, in the strength of your might."

> *Tg. Ps.-J.:* [35]When the ark desired to set out . . . he (Moses) said, "Let the Word of the LORD be now revealed in the power of your anger, and let the enemies of your people be scattered, and let those who hate them not have a foot to stand before you." [36]And when the ark desired to rest, . . . he said, "Return now, O Word of the LORD, in your good mercy, and lead the people of Israel, and let the Glory of your *Shekinah* dwell among them, and have compassion on [*or* love ורחים] the myriads of the house of Jacob, the multitudes of the thousands of Israel."

> *Frg. Tg. V:* [35]And when the ark would set out, Moses would raise his hands in prayer and say, "Arise, please, O Word of the LORD, in your mighty strength, and let the enemies of your people be scattered, and let those who hate you flee from before you." [36]And when the ark would rest, Moses would raise his hands in prayer and say, "Turn, please, O Word of the LORD, from your mighty wrath, and return to us in your good mercies, and bless the myriads, and multiply the thousands of the Israelites." (*Frg. Tg. P* only has v. 36, which is similar to *Frg. Tg. V* but has "LORD" instead of "Word of the LORD.")

People commonly take Jesus' promise, "I will come again," in John 14:3 as referring to the second coming, but commentators generally recognize that a more immediate coming is in view. In v. 19, for example, Jesus tells the disciples they will see him again. In v. 23 he promises that he and the Father will come to the one who keeps his word and dwell with that person. Jesus is promising to return to them on the third day.

As in the initial departure from Mt. Sinai, the divine Word is going on a three-day journey, going ahead of his disciples to prepare a place for his people, answering the plea of Moses in Num 10:35–36 and even the synagogue embellishments of that prayer, by scattering his enemies and those of his people, and he will return and bless and dwell among and love his people. Again we see that the *via dolorosa* is the divine warpath, from which Jesus will return victorious in three days, having prepared a place for his people. The way to the cross is not simply an ordeal or even a sacrifice, but also an offensive action carried to the enemy's camp, like Israel's assault on Jericho during the Passover season.

The connection between this passage and Num 10:33–36 may also help explain why Jesus says to the disciples, "You know the way where I am going" (John 14:4), whereas they claim that they do not know it (v. 5). Which is it? The way Jesus is going is a way he has traveled before, as "the Word of the LORD," about which they have heard descriptions in the synagogue from childhood. They know this way, but they may not yet have equated it with the way of which Jesus is speaking.

In John's account of Jesus' adaptation of the three-day journey from Sinai to his impending work in going to the cross, there are some differences that emerge. Israel followed the (Word of the) LORD during those three days, whereas Jesus' disciples cannot now follow him on this journey: "Where I go, you cannot follow me now; but you will follow later" (13:36). In the context of Num 10:33–36, the warfare carried out by the LORD is against human enemies (as in the case of Sennacherib discussed above): "Let your enemies be scattered, let those who hate you flee before you." By contrast, while Jesus does speak in the upper room of those who hate him (John 15:18, 23), his divine warfare will ultimately be against Satan himself and is to be accomplished by allowing those who hate him to put him to death. The adaptation from "your enemies" (Num 10:35) to "the ruler of the world" (John 14:30) is facilitated by a play on words in the Aramaic between "your enemies" in *Tg. Neof.* Num 10:35, בעלי דבבך (lit.: "masters of your enmity," idiomatic for "your enemies") and the name Beelzebub.[11]

The double interpretation (a typical practice of the Targums) of the Heb שׁוּבָה from the MT of Num 10:36 given in *Tg. Neof.* and *Frg. Tgs.* is also worthy of note. "Return" is translated both as "turn from your wrath" and "return to us," which fits perfectly the mission of Christ going to the cross to turn away the wrath of God from sinners and then returning to his disciples to bless, love, and dwell among them.

There is an evident connection between the *Pal. Tg.* renderings of Num 10:35–36 and John 14, portraying Jesus as the divine Word who is the divine Warrior. Once we see this, the appropriateness of the name "the Word of God" given to the returning, war-waging Christ in Rev 19:13 becomes clear. The connection is further strengthened when we remember that the visible symbol of the LORD going before his people in the wilderness as to war was the pillar of fire and cloud, in which the Word of the LORD shone upon his people according to *Tg. Neof.* and *Frg. Tg. P* Exod 13:21–22. In chapter one, we saw how this forms the conceptual background for John 1:4–5 (light of the Word shining and in conflict with darkness).[12]

---

[11] Peggy L. Day argues that it is on the basis of this wordplay that Beelzebub/ul became identified with Satan, a view which she traces back to E. K. A. Riehm, 1893. She finds support for this position in the fact that בעל דבבא originated in Aramaic as an Akkadian loanword meaning "accuser in court," which parallels the meaning of Hebrew שָׂטָן (see Ronning, "Curse on the Serpent," 19 n.47, commenting on Peggy L. Day, *An Adversary in Heaven: śāṭān in the Hebrew Bible* [Harvard Semitic Monographs 43; Atlanta: Scholars Press, 1988]), 152–59.

[12] In his *New Testament and the Palestinian Targum*, McNamara wrote that Rev 19:13a, 15b was "clearly dependent on Is 63, 1–6" (p. 231). Later, in his book *Palestinian Judaism,* he seems to have changed his mind ("It seems fairly certain that here the author is drawing on

In the next chapter, we will see that the portrayal of Jesus as warrior in Rev 19:13 grows out of the depiction of the divine warrior in Isa 59 and 63, where the Targum employs the concept of the divine Word.

ANOTHER LOOK AT JOSHUA 4 AND 2 SAMUEL 15

I mentioned above that in drawing out the parallels between the path of Jesus at the beginning and end of his ministry and the paths of Joshua at the Jordan and David at the Kidron, I left out the most important part. Perhaps after reading the section above, the reader can figure what was left out.

We saw that Jesus was at the same place as Joshua, and doing the same kind of things, and we saw how this fit in with and supplemented the synoptic material in recapitulating Israel's history at the Red Sea, the wilderness, and the Jordan. Of course, the crossing of the Jordan is not primarily about Joshua. We read in Josh 3:1–11 about the ark of the covenant going on ahead of the Israelites to the Jordan. It is when the feet of the priests carrying the ark touch the water that the water is cut off. "The (Red) Sea saw, and fled; the Jordan turned back" (Ps 114:3), not at the presence of Joshua, but of the LORD. The ark represented the presence of God among his people, and the ark going before them, as we saw above, represents the divine warrior going at the head of his army to defeat his foes. In the language of the Targums, the *Shekinah* dwelt, and the Word spoke, from between the cherubim, above the mercy seat of the ark. The parallels between the baptism of Jesus and *Tg. Ps.-J.* Num 7:89, which describes the Spirit descending over the ark to the place between the cherubim, and the Word speaking to Moses from there (see ch. 1 on John 1:32–33), confirm that this is the Word of whom John speaks in his Prologue.

The point is simply that in his return to the Jordan, Jesus is not just following the ancient path of his human namesake Joshua, but his own ancient path; the path of the pre-incarnate Word who has now become flesh, a man like Joshua. Joshua and Israel crossed the Jordan, but the ark of the covenant (thus also the divine Word in Targum thought) stayed in the Jordan while Israel crossed.

Similarly, in 2 Sam 15, where we saw that Jesus follows the same path as David, crossing the Kidron and going up the Mount of Olives, David and Jesus both being objects of betrayal. Again, however, we see that the path of David and Jesus was also the path of the ark. Second Samuel 15:24 relates how Zadok the high priest met David after crossing the Kidron, along with "all the Levites with him carrying the ark." Thus in leaving Jerusalem to the east and crossing the Kidron to the Mount of Olives, Jesus is retracing the path of the invisible Word of one thousand years before. But now the Word has become flesh, a person subject to betrayal and persecution, as was David.

---

the Wisdom of Solomon 18:14–16") and did not see Christ portrayed as the warring Word in the Gospel ("The term logos as applied here [Rev 19:13] to Christ has little in common with John 1:1–14" (p. 235).

There is, however, a difference between Josh 3–4 and 2 Sam 15. The paths of Joshua and the ark of the LORD may have been identical, but the path of David coincided with that of the ark only to a point, and that point is the Mount of Olives. There David sends Zadok with the ark back to Jerusalem (2 Sam 15:25–26). David recognizes this is not about him:

> Return the ark of God to the city. If I find favor in the sight of the LORD, then he will bring me back again, and show me both it and his dwelling place. But if he should say thus, "I have no delight in you," behold, here I am. Let him do to me as seems good in his sight.

If David dies, the LORD still reigns from Jerusalem. The LORD can bring David safely back to Jerusalem whether the ark is with him or not; the ark is for the nation, not just him.

Hereafter the paths of David and Jesus diverge. David is fleeing, and continues to flee, past the Mount of Olives, across the Jordan, then north, while the ark is taken back to Jerusalem. While Jesus had been following the path of both David and the ark when going to the Mount of Olives, now he follows the path of the ark (again, his own path as the targumic Word of one thousand years before), returning to Jerusalem. This time it is not the loyal high priest and Levites escorting him to his place of enthronement, however, but rather "officers from the chief priests and the Pharisees" (John 18:3) who have come to arrest him and have him put to death, as Absalom desired to do to David.

Why did David flee across the Jordan? To save his life. Why did Jesus not flee, but willingly return to Jerusalem? To give his life. Or to put it another way, for the very reason David fled, Jesus returned to Jerusalem to save David's life, and ours, eternally. David says, "If I find favor in the sight of the LORD, he will bring me back again and show me . . . his dwelling place." But how can David find favor in the sight of the LORD? By Jesus returning to Jerusalem "to give his life as a ransom for many" (Mark 10:45).

As noted previously, David had to flee for his life because he had been betrayed and his life was in danger. But an even more significant reason is that David was experiencing the judgment of God because of his sin against Uriah: "The sword shall not depart from your house, because you have despised me and have taken the wife of Uriah the Hittite to be your wife" (2 Sam 12:10). Jesus returned to Jerusalem to pay for such sins of those who believe in him, so that they might find favor in the sight of the LORD, and he might show them his eternal dwelling place.

When considering these OT texts about Joshua and David in light of their similarities to John's Gospel, I left out the most important part for propaedeutic reasons. I wanted to show how easy it is to see only a small part of the picture. The typical evangelical treatment of the subject of "Christ in the Old Testament" is confined to, or at least majors on, messianic prophecy and human typology. That is, the emphasis (often exclusive) is on the one who is to come, with little or no notice given to the fact that the one who is coming is one "whose goings forth are from of old, even from days of eternity."

JOHN 18:2–9; THE DISCIPLES SAVED BY THE PRESENCE OF THE LORD

When the officers come to arrest Jesus he asks them, "Whom do you seek?" and they say, "Jesus the Nazarene" (John 18:4–5). When he answers, "I am he," John says, "they drew back and fell to the ground." The sequence of actions of the enemies of Jesus parallels that of David's enemies in Ps 9:3: "When my enemies turn back, they stumble, and perish at your presence." In this case, the divine presence is indicated by "I am he," which on the one hand appears to be simply an identification as Jesus the Nazarene, but on the other hand must be related to the "I am he" of John 13:19, the prediction of that which is now taking place, and which sounds so much like the divine "I am he" of Isa 43:10.

One might object that the third action in the psalm, "they perish," does not apply to Jesus' enemies. In fact, they have come to make him perish and they seem to succeed. Of course, if they had perished then and there in the garden, we would perish too, since there would be no gospel. Judas did perish shortly afterward, and the fact that the officers drew back and fell to the ground was a sign that they also were in danger of perishing eternally. If the wording of *Tg. Ps.-J.* Num 10:35 noted above was found in first-century Targums, witnesses of their falling to the ground may have also remembered that passage: "Let the Word of the LORD be revealed . . . and let those who hate them (i.e., the LORD's people) not have a foot to stand before you."

We can also see parallels between David's experience in Ps 9 and the experience of the disciples. John takes note of the fact that Jesus saved their lives (John 18:8–9). That is, the disciples are saved by the presence of the LORD, as David spoke of his own experience. David went on to say that his deliverance was a result of the LORD vindicating him, sitting on his throne, judging righteously (Ps 9:4). In other words, Ps 9:4, as experienced by the disciples, can be interpreted sequentially: "You have accomplished my right and my cause (that is, by Jesus giving himself over to the will of his enemies, instead of making them perish right then and there, since there was a greater enemy that needed to be defeated first); you sat down on the throne, judging righteously" (at the ascension to the Father's right hand). The officers came to Gethsemane to make Jesus, the Word of the Lord, perish, but, as some mss of *Tg. Ps.* 9:7 say, "As for the Word of the LORD, his seat is in the highest heaven forever."

The situation in Gethsemane can be compared to the capture of the ark by the Philistines in 1 Sam 4. The Philistines interpreted this as a defeat for the God of Israel (vv. 8–9), but the broader narrative clarifies that it was the sins of the Israelites that led to the ark being captured. Likewise, our sins necessitated Jesus' being taken captive at this point. Both situations seem to represent a significant defeat, yet in both there are signs of military triumph. In 1 Sam 5, the LORD's triumph is indicated by what happens to the Philistine cities where the ark is taken, and by the fate of the idol of Dagon, which fell on its face and lost its hands and head due to the presence of the ark. The Egyptians cut off the hands of those they defeated in battle, to count those slain. The Assyrians cut off their heads. Both acts are done to Dagon.

Likewise, in John 18 Jesus appears to be defeated, but the actions of those who came to arrest him, and his saving the lives of his disciples, show that the reality is far different. In fact, one could say that these events at the Mount of Olives presage future events in which "The LORD will go forth (*Tg.*: "be revealed"; cf. John 18:4: "Jesus went forth") and fight against these nations, as he fights on a day of battle. On that day, his feet shall stand on the Mount of Olives" (Zech 14:3–4).

JOHN 19; THE WARRIOR PRIEST-KING IS
ANOINTED AND DOES BATTLE

The Anointing of Jesus as Priest-King

The contrast between reality and appearances continues into John 19. The first five verses describe how Pilate allowed Jesus to be scourged, dressed mockingly as a king in a royal (purple) robe and a crown of thorns, hailed mockingly as king, struck on the face, and finally presented as innocent before the people. As Jesus appears, Pilate says, "Behold the man."

The soldiers' intention was to mock Jesus and perhaps to take out on him their hatred of the Jews in general, inspired by previous rebellions and murders of Roman soldiers. Pilate's purpose was to appease the crowd, since he did not want to put Jesus to death. He was essentially asking them, "Have I not punished him enough already?" But what is God's purpose?

John, drawing from themes in targumic interpretation, may have been using irony to prefigure in this incident the anointing of Jesus as king and priest according to the order of Melchizedek. Just as Caiaphas "prophesied" that Jesus would die for the nation, Pilate's words may contain a deeper meaning.

"Behold the man" has been related by some to Zech 6:12, "Behold a man whose name is Branch; for he will branch out from where he is, and he will build the temple of the LORD." In this setting, the high priest Joshua is being addressed, and he has a crown of silver and gold on his head and is presumably wearing his priestly garments. The oracle goes on to say, "Yes, it is he who will build the temple of the LORD, and he who will bear the honor, and sit and rule on his throne. Thus he will be a priest on his throne, and the counsel of peace will be between the two of them."

Some translations (e.g., ESV) avoid the idea that Joshua represents the Messiah who is both priest and king. The title "Branch" for the Messiah was previously used in Isa 4:2; Jer 23:5; 33:15; and Zech 3:8. In the latter, it is clear that Joshua is not the Branch, but a symbol of "my servant the Branch" who is to come. Yet it is hard to avoid seeing the connections between this passage and Ps 110. Joshua the high priest has a royal crown (not the priestly turban) on his head. Likewise David's Lord in Ps 110 sits at the right hand of God as king, yet is also called a priest according to the order of Melchizedek. Melchizedek was the king-priest who brought out bread and wine to Abraham after his defeat of the coalition of kings who took Lot captive (Gen 14:18).

It was not unusual in those days for a pagan king to also be priest, but it was strictly forbidden for the king of Israel to be a priest to the LORD, as the examples of Saul and Uzziah show. Consequently, Psalm 110 must have seemed quite mysterious in OT times. What were the priestly activities of David's Lord? Nothing seems to be said of them in the psalm itself, which otherwise is all about his victory over his enemies. Zechariah 6 does not seem to answer this question, but the allusions to Ps 110 are hard to miss. The Messiah not only is a priest, but also will "sit and rule" (Zech 6:13), as the LORD says to David's Lord, "Sit at my right hand . . . rule in the midst of your enemies" (Ps 110:1–2). He can be both priest and king because in him there is no conflict between the two offices: "He will be a priest on his throne, and the counsel of peace will be between the two (offices)" (Zech 6:13). "Peace" in this context would also remind us of Solomon (whose name means "his peace"), who built the first temple after the victories of David, and of Melchizedek, king of Salem (Salem is similar to the Hebrew word for "peace") and of the messianic name "Prince of Peace" (Isa 9:6).

Zechariah 3:8 calls him "my servant the Branch," which may be a combination of the "Branch" title of Isa 4:2 and "my Servant" of the Servant Songs of Isaiah. Isaiah 52:13–53:12 is complementary to Ps 110 in that while Ps 110 has just one verse mentioning him as a priest, the rest describing him as a victorious warrior, Isa 52:13–53:12 has just one verse describing him as victorious warrior (53:12), the rest describing his priestly activity of bearing our sins as a guilt offering, pouring out his life to death. The two passages taken together make it clear that the Messiah's priestly activities are not separate from, but part of, his victorious warfare.

We can also see this combination of priestly and kingly activity if we look at four "behold" declarations about Jesus in John's Gospel, two by John the Baptist at the beginning of Jesus' ministry, and two by Pilate at the end:

1:29: Behold the Lamb of God, who takes away the sin of the world!

1:36: Behold the Lamb of God!

19:5: Behold the man!

19:14: Behold your king!

Pilate's declarations describe Jesus as the messianic priest-king by (unwitting) reference to Zech 6:12, while John's declarations describe his priestly activities.

Although some have said that John the Baptist's comments were not referring to substitutionary atonement, yet the clear connections of his words to OT texts make such a conclusion seem unavoidable. First, we recall Isaac's question to Abraham, "Behold, the fire and the wood, but where is the lamb for the burnt offering?" (Gen 22:7), and Abraham's prophetic answer, "God will provide for himself the lamb for the burnt offering, my son" (v. 8). God did provide a ram as an immediate substitute for Isaac, but there is a greater answer to Isaac's question, "Where is the lamb?" John gives that answer in his declaration, "Behold the Lamb of God."

Further, the phrase "takes away the sin of the world" points to Isa 53:4 ("Surely our griefs he himself bore") and 12 ("He bore the sin of many"). Isaiah's servant is likened to "a lamb led to the slaughter" (v. 7) who makes himself a guilt offering, which in the Law could be a lamb (v. 10; cf. Lev 5:6–7; 16). The Hebrew verb for "bore" in Isa 53:4, 12 is נשא, used commonly in the Law of one who must bear his own guilt for some offense. It is also used in Lev 10:17 of the sin offering, which is "to bear away the guilt of the congregation, to make atonement for them," and for the scapegoat bearing away the sins of the congregation into the wilderness (16:22).

The Greek verb translated "takes away" (αἴρω) in John the Baptist's declaration in John 1:29 is not the same as the ones that the LXX uses in Isa 53:4 and 12 (φέρω, ἀναφέρω) or in the passages in the Law that speak of bearing guilt. This might seem to weaken the case for connecting John 1:29, 36 to Isa 53. However, the majority of times in which αἴρω appears in the LXX, it is translating נשא. Recall that it is the *niphal* of this root that appears in the "lifted up" passages of Isaiah that we looked at above.

Finally, "the Lamb of God" points to Jesus as the Passover lamb. This connection is evident from John 19:36, "Not a bone of it shall be broken," which quotes the regulation of the Passover lamb from Exod 12:46 and Num 9:12.[13] While it is true that the legislation concerning the Passover lamb does not describe it as taking away sin, the original Passover lambs were slain as substitutes for the Israelite firstborn. Further, the Passover meal served as a model for the communion ordinance that remembers Christ's sacrificial death. Finally, the fact that the OT Passover lamb was not explicitly described as a sacrifice for sin did not keep Paul from saying, "Christ our Passover lamb has been sacrificed" (1 Cor 5:7). Such a statement is completely reasonable given his understanding that Jesus is "the Lamb of God who takes away the sin of the world," based on Gen 22 (Isaac as a model of the lamb), Isa 53, and the Passover lamb.[14]

The connection between Zechariah's statement and John's Gospel is made even more explicit when the former is viewed in light of the Targums. *Targum Zechariah 6:12* says, "Behold the man whose name is Messiah. He will be revealed, and he shall be anointed."[15] Perhaps some of those who heard Pilate, who believed that Jesus was the Messiah, thought of this passage as they heard Pilate's declaration. We can see some similarities between the anointing of OT kings and priests

---

[13] There is less agreement with Ps 34:20, though it is quite possible that we should consider all three passages as being referred to by John.

[14] Reim, *Alttestamentlichen Hintergrund*, 51–54.

[15] In The Aramaic Bible, the last verb (ויתרבי) is translated "he shall be raised up" (Kevin K. Cathcart and Robert P. Gordon, *The Targum of the Minor Prophets* [ArBib 14; Collegeville, Minn.: Liturgical Press, 1989], 198). The authors note Samson H. Levey's translation as "(destined) to be anointed" (*The Messiah: An Aramaic Interpretation. The Messianic Exegesis of the Targum* [Cincinnati: Hebrew Union College, 1974], 99), but they think that "raised up" is more likely as a translation of the Hebrew "branch out, sprout" (*Targum of the Minor Prophets*, 198 n.12). Since, however, this verb is from the same root as the noun which the Targum has interpreted as "Messiah," it seems reasonable that the targumist would render the verb as "he shall be anointed." While *Tg. Jon.* usually uses the Aramaic cognate to translate the Hebrew verb משח, it does sometimes have רבי (such as at *Tg. Isa.* 61:1), and other Targums usually use רבי for Hebrew משח.

and the things done to Jesus in John 19:1–5. Second Kings 11:12 (= 2 Chr 23:11) mentions putting a crown on the head of a king when he is anointed. We also find the following pious sentiment expressed in *Tg. Ps.-J.* Exod 15:18 (for MT: "The LORD will reign forever and ever"):

> When the people of the sons of Israel saw the miracles and wonders (at the Red Sea) . . . they spoke up and were saying to one another, "Come, let us place a crown of anointing upon the head of our Redeemer, who makes things pass away, but does not himself pass away; who makes things change, but is not changed; who is king of kings in this world, and the crown of kingship is also his for the world to come, and it is his forever and ever."[16]

Fragmentary Targum V Exodus 15:18 reads similarly. *Fragmentary Targum P* contains a reading schedule according to which Exod 13:19–15:26 was to be read on the seventh day of Passover.[17] Such a practice may have been in place in the first century. If so, perhaps some may have thought about the recent coronation of Jesus by Pilate, especially if the "good confession" of Jesus before Pilate (1 Tim 6:13) had been made known, when Jesus spoke with him about his kingdom which is not of this world (John 18:36) and then came out before the people with "the crown of his kingship" on his head. Ironically, the crown was put there not by his people anxious to "place a crown of anointing upon the head of our Redeemer," but by Roman soldiers in mocking cruelty, after he was delivered over to them by his people. When Jesus appeared before the people after being brought out by Pilate, and when he hung on the cross, onlookers steeped in targumic interpretation might have concurred with the sentiment expressed in *Tg. Neof.* Exod 15:18: "How the crown of kingship becomes you, O LORD!"

The Crucifixion as Victory

Finally, in the crucifixion itself—an agonizing and shameful death, a public exhibition and warning to potential criminals and revolutionaries—things are not as they appear. The crucifixion appears to be a total and final defeat, yet the reality is quite the opposite. The first promise of salvation in the Bible is the Lord's statement to the serpent: "He shall strike you on the head" (Gen 3:15). In several places in the OT, we see what could be called "literalistic" fulfillments of this ancient promise, as one of the "offspring of the serpent" meets his end in such a way as to remind us of this promise (though the promise itself is not to be fulfilled in literal terms). For example, Jael, the wife of Heber the Kenite, drove a tent peg

---

[16] "Crown of anointing" is כליל דרבו, which Maher translates "crown of greatness" (*Pseudo-Jonathan: Exodus*, 205). See the previous note for a similar issue. The word רבו in this verse is translated "anointment" on the CAL website (http://cal1.cn.huc.edu/). To view the lexical information, select "Search the CAL textual databases," then select "Targum Studies Module," then "Browse a single targum – with lexical analysis." After selecting *Targum Pseudo-Jonathan*, submit a query for text 215 (= Exod 15), then click on 21518 (v. 18).

[17] Klein, *Fragment Targums*, 1:19.

through the skull of Sisera (Judg 4–5).[18] David defeated Goliath with a blow to the head (1 Sam 17). As we saw above, Jesus came in the name of the LORD as David did against Goliath (1 Sam 17:45; Ps 118:26; John 5:43; 12:13). All four Gospels tell us that Jesus was crucified at "the place of a skull" (Matt 27:33; Mark 15:22; Luke 23:33; John 19:17), and here again we can see a literalistic fulfillment of Gen 3:15, with the cross of Jesus driven into this "skull." In the midst of apparent defeat, we see what is actually a sign of victory over the world and the devil, the crushing of the serpent's head, as the feet of the Son of God are pierced.

CONCLUSIONS

John's conscious use of OT allusions and typology show Jesus to be a "man of war" on both a human level (Jesus is like Joshua and David) and divine level (as in Exod 15:3, YHWH is a man of war), thus supporting the interpretation of John 1:14 as "YHWH became flesh." We saw that John 12:31–32 alludes to the LORD's deliverance of Jerusalem from Sennacherib, and that John 14:1–4 alludes to the initial departure of the LORD's people from Mt. Sinai on a three-day journey, in which the LORD was petitioned to scatter his enemies and return to his people. John views both of these events as prefigurements of Christ's defeat of the devil on the cross. In various Targum passages describing these divine victories, the figure of the divine Word is used, thus supporting the view that John's Logos title grew out of his understanding of the Targums and and that the Targums are essential in helping us understand a major theme in John's Gospel—Jesus as a victorious warrior. The idea that the death of Jesus is a sign of weakness and defeat is countered with an understanding of the crucifixion and resurrection as the greatest of all victories, over death and the devil, by which Christ's followers are freed from slavery to sin and death.

---

[18] Another parallel between Gen 3 and Judg 4–5 can be seen in the establishment of enmity between Sisera and the woman, whereas before there was peace. We also see some reversals of the situation of Gen 3: Sisera is deceived by the woman and led to his death; he drank, his eyes were closed (he slept), and he died.

6

Jesus the Bridegroom of His People

INTRODUCTION

In his first miracle, turning water into wine at a wedding (John 2:1–11), Jesus performed the duty of the bridegroom when the bridegroom fell short. We know that it was the bridegroom's duty to provide the wine because he was the one who got credit for the fine wine that Jesus provided (vv. 9–10). Later, in John 3:29 John the Baptist refers to Jesus as the bridegroom.[1] Likewise in some parables in the Synoptics Jesus is the bridegroom (Matt 22:2–14; 25:1–13; Luke 12:36), and he referred to himself as a bridegroom in answering the question about fasting (Matt 9:15; Mark 2:19–20; Luke 5:34–35). In what sense is Jesus a bridegroom?

Interpreters at least since Origen have noted that in John 4, where Jesus meets the Samaritan woman at a well, there is a potential connection to several OT accounts of a man meeting a woman at a well, whereupon the woman (Rebekah, Rachel, Zipporah) goes on to become the bride of a man of God.[2] In this chapter, we explore the development of the theme of the divine bridegroom in both the OT and the Targums and show its relationship to the corresponding theme of Israel as the bride of the LORD, and how both the human and the divine aspects of this theme have parallels in John 4. It is another example of what it means that the Word (interpreted as a divine title) has become flesh.

CONNECTION TO THE THEME OF JESUS AS WARRIOR

The themes of God as warrior and as the bridegroom of his people are found side by side in Isa 59:15b to 63:6, which has the following well-recognized chiastic structure:

---

[1] Paul D. Duke noted the significance of this miracle in portraying Jesus as the bridegroom in *Irony in the Fourth Gospel* (Atlanta: John Knox, 1985), 101, as did Craig R. Koester, *Symbolism in the Fourth Gospel: Meaning, Mystery, Community* (Minneapolis: Fortress, 1995), 48–49. Both also noted the connection to John 3:29. It should be added that at the conclusion of the Samaritan episode, John mentions Jesus' return to Cana and reminds us of the miracle done there (4:43–46).

[2] Jocelyn McWhirter cites Origen's *Genesis Homily* 10.5 to this effect (*The Bridegroom Messiah and the People of God: Marriage in the Fourth Gospel* [SNTSMS 138; Cambridge: Cambridge University Press, 2006], 1).

59:15b–21	**A** The Divine Warrior
60:1–22	**B** The Glory of Zion
61:1–11	**C** The LORD's Anointed
62:1–12	**B′** The Glory of Zion
63:1–6	**A′** The Divine Warrior

In section B′ (62:4–5), we see the LORD as bridegroom and redeemed Israel as bride:

> [4]You will no longer be called Azubah [Forsaken],
> And your land will no longer be called Shemamah [Desolate].
> For you will be named Hephzibah [My Delight is in Her],
> And your land, Beulah [Married].
> For the LORD delights in you,
> And your land will be married.
> [5]For as a young man marries a virgin,
> So your Builder will marry you.
> And as the bridegroom rejoices over the bride,
> So your God will rejoice over you.

In place of MT "your sons" in v. 5 (which does not fit the context), we read "Your Builder," as suggested by *BHS,* and which points to Ps 147:2, "the LORD is the builder of Jerusalem."[3] Hephzibah was the name of the mother of king Manasseh; thus she was a royal bride (of Hezekiah). Shemamah is what the LORD called Judah in Isa 1:7. Zion was called Azubah in Isa 60:15. Azubah was also the name of a royal bride, the mother of Jehoshaphat, therefore wife of Asa (1 Kgs 22:42; 2 Chr 20:31).

The sequence B′/A′ is essentially repeated in Rev 19. Verses 7–9 speak of the wedding supper of the Lamb (agreeing with B′ above), while vv. 11–16 portray Jesus as the divine warrior with imagery drawn from Isa 63:1–6 (A′ above):

> [2]Why is your apparel red,
> And your garments like the one who treads in the wine press?
> [3]"I have trodden the wine trough alone,
> And from the peoples there was no man with me.
> I also trod them in my anger
> And trampled them in my wrath;
> And their lifeblood is sprinkled on my garments,
> And I stained all my clothing." (Isa 63:2–3)

> [13]He is clothed with a robe dipped in blood,
> and his name is called The Word of God. . . .
> [15]and he treads the wine press of the fierce wrath of God, the Almighty. (Rev 19:13, 15)

---

[3]MT בָּנָיִךְ ("your sons") could be repointed as בֹּנֵיִךְ, with noun and verbs as honorific plurals (cf. "your Husband" and "your Maker" in Isa 54:5). It could also be that the י was originally the third root consonant, as one often sees III-ה verbs spelled with י in Isaiah, and the verb was mistakenly pointed as plural due to the misinterpretation of the noun as the plural "sons."

As Alec Motyer observed, "We rightly see the New Testament counterpart to this [passage in Isa 63] in the wrath of the Lamb (Rev. 6:15ff.) and the treading of the winepress of the wrath of God (Rev 14:17–20; 19:15)."[4]

A targumic interpretation of the warrior's name "the Word of God" (v. 13) is consistent with *Tg. Isa.* 63:5, where God's wrath in this warfare is rendered as "the Word of my pleasure." This expression is also found in *Tg. Isa.* 59:16 (from section A above) for MT "his own righteousness." The next verse says he will save and avenge by his Word, and v. 19 says "by the Word of the LORD they shall be plundered" (the MT refers to the breath of the LORD).

Sections A/A′ and B/B′ represent the two alternatives open to humankind, for which one could adapt the motto of the U.S. I Marine Expeditionary Force: "no better friend [section B/B′, he glorifies his people with righteousness and salvation], no worse enemy [section A/A′, he tramples his enemy underfoot]."

On a human level the two themes go together as well. We read, for example, that Caleb gave his daughter Achsah in marriage to Othniel as a reward for conquering Kiriath-Sepher (Josh 15:16–17; Judg 1:12–13). Likewise Saul promised his daughter Merab to the one who killed Goliath (1 Sam 17:25), then later gave Michal to David for slaying two hundred Philistines (1 Sam 18:27).

We saw in the last chapter that the Gospel of John shows Jesus to be a warrior, based on both human and divine analogies to the OT, particularly as they are read in light of the Targums. If the bride is the warrior's prize, and if Jesus is the greatest warrior, defeating Satan on the cross, what is Jesus' prize? The answer, of course, is the church.

THE WOMAN AT THE WELL IN THE OT

In three different OT incidents (Gen 24, Gen 29, and Exod 2), a man meets a woman at a well, and she goes on to become the bride of a man of God. We are interested in these passages because in John 4 Jesus meets a Samaritan woman at a well, and this encounter involves a number of parallels to each of the OT incidents, not only in the Bible itself but also as these accounts are embellished in Jewish tradition.[5] But before looking at these parallels, we want to see how the OT incidents themselves point to the bridegroom/bride relationship between the LORD and Israel.

In Gen 24, by far the longest of these accounts (sixty-seven verses), Abraham sends his servant back to his homeland in upper Mesopotamia to get a wife for Isaac, because Isaac must not marry a Canaanite woman (the promises to

---

[4] Motyer, *Prophecy of Isaiah*, 509.

[5] "The OT background suggests a parallel between the courtship meetings at a well of Abraham's servant and Rebekah (Gen 24:1ff.), Jacob and Rachel (Gen 29:1–14), Moses and Sipporah (Ex 2:15–22), and Jesus and the Samaritan woman" (Jerome H. Neyrey, "Jacob Traditions and the Interpretation of John 4:10–26," *CBQ* 41 [1979]: 425). "Allusions to the cross-gender well scenes of Gen 24, and secondarily to Gen 29 and Exod 2, are difficult to miss" (Keener, *John*, 586).

Abraham were conditional on a godly offspring following the ways of the LORD according to Gen 18:19). Stopping at a well outside the city of Nahor, Abraham's servant devises a test of character for the prospective bride and prays for success. Immediately Rebekah comes by and passes the test, volunteering to draw water for the servant's ten camels. The servant introduces himself to Rebekah, and she runs home and tells her family. After Laban comes to meet him at the well and invites him to stay, the servant secures their permission for Isaac to marry Rebekah.

All of this takes place for the benefit of Isaac who is the bridegroom, but very little notice is taken of him in this account, which focuses rather on Rebekah and the servant, both of whom are shown to be of exceptional character. Abraham's servant is the model servant who relies upon God and is concerned with only one thing, namely, doing his master's will. Rebekah is likewise the model bride, a woman of virtuous character—hard working, respectful, virginal, beautiful, and even willing to go and live in another land.

In the other two accounts, by contrast, the focus is on the bridegroom and the deeds that he does at the well for his prospective bride. In Gen 29, Jacob has left home on his twofold mission of saving his life and getting a wife. After stopping at a well near Haran, he sees Rachel coming, and being informed that she is Laban's daughter, he rolls away a large stone at the mouth of the well by himself and waters Rachel's flock (v. 10). Little attention is paid to the future bride here, but rather the focus is on Jacob and what he does for her, performing by himself what was normally done by a group of men.

In Exod 2, Moses is fleeing for his life, in the course of which he meets his future wife Zipporah and her sisters at a well. Again, the focus is not on the prospective bride, but on the bridegroom and the deeds that he does on her behalf. He waters her flock, as Jacob did Rachel's, but first delivered the sisters from shepherds who come to harass them. Verse 17 says that he saves them (הוֹשִׁעַ); v. 19 says he delivered them (הִצִּיל). Both verbs are commonly used of the LORD's salvation of Israel from Egypt.

The accounts can be considered as consisting of two types, as noted above, but they also have other common elements: a stranger (in danger in two of the accounts) goes to a foreign land and meets a woman at a well; a betrothal takes place; and the woman goes on to become the bride of a man of God.

There is a fourth case that should probably be understood in light of these other three. In Exod 17:1–6, the LORD miraculously brings forth water out of the rock for Israel, after he had brought them out of Egypt. In v. 6, the LORD says, "I will stand before you there on the rock," which may suggest a visible manifestation of the LORD, which, according to John 1:18 ("no man has seen God at any time"), would have been a manifestation of the Son. Here Israel (represented by its elders; v. 5) "meets" the LORD at this miraculous well. If a marriage ceremony is truly in view, this would be the earliest canonical reference in which the LORD refers to the relationship between himself and his people in terms of a marriage relationship. This is indicated not by any use of marriage terminology, but by analogy to the previous accounts of a man meeting a woman at a well. In fact, we can see a merging of the two narrative types mentioned above, since we have at this miraculous well both the bride (Israel) and the bridegroom (as in Gen 29 and Exod 2), along with his servant.

The bridegroom is the LORD, who has "saved" and "delivered" his people from the Egyptians, as Moses did for Zipporah in Midian. As Jacob and Moses drew water for their prospective brides, the LORD draws water for his people, his flock, which is also to become his bride. The servant is now Moses, who, like Abraham's servant, is concerned only with doing his master's will: "Moses did so" (v. 6). But what shall we say about the bride? We saw that Rebekah acted the model bride—she was tested by the servant to see what sort of character she had, and she passed the test. Here Israel is tested by thirst, and they respond by testing the LORD, grumbling and complaining, regretting their redemption (vv. 2–4)—and they are ready to kill Moses (v. 4)!

This incident took place at Horeb (v. 6; Horeb = Sinai), where shortly afterward the LORD made the following "proposal" to Israel:

> You yourselves have seen what I did to the Egyptians, how I bore you on eagles' wings, and brought you to myself. Now then, if you will indeed listen to my voice and keep my covenant, then you shall be my special treasure among all the peoples, for all the earth is mine; and you shall be to me a kingdom of priests and a holy nation. (Exod 19:4–6)

If Exod 17:1–6 can be interpreted in marital terms, then this proposal can be interpreted in part along the same lines: It is a betrothal proposal delivered through the servant of the LORD, much as Abraham's servant made the betrothal proposal concerning Rebekah.

Israel accepts the proposal, volunteering, "All that the LORD has spoken we will do" (v. 8, and again in 24:3, 7). For our purposes, we note that in targumic terms, Israel's accepting of this proposal involves a promise to receive the Word of the LORD, since the proposal is worded "if you indeed receive my Word" (*Tgs. Onq.* and *Ps.-J.* Exod 19:5), and in *Tg. Neof.* [mg.] and *Frg. Tgs.* P, V Exod 19:8, the people answer, "All that the Word of the LORD has spoken we will do" (similarly for *Tg. Neof.* [mg.] Exod 24:3, 7), adding, "We will listen" in Exod 24:7, which is "We will receive" in *Tgs. Onq.* and *Ps.-J.*

A few weeks later, Israel makes the golden calf, showing how different she is from Rebekah, who not only promised, but fulfilled her promise to do a good deed for Abraham's servant. Israel's refusal to enter the promised land is referred to as "fornication" (זְנוּתִים; related to זוֹנָה, "prostitute") in Num 14:33. In fact, Josh 2 shows that Israel compares unfavorably to Rahab the Canaanite prostitute with respect to her works, her faith, and her reward. Her works involved hiding the two spies and helping them escape. In this she is like the mother of Moses who hid him to save his life, and she is like the midwives who lied to Pharaoh in order to save the lives of the male Israelite children. In her works, she contrasts with the wilderness generation who wanted to stone to death the two spies who urged obedience to the LORD (Num 14:10). Rahab's faith also stands in contrast to the unbelief of the wilderness generation: "How long will they not believe in me?" (Num 14:11). Rahab, in contrast, unwittingly quotes Moses, whom she never heard or read: "The LORD your God, he is God in heaven above, and on the earth below" (Josh 2:11; cf. Deut 4:39).

As a result of her true faith and good works, Rahab the Canaanite prostitute receives the reward that the wilderness generation forfeited through unbelief and evil works, as she received an inheritance in Israel (Josh 6:22–25). According to Matt 1:5, Salmon, son of Nahshon, was the father of Boaz by Rahab. Nahshon was the leader of the tribe of Judah at the exodus (Num 1:7; 2:3), and thus would have been among those who died in the wilderness for their unbelief, while his son Salmon grew up in the wilderness and entered the land with Joshua and was allotted a portion of land in Judah. His (presumed) wife Rahab thus would have received the inheritance that her own father-in-law lost when he died in the wilderness.

Subsequent to the death of Joshua and the elders of his generation, Israel was characterized much more frequently as an unfaithful bride than as a faithful one. Ezekiel 16:33 says that Judah is even beyond prostitution, paying her lovers rather than being paid by them. The eventual result is exile, "divorce" in terms of the marriage analogy (Isa 50:1), and the promise of return from exile is given in terms of a restoration of the marriage covenant (e.g., Isa 54:4–8).

In light of this OT background and of the disasters that the Jews experienced in C.E. 70, it would have been reasonable for John's audience to conclude from historical events that the LORD's people had been unfaithful to the covenant, that they have not fulfilled the promise of Exod 19:8; 24:3, 7. In short, their calamities must have come because (in targumic terms) they have not received the Word of the LORD.

How the OT Background Illumines John 4

We will now look at each of the OT well scenes discussed above in relation to John 4, and see that the three stories of a man meeting a woman at a well sheds light on how Jesus, in his own encounter at a well, serves both as a servant and a bridegroom. Comparison with the account of Israel "meeting" the LORD at a well shows Jesus as the divine bridegroom.

Genesis 24

There are numerous parallels between the words and deeds of Abraham's servant in Gen 24 and the words and deeds of Jesus in John 4.[6] Genesis 24 focused on the servant, not the bridegroom, and the parallels between the two chapters highlight Jesus as Servant. First we can compare the larger theme of both chapters. The theme of Gen 24 is that a father (Abraham) is seeking a virtuous bride for his son Isaac, and sends his servant to another land to attain that goal. Jesus says in John 4:23 that the Father seeks those who worship him in spirit and in truth. To attain that goal, he has sent his Son as servant (v. 34). He has come not just to a

---

[6] Most of these parallels were set out by M.-É. Boismard in "Aenon, près de Salem," *RB* 80 (1973): 223–24, and by Bonneau in "Woman at the Well," 1254.

foreign land (John 4 does take place outside of Judea), but from his Father's house in heaven to earth. There are similarities of detail as well:

(1) Jesus begins his conversation with the Samaritan woman by asking her for a drink (v. 7), just as Abraham's servant did with Rebekah (Gen 24:17).

(2) Jesus speaks of gifts that he has to give her that she does not know about (v. 10). Likewise Abraham's servant brought out gifts for Rebekah when she had passed his test of character (Gen 24:22).

(3) After meeting the remarkable stranger at a well, the Samaritan woman goes into her city and invites the men of the city to come and meet this man; they then invite him to stay with them (vv. 28–29, 40). This parallels Rebekah's actions in telling her family about the servant of Abraham, and Laban coming to the well to meet him and invite him to stay with them (Gen 24:28–31).

(4) In both cases, the stranger refuses to eat when food is offered to him (vv. 32–34; Gen 24:33).

(5) In both cases, the stranger stays for two days (vv. 40, 43; Gen 24:54). Even though it seems that the visit of Abraham's servant was less than 24 hours, in the biblical way of counting this would be two days (the day he arrived and the day he left).

John 4 is missing some of the elements of Gen 24. There is no test of the woman's character; instead we see that Jesus already knows about her life and her character (vv. 17–18), about which we will say more later. Secondly, there is no betrothal as there is in the Genesis account. Instead, we read that the Samaritans believed in Jesus (vv. 39–42). Again, this is something about which we will say more later.

Genesis 29

Jacob, like Abraham's servant, travels to a foreign land on his mission. As noted in ch. 4, Jacob's twofold mission on this journey from his father's house (to save his life, to get a wife) can be compared with that of Jesus, who left his Father's house in order to give his life and to gain the church. Thus, in the case of Jesus, the two missions are one, and we might also note that his mission involved saving Jacob's (eternal) life (and ours) and that the Messiah's name is "Israel" (the true Jacob) in Isa 49:3. While his overall mission was to give his life, John 4:1–4 may imply that Jesus entered Samaria in order to avoid hostility with the Pharisees. If so, on his mission to give his life he is temporarily avoiding danger to his life, like Jacob.

John notes in v. 6 that this well is "Jacob's well," which would not be the well of Gen 29, of course, but would still bring to mind the figure of Jacob at a well. In Gen 29:10, Jacob waters the flock for Rachel, and in John 4:10–14 Jesus offers living water to the Samaritan woman—water that springs up to eternal life. As mentioned in ch. 1, the *Pal. Tgs.* preserve a legend about a miracle associated with Jacob at the well near Haran. According to *Tgs. Neof.* and *Ps.-J.*, and *Frg. Tgs. P, V* Gen 28:10, when Jacob removed the stone from the mouth of the well, the water surged up and overflowed all the time that Jacob was in Haran (thus twenty years).

The various accounts mention "Jacob our father" or "our father Jacob" six to seven times (except that *Tg. Ps.-J.*'s account does not use this phrase), so the Lord's description of his own water as "a spring of water welling up to eternal life" would have been an apt answer to the Samaritan woman's question, "You are not greater than our father Jacob, are you?" (v. 12). Perhaps this tradition was known among the Samaritans as well as the Jews. Of course, she also comes to see that Jesus is greater than Jacob, because as she herself says, he "told me all the things that I have done" (v. 29).

Exodus 2

Moses, like Jacob, draws water for the flock of his prospective bride; the accounts in Exod 2 and Gen 29 share this similarity to John 4, although Jesus does not draw water but in v. 10 offers better water. Moses also "saves" and "delivers" Zipporah, which we pointed to as analogous to the deliverance of Israel from Egypt, and which is also obviously analogous to the work of Christ in obtaining his bride.

A unique similarity between John 4 and Exod 2 is that the man in both accounts is sitting by the well (John 4:6; Exod 2:15). Abraham's servant is standing at the well (Gen 24:13) as Jacob seems to be (Gen 29:1–10). Here again, Jewish tradition adds to the similarity between the two accounts. Josephus relates information about Moses in Midian that also appears in John 4:6, namely, that Moses sat down at the well at midday to rest after his journey.[7]

To summarize, the OT parallels discussed so far bring together in the person of Jesus, as seen in John 4, both the ideal servant (by comparison to Gen 24) and the man of God as bridegroom (by comparison to Gen 29 and Exod 2). We might add that the bridegrooms in question were also servants in that they were servants of God (Gen 24:14; 32:10; Exod 4:10). John 4 shows Jesus as the servant-bridegroom.

Exodus 17

While the parallels between John 4 and Gen 24, Gen 29, and Exod 2 reveal Jesus as a human servant-bridegroom, the parallels to Exod 17 show him to be the divine-human servant-bridegroom. The deity of Christ is shown in several ways in this account.

As mentioned in ch. 3, John 4:26 is the first of the "I am he" (ἐγώ εἰμι) sayings in John, and a few interpreters have pointed to its similarity to the last of the divine "I am he" (אֲנִי הוּא) sayings in Isaiah:

Therefore my people shall know my name; therefore in that day (they shall know) that *I am he, the one who is speaking*, here I am. (Isa 52:6)	I am he, the one who is speaking to you. (John 4:26)

---

[7] Josephus, *Ant.* 2.257, noted by Bernard, *John*, 1:136.

Of course, the Samaritan woman would take "I am he" to mean only "I am the Messiah" (v. 25), but the similarity to Isa 52:6 is most suggestive. The promise involves God's people knowing his name. We noted earlier that the mission of Jesus was to reveal the Father's name (John 17:6, 26), that the Father's name is also given to the Son (John 17:11, 12), and that "I am he" was a way of evoking the divine name after it was no longer pronounced. As we see below, the Samaritan woman symbolically represents the people of God, so that John 4 contains a fulfillment of Isa 52:6, a revelation of the divine name to God's people. Further, Isa 52:6 can be read in its context as a promise of a revelation of the divine name that goes beyond what took place in OT times; God is going to speak in a way that he has not done before. "Here I am" (Isa 52:6) is also what Isaiah said when he volunteered to be sent by God as a prophet to his people (6:8). "Now the LORD God has sent me" (Isa 48:16) also indicates a new way of God speaking to his people, as the servant comes into the world.

Recall that *Tg. Neof.* Deut 32:39 reads "I, I in my Word, am he." It is possible, though speculative, that in the lost *Pal. Targ.* of the Prophets, such a paraphrase existed of the "I am he" sayings in Isaiah as well: "I, in my Word, am he, the one who is speaking to you." In any case, in light of this "I am he" saying by Jesus, we can look again at Exod 17:1–6 and see Jesus not as a mere human bridegroom who provides water to benefit an individual human bride, but as the divine bridegroom of his people. There we saw the divine bridegroom with his servant Moses miraculously bring forth water from the rock for his people (who are also his flock). In John 4, we see at the well the divine bridegroom who has become a servant, like Moses, a real man who grows weary and thirsty, yet who provides better water than could the patriarchs.

This interpretation receives added confirmation when we consider the title "Word" in light of *Tg. Neof.* Exod 17:6, where the LORD says to Moses, "Behold, my Word shall stand in readiness on the rock at Horeb." So whereas in this *Pal. Tg.* rendering of Exod 17, the divine Word and the servant Moses are at the miraculous well with Israel, in John 4 the Word who has become flesh is at the well with the Samaritan woman who represents his people, and he speaks of water that springs up to eternal life. Even without the rendering in *Tg. Neof.*, John 1:18 would indicate that it is the Son, the visible manifestation of God, whom Israel "met" at the well. We might add that in the Gospel Jesus is also seen as analogous to the rock, since he is the one who is struck, and he is the source of the life-giving water.[8]

---

[8] On another occasion, Moses struck the rock twice when he was only supposed to speak to it (Num 20:2–11). *Targum Pseudo-Jonathan* Num 20:11 explains why Moses struck it twice: the first time blood came out, the second time water. Günter Reim notes the connection to John 19:34–37 ("Targum und Johannesevangelium," *Biblische Zeitschrift* 27 [1983]: 9), as does Keener (*John*, 1153 n.757), who cites Thomas Francis Glasson with this observation (*Moses in the Fourth Gospel* [Studies in Biblical Theology 40; Naperville, Ill.: Allenson, 1963], 54). Glasson cites Westcott, who found this information in John Lightfoot's *Horae Hebraicae*, which cited the same tradition in *Psalms Rabbah* 78.2 (on Ps 78:20), where the interpretation is derived from the fact that the word for the water flowing out (זוב) is the same as that used for flow of blood in Lev 15:25.

Another feature that suggests that Jesus is the divine bridegroom in John 4 is the fact that in place of a betrothal, the Samaritans believed in Jesus. We noted above that this was also true of God's relationship with Israel. His proposal from Mt. Sinai was, "If you indeed listen to my voice," or in the targumic rendering, "If you indeed receive my Word." As noted in ch. 1, John 1:11–12 equates receiving the Word with believing in his name. The Samaritans, therefore, met the divine betrothal requirement by believing in Jesus.

THE SAMARITAN WOMAN AS SYMBOLIC OF THE BRIDE OF CHRIST

Probably most Christians have read John 4 with the thought, "this shows us that the worst of sinners can be saved." If, however, John 4 presents the woman at the well as a bride in keeping with the OT well encounters, she represents not the worst of sinners, but the bride of Christ, the people of God, the church as a whole. As such, she is not a very flattering picture!

In comparing the Samaritan woman to Rebekah, the ideal bride of Gen 24, we note that the reason for sending the servant to Abraham's homeland was that Isaac must not marry a Canaanite woman, because of the depravity of Canaanite culture, as the Canaanites were without knowledge of the true God. But in the minds of Jesus' countrymen and many of John's readers, the Samaritans were the equivalent of the Canaanites. As Jesus himself said to the woman, "You (Samaritans) worship what you do not know" (v. 22), and as the woman or the gospel writer note, "Jews have no dealings with Samaritans" (v. 9). Samaritans were off limits to observant Jews, just as the Canaanites were in the OT.

Beyond matters of race and culture, Rebekah was a chaste virgin, a woman of good character, while the Samaritan woman had had five husbands and was at that time living with a man to whom she was not married (vv. 17–18). Clearly, if Rebekah is the ideal bride, the Samaritan woman is the very opposite, the model of the undesirable bride. And in these very undesirable features, we can see how she is a fitting symbol for the church of Jesus Christ. The Samaritan woman is from the "wrong" family and cultural background. But the same is true about all the members of Adam's race. God looked upon that race before the flood and saw only corruption, and that race is the same today, because of the sin that entered the world through Adam.

The Samaritan woman had had one husband after another, and was now living with someone who was not her husband—an unmarried man or maybe some- one else's husband. When we examined the OT metaphor of God's marriage to his people we saw that idolatry, in God's sight, is tantamount to spiritual immorality, adultery, fornication, and prostitution. Since in this sense those who come to faith have all had many gods before coming to know the one true God, they come to him on the spiritual level like the Samaritan woman did on the physical level. In John's narrative, the immorality of the Samaritan woman symbolizes our idola- trous nature. Outwardly, one might be like Rebekah, highly regarded in society, good by human standards, but God sees the heart and knows that in the past each has had many gods before him. We are the undesirable Samaritan woman.

PAUL'S GREAT MYSTERY

In Eph 5:22–33, Paul expounds on the duties of Christian husbands and wives based on the analogy of the relationship between Christ and the church. Like John, Paul envisions Christ as divine bridegroom in continuity with the OT portrayal of the God of Israel as the nation's bridegroom. And as in Rev 19, this theme is closely associated with the theme of Christ as divine warrior. This may be inferred from the fact that just as in Isa 59:15–63:6 these two themes are put side by side, so also in his letter to the Ephesians, Paul flows from a discussion of Christian marriage relationships as analogous to the relationship between Christ and the church to a discussion of Christian warfare (Eph 6:10–17) that draws on terminology from the first of these two divine warrior sections in Isaiah (Isa 59:17; cf. Eph 6:14, 17).

In the course of his exposition on marriage relationships, Paul says "This mystery is great" (Eph 5:32), perhaps implying that there is much more to be said about Christ as bridegroom that the believer may investigate further, both from the OT portrayal of the divine bridegroom and from the NT work of Christ. John, writing later than Paul, may be seen as building on Paul's portrayal of Christ as bridegroom (this is not to suggest that Paul himself in his teaching ministry would not have said much more on this subject than we have record of in his writings). When Paul says that Jesus gave himself up for the church to make her holy (Eph 5:25–26), he may well be contrasting Christ to the patriarchs who did the opposite: Abraham and Isaac gave up their brides to potential defilement in order to save their own lives (Gen 12:11–15; 20:2; 26:7). As we saw in ch. 4, these episodes may be considered "fall narratives" that show the patriarchs to be unworthy to fulfill the role of "new Adam." Isaac's excuse is especially worth noting by way of contrast to the motivation of Jesus in fulfilling the role of divine bridegroom: Isaac lied about Rebekah, "because I thought, 'Lest I die on account of her'" (Gen 26:9). When John 4 presents the narrative of the immoral Samaritan woman (who is in effect an anti-Rebekah) as a model of the church, the contrast in the respective actions of the bridegrooms becomes much sharper. Jesus came to "die on account of her," yet not because of her worthiness, but in spite of her lack of it.

On the other hand, Jesus gave his life for her "to make her holy." That is, he died that she not remain in the spiritual condition of the Samaritan woman, but that she be transformed into a Rebekah, so to speak: "that he might present to himself a glorious church, having no stain or wrinkle, or any such thing, but that she should be holy and blameless" (Eph 5:27). We saw at the beginning of this chapter that the bride is the warrior's prize; therefore the church is the reward for the Son of God who won such a great victory over the devil on the cross. But if the church is represented by the Samaritan woman, she does not seem to be much of a prize! Who would risk his life for such a reward? Paul says to the Corinthians, whose cultural background had so much in common with that of the Samaritan woman, "I am jealous for you with a godly jealousy, for I betrothed you to one husband, so as to present you as a pure virgin to Christ" (2 Cor 11:2). In the physical realm, virginity is not something that can be gained once lost, but in the spiritual realm, it seems that Paul anticipates just such a thing. By this miracle of grace, the church can thus be in reality a prize worthy of the greatest of champions, the Son of God, as she is changed from a Samaritan woman to a Rebekah. Paul's words imply that it is the goal of the Christian ministry to prepare the church to become this glorious prize. This observation is a fitting introduction to the next chapter, where we see Jesus as the divine lawgiver, instructing his people how to live.

THE UPPER ROOM DISCOURSE IN LIGHT OF JESUS BEING THE BRIDEGROOM

While there is no overt marriage terminology in the upper room discourse of Jesus, the same may be said of the giving of the law from Mt. Sinai. Yet we have seen that the Sinai covenant is analogous to the marriage covenant, and in the next chapter we will see that in several ways the upper room is a "new Sinai." I close this chapter by mentioning several features of the upper room discourse that can be better understood with the idea of Jesus as the bridegroom as background.

In John 14:1, Jesus says to the disciples, "Believe in God; believe also in me." We saw in the previous chapter that there is good reason to believe that in John 4, trusting in Jesus takes the place of the betrothal found in the OT accounts of a man meeting a woman at a well. This observation raises the question of the role of faith in this divine-human marital relationship. The marriage supper of the Lamb is in the future, when the Lord returns. How do Christ's followers behave between now and then? The answer is that they get ready, in faith. By faith they pursue righteousness and holiness, believing that he is coming again.

A related matter is that of consecration. The section in the Talmud dealing with betrothal and marriage is called *Qiddushin*, "holy things" or "consecration/ sanctification." When a man and woman are engaged to be married, they consecrate themselves to one another. During the time of engagement, they remain faithful and will not consider any rivals. Jesus speaks of consecration in John 17:17, 19, where we learn that Jesus consecrates himself for the sake of his people, in order that his people might be consecrated (or, sanctified, v. 19). In v. 17, he asks the Father to consecrate the disciples in the Father's truth, his word. It is clear from this that believers are not able to consecrate themselves, and this is in keeping with what we have already seen concerning our undesirable origins. In *Tg. Neof.* [mg.] Lev 22:32, the LORD says he is the one "who sanctified you in my Word."

Customarily, a prospective bridegroom gives a ring to his beloved as a token of the seriousness of his promise. Before a ring became standard, he could give anything of value, including money. This engagement gift reminds the beloved of their commitment and should keep her from being tempted by any rival lover. In the upper room, Jesus also gives a gift of great value, in context also mentioning a great rival for the believer's affections: "Peace I leave with you; my peace I give to you. Not as the world gives, do I give to you" (John 14:27). The world can dazzle Christ's followers with enticing offers, but they are nothing like what Christ gives them—his peace. This peace is a token of his consecration for their sake. It is the gift of great value that he leaves his people as a sign that he will come again for them. Of course, the world is not just a rival, and it is not a legitimate rival, another who loves the followers of Christ. The world is an evil seducer who puts on a pretty face to entice them, to lure them away, to defile them and bring them misery and death. This desire may not be conscious on the part of the world, but it is Satan's desire, and he uses the world to speak to believers, to seduce them, that they might "be led astray from the simplicity and purity of devotion to Christ" (2 Cor 11:3).

CONCLUSIONS

By considering the theme of Jesus as bridegroom of his people in light of its OT background, with its typological analogies, both human and divine, we have seen yet another way in which the Gospel of John develops the theme, "the Word became flesh." As the divine Word met Israel at the well in *Tg. Neof.* Exod 17, as Jacob and Moses met their future brides at a well, and as Abraham's servant met Rebekah at a well, Jesus meets the Samaritan woman, symbolic of his bride, the church. In John's presentation, Jesus is the divine-human servant-bridegroom who saves and delivers his bride by his waging of war against the devil, and he consecrates himself so that she might be holy, faithful to him as she waits for his return.

7

Jesus the Lawgiver of His People

Introduction

God is the lawgiver of his people throughout the OT. He gave Adam and Eve, Noah, the patriarchs, and then Israel commandments to keep. Most prominently, God gave Israel his law on Mt. Sinai, but he gave his people laws at other times as well, such as the Sabbath commandment at the giving of the manna in Exod 16, the laws of Deuteronomy before they entered the land, and other laws at later times through other prophets.

In this chapter, we look at the words of Jesus in John in light of this OT background as another example of "the Word became flesh." As interpreted in the *Pal. Tgs.* of the Pentateuch, Israel heard the voice of *the Word* from Mt. Sinai, and Moses gave the law as a result of the Word commanding him what to say to Israel. In the ministry of Jesus, his people again heard the voice of the Word, the divine lawgiver, though speaking as a man like Moses.

Again we will see that there is not only continuity from OT to NT on this theme, but change as well, due to the Word (understood as God the Son) becoming flesh. Jesus speaks not only as lawgiver, but also as one who is sent by the Father. He is thus also the human lawgiver, as was Moses. Finally, we see that Jesus, as one who was born under the law, is also the law keeper; he kept the same law God gave to Israel through him. His perfect obedience to that law sent him to the cross and secured the salvation of those who believe in him.

Connection to the Theme of Jesus as Bridegroom

Why do we consider the theme of Jesus as lawgiver after considering the theme of Jesus as bridegroom? We have already seen that the Sinai covenant is analogous to the human marriage covenant. This idea is well attested in the Prophets (most obviously Hosea) and in Judaism. In the *Tg. Song*, the whole Song of Solomon is allegorized as a history of God's dealings with his people. We will see in the next chapter that "You will seek me but will not find me" (John 7:34) could relate to the theme of the withdrawal of the *Shekinah* as experienced by Israel as a result of the golden calf incident, which is the Targum's interpretation of Song 3:2, "I sought him, but did not find him." We can contrast this view of God as bridegroom of his people with that of polytheistic religions in which the gods literally had wives (goddesses) and produced children (other gods) by them.

If God's relationship to Israel is analogous to the marriage relationship, then God's law, as given through Moses, governs that relationship. We may think not only of a marriage contract, but also of the marriage vows. In the traditional marriage vows of English-speaking Christians, husband and wife in large part promise the same things, but there are also differences. The husband promises to cherish his wife, and the wife promises to obey her husband. This difference is also brought out in Exod 19:5–6, which, as has been mentioned before, can be viewed as God's "proposal" to Israel.[1] For his part, the LORD promises to regard Israel as his special treasure, chosen from among all the nations, just as a man should set his affection on one woman and forsake all others. The condition for this special affection from God is that Israel obey him. In v. 8, Israel accepts the proposal: "All that the LORD has spoken, we will do."

Is this idea applicable in the NT? Peter quotes Exod 19:5, referring to Christians as "a people for God's own possession" who have been called out of darkness into light (1 Pet 2:9), just as Israel was called out of Egypt to the promised land to keep God's law. We are called to be a holy people, just as Israel was, and this holiness is defined as keeping his law.

We have also seen how John 1:11–12 can be related to Exod 19:5, in which the proposal "if you will indeed listen to my voice" is rendered "if you will indeed receive my Word" in *Tgs. Onq.* and *Ps.-J.* ("listen to the voice of my Word" in *Tg. Neof.*). This means that the idea of receiving Christ the Word necessarily implies obedience, not merely receiving a gift with no conditions. Saving faith is necessarily accompanied by obedience, as we can see for example from John 17:6 ("they have kept your word") and 17:8 (the disciples received the words of the Father which Jesus gave to them, and they believed that he was sent by the Father).

THE OT LAW WAS GIVEN THROUGH THE SON

The Voice of the Word from Sinai

One way that John shows Jesus as the divine lawgiver is by calling him the Word. One major application of Word in the Targums is to the giving of the law, and we see in the words of Jesus numerous echoes of the targumic Word, that is, the divine Word, as lawgiver.

For example, according to *Tg. Neof.*, *CTg. F*, and *Frg. Tgs. P, V* Exod 19:3, God's "proposal" to Israel in Exod 19:5–6 was spoken by the Word (*Dibbera*) of

---

[1] The idea of Moses as matchmaker between God and Israel was presented in a class at Dropsie College by Sol Cohen (about 1985), and I have seen references to it in popular literature, but I do not know how far back this idea goes in Judaism.

the LORD. The people answered in v. 8 (*Tg. Neof.* [mg.], *C. Tg. F, Frg. Tgs. P, V*), "all that the Word of the LORD has spoken we will do." A similar response follows the giving of the law: "All that the LORD has spoken, we will do, and we will listen" (Exod 24:7). None of the Targums read "the Word of the LORD" here, but this verse is quoted in *Tg. Neof.* and *Frg. Tgs. P, V* Deut 33:2 as follows: "All that the Word of the LORD has spoken, we will do, and we will listen" (שמע; *Tg. Neof., Frg. Tg. V*); "we will receive" (קבל; *Frg. Tg. P*). In addition, dozens of times where the MT reads "the LORD said" in connection with the giving of the law, *Tg. Neof.* [mg.] indicates "the Word of the LORD said."

In connection with the giving of the Ten Commandments, God says in Exod 19:9, "I am going to come to you." Here *Tg. Neof.* and *Frg. Tgs. P, V* read, "My Word will be revealed to you" (similarly *Tg. Neof.* [mg.] and *Frg. Tgs. P, V* 19:11, for MT "the LORD will come down"). *Targum Neofiti* 19:20 says "the glory of the *Shekinah* of the LORD" (mg. and *Frg. Tgs. P, V:* "the Word of the LORD") was revealed on Mt. Sinai, where the Word of the LORD summoned Moses. The Ten Commandments are introduced by "the Word of the LORD spoke all these words" (*Tg. Neof.* [mg.]; *Frg. Tgs. P, V* Exod 20:1; *P* uses *Dibbera*).

Looking back at the giving of the Ten Commandments, Moses says in Deut 4:12, (1) "the LORD spoke to you from the midst of the fire"; (2) "you heard the sound of words, but you saw no form"—(3) "only a voice." For (1) *Tg. Neof.* [mg.] has "the Word of the LORD spoke to you." For (2) *Tg. Ps.-J.* has "you heard the voice of the Word" [*Dibbura*]. For (3) *Tg. Neof.* has, "only the voice of his Word."

Similarly, in Deut 4:36 Moses says, "From heaven he let you hear his voice . . . and you heard his words from the midst of the fire." The *Tgs. Onq., Ps.-J.,* and *Neof.* say "he let you hear the voice of his Word" from the fire. For "his words," *Tgs. Onq.* and *Ps.-J.* use פִּתְגָּם (*pithgam*), the usual translation of דָּבָר (*dabar*), but *Tg. Neof.* uses the plural of דִּבִּיר (*dibber*), to indicate the Ten Commandments. In *Tgs. Onq., Ps.-J.,* and *Neof.* Deut 5:5, Moses says that at Mt. Sinai "I stood between the Word of the LORD and you."

Moses recounts the response of the people to the Sinai revelation as follows in *Tg. Neof.* Deut 5:23–28:

> [23]When you heard the voice of his Word from the midst of the darkness . . . you came near to me . . . [24]and you said, "Behold, the Word of the LORD our God has shown us his glory and his power, and we have heard the voice of his Word from the midst of the flames of fire. This day we have seen that the Word of the LORD can speak with a son of man and he can live. [25]And now, why should we die? For this great fire will consume us; if we hear any more the voice of the Word of the LORD our God, we shall die. [26]For who is there of all flesh who has heard the voice of the Word of the living God speaking from the midst of the flames of fire, like us, and lived? [27]You go near and hear all that the LORD our God will say, and you shall speak with us all that the LORD your God will speak with you, and we will hear and do it." [28]And the Word of the LORD heard the voice of your words at that time.

This passage, or its first-century predecessor, might illumine two passages from John 5. Firstly, in 5:25 Jesus says "an hour is coming, and now is, when the dead shall hear the voice of the Son of God, and those who hear shall live." Taking the targumic "voice of the Word of the LORD" as "the voice of the Son of God," we can see a development from Deut 5:25–26 to John 5:25. On Mt. Sinai, the living heard the voice of the Son of God and continued to live (physically, but later died in their sin in the wilderness). They feared that if they heard the voice of the Son of God again they would die (physically). But Jesus says, "an hour is coming, and now is, when the (physically) dead shall hear the voice of the Son of God, and those who hear shall live."

Secondly, in John 5:38–39 Jesus tells the Jews (1) they have never heard the Father's voice; (2) nor seen his form; (3) the Father's word is not abiding in them, (4) for they do not believe in the one the Father sent. Clearly (3) and (4) are a sharp critique. But (2) is merely a statement of fact, not a criticism, since no one (except the Son), good or evil, has seen the Father. Is (1) part of the critique? Should they have heard the Father's voice, or is this also just a statement of fact—that no one except the Son, good or evil, has heard the Father's voice, just as they have not seen his form?

If we take "never" to mean that Jesus is speaking to the Jews collectively throughout history, the meaning would be that Israel never heard the Father's voice—not even from Mt. Sinai. The point could be that they heard the voice of the Son from Sinai. As noted above, they asked that they not hear his voice anymore, lest they die. They promised that if Moses would be God's representative, they would obey in everything. This ancient promise became an obligation for every generation; whenever that promise was read in the synagogue, an Israelite would say "amen" to it. Jesus is telling them in v. 38, "You have not kept that ancient promise." They did not believe God's representative, whether Moses (v. 46–47), John (v. 33), or the Word himself who has become flesh and speaks as a human sent by God.

The context of this passage confirms that Jesus is saying not that he is just another in the line of those sent by God, but that he is the one who spoke to Israel from Mt. Sinai. If one is not careful, one might think that John 5:36–46 portrays Jesus as merely a spokesperson for God like Moses. In accordance with the people's request, Moses was God's representative. In Deut 18:18–19, the LORD promised that there will be future prophets like Moses to fulfill the same role. Jesus is saying that he is one such, sent by the Father, authenticated by him, and that the Jews should therefore believe him (John 5:36–38). Jesus does a prophet's job of reproving the LORD's people: "You do not have his word abiding in you" (v. 38), "you do not have the love of God in yourselves" (v. 42). That is, they have not kept the great commandment of Deut 6:5–10, in which Moses commands Israel to love God with a whole heart and to keep the words Moses is commanding them on their hearts (i.e., that his word should abide in them). Further, they are commanded to listen to God's prophet (Deut 18:18–19), and they have not kept that. Jesus says he has come in his Father's name, which we related to Ps 118:26 (ch. 5), but which can also be related to Deut 18:19, which promises to send Israel prophets who will speak in God's name. In v. 46, Jesus says to "the Jews," "If you believed Moses (which they claim to do) you would believe me, for he wrote about me." That is, if they believed one genuine spokesperson for God, they should believe another, whom Moses wrote about in Deut 18:18–19. Likewise in v. 47, Jesus implies that his words are like the writings of Moses, the word of God delivered through a person.

But the passage goes farther; it shows Jesus as the God of Moses. Reflecting the word order of the Greek, v. 46 reads, "If you believed Moses, you would believe me, for it was about me that he wrote." What is the law of Moses all about? The law of Moses is about the LORD, and what he did to save his people, and what he will do for them, and how he requires them to live so that the promises will be fulfilled for them. There is very little written in the law of Moses about a man who was to come in the future that would justify the statement, "it was about me that he wrote." Moses wrote about the LORD, full of grace and truth (Exod 34:6), which is how John describes Jesus (John 1:14). Moses wrote about the LORD who revealed the meaning of his name to him, and through him, to Israel (Exod 3:14; 34:5–7), as did Jesus to the disciples, and through them, to believers today (John 17:6, 26). Moses wrote about the LORD who came down from heaven (Exod 3:8; 34:5), as John did about Jesus (John 6:38). Moses wrote about the LORD who as warrior fights for his people (Exod 34:11, etc.), as John did of Jesus (John 12:31–32, etc.). Moses wrote about the LORD as the bridegroom of his people (Exod 34:14–16, etc.), as is Jesus (John 4), and as the lawgiver of his people (Exod 34:7, etc.), as is Jesus.

Thus John 5:46 can be interpreted along human lines, as noted above: if the Jews believed one genuine spokesperson for God they should believe another. But more significantly, it could be interpreted along divine lines: "If you believed Moses, you would believe me, for *as my prophet, it was about me that he wrote.*" The Jews had a saying about Exod 14:31 that is similar to John 5:46 and tends to confirm this understanding of it (see *Mekilta* Exod 14:31 below). This is further confirmed by how Exod 14:31 is rendered in the Targums, keeping in mind that John has called Jesus the Word:

Exod 14:31	They believed in the LORD and in his servant Moses.
Tgs. Neof., Ps.-J., ***Frg. Tg. P, C. Tg. J***	They believed in the name of the Word of the LORD (cf. John 1:12) and in the prophecy of his servant Moses.
Tg. Onq.	They believed in the Word of the LORD and in the prophecy of his servant Moses.
Mekilta **Exod 14:31**	If they believed Moses, how much more did they believe the LORD.[2]
John 5:46	If you believed Moses, you would believe me, for it was about me that he wrote.

John 5:39 is similar to 5:46 in that Jesus is speaking of the Scripture's testimony to himself: "You search the Scriptures, because you think that in them you

---

[2] Morton Smith, *Tannaitic Parallels to the Gospels* (JBLMS 6; Philadelphia: SBL, 1951), 154; cited in M. Eugene Boring, Klaus Berger, and Carsten Colpe, eds., *Hellenistic Commentary to the New Testament* (Nashville: Abingdon, 1995), 271.

have eternal life. Yet it is these that testify about me." Again, it is easy to assume that the scriptural testimony to Jesus comprises a relatively few messianic passages that speak of a savior to come in the future. Is that what Jesus means, or does he mean the same thing as I suggested for v. 46, that the Scriptures testify to the God of Israel, to whom Israel must come to find eternal life? John 5:40, when compared to Isa 55:3 and its rendering in *Tg. Isa*, provides us a clear answer:

John 5:40	Isa 55:3	*Tg. Isa.* 55:3
And you are unwilling to come to me, so that you may have life.	Come to me, listen, so that your soul may live.	Receive my Word, listen, so that your soul may live.

The Voice of the Word in the Tabernacle

After the giving of the law code on Mt. Sinai, the LORD said he would continue to speak to Moses in the tabernacle, from the earthly model of his heavenly throne room. Thus, as on Mt. Sinai, the Word spoke to Moses, now from between the cherubim, in connection with the giving of his law to Israel (*Tgs. Neof.* and *Ps.-J.* Num 7:89; cf. *Tgs Onq., Neof.* and *Ps.-J.* Exod 25:22 and Num 17:4). Therefore, the laws given in Leviticus through Deuteronomy, in targumic thought, would have been given to Moses by the Word speaking to him from above the mercy seat in the holy of holies. As we saw in ch. 1, the rendering of *Tg. Ps.-J.* Num 7:89, when compared to John the Baptist's description of the baptism of Jesus (John 1:32–33), indicates that in John's understanding, Jesus is this law-giving Word who has now become flesh.

In light of the above, we can see the irony of John 9:29: "We know that God has spoken to Moses, but as for this man, we do not know where he is from." This "man" is the Word who spoke to Moses, who now has become flesh, a man like Moses. Jesus speaks as one sent by God, yet he also speaks as God. Thus in place of the OT concept of God and his prophet, John presents Jesus as the divine prophet, the Word become flesh.

THE UPPER ROOM AS A NEW SINAI

The Synoptic Material

From the Synoptic Gospels, John's readers would already know of the inauguration of the new covenant (Matt 26:28; Mark 14:24; Luke 22:20), which brings to mind the promise of Jer 31:31–34, but also (by way of contrast) the Sinai covenant, which the passage in Jeremiah refers to as the old covenant. As the sign of the new covenant, there is a new ceremonial law, the Lord's supper, for the purpose of remembering Jesus, based on the Mosaic Passover celebration, which was for the purpose of remembering the LORD and what he did for Israel (Deut 16:2–3, etc.).

The material in John corroborates the synoptic material to give an overall impression of the upper room as a "new Sinai."

The New Commandment

"A new commandment I give to you, that you love one another, even as I have loved you, that you also love one another" (John 13:34; similarly 15:12, 17). Along with the new covenant is a new commandment. The question often asked is, what is "new" about it? It sounds like a very good paraphrase of several Mosaic ethical laws, as we shall see. And if that is the case, one might say that it is not really new, but in fact would have been given through the Word to Israel already, before his incarnation. In fact, this commandment was first given at Mt. Sinai in Exod 22–23, and again given in Lev 19, and then expounded several times by Moses in Deuteronomy before Israel entered the promised land.

Exod 22:21–22; 23:9

You shall not mistreat or oppress [לחץ] a sojourner, for you were sojourners in the land of Egypt. You shall not oppress [ענה] any widow or orphan. If you do oppress [ענה] him at all, if he cries out to me, I will surely hear his cry, and my anger will be kindled, and I will kill you with the sword, and your wives will become widows, and your children orphans. . . . You shall not oppress [לחץ] a sojourner, since you yourselves know the soul of a sojourner, for you were sojourners in the land of Egypt.

Israelites were oppressed sojourners in Egypt (לחץ is used for Egyptians oppressing Israel in Exod 3:9; ענה is used in Gen 15:13; Exod 1:11–12) but are no longer oppressed or sojourners. Why? Because the LORD loved them and brought them out of Egypt. They should not act towards others as the Egyptians acted towards them. Rather, they should love the sojourner in their midst as the LORD loved them. If they act like the Egyptians did, and the oppressed cry out to the LORD as the Israelites did, then he will hear and act against them as he did against the Egyptians.

Lev 19:33–34

[33]When a sojourner resides with you in your land, you shall not oppress him. [34]The sojourner who resides with you shall be to you like the native among you. You shall love him as yourself; for you were sojourners in Egypt; I am the LORD your God.

This command expands somewhat on Exod 23:9. Verse 34 contains what Jesus later called the second great commandment (Lev 19:18; Matt 22:39; Mark 12:31; Luke 10:27) and applies it to the sojourner in Israel, so that an Israelite should not need to ask, "Who is my neighbor?" (cf. Luke 10:29). To love one's neighbor as oneself is to treat one's neighbor as one would like to be treated, so the Golden Rule (Matt 7:12//Luke 6:31) is simply another way of stating the second great commandment. Leviticus 19:33–34 gives a specific application of the Golden Rule. The

Israelites were sojourners in Egypt, deprived of rights, and made slaves. Did they like to be treated this way? Obviously not. They cried out to the LORD, and he delivered them, gave them freedom, gave them rights such as to a just legal system. They should keep this in mind when they deal with the sojourner in their midst. We might say Lev 19:33–34 is the Golden Rule beyond the plane of human relationships. The LORD is really saying to Israel, "Love the sojourner as I loved you when you were sojourners." The example of his love to which "as I loved you" refers is the exodus from Egypt, and the law is an example of the ideal of moral, ethical godlikeness expressed in biblical law.

Again, the paraphrase of Exod 23:9 and Lev 19:34 given above sounds very much like the "new" commandment of John 13:34. Further, according to the marginal readings of *Tg. Neof.* Exod 20:22 and Lev 19:1, this command was spoken to Moses by the Word of the LORD. Apart from those verses, however, we have the general statement in the Targums of Exod 25:22, Num 7:89, etc., that this law was given to Moses by the divine Word speaking to him from between the cherubim in the holy of holies. So it sounds like the same commandment from the same lawgiver. In what sense is it new?

Deut 5:14–15

The rationale for keeping the Sabbath commandment is godlikeness in both Exod 20 and Deut 5, but the aspect of godlikeness brought out in the two chapters is not the same. In Exod 20:11, the Israelite rests in imitation of God's rest after creating the universe. In Deut 5:14–15, however, godlikeness consists of giving rest to others, as God gives them rest: "so that your male servant and female servant may rest, as well as you. And you shall remember that you were a slave in the land of Egypt, and the LORD your God brought you out from there."

Israel had no Sabbath in Egypt; the Sabbath rest was given to them by God as part of their redemption. Israelite heads of households were masters, not slaves, because the LORD loved them and gave them freedom and rest. Likewise, they must be good masters in giving the Sabbath rest to members of their households, as he was a good Master in giving them a Sabbath day of rest. They must love the members of their households as God loved them. God is saying to them, "Love your households (by giving them a Sabbath rest) as I have loved you (by giving you this rest)."

Deut 10:18–19; 24:17–18

These two laws are similar to each other and to Exod 22:21–22; 23:9 and Lev 19:33–34:

> (The LORD) executes justice for the orphan and widow, and loves the sojourner, giving him food and clothing. So you love the sojourner, for you were sojourners in the land of Egypt (and I loved you). (Deut 10:18–19)

> You shall not pervert the rights of a sojourner or orphan, nor take a widow's garment in pledge. But you shall remember that you were a slave in Egypt, and that the LORD your God redeemed you from there. (24:17–18)

Again, one can paraphrase, "Love the orphan, the widow, the sojourner as I have loved you; love one another as I have loved you."

Deut 15:12–18

This law could be summarized, "Give your servant an exodus, as I gave to you." That is, "Love him as I have loved you." Italicized words with explanatory notes, marked by brackets here and just below, highlight the exodus theme in this law:

> [12]If your brother, a Hebrew man, or a Hebrew woman, is sold to you, he shall *serve*[1] you six years, and in the seventh year you shall *let him go*[2] free from you. [13]And when you *let him go*[2] free from you, you shall not *let him go*[2] *empty-handed*[3]; [14]you shall furnish him liberally out of your flock, out of your threshing floor, and out of your wine press; as the LORD your God has blessed you, you shall give to him. [15]*You shall remember that you were a slave*[1] *in the land of Egypt, and the LORD your God redeemed you*; therefore I command you this thing today. [16]But if he says to you, "I will not *go out*[4] from you," because he loves you and your household, since he fares well with you, [17]then you shall take an awl, and thrust it through his ear into the door, and he shall be your *servant*[1] for ever. And to your servant girl you shall do likewise. [18]*It shall not seem hard*[5] in your eyes, when you *let him go*[2] free from you; for at half the cost of a hired servant he has *served you*[1] six years. So the LORD your God will bless you in all that you do.

[1] The servant's servitude is analogous to Israel's servitude in Egypt (note that "servant" and "slave" are the same word in Hebrew; the word also is used generally for an employee). But if the servant considers himself better off under his master (because like the LORD he is good to him), he can remain a servant. The master remembers that it is by the LORD's grace that he himself is not a slave in Egypt.

[2] The verb שִׁלַּח (*šillaḥ*), used repeatedly for the exodus: "Let my people go."

[3] Same word as in Exod 3:21: "When you leave, you shall not leave empty-handed."

[4] The verb יָצָא (*yāṣāʾ*), used repeatedly for the exodus (mostly in the *hiphil* [causative] form, "bring forth").

[5] The verb קָשָׁה (*qāšâ*), used occasionally for Pharaoh's stubbornness about letting Israel go (Exod 7:3: "I will *harden* Pharaoh's heart"; 13:15: "Pharaoh *was stubborn* about *letting us go*"). The Israelite master, the household head, is enjoined to be like his God, not like Pharaoh: "As the LORD your God has blessed you, you shall give to him" (v. 14). That is, love him as the LORD has loved you; do not oppress him, as Pharaoh did you.

Why Is the Old Commandment Called "New"?

It would therefore appear that the *new* command, "love one another, as I have loved you," is a good paraphrase of several OT laws. Further, being derived from the second great commandment, "love your neighbor as yourself," and being based on the principle of ethical likeness to God, that the LORD's people, as his beloved children, should imitate him, it is at the very heart of OT ethical law. It appears to be an *old* commandment. And by identifying Jesus as the Word who is the lawgiver, John shows us that the "I" in the new commandment is the same as in the old. In light of this, Christopher J. Wright's comment on Deut 15:12–18 is quite ironic: "This wonderful text . . . could have come from the lips of Christ himself."[3] The OT and targumic roots of John's theology have revealed that in fact it did!

In what sense, then, is this a *new* commandment? Even if John 13:34 contained the exact wording of a command from the OT, the context of the verse shows us how it can be called a new commandment. The wording could be identical, but the meaning of "as I have loved you" is new. In every case, in these OT laws which can be paraphrased "love others as I have loved you," the expression "as I have loved you" refers to God's love for Israel expressed in the exodus. In the exodus of Israel from Egypt, the LORD showed himself to be a gracious, loving Lord and Master, giving an example to Israelite masters, heads of households, judges, etc., so that they should be like him in the exercise of their power and authority. In John 13:34, however, "as I have loved you" refers to the fact that the eternal Son of God laid aside his privileges of deity and took upon himself the form of a servant. In the context of John 13, Jesus has just graphically illustrated this to the disciples by laying aside his garments and washing their feet. So this commandment is new in the sense that it requires Christ's followers to imitate not the heavenly *Master* who freed his people from Egypt, but the heavenly *Servant* who laid down his life for them and for their salvation.

Israel's Failure to Receive the Word of the LORD

Another passage that forms an important background for understanding the significance of Jesus' words in the upper room is Deut 15:12–18. Since this passage, dealing with the manumission of Hebrew slaves, is essentially an expansion of Exod 21:2–6, it is the first ordinance in the law code of Exod 21–23. It is appropriate that this law comes first because of the circumstances of Israel's deliverance from Egypt. It reminds them that they were slaves in Egypt, and the LORD set them free.

This law is reflected in Jer 34:8–22, a passage that, in the synagogue reading schedule that has come down to us, was read along with Exod 21:2–6. Jeremiah had been preaching submission to the Babylonians and prophesying defeat and the destruction of the city and the temple if they resisted. Jeremiah 34:7 indicates that his prophecy was well on its way to fulfillment; only three fortified cities (including Jerusalem) had not fallen to the Babylonian army. Verses 8–11 describe how Zedekiah had enforced the law of manumission, so that the people set their Hebrew servants free, and how they then changed their minds (like the Egyptians in Exod 13!) and brought their servants back into bondage, despite having made a very solemn self-maledictory covenant to set them free (Jer 34:18). Apparently

---

[3] Christopher J. Wright, *Deuteronomy* (NIBCOT; Peabody, Mass: Hendrickson, 1996), 193.

the people changed their minds when the coming of the Egyptian army resulted in the temporary lifting of the Babylonian siege on Jerusalem (vv. 21–22; 37:5–11).

In vv. 12–16, the LORD reminds them of the connection between the manumission law and Israel's exodus from Egypt and tells them that their forefathers did not keep this law, or as it is put in *Tg. Jer.* 34:14, their fathers "did not receive my Word." Likewise, the present generation, after temporarily obeying, repented of their repentance, and in v. 17 the "measure for measure" judgment was pronounced on them because they "have not received my Word" to love their neighbor as the LORD loved them. The curse that the king, the priests, the officials, and the people pronounced upon themselves in the covenant (v. 18) would come true; they would be "released" to judgment, terror, disease, famine, and death.

The situation in the upper room has a number of similarities to that of Jeremiah's time. Jesus had predicted the destruction of Jerusalem and the temple a few days earlier (Matt 24:2; Mark 13:2; Luke 19:43–44; 21:20). The Word of the LORD has become a servant, and as such he reiterates the old commandment to love "as I have loved you," but he gives it a new meaning. It now grows out of the reality that he himself is going to the cross as a result of a gross violation of that commandment. Jesus will not merely be taken advantage of, as Israel was warned not to take advantage of the widow, the orphan, the sojourner, or the servant. He will be subject to a total denial of justice, and of the most basic of rights—the right to live. That is, Israel will once again refuse to receive the Word of the LORD, who commanded them to "love one another as I have loved you," but they will treat him worse than their fathers treated their servants in the time of Jeremiah. Jeremiah's words thus would come to have new meaning: "You have done evil more than your fathers" (Jer 7:26).

The Obedience of the Son

Finally, we note that Jesus, through whom this command was given to Israel in OT times, himself kept the command. The commandment given by God to Israel, "love one another as I have loved you," becomes, in the incarnation, a command from the Father to the Son, for the Son to love others as the Father has loved him. In John 15:9–10, Jesus says that he has obeyed that command: "Just as the Father has loved me, so I have loved you. . . . I have kept my Father's commandments." Two verses later, he repeats the "new" commandment to the disciples. This obedient love of Christ for people is what sent him to the cross, so that his law-keeping becomes an example for his followers of how to keep his law.

Loving God Means Keeping His Commandments

The Second Commandment and the Great Commandment

Another way in which the upper room appears as a new Sinai, with Jesus as lawgiver, is in the connection Jesus makes between love for him and keeping his commandments. In the second commandment from the old Sinai, the LORD says,

"I the LORD your God . . . show kindness to thousands, to those who love me, and to those who keep my commandments" (Exod 20:5–6; Deut 5:9–10). The conjunction translated "and" could also be rendered "that is," so that love for God is defined as keeping his commandments. This seems clearly to have been the case in the great commandment expounded by Moses in Deut 6:5–9, where he commanded Israel to "love the LORD your God with all your heart, with all your soul, and with all your strength" and immediately followed this with the requirement to keep his commandments upon their hearts, to speak of them throughout the day, and to teach them to their children.

Jesus makes the same point in the upper room, speaking not as a prophet, but as the lawgiver: "If you love me, you will keep my commandments" (John 14:15). Keener comments that "Biblically literate Jewish hearers would immediately think of the associations between obeying God's commandments and loving God (Exod 20:6; Deut 5:10; 7:9; 10:12; 11:1, 13, 22; 19:9; 30:16; Neh 1:5; Dan 9:4 . . .)."[4] According to the *Pal. Tgs.* of the Pentateuch, Israel heard the voice of the Word from Mt. Sinai make this connection between loving him and keeping his commandments. Later they heard this same connection made by Moses in Deuteronomy, since they requested that they hear from a person, not directly from the Word. And now the Word who has become flesh, a man like Moses, makes the same connection between loving him and keeping his commandments in the upper room, the new Sinai.

Similar ideas appear in John 14:21: "He who has my commandments and keeps them, he it is who loves me"; in 14:23: "If anyone loves me, he will keep my word"; and (framed negatively) in 14:24: "He who does not love me does not keep my words." In John 15:14, Jesus says, "you are my friends if you do what I command you." God calls Abraham "my friend" in Isa 41:8. The Hebrew word translated "my friend" is the singular form of the word translated "those who love me" in the second commandment. Thus John 15:14 is saying essentially the same thing as the verses cited above.

The second commandment also speaks of those who hate God: "I, the LORD your God, am a jealous God, visiting the iniquity of the fathers on the children, to the third and fourth generation of those who hate me." Jesus also speaks in the upper room of those who hate him: "If the world hates you, know that it has hated me before you." "He who hates me, hates my Father also. . . . Now they have both seen and hated me and my Father as well. But this is in order that the word may be fulfilled that is written in their law, 'They hated me without cause'" (John 15:18, 23–25).

Should these words be interpreted along the same lines as those in which Jesus speaks of love for him? That is, is this divine speech? One might say that by quoting from Ps 35:19 (= 69:4), Jesus is speaking of hatred of one human by another, like that experienced by David. Yet there is another potential OT background for these words, where God is speaking. In John 15:24, Jesus says, "If I had not done among them the works which no one else did, they would not have sin." This sounds very much like Exod 34:10, where the LORD says, "Behold, I am

---

[4] Keener, *John*, 2:974.

going to make a covenant. Before all your people I will do miracles which have not been done in all the earth." Just three verses earlier, the LORD quotes partially from the second commandment (20:5), ending with "visiting the iniquity of the fathers on the children, to the third and fourth generation." The verse finishes with the words (spoken, according to the Targums, by the Word from Mt. Sinai) "of those who hate me." Read in the light of the Targums, then, Jesus speaks the words, "the world . . . has hated me," as both God and man, as the lawgiver who gave the law on Mt. Sinai and a man like David who experienced hatred from other men who forsook the law. The targumic Word has become flesh.

The Obedience of the Son

As the Son through whom the law was given said that Israelites would show their love for him by keeping his commandments, he, too, when he took on human flesh, must show his love for the Father by keeping his commandments. In John 14:31, Jesus expresses this truth by saying, "That the world may know that I love the Father, and as the Father gave me commandment, even so I do. Arise, let us go from here."

Isaiah prophesied the obedience of the Servant of the LORD in submitting to beating and humiliation in Isa 50:5-6. Yet Christ's obedience did not consist of arranging for someone to mistreat him. Rather, it consisted of following the law of Moses, loving the church as the Father loved him, and telling the truth as God's representative. This obedience itself led to enmity and hatred, from which he did not shrink back. "The world cannot hate you, but it hates me because I testify of it, that its deeds are evil" (John 7:7).

Jesus did not go around trying to get himself killed. Before his hour came, in fact, he hid himself or avoided his persecutors who wanted to kill him (e.g., John 8:59). He obeyed the command to go to the cross by going to a certain place (Gethsemane), at a certain time (after the last supper), and submitting to arrest and all that followed. The divine lawgiver became the divine law keeper, an example for his people of showing love for God by keeping his commandments.

These comparisons of Jesus' statements in the upper room with passages from the OT have shown that there is no conflict between the requirements of the OT law and the NT ideal of Christlikeness. When the LORD gave Israel the command to "love others as I have loved you," moral likeness to God was the basis for that law, as it was for all of the other moral laws. Reading Jesus' upper room discourse in the light of the Targums shows that the OT laws were given to Israel through the Word of God—the Son. Therefore, moral likeness to the Son was the basis for the ethical laws of Moses. To suggest that this basis for NT ethical conduct is a change from the OT period is therefore to overlook the implications of Christ's deity.

The Blessings and Curses

A significant portion of the law consists of promises of blessing for obedience and warnings of curses for disobedience. The major passages of blessings and curses in the law are Lev 26 and Deut 28, and we can also see some similarities between these passages and the upper room discourse.

In John 13:17, Jesus gives a general promise of blessing for obedience: "If you know these things, blessed [*or* happy] are you if you do them." This may be compared to the general promise of blessing in Deut 28:2, "All these blessings will come upon you and overtake you if you listen to the voice of the LORD your God," which *Tg. Neof.* renders ". . . if you diligently listen to the voice of the Word of the LORD your God" and *Tgs. Ps.-J.* and *Onq.* render ". . . if you receive the Word of the LORD your God."

In John 14:23, Jesus promises, "If anyone loves me, he will keep my word, and my Father will love him, and we will come to him, and make our dwelling with him." This promise contains parallels to Lev 26:11–12, which we noted in ch. 2, because of its rendering in the Targums:

MT	Targums
I will make my dwelling among you	*Tg. Neof.:* I will make the glory of my *Shekinah* dwell among you (similarly *Tg. Ps.-J.*)
and my soul	*Tgs. Onq.* and *Ps.-J.:* my Word
will not reject you.	
I will also walk among you	*Tg. Neof.:* my Word will go among you
	Tg. Ps.-J.: I will make the glory of my *Shekinah* dwell among you (similarly *Tg. Neof.* [mg.])
and be your God	*Tgs. Neof.* and *Ps.-J.:* my Word will be to you a redeeming God
and you shall be my people.	

In John 14:21, 23; 15:10, Jesus promises the disciples that if they keep his word, they will be loved by the Father and the Son. This promise can be compared to Deut 7:12–13, where Moses says that if the Israelites obey the LORD, "he will love you and bless you and multiply you," and *Tg. Ps.-J.* Lev 26:44, "I will love them in my Word" (MT: "I will not reject them"). In John 14:27; 16:33, Jesus promises the blessing of peace, which reminds us of Lev 26:6, "I will grant peace in the land, so that you may lie down with no one making you tremble." In John 15:5, Jesus promises the blessing of fruitfulness, just as Lev 26:9 says "I will make you fruitful and multiply you."

Another way the theme of blessings and curses is brought out by Jesus is in his use of the vine and branches analogy and its basis in (primarily) Ps 80, in which Israel is the vine transplanted from Egypt into the promised land. There the vine initially prospered and filled the land but has since been despoiled by passersby and wild beasts, who came through its broken walls (vv. 12–13), and burned it with fire so that the people perish (v. 16). God does not answer their prayers (v. 4); they are fed the bread of tears (v. 5) and scorned by their neighbors (v. 6). In short, Israel has experienced the covenant curses.

Jesus uses the same figure to speak of the blessings and curses. In Ps 80, the vine is ruined, but the success of Jesus as vine is not in doubt: "I am he, the true vine" (John 15:1). The true vine stands in contrast to fallible and/or false predecessors such as Zedekiah, the false vine of the parable of Ezek 17. However, the success of the branches is in doubt. The interpretation of the branches as disciples in *Tg. Ps.* 80:11 may have been current as Jesus spoke, and if so the figure would be familiar to the disciples.[5] If the disciples are obedient, they will bear much fruit (John 15:5) and their prayers will be answered, unlike the situation of Ps 80:4 (cf. John 15:7; 16:23–24). As with the targumic vine (along with its branches) in Ps 80, if they are not obedient, they will be burned up (v. 6).

Despite the many OT parallels, there is something new about the blessings and curses in the upper room discourse. Jesus warns the disciples that even though they are blessed by doing his will and bearing fruit, they may be killed precisely because of their obedience (John 15:21; 16:2–3). This is important since if one defines blessings and curses only according to the terminology of the law, one might rather conclude that those killed for the sake of Christ are cursed. Of course, the believer's example in this matter is Jesus himself, put to death as a notorious criminal, but endlessly blessed:

> May his name endure forever,
>   May his name increase as long as the sun shines.
> Let men bless themselves in him,
>   Let all nations call him blessed. (Ps 72:17)

The Command to Depart

John is the only Gospel writer to report that the disciples left the upper room at the command of Jesus (John 14:31). John might have mentioned this simply as a way of highlighting the obedience of Jesus to the Father, as noted above. But he may also have wanted to draw the attention of his followers to another parallel between his teaching in the upper room and Mt. Sinai. We have already seen that the Lord's promise of going to prepare a place for the disciples parallels the LORD going before Israel on a three-day journey from Mt. Sinai (Num 10). In highlighting the command to depart, John may be completing the picture.

Numbers 10:13 says that Israel "moved out for the first time according to the mouth of the LORD through the hand of Moses." The Targums say that they departed according to "the Word of the LORD" (*Tgs. Onq.* and *Ps.-J.*) or "the decree of the Word (of the LORD)" (*Tg. Neof.*). The command to depart is recalled by Moses in Deut 1:6, and here the Targums do not ascribe the command to the Word of the LORD. However, one could infer from the *Pal. Tgs.* Num 7:89 that this command was communicated to Moses by the Word, speaking to him from the holy of holies.

---

[5] "You made branches grow, you sent out her (Jerusalem's) disciples to the Great Sea, and her children to the River Euphrates." The previous verse mentions Jerusalem and the academies. Saul of Tarsus is a good example of these "branches" from the academies who would persecute the true branches.

Numbers 9:18–23 also makes the point several times that the Israelites set out and camped throughout the wilderness period "according to the mouth of the LORD" (vv. 18, 20, 23), which the Targums render, as in Num 10:13, "according to the Word of the LORD" or "according to the decree of the Word of the LORD."

THE OBEDIENCE OF JESUS AT THE FEASTS

Besides details such as the time and place of the three annual feasts, the sacrifices to be offered, and the like, Deut 16 prescribes certain duties that the Israelites are to carry out. Of primary importance was the duty to remember their deliverance from Egypt, mentioned in connection with the feasts of Passover/Unleavened Bread (v. 3b) and Pentecost (v. 12). We may presume that this duty was intended to be part of the Feast of Booths as well, though it is not specifically mentioned; if nothing else, says Deut 16:3, they should remember every day of their lives their deliverance from Egypt. In light of this, the statement by Jesus' critics in John 8:33, "We have never been enslaved to anyone," implies that they had failed in their duty to be thankful to God for their redemption.

Jesus' status as the Word of the LORD raises the question as to whether he was obligated to keep this command of remembrance. The OT redemption from Egypt was, after all, accomplished through him, and he came to the feasts as the redeemer. Malachi had prophesied, "The Lord whom you seek will suddenly come to his temple" (3:1), and John seems to indicate that this prophesy was fulfilled at the Feast of Booths (John 7–8). John 7:11 says that the Jews were seeking him at the feast, and then in v. 14 he suddenly appears in the temple in the middle of the feast. He comes to the feast as redeemer, not as one needing to remember redemption. His saying, "I am he, the light of the world; he who follows me shall not walk in the darkness, but shall have the light of life" (8:12) may serve as a reminder that Israel had followed the Word of the LORD in the pillar of fire and cloud out of Egypt, according to *Tg. Neof.* and *Frg. Tg. P* Exod 13:21–22. In John 8:32–36, Jesus offers redemption from slavery to sin, a greater deliverance than that from Egypt, since one can be free from Egypt, but not be "free indeed" (v. 36). How should Israel have responded to their redemption? They should have been thankful. Yet as previously noted, John 8:33 indicates that they are not thankful. Indeed, they seek to kill the redeemer at the feast (7:19, 25; 8:59)!

Deuteronomy 16 also obligates the Israelites to rejoice at the feasts. While this duty is mentioned specifically for only two of the three feasts (Pentecost, v. 11; Booths, vv. 14–15), it is again safe to presume that this was an obligation for all three. Further, the celebrant was not to think only of himself and his family when rejoicing; he was to ensure that all could rejoice, including those most likely to be poor and unable to provide for the festivities—servants, orphans, widows, sojourners, and Levites.

John highlights the obedience of Jesus to this obligation of rejoicing at the Feast of the Passover/Unleavened Bread, his last feast, during which he was crucified and rose again. John 13:29 says that the disciples thought that Jesus had sent

Judas out to buy provisions for the feast or to give something to the poor. That the disciples would think this shows that it was the practice of Jesus to give to the poor. This general obligation of the Israelite is especially important at the feasts so that the poor might rejoice along with everyone else.

Psalm 41:1 pronounces a blessing on the one who considers the poor (or the helpless): the LORD will deliver him in a day of trouble, protect him, and keep him alive. This blessing would apply to Jesus, as one who considered the poor. Jesus has just quoted from this psalm (John 13:18), saying that he would be betrayed as David was. Would the psalm's promise of being kept alive be fulfilled for him? As some commentators have noted, the Hebrew, "you will keep him alive" (v. 2), can also mean "you will make him alive," and so yes, the promise was fulfilled, in resurrection.[6]

The disciples, as itinerant ministers, would be like the Levites whom the Israelites were to provide for so that they too could rejoice in the feast. Because Jesus was going to die, they would instead be filled with sorrow. Nevertheless, Jesus assures them that he will not leave them as orphans (John 14:18; orphans, again, are to be Israel's special concern during the feasts); their sorrow will be turned to joy (16:20–22). But Jesus also promises joy beyond the feast days, joy that comes from keeping his commandments and abiding in his love, joy that comes from answered prayer (15:10–11; 16:24). "That your joy may be made full" (cf. 15:11; 16:24) sounds very much like Deut 16:15, "that you may be altogether joyful."

Widows were also singled out for special concern at the feasts, and in John 19:26–27 we see Jesus caring for his mother by appointing someone to care for her, which may indicate that she was a widow. If her husband Joseph were in fact deceased, then a widow losing her oldest son during the feast would have been a special cause of sorrow for Mary. Jesus provides for her, asking the "beloved disciple" to serve as her son. Like the sorrow of the disciples, her sorrow too will be turned to joy during the feast.

In providing for Mary, Jesus is also keeping the fifth commandment. As Paul says, this is the first commandment with a promise, and the promise is long life upon the land. Even while dying, Jesus paradoxically fulfills the command that promises long life for those who keep it. The same paradox exists in the fourth Servant Song, Isa 52:13–53:12. The passage makes it clear that the servant would suffer to the point of death: "he was cut off out of the land of the living" (53:8); his grave would be assigned to be with wicked men, yet he would be with a rich man in his death (v. 9). Yet, despite his suffering, "he will prolong his days" (the reward for keeping the fifth commandment, and the law in general). The promise is fulfilled in the resurrection.

The law was given through the Son in OT times, and from the time he left his Father's house until the time he returned to the Father, Jesus fulfilled the role of a servant, always obeying the law, always doing the will of the Father as his representative, and, when the appointed hour had come, surrendering himself to the powers of darkness to make his obedience complete for the salvation of his people.

---

[6] See, e.g., Hanson, *Prophetic Gospel*, 174.

Conclusions

Again we have seen that Jesus, as he is presented as the lawgiver in the fourth Gospel, has both divine (YHWH) and human (Moses) parallels to the OT. The divine parallels involve OT texts wherein the divine Word figures prominently in the corresponding Targums. John portrays Jesus as the one through whom the OT law was given on Mt. Sinai and in the holy of holies. He remains the divine lawgiver, but, having become flesh, he is also a human lawgiver, as well as the perfect law keeper, all to provide salvation and set an example for his followers.

8

Jesus as the One in Whom We Must Believe

Introduction

We have seen in previous chapters that John portrays Jesus Christ in various divine roles (the one who comes down from heaven to save his people by warfare, to be their glorious bridegroom, to be their lawgiver, and to dwell among them and be their God), that Jesus' performance of these roles reveals the name of God, and that in the work of Christ there is continuity with the works of God throughout the OT, as well as change due to the incarnation. "The Word became flesh and dwelt among us" summarizes this message. This revelation calls for a response of faith, and in this chapter we examine language in John that speaks either of those who believed in Jesus or of the need to believe in Jesus in order to have life. We will also look at similar language of response in the OT and as it is developed in the interpretations of the OT found in the Targums. Again we will see that there is continuity between the OT and the Gospel of John on the theme of believing in YHWH, as well as change that results from the fact that the Word of God has become flesh.

Believing in Jesus the Son of Man

In the OT, resting one's faith on humans is not generally commended; more often it is condemned (e.g., Jer 17:5). Sometimes, however, faith in humans, specifically God's spokespersons the prophets, is viewed positively. This raises the question whether OT passages that commend faith in the prophets or passages that focus on faith in the LORD are more relevant to John's language about trusting in Jesus. In keeping with John's overriding theme that "the Word became flesh," we shall see that the answer is that both are relevant.

Faith in Moses and the Prophets (Exod 14:31; 19:3; 2 Chr 20:20)

Moses is singled out as a man in whom Israel should believe. After crossing through the Red Sea, "the people believed in the LORD, and in Moses his servant" (Exod 14:31). On Mount Sinai the LORD says to Moses, "I will come to you in a thick cloud, that the people might hear when I speak with you, and may also believe in you forever" (Exod 19:3). Clearly, believing in Moses is viewed positively and is grounded in the fact that Moses is a faithful spokesperson for the LORD. Similarly, Jehoshaphat urges the people of Judah, "Believe in the LORD your God, and believe in his prophets," using wording much like Exod 14:31 and addressing a similar situation (2 Chr 20:20; compare v. 17 with Exod 14:13–14).

John 14:1 is closely analogous to Exod 14:31, substituting Jesus as servant of God for Moses, as can be seen from the following comparison:[1]

Exod 14:31	John 14:1
The people . . . believed in the LORD and in Moses his servant.	Believe in God, believe also in me (a servant like Moses).

John 5:46 points in the same direction: "If you believed Moses, you would believe me, for he wrote about me." That is, if Jesus' hearers believed in Moses the spokesperson for God, they should believe in Jesus, another spokesperson for God. After all, Moses promised in Deut 18:15–18 that God would raise up prophets like Moses in the future to speak to the people. However, passages like John 9:35, "Do you believe in the Son of Man?" that are followed by profession of faith and worship (v. 38), clearly contrast with OT expressions of faith in Moses, which are subordinated to faith in the God of Moses.

Faith in the Divine Word

John 14:1; Num 10:33; Deut 1:32–33

We saw in our examination of John 14:2 in ch. 5 that the Lord's language, "I go to prepare a place for you," depends on Num 10:33, where the Targums say "prepare" instead of "search out" a resting place. Jesus' going to the cross and returning in the resurrection is analogous to Israel's three-day journey on their initial departure from Mt. Sinai, with the LORD going before them to defeat their enemies and returning to dwell among them. Specifically, Jesus's death and victorious return answers the petition of Moses as rendered in the Targums that the Word of the LORD would rise up and scatter the enemies of God's people, turn away his wrath, and return to dwell among them and bless them (*Pal. Tgs.* Num 10:35–36). In Deut 1:32–36, Moses reminds Israel of how the previous generation refused to enter the promised land through unbelief, borrowing language from Num 10:33 and mentioning Caleb as an exception. Comparing this passage in *Tg. Neof.* with John 14, in light of John's designation of Jesus as the divine Word, is most suggestive:

---

[1] Reim, *Alttestamentlichen Hintergrund*, 106, 111, 139, 143.

MT	Tg. Neof.	John 14:1–3
[32]Yet in this matter you were *not believing in the* LORD *your God,* [33]who goes before you on the way, *to seek out a place for you to camp.* . . . [36]Caleb . . . has *followed the* LORD fully.	Yet in this matter you were *not believing in the name of the Word of the* LORD *your God, who led* before you on the way to prepare a place for your encampment. . . . Caleb . . . has *followed the Word of the* LORD *completely.*[2]	Let not your heart be troubled; *believe in God,* believe also in me. In my Father's house are many dwelling places; if it were not so, I would have told you; for *I go to prepare a place for you.*

Thus while John 14:1 can be taken along the lines of Exod 14:31 to mean "Believe in God and in me his servant and representative," it can also be taken along the lines of *Tg. Neof.* Deut 1:32 to mean "Believe in me, the divine Word." Again we recall that John's Prologue speaks of "those who believed in his (the Word's) name" (John 1:12). But since John has told us "the Word became flesh," we do not have to choose between these two options; both are true. Jesus is warning the disciples implicitly not to be like the wilderness generation; instead, they should be like Caleb, who, long before them, followed the invisible Word fully by obeying his word given through the human representative, Moses.

John 5:46; Exod 14:31

Likewise, as we saw in ch. 7, the Targums of Exod 14:31 suggest another way of reading John 5:46:

Pal. Tgs. Exod 14:31	John 5:46
The people . . . believed *in the name of the Word of the* LORD and in the prophecy of his servant Moses.	If you believed Moses, you would *believe me,* for he wrote about me.

Again, John's designation of Jesus as the divine Word helps us make the proper connection. Two further factors of which we took note in ch. 7 point to this interpretation: (1) If we follow the emphasis of the Greek text, a better translation of John 5:46 would be, "If you believed Moses, you would believe me, for *it was about me* that he wrote.[3] This is most naturally understood, "Moses was my spokesperson" (similarly John 12:41: Isaiah "spoke of him," i.e., of Christ, referring to Isa 6). Moses wrote, for example, about the LORD who was "full of grace and truth" (see ch. 2 above), who came down from heaven to reveal his name (chs. 3 and 4), to save his people (ch. 5), to take them as his bride (ch. 6), to give them his law (ch. 7), and to be their God. (2) Jesus may have been alluding to a rabbinical saying on Exod 14:31 (cited above), "If they believed Moses, *a fortiori* (they believed the Lord . . .)."

---

[2] *Tgs. Ps.-J.* and *Onq.* have "the Word" instead of "the name of the Word."
[3] περὶ γὰρ ἐμοῦ ἐκεῖνος ἔγραψεν.

John 12:37; 2:11, 23; Num 14:11, 22

As we have noted several times, the wording of John 12:37 seems to be influenced by Num 14:11, and again the reference to the divine Word in the Targums of this verse is suggestive:

John 12:37	Num 14:11 (MT)	*Tgs. Ps.-J.* and *Onq.*
Though he had performed so many *signs* before them, they were *not believing* in him.	How long will they *not believe* in me, despite all the *signs* which I have done in their midst?	How long will they *not believe* in my Word, despite all the *miracles* which I have worked among them? (Cf. *Tg. Neof.*: How long will they not believe in the name of my Word?)

Such a comparison would serve to draw a parallel between the generation that rejected Jesus and the generation that died in the wilderness: "this evil generation" (Deut 1:35); "this evil congregation which is gathered together against me" (Num 14:35). Likewise, the threat, "you will die in your sins" (John 8:24), while reminiscent of similar warnings in Ezek 3:18–20; 33:8, 9, 18, should also remind us of the wilderness generation, as the daughters of Zelophehad, presenting their petition before Moses, said that their father had not participated in the rebellion of Korah, but "he died in his own sin" (Num 27:3). That is, he was like the rest of the generation that "did not believe in the LORD" (or, according to the Targums, "[the name of] his Word") and died for this unbelief. The way John describes those who believed in Jesus inverts the way Num 14:22 and 14:11 describe the wilderness generation, speaking of their faith instead of their unbelief:

Num 14:22	*Tgs.* Num 14:11	John 2:11, 23
Surely, all the men who have seen *my glory and my signs* which I have done in Egypt and in the wilderness, yet have tested me these ten times and have not listened to my voice (*Tgs. Ps.-J.* and *Onq.*: have not received my Word), shall by no means see the land.	How long will they not believe in [the name of] my Word?	This beginning of signs Jesus did in Cana of Galilee, and manifested *his glory,* and his disciples believed in him. . . . Many believed in his name, observing *his signs* which he was doing.

"His glory" and "his signs" seem naturally related to "my glory and my signs" of Num 14:22, since there is no scriptural reference to the glory of Moses being manifested in the miracles of the exodus and wilderness. The "beginning of signs"—turning water into wine—also points to the exodus miracles, which began with the waters of the Nile being turned to blood (Exod 7:17–19). Another possible parallel is that the Nile waters were used for purification and could be stored in vessels in a temple for that purpose.[4] The two miracles form a contrast in that one was a disaster

---

[4] A connection between the first miracle of Jesus and the first plague in Egypt has been noted by Harald Sahlin (*Zur Typologie des Johannesevangeliums* [Uppsala: Lundequistska Bokhandeln, 1950], 330) and Robert Houston Smith ("Exodus Typology in the Fourth Gos-

for Egyptians, the other a blessing for Israelites. In the same way, the first plague in Egypt, which killed the fish in the Nile (Exod 7:18, 21), can be contrasted to the last sign mentioned by John, the miraculous catch of fish (John 21:5–6).

The other miracles of Jesus in John may likewise also be related to "my signs which I have done in Egypt and in the wilderness." The feeding of the five thousand is like the miraculous feeding of the Israelites in the wilderness (6:11). The healing miracles and the resurrection of Lazarus can be understood in light of the LORD's promise in Exod 15:26: "If you diligently listen to the voice of the LORD (*Tgs. Onq.* and *Ps.-J.*: "receive the Word of the LORD"; *Tg. Neof.*: "listen to the Word of the LORD") . . . all the afflictions which I put upon the Egyptians I will not put upon you, for I, the LORD, am your healer" (*Tg. Neof.* [mg. 1] and *Frg. Tgs. P, V*: "who by my Word heals you"; *Tg. Neof.* [mg. 2]: "who heals by the Word of the LORD"). Jesus' walking on the water is like the LORD leading the Israelites through the Red Sea, as we shall see below. The healing of the man born blind brought this man out of perpetual darkness; the ninth plague brought darkness upon the Egyptians (Exod 10:23; they did not see one another) while the Israelites experienced light. Even the crucifixion of Jesus, on Passover Eve, can be compared to the tenth plague, since in it he destroyed the works of the devil by enduring the fate of the Egyptian firstborn (see ch. 5).

Two additional parallels between the two generations may have come to mind. First, Moses' generation perished over a period of forty years, and, more specifically, they fought after being warned not to fight since they would be defeated (Num 14:40–42). According to all the Targums of this passage, Moses warned them that they would be defeated because the LORD's *Shekinah* was not among them, and the Word of the LORD would not be their helper. Second, we note that the Talmud preserves a tradition that certain miracles interpreted as indicating the presence of the *Shekinah* in Israel ceased forty years prior to the destruction of Jerusalem, and perhaps that tradition was already current when John wrote.

John 2:23–25; Gen 40:23; Jer 17:5, 7, 10; Ps 118:8–9

As noted above, John 2:23 speaks about those who believed in Jesus at the Passover feast in a manner that contrasts with Israel's unbelief in the LORD described in Num 14:11, 22. The appropriateness of such faith in the man Jesus could be questioned on the basis of Jer 17:5, which says, "Cursed is the man who trusts in mankind, who makes flesh his strength," in contrast with "the man who trusts in the LORD, and whose trust is the LORD," who is blessed (v. 7), and Ps 118:8–9, which says that it is better to trust in the LORD than to trust in men, even princes. A

---

pel," *JBL* 81 [1962]: 334). For the Nile waters being used for purification, see Coffin Spell 439: (the priest says) "Wash yourself in the swamp-waters of the inundation and in the waters of the Nile which are in the Broad Hall." This was cited by Rodger Wayne Dalman, "The Theology of Israel's Sea Crossing" (Th.D. diss., Concordia Seminary, Saint Louis, 1990), 130–31, in connection with Exod 7:15. Similarly, Rosemary Clark describes "The Nile Room" of an Egyptian temple where Nile waters were stored for purification (*The Sacred Tradition in Ancient Egypt: The Esoteric Wisdom Revealed* [Saint Paul, Minn.: Llewellyn, 2000], 240).

look at the Targum renderings of these passages suggests that John may have met such objections in part by identifying Jesus as the divine Word. In the case of Jer 17:5, 7, we are most interested in a quotation of these verses in the *Pal. Tgs.* Gen 40:23, where there is an attempt to explain why Joseph had to remain in prison two more years after asking the cupbearer to remember him to Pharaoh:

> Joseph forsook the grace which is from above and the grace which is from below and the grace which accompanied him from his father's house, and *he trusted* in the chief cup bearer, *in flesh that passes, in flesh that tastes the cup of death*. And he did not remember the Scripture, for it is written in the book of the law of the LORD, which is like the Book of the Wars, "*Cursed is the son of man who trusts in flesh and who places his trust in flesh. <And blessed shall be the man who trusts in the name of the Word of the LORD, and who makes the Word of the LORD his trust.>*" Therefore the chief cup bearer did not remember Joseph and he forgot him until the appointed time to redeem arrived. (*Tg. Neof.* Gen 40:23).[5]

In saying that Jesus did not entrust himself to any person (John 2:24), John is telling us that Jesus himself was obedient to Jer 17:5. In identifying Jesus as the Word who became flesh, John also answers the objection that trusting in Jesus is trusting in flesh that passed away and tasted the cup of death, and that the person (son of man) who does so brings a curse upon himself or herself. To the contrary, those who trust in Jesus are blessed, not cursed, for they are trusting in the name of the Word of the LORD (John 1:12), making the divine Word their trust, who, though he tasted the cup of death, did not pass away but abides forever.

Likewise *Tg. Ps.* 118:8–9 says that it is better to trust in *the Word of the LORD* than to trust in *a son of man*, even princes. Because of the incarnation, however, it is not an either-or situation; *the* Son of Man is now the divine Word, and trust in him is not only commended, but required, for eternal life.

John goes on to say that Jesus "knew all men" and "knew what was in man" (2:24–25), which agrees with another passage in Jer 17: "The heart is more deceitful than all else, . . . who can know it? I, the LORD, search the heart, I test the mind, even to give to each man according to his own ways" (vv. 9–10).[6] In relation to Jer 17 and Ps 118, then, Jesus as a person was obedient to the command not to trust in any human, but those who trust in him are not guilty of trusting in a human, or a son of man, or in flesh that passes away; rather, they are obeying these passages because they are trusting in the name of the divine Word who has become flesh.

John 3:14, 18; Num 21:8–9

In John 3:14, Jesus says to Nicodemus that he will be lifted up like the bronze snake in the wilderness, so that those who believe in him may have eternal life. He

---

[5] Text in angled brackets is supplied from *Frg. Tg. P* (it was probably accidentally omitted in *Tg. Neof.*); *Frg. Tg. V* is similar but omits "and who makes the Word of the Lord his trust."

[6] As noted in ch. 3, Jer 17:10 is also paraphrased by Jesus in Rev 2:23, where "I am he" (ἐγώ εἰμι; i.e., Jesus) substitutes for "I, the LORD" (אֲנִי יהוה; LXX: ἐγὼ κύριος).

goes on to say that those who do not believe are condemned already, since they have not believed in the name of the only Son of God. Numbers 21:5, "The people spoke against God and against Moses," is a reversal of Exod 14:31, when they believed in the Lord and in Moses. Numbers 21:8–9 does not mention any requirement of faith on the part of the Israelites who looked to the snake in order to live, and *Tg. Ps.-J.* apparently tried to make up for this perceived lack by adding that in order to live, the one who was bitten must direct his heart toward the name of the Word of the Lord. Based on this Targum reading, some scholars have suggested the possibility that "the name of the only Son of God" in v. 18 is the same as "the name of the Word of the Lord," that is, the Tetragrammaton.[7] That the name of the Son of God is the Tetragrammaton rather than a new name (i.e., Jesus) would explain why the one who does not believe in this name "is condemned already." In the OT, Israelites were not required to believe in the name Jesus, but rather in the name YHWH, which is here called "the name of the only Son of God." This is further supported by John 17:11–12, where Jesus says that the Father has given him his name (see ch. 3).

John 6:20; 8:24, 28; 13:19; Isa 43:10

In Isa 43:10, the Lord summons Israel as witness to the fact that he alone (in contrast to the idols) foretells the future, "So that you might know and believe me, and understand that I am he. Before me there was no God formed, and there will be none after me." As noted in ch. 3, "I am he" is אֲנִי הוּא, which is rendered idiomatically in the LXX as ἐγώ εἰμι. The Aramaic is אֲנָא הוּא. Consequently, when Jesus says ἐγώ εἰμι, the possibility exists that these Greek words represent an originally spoken Aramaic אֲנָא הוּא. When the language of Jesus alludes to MT language where God says "I am he" and the LXX has ἐγώ εἰμι, it is commonly accepted that we should understand ἐγώ εἰμι as the divine "I am he." In the next chapter, I will argue that all the ἐγώ εἰμι sayings of Jesus should be so understood and translated, but for now I will note those which seem to depend on Isa 43:10.

The clearest NT allusion to Isa 43:10 is found in John 13:19: "From now on I am telling you before it comes to pass, so that when it does occur, you will know that I am he." The premise of these two verses is the same—that prediction of the future is proof of the genuineness and uniqueness of the God of Israel. The language moves beyond a mere claim to be a genuine prophet, although Jesus might have borrowed part of the language of this verse from Ezek 33:33: "When it comes to pass—behold, it is coming—they will know that a prophet has been in their midst." When Jesus says "you will know that I am he," he is speaking to his disciples in his own person in the same way that God spoke to Israel through Isaiah.

---

[7] M.-É. Boismard, "Les citations targumiques dans le quatrième évangile," *RB* 66 (1959): 378, cited by Brown, *John*, 1:133; also noted by McNamara, *Targum and Testament*, 147–48. Reim also noted the targumic rendering of Num 21:8 as background to John 3:14, 18, but incorrectly ascribed it to *Tg. Onq.* (*Alttestamentlichen Hintergrund*, 152).

John 8:24, like 13:19, contains an "absolute" use of "I am he." That is, the word "he" (presumably underlying ἐγώ εἰμι in the Aramaic) does not have a precise antecedent or predicate. "Unless you believe that I am he, you will die in your sins." Because his hearers do not immediately see the connection to the divine "I am he" of Isaiah, and because there is no predicate or antecedent, they do not understand who he is claiming to be (v. 25). In contrast, the saying in 8:28 has a clear antecedent: "When you lift up the Son of Man, you will know that I am he." Although the antecedent is "the Son of Man," the allusion to Isa 43:10 is much like John 8:24; together they reflect the "know" and "believe" of that verse:

Isa 43:10	**John 8:24**	**John 8:28**
So that you may *know and believe* me, and understand *that I am he.*	Unless you *believe that I am he.*	Then you will *know that I am he.*

The parallel to Isa 43:10 is slightly closer in the LXX: "So that you may know and believe and understand that I am he."[8]

Another reason for linking John 8:28 with Isa 43:10 is that it is a prediction of the future, just as in the context of John 13:19. In addition, we saw in ch. 5 that the lifting up of the Son of Man is an offensive act of war on the part of Christ. Jesus' words in John 8:28 are tantamount to saying, "When I defeat Satan on the cross, then you will know that I am he." In this form it can be compared to the idea that through God's acts of war against the Egyptians, they will know "that I am the Lord." In the *Pal. Tgs.* of the Pentateuch, "I am [אני] the Lord" from the MT is often rendered by "I am he [אנא הוא], the Lord." In the next chapter, we will see that John 8:28 is also similar to several such divine sayings in *Tg. Neof.* Exodus, and some of these are spoken by the divine Word, according to the marginal glosses of *Tg. Neof.*

In John 6:20, when Jesus walks on the water and greets the disciples with "It is I [ἐγώ εἰμι], do not be afraid," the most obvious intent is to identify himself (by the sound of his voice) to his disciples as someone they know. However, there are also a number of reasons to understand this verse as echoing the divine "I am he" of Isa 43:10: (1) The divine assurance, "do not be afraid," also occurs in the context of Isa 43:10 (vv. 1 and 5). (2) That assurance is given to Israel for comfort when they are passing through the waters (v. 2), which is what the disciples are doing when Jesus comes to them.[9] (3) "Do not be afraid, I am with you" of Isa 43:5 is in *Tg. Isa.* "Do not be afraid, for my Word is your help." Jesus the Word helps the disciples get to the other side (v. 21). (4) The Targum also interprets Isa 43:2 historically: "at the

---

[8] See David Mark Ball, *"I Am" in John's Gospel: Literary Function, Background and Theological Implications* (JSNTSup 124; Sheffield: Sheffield Academic Press, 1996), 188–89.

[9] See, e.g., Ball, *"I Am" in John's Gospel,* 183–85, and John Paul Heil, *Jesus Walking on the Sea: Meaning and Gospel Functions of Matt 14:22–33, Mark 6:45–52 and John 6:15b–21* (AnBib 87; Rome: Biblical Institute Press, 1981), 59.

first, when you passed through the Red Sea, my Word was your help." When Israel crossed the sea, there was a strong wind blowing, and it was dark (Exod 14:21), just as in John 6 (vv. 17–18). Thus, while scholars have noted a connection between John 6:20 and Isa 43:10 based only on the MT, the connections are even stronger when we take into account *Tg. Isa.* 43 and John's designation of Jesus as the divine Word.

In *Tg. Isa.* 43:1, God calls Israel "my own." The Aramaic is דילי, and the third person (his own) would be דיליה, which, as noted in ch. 1, has been suggested as the Aramaic which underlies "his own" of John 1:11–12, where John says that the divine Word came to his own, who did not receive him, but to those who did receive him, he gave the right to become children of God. In John 6:17–21, Jesus *comes to* the disciples (v. 17), they *receive him* (v. 21), and they immediately arrive at their destination (John uses the verbs ἔρχομαι and λαμβάνω, as in 1:11–12). The event thus echoes the language of 1:11–12, that Christ has come, and those who receive him are given eternal life.

The crossing of the Red Sea is also mentioned in Ps 77:14–20. Verse 19 of the psalm says, "Your path was through the sea, your way through mighty waters; Your footsteps could not be discerned," and some have related this to Jesus' walking on the sea.[10] Some Targum passages speak of the presence of the divine Word in the crossing of the sea. *Targum Neofiti* [mg.] and *Frg. Tg. V* Exod 14:24 say that the divine Word looked upon the Egyptians and confounded them. In *Tg. Ps.-J.* Exod 14:25, the Egyptians acknowledge that the divine Word is fighting against them. At that time, his footsteps could not be seen on the dry ground because, of course, he had no physical feet. When the Word became flesh, his footsteps could not be discerned because water does not sustain footprints.

The Targums render Ps 77 in some interesting ways: *Targum Psalms* 77:14 says, "You are he, the God who works wonders." "You are he" is את הוא, spoken of God, who says in Isa 43:10 (among many places), "I am he." While v. 16 of the MT says that the waters saw God and trembled, the Targum says that the Israelites saw his *Shekinah* in the midst of the sea, and the Gentiles trembled. The disciples did both of these things when they saw Jesus.

COMING TO JESUS IN ORDER TO HAVE LIFE
(JOHN 5:40; 6:45; 7:37; ISA 55:1–3)

Believing in Jesus and coming to him are essentially the same. This fact is seen in the parallelism within John 6:35, "He who *comes to me* will not hunger, and he who *believes in me* will never thirst," as well as in John 7:37–38, "Let him *come to me* . . . he who *believes in me*." While language about believing in Jesus is found throughout the Gospel, the idea of coming to him is found in John 5:40 and 7:37 and six times in the bread of life discourse (6:35, 37 [2x], 44, 45, 65). We have already noted in ch. 4 the dependence of John 5:40 and 7:37 on Isa 55:1–3:

---

[10] Brown, *John*, 1:255.

John 5:39–40	John 7:37	Isa 55:1–3
You search the Scriptures because you think that in them you have eternal life; it is these that testify about me. But you are unwilling to *come to me,* that you might have life.	If anyone is thirsty, let him *come to me and drink.*	*Everyone who thirsts, come* to the waters. . . . Incline your ear and *come to me.* Listen, that your soul may live.

This dependence makes it clear that Jesus' statement that "the Scriptures . . . testify about me" does not refer primarily to a relatively few messianic prophecies scattered throughout the OT, but should be taken in the same way as "it was about me that Moses wrote" a few verses later (v. 46). Hanson notes: "Thus we are not to seek for prophecies about the Messiah in the Pentateuch, where they are notoriously difficult to find."[11] The OT Scriptures testify primarily about the person and work of YHWH, the God of Israel. "Come to me" is thus divine speech.

That the "come to me" language of John 6 also depends on Isa 55:1–3 is not so obvious. The more obvious OT background here is the giving of the manna in the wilderness. However, we note that the thought of John 6:27 ("Do not work for the food which perishes, but for the food which endures to eternal life") is very much along the lines of Isa 55:2 ("Why do you spend money for what is not bread, and your wages for what does not satisfy? Listen carefully to me, and eat what is good"). For "listen carefully to me," *Tg. Isa.* has "diligently receive my Word."

In John 6:45, Jesus also draws his hearers' attention to the context of this divine invitation by quoting the promise of Isa 54:13, "All your sons will be taught of the LORD," which appears just a few verses before that invitation. In the same verse, Jesus goes on to make another allusion to Isa 55:1–3 which becomes apparent only when we look at the Targum of that passage. "Come to the waters" of Isa 55:1 is rendered "*come* and *learn,*" while "come, buy, and eat" becomes "*come, hear,* and *learn.*" Jesus seems to allude to this targumic interpretation when he says "Everyone who has *heard* from the Father, and *learned, comes* to me" (v. 45b).

Seeking Jesus but Not Finding Him

John 7:34, 36; 8:21

Hosea 3:4–5 says that in the last days, after many days without king or prince, sacrifice, sacred pillar, ephod, or household idols, "the sons of Israel will return and seek the LORD their God and David their king." The Targum interprets David as "Messiah, son of David." When Jesus speaks about the Jews seeking him, it may simply reflect the idea that they will seek him, the (human) Messiah, just as Prov 29:26 says that many seek the face of a ruler. On the other hand, there is good reason to relate such words of Jesus to the OT idea that people must seek the LORD with a whole heart; that is, it is divine speech.

---

[11] Hanson, *Prophetic Gospel,* 82.

Exodus 33:7 says that Moses set up a "tent of meeting" a good distance outside the camp and that those who sought the LORD would go there. That this tent was set up "outside the camp" contrasts with the purpose of the tabernacle, for which Moses had just received building instructions and which would also be called the "tent of meeting"—that God would dwell in the midst of his people, not outside the camp. This observation gave rise to the interpretation in Jewish tradition that the tent was set up outside the camp because God himself had withdrawn his presence outside the camp, in effect excommunicating the nation after their worship of the golden calf (Exod 32). Moses, the servant of God, was therefore following his Master outside the camp. As noted in ch. 2, this interpretation is found in *Exodus Rabbah* 45.3.[12] It is also reflected in *Tg. Song* 3:2, where the words of the bride concerning her bridegroom, "I sought him but did not find him," are allegorized as the words of Israel after the sin of the golden calf: "'Let us request instruction from the LORD and the holy *Shekinah* which has been removed from us.' Then they went around in the towns, streets, and squares, but they did not find it."[13] The bride repeats these words in 5:6, which are there allegorized as the words of Israel during the Babylonian captivity: "I sought the *Shekinah* of his glory, but did not find it."

For several reasons, the words "I sought the *Shekinah* of his glory but did not find it" invite comparison to the words of Jesus, "You will seek me and will not find me; and where I am, you cannot come" (John 7:34). These reasons include the conceptual overlap between the targumic Word and *Shekinah*, John's identification of Jesus as the divine bridegroom (ch. 6), the implication that the bridegroom in *Tg. Song* symbolizes the divine bridegroom, and the similarity of historical period of John to the Babylonian exile and the golden calf incident. John underscores the significance of Jesus' statement by recording the crowd's question, "What is this statement that he said, 'You will seek me, and will not find me; and where I am, you cannot come'?" (v. 36). Jesus' contemporaries interpret the statement as mere human speech: "Where does *this man* intend to go that we will not find him?" If the interpretations reflected in *Tg. Song* 3:2; 5:6; and *Exodus Rabbah* 45.3 were current as Jesus spoke, then it is quite possible that Jesus was speaking of the withdrawal of the divine presence and indicating that when the Jews seek God through their regular religious observance in the synagogue and at the temple (as in Isa 58:2), they will not find him, for he will withdraw his presence from Israel.

Interpreting John 7:34 as divine speech would also call to mind the promise of Moses in Deut 4:29, that from exile "You will seek [בקש] the LORD your God, and you will find him if you seek [דרש] him with all your heart and all your soul." If they do not find him, then, it is not because he is going to a particular place that they do not have the physical means to get to (e.g., "among the dispersion," John 7:35), but rather because they are not seeking their God with all their heart and

---

[12] "The excommunicated was cut off entirely from the camp; here, Moses removes himself afar off from those excommunicated by God" (Lehrman, *Midrash Rabbah: Exodus*, 520 n.5).

[13] The similarity to the interpretation in *Exodus Rabbah* was noted by Philip S. Alexander, *The Targum of Canticles* (ArBib 17A; Collegeville, Minn.: Liturgical Press, 2003), 117 n.6.

soul. The promise is repeated in Jer 29:13, where it is spoken of the generation that will return from Babylon. It is also given with slight changes in 1 Chr 28:9 (David to Solomon) and 2 Chr 15:2 (the prophet Azariah to king Asa).

Confirming that John 7:34 is divine speech is the similar statement in 8:21, where "you will die in your sin" stands in place of "you will not find me": "I go away, and you will seek me, and you will die in your sin. Where I am going, you cannot come." As we saw above, "you will die in your sins" from a few verses later is prefaced by "unless you believe that I am he" (8:24), which is likewise divine speech, though not understood to be so by his hearers.

Another example of seeking but not finding is in Hos 5:6–7: "They (the rebellious Israelites) go with their flocks and their herds to seek the LORD, but they will not find; *he has withdrawn from them*. They have dealt treacherously *against the LORD*." The mention of going with flocks and herds refers to sacrifice such as they would make at a feast (v. 7 mentions the new moon); similarly John 7:34; 8:21 is spoken in the temple at the Feast of Booths. The Targum of this passage in Hosea is most suggestive: "He has *withdrawn his Shekinah* from them; *against the Word of the LORD* they have dealt falsely." Similarly, v. 15: "*I will withdraw my Shekinah*; I will return to my holy dwelling in heaven, until they acknowledge their sin" (MT: "I will go away and return to my place"). John 7:34 and 8:21 can be interpreted along the same lines. Because Israel is going to deal falsely with the divine Word (Matt 26:59: "The chief priests and the whole Sanhedrin kept trying to obtain false testimony against Jesus, in order that they might put him to death"), he will return to heaven. The ascension of Jesus is the withdrawal of the *Shekinah*, the manifest presence of God.[14] John 7:34, 36; 8:21 therefore do not speak merely of the physical departure of a person, but of the withdrawal of the divine presence, and they implicitly warn of the disasters that must follow that withdrawal.

We read in John 8:59 that to avoid being stoned, "Jesus hid himself and went out of the temple." This could be seen as a foreshadowing of the withdrawal of the *Shekinah*, soon to occur for the same reason (that they sought to kill him). In Isa 45:15, Isaiah exclaims, "Truly, you are a God who hides himself, O God of Israel, (its) savior." The Targum interprets this as saying that God caused his *Shekinah* to dwell in heaven, though it does not explicitly speak of the withdrawal of the *Shekinah*, as in other passages in the MT where God says he will hide his face from Israel: "When the priests spread out their hands to pray for you, I will take up the face of my *Shekinah* from you, and when you multiply your prayers, I will not be pleased to receive your prayers, because your hands are full of innocent blood" (*Tg. Isa.* 1:15). That John says Jesus (whom he has called "the Word") hid himself could also be related to *Tg. Neof.* Deut 31:18, where, instead of saying he will withdraw his *Shekinah*, God says, "I in my Word will surely hide the face of my good pleasure in that day." A first-century Targum might have used such language in other passages where in MT God hides his face, or hides himself, including Isa 1:15;

---

[14] This would also be implied from Matt 18:20, if this Talmud saying was current in the first century: "If three are sitting as a court of judges, the Divine Presence (*Shekinah*) is with them" (*b. Berakot* 6a).

45:15 (see also Deut 31:17, 20; Isa 8:17; 54:8; 57:17; 64:7; Jer 33:5; in Ezek 39:29 he promises not to do so).

John 12:26

Further corroboration for the theme of a divine withdrawal from Israel can be found in John 12:26: "If any one serves me, let him follow me; where I am, there shall my servant also be." Of course, "where I am" is going to be in heaven, at the right hand of the Father (7:34: "I go to him who sent me"). But Jesus is obviously not telling his servants they must be in heaven; we are to serve him in the world. Jesus is going to be in heaven, but also "outside the camp" (Heb 13:13). Again we note that *Exodus Rabbah 45.3* says that Moses set up the tent of meeting outside the camp because God had withdrawn his *Shekinah* from the camp in response to the sin of the golden calf, and that Moses the servant must regard as excommunicated those whom his Master had excommunicated. Moses, the servant, followed his Master outside the camp when God withdrew his *Shekinah* from Israel's midst, under the principle "Where I am, there shall my servant also be," a principle Jesus repeats as he is preparing to again withdraw his presence from Israel, this time for a sin greater than that of worshiping the golden calf. It was outside the camp, at the tent of meeting which Moses set up, that the Israelites went to seek the Lord (Exod 33:7). Here "the Word of the Lord spoke to Moses" (*Tg. Ps.-J.* Exod 33:9 and *Tg. Neof.* [mg.] Exod 33:11) and Moses saw the Word (*Dibbura*) of the glory of God's *Shekinah* (*Tg. Neof.* and *Frg. Tgs. P, V* Exod 33:23). At this place outside the camp, says *Tg. Ps.-J.* Exod 33:11, "Moses heard the voice of the Word [*Dibbura*]."

As in John 8, where Jesus hid himself after announcing that his people will seek him in vain, so also in John 12, Jesus hides himself after telling his servants that they must follow him where he is going: "These things Jesus spoke and, going away, hid himself from them" (v. 36). This is immediately followed by the allusion to Num 14:11, a context which (in the Targums) also speaks of the departure of God's presence and the lack of help from the divine Word (vv. 42–43).

If the targumic belief that the *Shekinah* departed from Jerusalem forty years before its destruction was current when John wrote, it would explain his preservation of these sayings of Jesus. Of course, an observant Jew could also posit after the destruction of Jerusalem by the Romans that the cause must have been a great sin on the part of God's people that resulted in the withdrawal of his *Shekinah*. By identifying Jesus as the Word, John suggests that the nature of that great sin is identified in the Scriptures recited in the synagogue, such as *Tg. Neof.* Num 14:42–43, where Moses warns Israel after their refusal to go into the promised land, "Do not go up (to fight), for the glory of the *Shekinah* of the Lord does not dwell upon you, lest you be struck down before your enemies. . . . You have turned back from the Word of the Lord, and the Lord will not be with you" (mg.: "the Word of the Lord will not be your helper"). According to talmudic tradition, that rejection of the divine Word would have been about c.e. 30. This advice Moses gave Israel before precipitously entering the promised land (as well as the advice of Jeremiah during the Babylonian invasion) was equally timely before the Jewish rebellion against Rome.

Isaiah 55:6 also expresses the idea that seeking the LORD is no guarantee of success: "Seek the LORD while he may be found; call upon him while he is near." This verse is just a few verses after the divine invitation "come to me" (55:3). Jesus issues a similar invitation at the feast shortly after warning, "you will seek me and not find me" (John 7:34). And of course, Isaiah's admonition to call on the LORD "while he is near" would be especially appropriate to the ministry of the incarnate Son, who is "God with us" (Matt 1:23), a designation possibly alluded to in v. 33: "for a little while longer, I am with you."

In the case of Isa 55:6, the Targum does not help us make the connection to John 7:34 by using language about seeking the divine Word. It does not say, "Seek the Word of the LORD," but rather, "Seek *the fear of the LORD* while you are alive." As far as I know, only one Targum passage talks about seeking the divine Word, *Tg. 1 Chr.* 16:10b–11a: "Let the heart of those who *seek the Word of the LORD* rejoice. *Seek the Word of the LORD* and his strength." This one example would not count much by way of precedent, especially since there is no evidence that the books of Chronicles were read publicly in the synagogue. This passage in 1 Chronicles is identical (in the MT) to Ps 105:3b–4a, and the corresponding *Tg. Ps.* passage illustrates another common way of rendering the "seek" language: "Let the heart of those who *seek instruction from before the LORD* rejoice. *Seek the instruction of the LORD*, and his Torah" (*Tg. Ps.* 105:3b–4a).

The circumlocution used in *Tg. Isa.* 55:6, "Seek *the fear of the LORD*," was also used in *Tg. Onq.* Deut 1:36 with another verb: "Caleb . . . has *followed the fear of the LORD* fully (MT: he followed the LORD fully)." In *Tg. Neof.*, however, it says that Caleb "*followed the Word of the LORD* fully." Although it is speculative, it may be the case that in the first-century Targums the idea of seeking the Word of the LORD may have been more common than in our extant Targums. For example, there could have been an alternative reading to Isa 55:6 in the extant *Tg. Isa.* (or a Palestinian version), "Seek the Word of the LORD while he may be found." We noted previously that there is some basis for thinking that there was a more "Palestinian" Targum of the Prophets. Besides the evidence from the *Tos. Tgs.*, above we noted a quote from Jer 17 in *Pal. Tgs.* Gen 40:23 which uses the expression "the name of the Word of the LORD," an expression not found anywhere in *Tg. Jon.* (or *Tg. Onq.* of the Pentateuch, the other "official" Targum). We also saw in ch. 1 that *Tg. Ps.-J. Deut* 4:7 says "the Word of the LORD sits upon his throne, high and lifted up," which is obviously borrowed from Isa 6:1 but does not agree with *Tg. Jon.*'s wording (*Tg. Isa.* 6:1 says, "I saw the glory of the LORD, sitting upon his throne, high and lifted up").

John 13:33

In John 13:33, Jesus repeats some of his words in 7:34 to the disciples: "Little children, I am with you a little while longer. You will seek me, and as I said to

the Jews, now I also say to you, 'Where I am going, you cannot come.'" Notice
that he does not say, "You will seek me, and you will not find me." Moreover, he
goes on to say, "Where I go, you cannot follow me now, but you will follow later"
(v. 36). Again, if we understand these words as divine speech, Jesus is saying that
the disciples will seek the LORD. Jesus is going outside the camp, and the disciples
will be like those who sought the LORD outside the camp after the incident of the
golden calf (Exod 33:7), where, according to the *Pal. Tgs.*, the divine Word spoke
to Moses. They cannot go there now, as Jesus is going to the cross to do battle alone
and to return in resurrection, but later they too will bear his reproach outside the
camp (Heb 13:13).

In the OT, people sought the LORD because of some need. Often that need
was to restore God's favor after some sin (e.g., Exod 33:7; 2 Sam 21:1; 2 Chr 15:4;
Isa 26:16; Dan 9:3; Hos 10:12). Since the disciples were about to abandon Jesus at
his arrest, they would have such a need. In this context, "You will seek me" could
be a prediction that the disciples would (unlike Judas) return in repentance and
find him.

To sum up, Jesus' expression in John 7:34, "You will seek me, and you will
not find me," is not merely a prediction that the Jews will go looking for a certain
person whom they know. Against the background of the Jewish understanding of
Exod 33:7, Jesus is saying that he is going to excommunicate the nation of Israel,
just as in the aftermath of the golden calf incident. Those who want to find the
LORD must seek him "outside the camp," as did Moses at the tent of meeting. By
using the language of the Targums (identifying Jesus as the divine Word), John
witnesses to his fellow Jews that OT history has repeated itself; the divine Word
is to be sought and found outside the camp. The historical proof of the excom-
munication of Israel would follow in the destruction of Jerusalem and the temple.
An application to the Gentile church would also be implied: history will again be
repeated if the church stops following Christ "outside the camp," for example by
engaging in syncretism. The Lord's messages to the seven churches of Asia Minor
contain such threats: "Unless you repent, I will remove your lampstand," etc. (Rev
2:5, 16, 22–23; 3:3, 16).

FOLLOWING JESUS

Language about following Jesus is also susceptible to interpretations from two
perspectives, human and divine, and again we find that the two come together in
the fact that the Word became flesh. When Jesus says at the beginning of his ministry, "Follow me" (Matt 4:19; Mark 1:17; 2:14; Luke 5:27; John 1:43), his words are
completely understandable from a human perspective; the disciples would literally
follow Jesus around as others might follow another rabbi to learn from him. This
charge is repeated to Peter, shortly before Jesus' ascension, in John 21:19–22, in
keeping with the idea that the disciples must continue to follow Jesus (now not literally) even after he has ascended; they must follow his example and his teaching,
and they must follow him to a similar destination of persecution.

John 8:12

Other passages, however, may be related to OT language about following the God of Israel that in some Targums has become language about following the divine Word. On the last day of the Feast of Booths, Jesus says, "I am he [ἐγώ εἰμι], the light of the world. He who follows me will not walk in darkness, but will have the light of life" (John 8:12). "Light of the world" is not necessarily a divine designation, as Matt 5:14 makes clear (the disciples are the light of the world). The designation could simply be a claim to be the Messiah, the Servant of the LORD who is "a light to the nations" (Isa 42:6; 49:6). When the claim is repeated in John 9:5, the allusion to Isa 42:6–7 is hard to miss:

Isa 42:6–7	John 9:5–7
I will appoint you . . . as a light to the nations, to open blind eyes.	"I am the light of the world." (Jesus then goes on to open blind eyes.)

The saying in John 8:12 could also point to the Messiah of prophecy, as it has been noted that it could be an ironic response to the objection in 7:52, "Search and see that no prophet arises out of Galilee," drawing the attention of the listeners to the prophecy of a great light coming out of Galilee (Isa 9:2, connected to Christ's coming in Galilee in Matt 4:16). But John 8:12 has another context and is worded differently from 9:5. In 9:5, "I am" is simply εἰμι, while 8:12 has ἐγώ εἰμι, which, again, could reflect Aramaic אנא הוא, "I am he," and could be meant to echo the divine "I am he" of the OT.

In the time of Jesus' ministry, a great celebration of lights was held during the Feast of Booths (*m. Sukkah* 5:2–3), the significance of which is often assumed to include a reminder of the pillar of light that led the Israelites throughout their wilderness wanderings. This celebration would form a fitting backdrop for Jesus' words, "he who follows me," not only because of the idea of following the light, as Israel did in the wilderness, but also because this light ceremony utilized an arrangement of four golden lamps in the temple court of women. Towering fifty cubits high and illuminating every courtyard in Jerusalem, this arrangement would have been an appropriate representation of the pillar of fire that Israel followed for forty years. Now we may recall that *Tg. Neof.* Exod 13:21–22 says, "The Word of the LORD was leading before them during the daytime in a pillar of cloud, to lead them on the way, and by night in a pillar of fiery cloud to give them light, that they might journey by day and night. The pillar of cloud did not cease during the daytime, nor the pillar of fire by night, leading and standing in readiness and shining before the people" (similarly *Frg. Tg. P* for v. 21). The idea of following Jesus, the light of the world, can thus be associated with the OT ideas of Israel following God in the wilderness and of following the Servant of the LORD in Isaiah. Both associations are valid because the divine Word has become flesh. Those who followed the LORD in the wilderness were on their way to the promised land. Most did not arrive at their destination. Jesus promises that those who persevere in following him will arrive at the destination of eternal life; they have "the light of life."

John 12:26; 13:36

We have already discussed John 12:26 and 13:36 and their allusions to the OT pattern of Moses following the LORD outside the camp. We also noted above that in *Tg. Neof.* Deut 1:36 the LORD says "Caleb followed my Word fully" and thus did not die in his sins but entered the promised land (cf. *Tg. Neof.* Num 14:24).[15] The text in Num 32:11 that describes the generation that died in the wilderness as not following the LORD was accidentally omitted in *Tg. Neof.*, but the following verse describes Joshua and Caleb as following the Word of the LORD fully. *Targum Neofiti* Deut 7:4 forbids intermarriage with the native peoples of the promised land because "they would lead your sons away from following [lit.: *from after*] my Word." In *Tg. Neof.* Deut 31:27, Moses says, "Behold, while I am still alive with you today, you have rebelled from following [lit.: *have been rebellious after*] the Word of the LORD; how much more, then, after my death?" In the ministry of Jesus, when the Word became flesh, we find out the answer to this question: the leaders of Israel would put him to death, just as they planned to do at various times to those who followed the LORD fully in the days of Moses (Num 14:10, etc.).

John 10:27

"My sheep hear my voice, and they follow me" (John 10:27). Here again we could relate these words to both a human and a divine OT precedent. Though all the LORD's people are his sheep (e.g., Ps 78:52), their human leaders are often called shepherds. God's promise, made through Ezekiel, to "set over them one shepherd" and that "my servant David himself will tend them, and be their shepherd" (Ezek 34:23), can be naturally understood as fulfilled in Jesus' claim, "I am the good shepherd" (John 10:11, 14). The contrast that Jesus makes between himself and hirelings also fits the theme of Ezek 34 with its extensive condemnation of self-seeking shepherds.

But in John 10:11, 14 we again have ἐγώ εἰμι, and this again raises the question of whether Jesus is using divine speech, in which case we would translate, "I am he, the good shepherd." There is good reason from the context to answer in the affirmative. John 10:27 can be interpreted as divine speech because of what Jesus goes on to say in v. 28, and because of how vv. 27–28 compare with two OT texts, one of which is a divine "I am he" claim; further, one of the Targum translations of it speaks of the divine Word as the source of life in the world to come:

John 10:27–28   *My sheep hear my voice,* and I know them, and *they follow me.* And *I give eternal life to them,* and they will never perish; and *no one will snatch them out of my hand.*

---

[15]The MT actually has מִלֵּא אַחֲרֵי יהוה: "he filled up after the LORD," i.e., he was fully after (following) the LORD. The Aramaic has a similar idiom with אשלם בתר.

Ps 95:7	For he is our God, and we are the people of his pasture, *and the sheep of his hand.* Today, if you would *hear his voice* (*Tg.*: receive his Word), do not harden your hearts as at Meribah.
Deut 32:39	See now that *I, I am he,* and there is no God besides me. I put to death, and *I give life,* . . . and there is *no one who can snatch away from my hand.*
Tg. Neof. Deut 32:39 (similarly *Frg. Tg. V*)	See now that *I, I in my Word, am he,* and there is no God besides me. *I am he* who puts to death the living in this world *and who brings to life the dead in the world to come.*

Based on the parallels above, it seems likely that Jesus has taken the idea of "sheep of his hand" and of those sheep hearing his voice from Ps 95 and used them as a bridge to the MT of Deut 32:39, "no one . . . can snatch away from my hand" and to the inference in *Tg. Neof.* of resurrection from the MT "I give life" or "I make alive." "Snatch away" is the literal meaning of the Hebrew verb הִצִּיל, more often translated "delivered." The Aramaic verb used to translate הִצִּיל does not have this literal meaning. Thus the words of Jesus relate to both the Hebrew ("snatch away") and the Aramaic (the interpretation of "give life" as referring to resurrection) of Deut 32:39. It seems reasonable to conclude, then, that the ἐγώ εἰμι of John 10:11, 14 is, as in Deut 32:39, the divine I am he, especially when *Tg. Neof.* and *Frg. Tg. V* of this verse say "I, in my Word, am he."[16]

FORGIVENESS AND THE DIVINE WORD

The theme of Jesus as forgiver of sins is not as overt in John as in the Synoptics. So our focus will be on a single verse, John 8:24: "Therefore I said to you that you will die in your sins, for unless you believe that I am he, you will die in your sins." We have noted the allusion to the idea in Num 27:3 that those who died in the wilderness died in their sin, like Zelophahad. The alternative to dying in one's sin is to receive forgiveness for one's sins. We also saw that this passage, among several in John, alludes to Isa 43:10, a divine "I am he" saying. Isaiah 43:25, just a few verses later, is another I am he saying: "I, even I, am he who wipes out your transgressions for my own sake," or in *Tg. Isa.,* "I, even I, am he who forgives your sin for my name's sake." Again we note that in 1 John 2:12–14, John uses the Targum language of both of these verses together—"he who is from the beginning" (agreeing with *Tg. Isa.* 43:10), and "your sins are forgiven you for his name's sake"

---

[16] Ironically, the verse following the divine promise, "no one can snatch them out of my hand," is often quoted by Arians to contradict the doctrine of the deity of Christ: "My Father . . . is greater than all." But the divine statement "no one can snatch them out of my hand" from Deut 32:39 applies both to the Son (John 10:28) and to the Father (v. 29), showing that the manner in which the Father is greater than the Son is as has been understood by orthodox Christians throughout church history, a subordination within the Godhead, not a contrast between the One who is uncreated and his creation. "Follow me" is thus the command of the divine shepherd to his sheep.

(agreeing with *Tg. Isa.* 43:25). The implication, then, is that the one who says "unless you believe that I am he" is also the one who says "I am he who wipes out your transgressions for my own sake," or, in Targum language, "I am he who forgives your sins for my name's sake."

John's description of Jesus as "full of grace and truth" also implies that he is the forgiver of the believer's sins, since it is taken from God's self-description in Exod 34:6—a comprehensive summary of the moral attributes of God that includes, "who forgives iniquity, transgression, and sin." Recall that in the *Pal. Tgs* this is part of the revelation to Moses of the divine Word. In Num 14:19, after quoting from the Lord's description of himself as a forgiving God (Exod 34:7), Moses asks the Lord to forgive the people instead of destroying them for their refusal to follow him into the promised land (or, in language often used in *Pal. Tgs.*, their refusal to follow the divine Word into the promised land). To this, the Word of the Lord replies to Moses, "I have pardoned [שרי] and forgiven [שבק], as you have spoken/according to your word" (*Tg. Neof.* [mg.] and *Frg. Tg. V* Num 14:20).

These two words used to express forgiveness are also used in *Tg. Ps.-J.* Lev 9:23. In the MT of this verse, Moses and Aaron go into the tent of meeting and then come out and bless the people. The glory of the Lord then appears to all the people. *Targum Pseudo-Jonathan* embellishes this account to explain why the *Shekinah* was not immediately revealed after the offerings of v. 22, and why Moses and Aaron went into the tent:

> Aaron was ashamed, and said to Moses, "Perhaps the Word of the Lord is not pleased with the works of my hands." Then Moses and Aaron went into the tent of meeting, and prayed for the people of the house of Israel, and they came out and blessed the people, and said, "May the Word of the Lord receive your offerings with favor, and pardon and forgive your sins." Immediately the glory of the *Shekinah* of the Lord was revealed to all the people.

In John's presentation, when the Word became flesh, he *became* the offering that secures the believer's pardon and forgiveness, and the glorification (or "lifting up") of the Son on the cross can be interpreted as a divine sign that this offering was accepted, along the lines of *Tg. Ps.-J.* Lev 9:23.

Conclusions

Jesus speaks as both God and human in calling people to believe in him, come to him, seek him, follow him, in order to have eternal life. Knowledge of the Targums has again been helpful in illuminating the words of Jesus, disclosing them as divine speech. As a general rule, faith or trust in humans is not commended in the OT, but this rule should not be a stumbling block to Jews (or Gentiles) in believing in Jesus, since to believe in Jesus is in fact to follow the example of the OT faithful who believed in the Lord, or, as the Targums put it, in the Word of the Lord, or in the name of the Word of the Lord. The way of salvation has not changed from OT to NT; faith in YHWH has always been the essence of covenant keeping for

God's people: "He believed in the LORD, and he counted it to him as righteousness" (Gen 15:6). The language of the targums highlights the continuity present when the Word became flesh: "He believed in the Word of the LORD, and he counted it to him as righteousness" (*Tgs. Onq.* and *Ps.-J.* Gen 15:6; *Tg. Neof.*; "He believed in the name of the Word of the LORD"). For John, the name of the Word of the LORD, the Tetragrammaton, is "the name of the only Son of God" (John 3:18), through whom believers, by trusting in that name (John 20:31), may have life and receive the forgiveness of sins.

9

The "I Am He" Sayings

INTRODUCTION

In chapters three and eight, we looked in some detail at the divine "I am he" sayings of the OT (Deut 32:39 and Isaiah) and observed that MT "I am he" (אֲנִי הוּא) is rendered idiomatically in the LXX as ἐγώ εἰμι, and that a number of ἐγώ εἰμι sayings of Jesus seem to depend on the divine "I am he" of the OT, especially that of Isa 43:10. In addition, we noted that *Pal. Tgs.* associated with Deut 32:39 associate the divine Word with the divine "I am he" in different ways. *Targum Pseudo-Jonathan* Deut 32:39 says, "When the Word of the LORD shall be revealed to redeem his people, he will say to all the peoples, 'I am he who is and was, and I am he who will be.'" As we saw, the threefold "I am he" of John 8:24, 28, 58, present, future, past, could be seen as a fulfillment of this quasi-biblical prophecy. In this Targum God goes on to say, "I through my Word put to death and make alive" (v. 39) and that God "through his Word will make atonement for the sins of his land and of his people" (v. 43).

Targum Neofiti Deut 32:39 reads quite differently but is also of interest: "See now that I, *I in my Word, am he*, and there is no other God besides me. *I am he* who puts to death the living in this world, and brings to life the dead in the world to come. *I am he* who strikes, and *I am he* who heals, and there is no one who delivers from my hand." Verse 40 adds, "As I live and exist in my Word forever." The *Frg. Tg. V* Deut 32:39–40 is almost identical to *Tg. Neof.*

By now I hope my reader is becoming sympathetic to the idea that John calls Jesus "the Word" because of the use of *Memra* and *Dibbera/Dibbura* in the Targums. Such a conclusion helps resolve one of the problems of John's Gospel, namely, that Jesus is not identified as the Word outside of the Prologue. If "the Word" is targumic, then we can see that Jesus repeatedly saying "I am he" in the body of the Gospel, in contexts that echo the divine "I am he" of the OT, amounts to the same thing as John's designation of him as the Word who is God in the prologue. Both expressions identify Jesus as the God of Israel, the one true God, so that the divine "I am he" sayings in the body of the Gospel complement the Logos title in the Prologue. References to the divine Word in the "I am he" sayings of *Pal. Tgs.* Deut 32:39 serve to make this connection.

Strengthening the idea that John is using the language of the Targums in the Prologue (calling Jesus the Word) that corresponds to MT language in the body of the Gospel (Jesus echoing the divine "I am he" language of the MT not found in the Targums) are other examples where John uses targumic language in place of an MT equivalent in sayings of Jesus. We have seen that the "come to me" language of Jesus in John 5–7 depends on "come to me" in the divine invitation of Isa 55:3, whereas John, speaking of the same spiritual transaction, uses targumic language from Isa 55:3 (and elsewhere) that speaks of those who receive Jesus (the Word). Similarly, Jesus says "believe in me," whereas John speaks of believing in "his name," which is the Targums' way of referring to the divine Word. As we noted, outside the Gospel, John calls Jesus "he who is from the beginning" (1 John 2:13, 14), which is how God describes himself three times in *Tg. Isa.* Generally, this expression stands for MT "I am the first," which forms part of "I am the first and the last," an expression used by Jesus three times in Revelation (1:17; 2:8; 22:13).

In this chapter, we will look at references to the divine Word not only in *Pal. Tgs.* Deut 32:39 but also in the context of the "I am he" sayings in *Targum Isaiah*, which, for the most part, agree with the MT sayings. We will also look at the several dozen divine "I am he" sayings which were added in the *Pal. Tgs.*, almost always rendering MT expressions such as "I (am) the LORD" as "I (am) he, the LORD." Many of these sayings may provide additional illumination regarding the "I am he" sayings of Jesus, and some of them, according to one *Pal. Tg.* tradition (*Tg. Neof.* or a marginal gloss in *Tg. Neof.*), are spoken by the divine Word, making them potentially relevant to understanding the sayings of Jesus in John. Past studies have (rightly) examined the "I am he" sayings in John from the background of the MT and LXX, but scholars have overlooked the substantial number of additional "I am he" sayings from the *Pal. Tgs.* of the Pentateuch, as well as references to the targumic Word in the context of the "I am he" sayings in Isaiah.

We will also see that there are "I am he" sayings in the *Pal. Tgs.* that, although not echoed in any "I am he" saying of Jesus, nevertheless speak to some aspect of the person and work of Christ in John's Gospel. For this kind of example, we can compare John 10:27, "No one can snatch them out of my hand," which (as noted in ch. 8) seems to be taken from the MT of Deut 32:39 (= Isa 43:13), without quoting the "I am he" portion of those passages. *Targum Neofiti* and *Frg. Tg. V* Deut 32:39 are of interest because they speak to the issue of eternal life, which also figures in the context of John 10:27. Conversely, there are references to the divine Word in the Targums that, apart from any "I am he" saying, may nevertheless illuminate one of these sayings in John.

It should be acknowledged that there is no inherent divine claim in the mere utterance of the words "I am he." The man born blind, for example, kept saying "I am he" (ἐγώ εἰμι) when asked whether he really was born blind (John 9:9). David says, "I am he who sinned" (1 Chr 21:17 MT and *Tg.*). *Targum Lamentations* 3:1 says, "I am he, the man who has seen affliction." Similarly, there are a few human "I am he" sayings in the *Pal. Tgs.* of the Pentateuch. In *Tg. Ps.-J.* Gen 45:3, we find, "I am he, Joseph" (spoken when Joseph reveals himself to his brothers). In *Tg. Ps.-J.* and *Frg. Tg. V* Lev 10:20, Moses says, "I am he from whom the practice was hidden, and my brother Aaron taught it to me." In *Tg. Neof.* Deut 5:5, Moses says, "I was standing between the Word of the LORD and you" (referring to Exod 20); a gloss adds הוא to אנה. אנא הוא is also used ten times in a tale told in *Frg. Tg. P* Exod 12:2, where the various months of the year issue their claims as to why they should be the first month of the year. This raises the question, are passages in the *Pal. Tgs.* where God says אנא הוא relevant to the present investigation?

In most of the passages in the *Pal. Tgs.* where God says אנה הוא, in MT of the passage he says אֲנִי. For example, in Exod 6:2, the LORD says to Moses, "I am the LORD" (אֲנִי יהוה), while *Tg. Neof.* has אנה הוא ייי (*CTg. D* also adds הוא). Is the "addition" of הוא a matter of Aramaic idiom, of no more significance than the "added" הוא in "I am Joseph," or is it theologically motivated, perhaps as a way of referring to the name of God, based on the importance of this phrase in Deut 32:39 and Isa 41–52?

In considering Hebrew phrases such as אַתָּה הוּא מַלְכִּי, "you are [he] my king" (Ps 44:4), S. R. Driver raised the question whether הוּא should be considered the *copula*, in which case אַתָּה הוּא should simply be understood "you are," or is הוּא an anticipation of the predicate, in which case the sense would be "you are he, my king." Driver opted for the latter.[1] We have the same choices in considering the אנה הוא phrases in the *Pal. Tgs.* outside of Deut 32:39. Even if one decides that there is an anticipation of the predicate in these passages, justifying the translation "I am he" as opposed to "I am," it is still possible that the phrase is merely an expression of Aramaic idiom, rather than something meant to point to the name of God. So there is some uncertainty as to whether the additional אנה הוא passages in the *Pal. Tgs.* of the Pentateuch are relevant to an investigation of the ἐγώ εἰμι sayings of Jesus.

On the other hand, the fact that the divine "I am he" greatly predominates over the human "I am he" in the MT and the Targums would seem to give warrant for their inclusion in this study as at least potentially of interest. *Targum Jonathan* does not use "I am he" except in translating MT "I am he," spoken in the prophets only by God (perhaps unintentionally, "I am he" in its first occurrence, Isa 41:4, is not translated), with the exception of three places where a divine "I am he" is added: once each in *Tg. Isa.* 43:10 and 48:12 (where there is already one "I am he") and twice in *Tg. Isa.* 44:6. The effect of these additions is to make *Tg. Isa.* 43:10; 44:6; 48:12 all say, "I am he, I am he who is from the beginning." As we have noted, the designation of Jesus as "him who is from the beginning" in 1 John 2:13–14 seems to come from this targumic expression, confirming evidence being that 1 John 2:12 draws from another targumic "I am he" saying from this context, "I, I am he who forgives your sins for my name's sake" (*Tg. Isa.* 43:25).

In *Tg. Onq.*, "I am he" is used only for MT "I am he," which means it is found only in *Tg. Onq.* Deut 32:39. In *Tg. Neof.*, however, including glosses, "I am he" occurs forty-seven times (in forty-two verses), forty-six of them spoken by God.

---

[1] Driver, *Tenses*, 271–72 (§200). For a discussion of the copula in Syriac, see Theodore Nöldeke, *Compendious Syriac Grammar* (trans. James A. Crichton; London: Williams and Norgate, 1904), 248–49 (§§312 C and D). In the Peshitta, *'n' 'n'* is the usual way of rendering the pronoun, אני in "I am the LORD" as well as the expression אני הוא in the OT, and ἐγώ εἰμι as spoken by Jesus in the NT.

Targum Pseudo-Jonathan has the expression forty-four times (in forty verses), forty-two of which are spoken by God. The *Frg. Tgs.* have a number of divine "I am he" sayings (in five verses), but they are not unique, agreeing with *Tgs. Neof.* or *Ps.-J.*, or both. The Cairo Genizah Targum fragments likewise have some "I am he" sayings that agree with other *Pal. Tgs.* The *CTg.* F Lev 22:33 is of special interest, since it reads much like *Tg. Neof.*, but its added text well illustrates why John might have been interested in the targumic Word. The following is from *Tg. Neof.* Lev 22:32–33, with bracketed text added by *CTg.* F:

> I am he, the LORD, who sanctified you, who redeemed you and brought you out redeemed from the land of Egypt to be to you in my Word a redeeming God. I am he, the LORD who redeemed your fathers, and will in the future redeem you <by my Word>.

There is considerable agreement between *Tgs. Neof.* and *Ps.-J.* in usage, so that the total number of distinct "I am he" sayings in the *Pal. Tgs.* of the Pentateuch is sixty-four (in fifty-seven verses). Six of these are in *Pal. Tgs.* Deut 32:39, so there are still almost sixty that we have not yet considered in this study.

In most cases where the additional "I am he" sayings from the *Pal. Tgs.* seem relevant to John, they reinforce the "divine" interpretation already attributed by scholars to some of the ἐγώ εἰμι sayings of Jesus, especially those of John 8:28, 58. In addition, certain ἐγώ εἰμι sayings in John that would not appear to be divine speech based merely on an examination of the MT and LXX would, however, appear to be so based on examination of one or more passages in the *Pal. Tgs.*

Various translations of the MT phrases אני הוא/הוא אנכי אנכי (I am he, I am the one, I am the same) and the NT phrase ἐγώ εἰμι (I am he, it is I, I am) may be justified grammatically.[2] The approach taken here assumes that every instance of ἐγώ εἰμι in the Gospel reflects a spoken Aramaic אֲנָא הוּא, and that ἐγώ εἰμι is used by John in translation because that is how the LXX renders the divine אֲנִי הוּא of Deut 32:39 and Isaiah. We will be considering all twenty-two of the sayings together, rather than just the so-called "divine sayings" or the so-called "I am" sayings (the good shepherd, etc.).[3] It is possible that the number twenty-two itself signals that this is John's intent, since this is the number of letters in both the Hebrew and the Aramaic alphabet and could therefore convey the "first and the last" claim that accompanies the divine "I am he" sayings in Isaiah and Revelation, the last of which accompanies, "I am the Alpha and the Omega" (Rev 1:8; 21:6; 22:13).

Given this possibility, it is important first to verify that there are indeed twenty-two sayings, since others might count them differently. If we just count ἐγώ εἰμι spoken by Jesus, or in words of Jesus quoted by his hearers, there are actually twenty-three occurrences (John 4:26; 6:20, 35, 41, 48, 51; 8:12, 18, 24, 28, 58; 10:7, 9, 11, 14; 11:25; 13:19; 14:6; 15:1, 5; 18:5, 6, 8). But the second-to-last of

---

[2] Burkett has a good discussion of this in *Son of the Man in the Gospel of John*, 142–50.

[3] The reader may be familiar with the seven "I am" statements of John: the bread of life (6:35, 41, 48, 51), the light of the world (8:12; cf. 9:5), the gate of the sheep (10:7, 9), the good shepherd (10:11, 14), the resurrection and the life (11:25), the way, truth, and life (14:6), and the true vine (15:1, 5). Together these encompass thirteen of the ἐγώ εἰμι sayings numbered here.

these (18:6) is just a reiteration of 18:5 rather than a truly separate saying, the two verses being counted together as the twenty-first.

Someone might object to this, "But John 6:41 is also a quote of an earlier saying, so if you do not count John 18:6 separately you should not count John 6:41 separately. This leaves twenty-one sayings rather than twenty-two." I count John 6:41 because it is not a quote of the previous ἐγώ εἰμι saying (v. 35), but at best may be a conflation of vv. 35 and 38:

V. 35   I am he, the bread of life.

V. 38   I have come down from heaven.

V. 41   At this the Jews began to grumble about him because he said, "I am he, the bread that came down from heaven."

But v. 41 is very close to what Jesus says later, "I am he, the living bread that came down from heaven" (v. 51). It may be, then, that John 6:41 is quoting something that Jesus said earlier that was not recorded by John in vv. 35–40. This is why I count it as a separate saying. For comparison we can look again at the "Son of Man" saying in John 12:34, when the crowd asks, "How can you say, 'The Son of Man must be lifted up'?" But John has left those words of Jesus out of John 12:23–32 (though they agree with John 3:14). Here too John might be counting, since he includes twelve "Son of Man" sayings by Jesus (the second "Son of Man" in John 12:34 is not a saying of Jesus but part of the question from the crowd).

CATEGORIZING THE ἐγώ εἰμι SAYINGS

The ἐγώ εἰμι sayings in John could be categorized grammatically as to whether they have an antecedent or predicate, whether they are followed by a participle, etc. However, I think it will become apparent in this study that grammatical categories do not coincide with what the sayings tell us about the person and work of Christ. It is too simplistic to suggest, for example, that the "absolute" sayings of John 8:24, 58; 13:19 are divine sayings, but those that have an antecedent or predicate are not. The categories I will be using here are those suggested by the analysis of John 1:47–51 carried out in ch. 1 (the revelation of Jesus to Nathanael). Recall that comparing John 1:47–51 to Gen 28:10–22 suggested three perspectives: (1) Jesus is divine (that is, Jesus' speaking to Nathanael is like the LORD speaking to Jacob); (2) Jesus is human (that is, Jesus is the Son of Man, a title related to the figure of Jacob in the OT; Nathanael calls Jesus Son of God and king of Israel, which he probably understood as equivalents of "Messiah"); and (3) Jesus is a means (that is, Jesus is the way to heaven, like Jacob's ladder). The divine perspective was further illuminated by the *Pal. Tgs.* of Gen 28:10, which indicate that a miracle took place so that Jacob would stop for the night at Bethel, "because the Word [*Dibbera*] desired to speak with him." This triple perspective agrees also with what John gives us more straightforwardly in 1:12, 14 of the

Prologue: the Word (Jesus is divine) became flesh (Jesus is human); by believing in him we become children of God (Jesus is a means).

By speaking of categories, I do not mean to suggest that the ἐγώ εἰμι sayings could be divided up neatly and each one put into one or the other of the three different categories describing the person and work of Christ. Some scholars have observed that a number of these sayings are double entendres,[4] and I have suggested that John 1:47–51 is a triple entendre. What I mean by three categories, then, is that when the saying was heard by those listening to Jesus or read by later readers, it will immediately suggest to a biblically literate person (one familiar with the OT, especially the "I am he" sayings) that Jesus either is speaking either as divine (like various OT sayings in the MT and in the Targums), or is claiming to be a certain human being (the Son of Man, the Messiah, Jesus of Nazareth), or is representing himself as the way to the Father, to heaven, or to eternal life. Further reflection on the sayings and their contexts, however, may suggest double and triple entendres, just as is the case in John 1:47–51. Together all of this suggests simply that the ἐγώ εἰμι sayings of Jesus are the "I am he" of the Son. Those in the first category could be spoken also by the Father and the Holy Spirit, but those in the second and third categories are unique to the Son. They should be considered not separately, however, but together as they appear in the Gospel. Together they tell us what it means that Jesus is the Messiah: he is fully God, he is a real man, and he is the way to the Father. He is the divine Messiah, and the Way who is divine.

Are we justified in basing these three categories on John 1:47–51, a passage that does not contain an "I am he" saying? Even if one acknowledges the triple perspective of John 1:47–51, it could nevertheless be mere coincidence that the "I am he" sayings can be categorized in the same way. A couple of observations will strengthen the probability that John did indeed intend us to recognize these three categories. The first is that, as mentioned before, John 1:47–51 is paradigmatic to the Gospel in certain ways. It contains the first Son of Man saying, which we saw alludes to both Ps 8 and to the figure of Jacob at Bethel. We noted that Jacob's journey when he stopped at Bethel provides a paradigm for the work of Christ: Jacob left his father's house on a twofold mission, to save his life and to get a wife, after which he would return in peace to his father's house, all with the help of the divine Word, according to the Targums. Jesus left his Father's house (the divine Word became flesh) to save Jacob's (eternal) life, and to win a bride for himself (the church), so that in Jesus the twofold mission of Jacob becomes one and the same. So it would not be surprising if this passage also gave us a key to interpreting the ἐγώ εἰμι sayings of Jesus. We could add to this observation the fact that the first of these sayings occurs when Jesus meets a woman at a well, evoking the theme found in Gen 29 (see ch. 6, Introduction and The Woman at the Well in the OT), where Jacob met his bride-to-be at a well.

A second observation is that there is in fact an indirect connection between John 1:47–51 and the divine "I am he." In both *Tg. Neof.* and *Tg. Ps.-J.* (also *CTg. E*)

---

[4] Burkett, e.g., lists John 4:26; 6:20; 18:5–8 under this description (*Son of the Man in the Gospel of John*, 147–48).

Gen 31:13, the angel of the LORD says to Jacob in Haran, "*I am he*, the God who was revealed to you at Bethel." This statement seems to point back to Gen 28:10–21, which *Tg. Neof.* and *Tg. Ps.-J.* (as well as both *Frg. Tg.* traditions) narrate as a divine revelation based on the fact that "the Word desired to speak with him" at Bethel.

ANALYSIS OF THE TWENTY-TWO "I AM HE" SAYINGS IN JOHN

John 4:26

> "I know that Messiah is coming" (he who is called Christ). "When he comes, he will disclose all things to us." Jesus said to her, "I am he, the one speaking to you."

Human: The Samaritan woman would take John 4:26 as Jesus' claim to be a certain man, one who was not understood to be divine by Jews or Samaritans. Jesus also speaks as a servant ("My food is to do the will of him who sent me," v. 34), which could recall the figure of the Servant of the LORD in Isaiah, and there are numerous parallels between the events at the well in John 4 and those of three OT scenes where a man meets a woman at a well (Gen 24; Gen 29; Exod 2), as discussed in ch. 6.

Divine: The echo of Isa 52:6 has already been noted: "Therefore, my people will know my name. In that day (they will know) that I am he, the one who is speaking, here am I."[5] *Targum Isaiah 52:6* reads, "Therefore my name shall be exalted among the peoples; therefore in that time you shall know that it is I who speak, and my Word endures." David Mark Ball notes that the two levels of meaning in John 4:26 result in two levels of irony. The first level of meaning, that Jesus is the Messiah, is there for all to see. The irony is that the Samaritan woman has been talking about the Messiah to the Messiah himself without knowing it. The second level of meaning depends on a knowledge of the connection between John 4:26 and Isa 52:6, and the irony is that the reader who is unaware of this connection, though ahead of the Samaritan woman in already understanding that Jesus is the Messiah, may nevertheless be like the Samaritan woman in not knowing the depth of who it is that she is talking to.[6] Such a theme is made explicit in the Lord's words to Philip in John 14:9 and in my opinion reflects one of John's burdens as he observes the church in its second or third generation. John addresses members who have been raised as Christians, who are familiar with the stories of Jesus from the Synoptic Gospels, and would acknowledge that Jesus is the promised Messiah, yet do not know who Jesus really is. Some may be teachers in the church who, like Nicodemus, are unregenerate; some may be leaders in the church who, like the Jews who persecuted Jesus, excommunicate true brethren (cf. 3 John 9–10). In line with this burden, it is lamentable to see how rarely the connection between John 4:26 and Isa 52:6 has been recognized in commentaries and Bible translations.

---

[5]"I am he, the one who is speaking to you" is Ἐγώ εἰμι ὁ λαλῶν σοι. The corresponding part of Isa 52:6 (LXX) is ἐγώ εἰμι αὐτὸς ὁ λαλῶν πάρειμι, for MT אֲנִי־הוּא הַמְדַבֵּר הִנֵּנִי.

[6]Ball, "*I Am*" *in John's Gospel*, 180–81.

"My name" in Isa 52:6 refers to the Tetragrammaton, to which "I am he" also refers. This verse is a prediction that at some future point, God's people will know this name. The observation that Israel has known this name from the beginning could be seen as a difficulty, which *Tg. Isa.* resolves by modifying the prediction to read "my name will be exalted among the peoples." The Targum also renders "here I am" with "my Word endures," which may have relevance to John 4:26. That John 4:26 is spoken to the Samaritan woman, who represents a broader definition of "my people" (as noted in ch. 6) that foreshadows a largely Gentile church, could indicate that Isa 52:6 is fulfilled by people who have not previously known God's name (Gentiles) coming to know it and to be his people. Another possibility is that in the person and work of Jesus Christ in the days of his flesh, there was an extended proclamation of the divine name, much as when the LORD came down on Mt. Sinai and passed before Moses, proclaiming his name, describing his attributes, "full of grace and truth," etc., at which time, according to the *Pal. Tgs.*, Moses saw the glory of the Word (*Dibbera/Dibbura*; Exod 33:23). The ministry of Jesus is an extended fulfillment of Exod 33:19: "I will make all my goodness pass before you, and will proclaim the name of the LORD before you. . . ." As discussed in ch. 3, the mission of Jesus is described in John 17:6, 26 as making known the Father's name (YHWH), which is also his own name given him by the Father (17:11–12). Since Isa 52:6 is the last "I am he" saying of Isaiah, and John 4:26 (which is dependent on Isa 52:6) is the first "I am he" saying in John, we can see that in revealing the name and character of God in the flesh, Jesus is basically picking up where he left off in Isaiah.

We have seen, and will see in more detail, that a number of the "I am he" sayings in John depend on the divine "I am he" of Isa 43:10, and John 4:26 is unique in depending on Isa 52:6. However, there is also an indirect connection between John 4:26 and *Tg. Isa.* 43:10, because *Tg. Isa.* 43:10 mentions the Messiah:

> "You are witnesses before me," says the LORD, "and my servant the Messiah with whom I am pleased, that you might know and believe before me and understand that I am he. I am he who is from the beginning, even the ages of ages are mine, and there is no God besides me."

For the targumist, the Messiah is witness, as Israel is, that "I am he; I am he who is from the beginning."[7] But for the Messiah to say of himself "I am he" with the same divine implications goes far beyond the Targums' idea of the person of the Messiah. Yet the "I am he" sayings of Jesus that depend on Isa 43:10 clearly point in this direction, and, as we have noted before, John himself identifies Jesus as "the one who is from the beginning" (1 John 2:13–14).

The divine dimension to "I am he" in John 4:26 is also brought out by considering Exod 17, where the divine bridegroom, so to speak, met Israel at a miraculous well. In ch. 6, we took note of the reading of *Tg. Neof.*, where the divine Word stood in readiness by the rock which, when stuck by his servant Moses, poured out

---

[7] Reim, in contrast, thought that *Tg. Isa.* 43:10 was read by John to indicate that the Messiah was the "I am he" ("Targum und Johannesevangelium," 11).

water for his people. In John 4, the Word and servant come together in the Word who became flesh.

Means: In the context, Jesus is the one who gives living water that wells up to eternal life (vv. 10, 14). The giving of water, we saw, was actually the bridegroom's role (Gen 29; Exod 2; Exod 17), and the giving of gifts was what Abraham's servant did; Jesus' giving of water parallels the servant's giving of gifts in Gen 24:22. To bring out the dimension of means one would need to identify Jesus more specifically as *the source* of the water. This is actually accomplished not here but in John 19:34: "One of the soldiers pierced Jesus' side with a spear, and out came blood and water." Above (ch. 6) we noted the reading of *Tg. Ps.-J.* Num 20:11, which says that the first time Moses struck the rock, it dripped blood; the second time, abundant water flowed forth.[8] Perhaps, then, John recorded the flow of blood and water because he saw it as pointing to the identification of Jesus not just as the giver of the living water of which he spoke to the Samaritan woman, but also as the source of that water.

If we accept that John 4 alludes to Exod 17, where we see the divine bridegroom and his servant Moses at the rock from which water came forth, then we can see in the Gospel the three perspectives come together in the person of Christ: the divine bridegroom, the servant, and the rock. Or if we look at *Tg. Neof.* Exod 17, where we have God and his Word, his servant (Moses), and the rock, in John 4 we have corresponding to this scene the Father and the Son, who is divine bridegroom, servant, and source of life-giving water.

John 6:20

> He said to them, "I am he, do not be afraid."

Human: Most obviously, Jesus is identifying himself as a certain man known to the disciples, who would recognize Jesus by the sound of his voice, thus assuring them that they are not seeing an apparition. Any other hypothetical human observer who did not know Jesus would likewise assume that a man is simply identifying himself as a man known to the men in the boat.

Divine: In the previous chapter I presented reasons for relating this saying to the divine "I am he" saying in Isa 43:10. In 43:1, the LORD says to Israel, "Do not be afraid." In 43:2, he says he will be with them when they pass through the waters, which is what the disciples were doing at the time John 6:20 is spoken. In Isa 43:3, he says he is their savior. In 43:5, he says, "Do not fear, for I am with you." Finally, there is the "I am he" saying of 43:10, which is of great significance to other ἐγώ εἰμι sayings in John.[9] *Targum Isaiah* 43:2 takes God's promise of being with his people when they cross through the waters to refer back to the crossing of the

---

[8] Noted by Reim, "Targum und Johannesevangelium," 9.

[9] Ball, *"I Am" in John's Gospel*, 182. Ball notes that in six LXX verses, "do not fear" occurs with ἐγώ εἰμι, all of which are spoken by God. The passages are Gen 26:24; 46:3; Jer 1:8, 17; 42:11; 46:28 (MT numbering).

Red Sea. When Israel crossed the sea, it was dark, with a strong wind blowing, as in John 6:16–21. Several *Pal. Tg.* Exod 14 passages point to the help of the divine Word in Israel's sea crossing (see ch. 2, p. 53, no. 13). *Targum Isaiah 43:2* says, "My Word was your help" (in crossing the sea), and v. 5 says, "My Word will be your help" (referring to the future). Thus biblical history is being repeated with the divine Word helping the disciples cross the sea.

Psalm 77:19 says that God's way was in the sea (i.e., the Red Sea) and his footprints were not evident, and Ps 107:4–30 describes sailors being saved from stormy waters by the LORD and brought safely to their destination, all in a context of the LORD filling the hungry with good things. These passages pertain to the previous and next episodes in John.[10]

Means: The dimension of means is brought out in the detail that when Jesus enters the boat, immediately they reach the other side (John 6:21). As we have observed previously, John uses words found also in the Prologue to give us a literal picture of Jesus *coming to* (v. 17) his own, of his own *receiving him* (v. 21), and of his own being helped to their destination. The disciples' act of receiving Jesus into the boat and reaching the other side reminds us of John 1:11–12: he came to his own and they did not receive him, but to those who did receive him, he gave the right to become children of God and thus to receive eternal life.

John 6:35, 41, 48, 51

The discourse on the bread of life, which presents Jesus as the true manna that brings eternal life, shares the same OT background of the feeding of the five thousand as the account of the giving of the manna, discussed in ch. 6. The audience of Jesus' discourse is clearly seeking more of the bread they received (6:30–31). In Num 21:5, the divine, the human, and the means of life come together as objects of the people's complaining, when "the people spoke against God and against Moses" and complained, "we loathe this miserable food." In *Tg. Neof.* and a variant of *Tg. Onq.*, they speak against the divine Word (*Tg. Neof* [mg.]: they speak against "the name of the Word of the LORD") and complain against Moses, saying, "our soul is distressed by this bread, the nourishment of which is little." In *Tg. Ps.-J.*, they complain in their hearts, speak against the Word of the LORD, and quarrel with Moses. Their soul loathes the manna, which is meager food. The complaints registered against Jesus in John 6:41, 43, 61 bring out this threefold perspective again, as the wilderness experience is repeated in the history of Israel: the people complain against the divine Word, the servant of God, and the means of life God gave to them.

Means: The predicates of ἐγώ εἰμι in these passages are "the bread of life" (vv. 35, 48), "the bread that came down from heaven" (v. 41), and "the living bread that came down from heaven" (v. 58). These "I am he" sayings most obviously fit the category of means. Using the metaphor of bread, they describe Jesus as the means to eternal life. The manna in the wilderness enabled men to live only a few years longer, but by eating of this bread, one may live forever. This bread also "came

---

[10] Brown, *John*, 1:255.

down" from heaven, as in Exod 16. In the MT of Exod 16:4, the verb "cause to rain" is used, but the Targums use the verb "bring down," so that the language in John of bread that came down from heaven (6:35, 48, 58) is closer to Exod 16:4 in the Targums than it is to the MT. In MT Exod 16:15, Moses answers the question "What is it?" (the question from which the manna was named) by saying, "It is the bread which the LORD has given you to eat." *Targum Neofiti* [mg.] says that the manna "is by the Word of the LORD for you as food." In John 6, the situation is altered so that the divine Word becomes the food, the flesh which the Father and he give for the life of the world (vv. 32, 51). A jar of manna was kept in the holy of holies, the place where the Word spoke to Moses; in the incarnation, the Word leaves the holy of holies, so to speak, and becomes a new kind of manna to give life to his people.

Divine: The manna began in Exod 16. The *Pal. Tgs.* Exod 16:12 say, "At twilight you shall eat flesh, and in the morning you shall eat bread, and you shall know that *I am he*, the LORD your God." This "I am he" is spoken by the divine Word according to *Tg. Neof.* [mg.] v. 11. The Logos title given by John to Jesus also brings out the divine aspect, since, as mentioned above, the people's complaint against Jesus is like the complaint against the Word of the LORD in the Targums.

We earlier made mention of the fact that Jesus' statement, "I have come down from heaven" (John 6:38), is a divine statement based on its OT background (ch. 4); the manna came down from the sky, Jesus came down from the divine dwelling place, as in OT times. We also noted (ch. 8) that the "come(s) to me" language in this chapter (vv. 35, 37 [2x], 44, 45, 65) has its basis in the divine invitation "come to me" and "eat what is good" of Isa 55:1–3. If ἐγώ εἰμι in these passages is meant to represent the spoken Aramaic "I am he," then we can note that "I am he" is also associated with life in the world to come in *Tg. Neof.* Deut 32:39: "I, I in my Word, am he. . . . I am he . . . who brings to life the dead in the world to come." This Word has become flesh, John tells us, and Jesus tells us in John 6:51, "This bread which I shall give for the life of the world, is my flesh," or, in terms of John 1:14, this bread is the Word who became flesh for the life of the world. *Targum Neofiti* Deut 32:40 says, "I live and exist in my Word forever," and Jesus says, "I am the living bread" (v. 51) and "Just as the living Father sent me, and I live because of the Father . . ." (v. 57). *Targum Pseudo-Jonathan* Deut 32:43 says, "By his Word he will make atonement for the sins of his land and of his people," which may be echoed in Jesus' identification with "the bread of God, which gives life to the world" (John 6:33). The "bread of life" is thus "the Word of life," that is, the Word who gives life. This is what John calls Jesus in 1 John 1:1, and he goes on, using targumic language associated with the Word in *Tg. Ps.-J.* Deut 32:39, to say that this life was "revealed" (1 John 1:2). Taken together, these parallels indicate that the fourfold ἐγώ εἰμι of John 6 can be indirectly linked to the divine "I am he" sayings of *Pal. Tgs.* Deut 32:39.

Human: As always when Jesus spoke, the human aspect was obvious to the people: "Is this not Jesus, son of Joseph, whose father and mother we know?" (John 6:42). After saying "I have come down from heaven," Jesus goes on to say "not to do my own will, but the will of him who sent me" (v. 38). This is again servant language, and could recall the figure of the Servant of the LORD of Isaiah who, though he dies, sees his offspring (Isa 53:9–10). Jesus refers to himself as the Son of Man, the progenitor of this offspring (see ch. 4), in 6:27, 53, and 62.

The human aspect is brought out also by OT analogy: Moses was the miracle worker who gave bread in the wilderness. The Jews asked Jesus, "What sign do you perform, so that we might believe?" (John 6:30), and they go on to suggest that he offer them something like manna. It is interesting, though, that it is Philip, not Jesus, who is Moses-like in his unbelief when Jesus tests him (John 6:5–7; cf. Num 11:13, 21–22).

John 8:12, 18, 24, 28, 58

Human: The human aspect seems to be at the forefront in John 8:12, 18, and 28. In ch. 8, we saw how Jesus' claim to be "the light of the world" could be related to prophecies of the Servant of the LORD in Isa 42:6; 49:6 and to the prediction that those who walk in darkness will see a great light in Isa 9:2 (thus John 8:12 is an ironic response to 7:52, "no prophet comes from Galilee"; cf. Matt 4:16).

In John 8:18 ("I am he, the one who testifies concerning myself") the human interpretation seems most obvious in light of the context, in which Jesus says, "the testimony of two men is true" (v. 17). And in v. 28 ("When you lift up the Son of Man, then you shall know that I am he") "I am he" obviously points back to "the Son of Man."

One could also say that the words of Jesus throughout this chapter (as well as chs. 7 and 9) identify him as the Servant of the LORD promised in Isaiah:

	Isaiah	John
Sent by the Father	48:16	7:16, 18, 28–29, 33; 8:16, 18, 26, 29, 42; 9:4
Taught by the Father	50:4–5	7:16; 8:26, 28, 38, 40
A teacher with disciples	50:4	7:14–17; 8:12, 31
Light of the world	42:6; 49:6 (cf. 9:2)	8:12; 9:5
Opens blind eyes	42:7; 49:6	9:1–41 (esp. 39)
Sets prisoners free	42:7; 49:9	8:32–36
Cannot be convicted of sin	50:8; 53:9	8:46
Honors and pleases the Father	53:10	8:29
Honored, glorified by the Father	42:1; 49:5; 52:13	8:54
Dishonored by Israel	49:7; 53:3	7:19–20; 8:37, 40, 48–49, 52, 59
Israel blind, deaf (unbelieving)	42:16, 19	8:43, 45–47; 9:41
Came for judgment	42:1, 3–4	9:39

Divine: Before looking at the individual verses, we can take note again that according to *m. Sukkah* 4:5, a modified form of "I am he" was used to address God in a daily procession during this feast, calling upon him to save his people (see ch. 3). Jesus' coming to the temple halfway through the feast can be seen as a fulfillment of the request, "Come to our aid," and his repeated claim of "I am he" as identifying him as the one who would answer this request, which is ironic in terms of the reception he received.

John 8:12, 18

As we saw in ch. 8, the claim "I am he, the light of the world; he who follows me shall not walk in the darkness, but shall have the light of life" (John 8:12) should be interpreted in light of the fact that it is spoken at the Feast of Booths, a time when Israel would be especially mindful of the LORD's care for them in the wilderness and when the light ceremony could evoke thoughts of the pillar of fire leading Israel during the forty years of wilderness wanderings, a fire which the Targums connect with the divine Word. Read in the light of the Targums, this verse is a divine claim. The alternative to having the light of life is to walk in darkness and, as stated in vv. 21 and 24, to die in one's sin, an expression also applicable to those who died in the wilderness in their unbelief (Num 27:3) in contrast to those who, like Joshua and Caleb, followed the divine Word (*Pal. Tgs.*) into the promised land.

Similarly, "I am he, the one who testifies concerning myself" (John 8:18) can be seen as a divine claim, since in the OT divine "I am he" sayings, God is testifying concerning himself that he is the one true God and that all other gods are false. Deuteronomy 32 is a prophetic testimony to the apostasy of Israel, which, when it comes true, will prove that "I am he" (v. 39). The "I am he" sayings in Isaiah function in a similar way.[11] Like the OT "I am he" contexts, Jesus here predicts apostasy (see below on 8:28).

One might respond that the "I am he" of Isaiah is the "I am he" of the Father, since part of the divine testimony in that context is "Behold, my servant" (Isa 42:1), which must represent the Father speaking about the Son, not the Son speaking about himself. Thus, in the "I am he" sayings of Isaiah, it must be the Father testifying concerning himself, not the Son. Indeed, Jesus' statement that "the Father testifies concerning me" could refer not only to the miracles that the Father gave the Son to perform, but also to the Father's testimony concerning the Son found in the book of Isaiah that, for example, he would open blind eyes (obviously relevant to John 9). I would grant this point, but also point out that we see in John that the Son shares the divine "I am he" of the Father; what the Son sees the Father doing, he does (John 8:38; 10:37), and so the Son also testifies concerning himself. From OT to NT there is a progression in revelation, though this is already hinted at in Isaiah in the divine names given to the Messiah (9:6) and the description of the servant as "high and lifted up" (52:13), the same way God is described elsewhere (6:1; 33:10; 57:15), in contrast to men who are high and lifted up with pride and idolatry (Isa 2:12–17).

---

[11] As T. Keiser notes, "not only is this expression used in reference to the Lord only in Deuteronomy xxxii and II Isaiah, but all of Isaiah's usages emphasize the same features of its occurrence in the Song of Moses," those features being that the Lord's people are called to recognize that "I am he," and that he is the one true God who is in control of history.

There are also some suggestive passages in the Targums that speak of the divine Word as a witness. The people ask Jeremiah whether they should go to Egypt or stay in Judah after Nebuchadnezzar conquers Jerusalem, and they promise to obey the word of the LORD through Jeremiah: "*May the Word of the LORD be among us* as a true and faithful witness, if we do not act according to every word in which the LORD your God has sent you to us, whether good or evil; *we will receive the Word of the LORD our God* before whom we are sending you, so that *it will be well for us when we receive the Word of the LORD our God*" (*Tg. Jer.* 42:5–6). As it turned out, they did not receive the Word of the LORD, but went to Egypt in rebellion and, ironically, the divine Word did appear among them as a true and faithful witness when the Word became flesh hundreds of years later, and again they did not receive him (John 1:11).

Micah 1:2 says, "Let the Lord GOD be a witness against you, the LORD from his holy temple. For behold, the LORD is coming out of his place, and will come down and tread upon the high places of the earth." The Targum says, "Let the Word of the LORD God be a witness against you," and for the next phrase a textual variant says, "the Word of the LORD from his holy temple." In the next ·verse, the idea of the LORD coming and descending is changed in both cases to the idea of the LORD being revealed: "For behold, the LORD is being revealed from the place of the house of his *Shekinah*, and he will be revealed and will tread upon the strongholds of the earth." One could easily imagine a Palestinian version of this verse speaking of the divine Word being revealed, but even without such a reading in v. 3, v. 2 as it is in *Tg. Jon.* could be viewed as another "Caiaphas (i.e., unwitting) prophecy," fulfilled in the Word becoming flesh and being revealed as a witness against his people in the earthly temple, where so much of the dialogue in John's Gospel takes place (including ch. 8).

John 8:24, 28, 58

The divine import of the words of Jesus is most obvious in vv. 24 ("Unless you believe that I am he, you will die in your sins") and 58 ("Before Abraham came into being, I am he"). At the time of the first hearing of these words, the divine claim of v. 58 was immediately recognized (they picked up stones to kill him), but v. 24 was obscure to his hearers and brought the response, "Who are you?" (v. 25). The Lord's response is regarded as some of the most difficult Greek to interpret in John.[12] The translation adopted here follows a singular reading from an early papyrus and assumes that "the beginning" is as in, for example, Isa 48:16:

Isa 48:16	John 8:25–26
From the beginning I have not spoken in secret. . . . And now, the Lord GOD has sent me, and his Spirit.	(I said to you) in the beginning that which I am also speaking to you (now) [Τὴν ἀρχὴν ὅ τι καὶ λαλῶ ὑμῖν]. . . . He who sent me is true.

---

[12] A wide variety of translations of v. 25 has been suggested since early times. Τὴν ἀρχὴν translates בְּרֵאשֹׁנָה (Gen 13:4) and בַּתְּחִלָּה (Gen 41:21; 43:18, 20; Dan 9:21) in the LXX, supporting the sense here of "formerly" or "in the beginning," but it could also bear other adverbial meanings such as "principally."

The words "I said to you" are found only in the margin of Bodmer Papyrus II ($\mathfrak{P}^{66}$), which has "I said to you" (Εἶπον ὑμῖν) before "in the beginning" (τὴν ἀρχὴν).[13] Interpreting "the beginning" not as the beginning of Jesus' earthly ministry but as the beginning of his revelation to Israel allows us to see a parallel to the divine revelation to Moses at the burning bush, in the context of which the issue of "Who are you?" was also raised (Exod 3:13: "They may say to me, 'What is his name?'"). Recall from ch. 3 that the *Pal. Tgs.* import the divine "I am he" into the explanation of the divine name at the scene of the burning bush. In *Tg. Ps.-J.* Exod 3:14, "I am he [אנא הוא] who is and who will be" stands for Hebrew אֶהְיֶה and, as I suggested in ch. 3, could be echoed in the present and future "I am he" of John 8:24, 28. In a lengthy marginal reading of *Tg. Neof.* Exod 3:14, God says, "I am he who was for your help in the captivity of the Egyptians, and I am he who is yet to be for your help in every generation."

Whether or not John 8:25 is meant to recall the revelation of the divine name at the burning bush, an allusion in the previous verse to the divine "I am he" of Isa 43:10 is frequently noted and was discussed in ch. 8. There it was also noted that vv. 24 and 28 together give a nice parallel to the "know and believe" of Isa 43:10. The allusion to Isa 43:10 was not immediately obvious, no doubt because the Jews were stuck on the expectation of an answer to a different question, "Are you the Messiah?"; but the echo of Isa 43:10 should be obvious upon reflection, especially since we have the advantage of John's opening statement, that the Word was in the beginning with God and was God. The reference to "the beginning" in John 8:25 might also be meant to allude to Isa 43:10, not the MT but the Targum, which reproduces MT "I am he," then interprets "before me was no god formed" as "I am he who is from the beginning" (a claim also found at *Tg. Isa.* 44:6 and 48:12).[14]

---

[13] The reading of $\mathfrak{P}^{66}$ was accepted by Robert W. Funk, who says that with this reading "the insurmountable difficulty felt by every commentator since Chrysostom is thereby alleviated." He notes that though the added text is a marginal correction, the editor of the papyrus is certain that they were added by the original scribe and that a majority of such marginal corrections contain text universally attested; only that of 8:25 is not attested elsewhere ("Papyrus Bodmer II [$\mathfrak{P}^{66}$] and John 8, 25," *HTR* 51 [1958]: 95–100). E. R. Smothers notes that in John 11:33 the scribe revised his original text, which agreed with one text tradition, to one that agreed with that of $\mathfrak{P}^{45}$, that is, that the scribe of $\mathfrak{P}^{66}$ went beyond simply copying one MS before him, but he went back and checked it against at least one other as well ("Two Readings in Papyrus Bodmer II," *HTR* 51 [1958]: 121). Smothers is not sure that $\mathfrak{P}^{66}$ is original: It "may be an interpolation; it may be primitive. Without it, the obscurity of our common text remains. With it, we have a simple and an adequate solution" (ibid., 122). See also Metzger, *Textual Commentary*, 191, and the major commentaries. Burkett suggests that Εἶπον ὑμῖν was added by mistake "from the previous verse, where $\mathfrak{P}^{66}$ also reads εἴ πον ὑμῖν" (*Son of the Man in the Gospel of John*, 152 n.2). He thinks that as an answer to the question "Who are you?" Jesus' response, "just what I am speaking to you," is a way of saying "I am the Word of God" (ibid., 151–52).

[14] Consequently, NIV's "Unless you believe that I am who I claim to be" (wording which completely obscures who he is claiming to be) is disappointing to say the least. The correct reading, "I am he," is given in an NIV text note and is in Today's New International Version (International Bible Society, 2001, 2005) as well.

In John 8:28, Jesus says: "When you lift up the Son of Man, then you will know that I am he." Here "I am he" seems simply to point back to "the Son of Man," just as in 4:26 it seems to simply point back to "the Messiah." As J. H. Bernard noted, in 8:28 "I am he" could refer back to "the Son of Man" or could be used as in 8:24, "the phrase being then identical with the self-designation of Yahweh in the Prophets, אֲנִי הוּא. . . . On either interpretation, the style of the sentence is that of Divine proclamations" (referring to Ezek 11:10).[15] As confirmation that the style of John 8:28 "is that of Divine proclamations," the sequence γνώσεσθε ὅτι ἐγώ from·v. 28 occurs eight times in the LXX (sometimes also followed by εἰμι), the MT equivalent of which is always followed by "YHWH" or "YHWH your God" (Exod 6:7; 10:2; 16:12; Ezek 13:23; 36:11; 37:6, 13, 14). In NASB, the expression "you/they might/may/will/shall know that I am" occurs eighty-one times, always spoken by the LORD in the OT (seventy-eight times, sixty-three of which are in Ezekiel), Christ in the NT. The other NT occurrences (besides John 8:28) are also spoken by Jesus in John's writings: John 14:20 ("on that day you shall know that I am in my Father") and Rev 2:23 ("the churches will know that I am he who searches [ἐγώ εἰμι ὁ ἐραυνῶν] the minds and hearts; and I will give to each one of you according to your deeds"), which is based on Jer 17:10 ("I, the LORD, search the heart. I test the mind. Even to give to each man according to his ways").

We can also compare John 8:28 to similar sayings of *Tg. Neof.*, where eight times in Exodus the LORD says, "you/they will know that I am he, the LORD," usually spoken by the divine Word (as in John 8:28), as indicated by the marginal glosses (marked by square brackets):

Tg. Neof. Exod 6:2–7	And the [Word of the] LORD spoke with Moses and said to him, "I am he, the LORD. . . . And my Word will be to you a redeemer God and *you will know that I am he*, the LORD your God who redeemed and brought you out from beneath the yoke of the servitude of the Egyptians." (also *CTg. D*)
Tg. Neof. Exod 7:1, 5	And the [Word of the] LORD said to Moses, ". . . And the Egyptians *will know that I am he*, the LORD, when I set the plagues of my punishment upon Egypt." (MT: "when I stretch out my hand against Egypt"; cf. John 21:18)
Tg. Neof. Exod 7:17	And the [Word of the] LORD said, "In this *you will know that I am he*, the LORD: behold, I strike the waters of the river with the staff that is in my hand and they shall be turned into blood" (also *CTg. D*, except not spoken by the divine Word; cf. John 2:11; 8:28)
Tg. Neof. Exod 8:20–22	Thus says the [Word of the] LORD, ". . . I will do signs and wonders . . . so that you may *know that I am he*, the Lord, whose Word dwells [the glory of whose *Shekinah* dwells] within the land."
Tg. Neof. Exod 10:2	And the [Word of the] LORD said to Moses, ". . . and you *will know that I am he*, the LORD."

[15] Bernard, *John*, 2:303.

***Tg. Neof.* Exod 14:1, 4**	And the [Word of the] Lord spoke with Moses, saying ". . . and the Egyptians *will know that I am he*, the Lord." (likewise Exod 14:15, 18)
***Tg. Neof.* Exod 16:12**	And the [Word of the] Lord spoke with Moses, saying ". . . and in the morning you shall be filled with bread, and you shall *know that I am he*, the Lord your God." (cf. John 6:35, 48: "I am he, the bread of life"; 6:41: "I am he, the bread that came down from heaven"; 6:51: "I am he, the living bread that came down from heaven")
***Tg. Neof.* Exod 29:43, 45–46**	"And my *Word* will meet the children of Israel there (= at the tabernacle, in context). . . . And I shall make my *Shekinah* dwell in the midst of the children of Israel, and my *Word* will be for them a redeeming God. *And they shall know that I am he*, the Lord their God, who brought them out of the land of Egypt, so that the glory of my *Shekinah* might dwell among them. I am he, the Lord their God." (cf. John 8, where Israel meets the Word at the temple and hears him say, "Then you shall know that I am he," referring to when he accomplishes his people's redemption).

Another "I am he" saying in *Tg. Neof.* (Exod 12:12) does not have "you/they will know" but can be related to John 8:28 because of its reference to the Passover:

And I will pass in my Word through the land of Egypt this night of the Passover and I will kill all the firstborn in the land of Egypt. . . . The Lord has said; [I am he].

John 8:28 is fulfilled at the Passover when Jesus destroys the works of the devil.

In the passages listed above, "I am he" is also found in *Tg. Ps.-J.* Exod 7:5; 14:4; 29:46, and the lxx has ἐγώ εἰμι in Exod 7:5; 14:4; 16:12; 29:46.

John 8:58 is often related directly to Exod 3:14, where the Hebrew is often interpreted "I am who I am" and the lxx translates with ἐγώ εἰμι. Such a connection would explain why the Jews took up stones. But as I argued in ch. 3, Exod 3:14 is better understood as "I will be who I have been," and ἐγώ εἰμι in John is more likely to be related to the divine "I am he" of Deut 32:39 and Isaiah as well as the additional "I am he" sayings in the *Pal. Tgs.* We noted there as well that John 8:24, 28, 58 could be related to *Tg. Ps.-J.* Deut 32:39, seen as fulfilled at the Feast of Booths, as the divine Word is revealed to redeem his people and says, in effect, "I am YHWH" through the past, present, and future "I am he" reference of these three verses. Like John 8:28, John 8:58 has additional points of reference in the Targums. Firstly, there are references to Abraham added to *Tg. Isa.* among the "I am he" sayings found there. Secondly, there are many "I am he" sayings in the *Pal. Tgs.* involving Abraham and the divine Word, which, if Jesus' listeners were accustomed to hearing them recited in the synagogue, would be further reason for taking this verse as a claim to being the God of Abraham, and would explain John's motivation for identifying Jesus as the divine Word. For example, *Tg. Isa.* 43:12 reads: "*I declared to Abraham your father* what was about to come. I saved you from Egypt, just as I swore to him between the pieces . . ." This is immediately followed by the second "I am he" saying of this chapter (third in the Targum of this chapter): "and also *from eternity I am he*." Likewise, *Tg. Isa.* 48:15 says, "I, even I, by my Word decreed a covenant with Abraham your father and exalted him." This comes just three verses after the "I am he" saying of 48:12, which in the Targum reads, "I am he, I am he who is from the beginning," as in *Tg. Isa.* 43:10.

Both of these passages might explain what Jesus meant by "Abraham rejoiced to see my day, and he saw it and was glad" (John 8:56), which leads to the claim of 8:58. What is the "day" of Christ the Word? *Targum Isaiah* 43:12 refers to the covenant of Gen 15, a foreshadowing of the passing through the Red Sea, an OT "Day of the LORD"; and *Tg. Isa.* 48:15 speaks of God in his Word making a covenant with Abraham. *Fragment Targum V* Exod 12:42 identifies the second of the four nights of remembrance as reminiscent of the time "when the Word of the LORD was revealed upon Abraham between the pieces," that is, the event of Gen 15. (The passage in *Frg. Tg. V* goes on to conflate this night with Gen 17, the promise of the birth of Isaac). Thus Abraham saw the Day of the LORD, the day of redemption from Egypt. Genesis 15 does not say that Abraham was glad to see this earlier day, but there is no reason to doubt that this was the case.

Several other passages from *Tg. Neof.* connect the divine Word with an "I am he" saying to or about Abraham:

***Tg. Neof.* Gen 17:1**	When Abram was ninety-nine years old, *the Word of the LORD* was revealed to Abram, and he said to him, "*I am he*, the God of Heaven."
***Tg. Neof.* Gen 26:24**	And *the [Word of the] LORD* was revealed to him that night, and he said, "<I> *am he*, the God of Abraham your father."
***Tg. Neof.* Exod 3:4–6**	*The Word of the LORD* called to him from the midst of the thorn bush, . . . and he said "*I am he*, the God of your father, *the God of Abraham*, the God of Isaac, and the God of Jacob." And Moses hid his face because he was afraid to look on the glory of the *Shekinah* of the LORD.
***Tg. Neof.* Exod 6:2–3**	And the [Word of the] LORD spoke with Moses and said to him, "I am he, the LORD. And I was revealed in my Word to Abraham. (also *CTg. D*)

Deuteronomy 32:39 and the Feast of Booths

I have been suggesting that, although none of the individual "I am he" sayings of John 8 seem to depend on the prototypical "I am he" of Deut 32:39 as it is worded in the MT, nevertheless, the threefold "I am he" of John 8:24, 28, 58, with present, future, and past reference, could be related to the prophecy in *Tg. Ps.-J. Deut* 32:39, which predicts that when the divine Word is revealed, he will say, "I am he who is and was, and I am he who will be in the future." We have also seen that in the OT, the divine "I am he" is God's testimony concerning himself, which has potential relevance to John 8:18, "I am he, the one who testifies concerning myself." Deuteronomy 32:39 is part of the Song of Moses, in which the apostasy of Israel is predicted.

Now we can mention the additional fact that there is a connection between Deut 32:39 and the Feast of Booths (the setting for all the "I am he" sayings of John

8) for the simple reason that the book of Deuteronomy was to be read every seven years at the Feast of Booths (Deut 31:10–13). The initial recitation of the song is also connected to the succession of Moses by Joshua, the namesake of Jesus. Deuteronomy 31 has the following structure:[16]

vv. 1–8	Introduction: There is a discussion of both divine and human leadership; Joshua is to succeed Moses so that Israel will not be like sheep without a shepherd (cf. Matt 9:36; Mark 6:34); the LORD will go before Joshua and be with him (Targums: the Word of the LORD will be his help).
vv. 9–13	A Future assemblies: The law is to be safeguarded by the ministers who carry the ark and read it publicly every seven years at the Feast of Booths, so that coming generations will learn to fear the LORD.
v. 14	B Joshua is presented for commissioning.
vv. 15–22	C The Song of Moses is to be learned and sung so that this prediction of apostasy will stand as a witness against future generations.
v. 23	B′ Joshua is commissioned.
vv. 24–29	A′ Present assembly: The law is put in the ark as a witness against Israel; the assembly will hear the song.

With regard to A/A′ we can note that the dialogue of John 8 takes place at the Feast of Booths, the occasion on which the law was to be read every seven years. Further, as already observed, 8:33 succinctly highlights a fundamental disregard of a major theme of Deuteronomy on the part of those attending the feast: "We have never yet been enslaved to anyone." Moses commanded Israel to remember at all times (Deut 5:6; 6:12, 21; 7:8; 8:14; 13:5, 10; 15:15; 24:18–22) and particularly every Sabbath (5:15) and at the feasts (16:12) that they had been slaves in Egypt. Since most in Moses' audience actually had never seen Egypt, it is clear that he nevertheless expected them (and thus future generations) to identify themselves as freed slaves.

B/B′ is of interest in light of what we have observed above about Jesus' human namesake. Joshua represents human leadership under the LORD; in Jesus we have leadership that is both divine and human.

In C it is ironic to observe that where the MT of Deut 31:15 says that the LORD appeared to Moses and Joshua and told Moses of the apostasy of the nation after his death, *Tg. Neof.* says that the Word of the LORD was revealed (*Tg. Ps.-J.*: "the glory of his *Shekinah*") and said these things. In John 8:28, the Word who became flesh predicts the ultimate apostasy, the ultimate rejection of the Word of the LORD: "When you lift up the Son of Man, then you will know that I am he." Thus in both Deut 32 and John 8, the fulfillment of the prediction of the apostasy of Israel proves Jesus' claim that "I am he." The *Tgs. Neof.* and *Ps.-J.* Deut 31:17 speak of the withdrawal of the *Shekinah* as a result of Israel's disobedience; *Tg. Neof.*

Deut 31:18 says, "I in my Word shall hide the face of my good pleasure," and in v. 27 Moses says, "While I am still alive with you this day, you have refused to follow the Word of the LORD, so how much more after my death!" Again we see the appropriateness of a targumic background to the Logos title and a specific fulfillment (when the Word became flesh) of this general prediction of Israel's failure to follow the divine Word after the death of Moses. In a manner reminiscent of the prophecy of Caiaphas, *Tg. Neof.* is unwittingly worded in a way that is particularly applicable to the time when the Word became flesh. "How much more" did they refuse to follow the divine Word then? As foretold at the feast in John 8:28, they crucified him!

The content of the song itself is also of interest in light of John 8. The Jews could appeal to Deut 32 for their claim, "We have one Father, God" (John 8:41), but Jesus could also appeal to Deut 32 for his claim that they are not children of God (8:42–47). On the one hand, Moses says or implies that Israelites are the children of God in Deut 32:6 ("Is he not your Father, who created you?"), v. 8 (Jacob's household of seventy, matching the seventy nations of Gen 10, is called the children of God), v. 18 (God begot them), v. 19 (they are "his sons and daughters"), and v. 20 (they are "sons"). On the other hand, v. 5 says that since "they have acted corruptly toward him, they are not his children (because of) their defect; a perverse and crooked generation."[17] Jesus' statement that "You are of your father the devil" (John 8:44) is probably based on the example of Cain as the first example of the offspring of the serpent, whose deeds they imitate when they take up stones to stone him (8:59). *Targum Pseudo-Jonathan* Deut 32:32–33 makes a similar point: "Their thoughts are evil like the poison of venomous snakes . . . like the venom of adders, so they are cruel." There is a clear link between this earlier incident and the issue raised in John's Prologue as to who are the true children of God.

Moses and Joshua gave the first recitation of this song to Israel (Deut 32:44); now Jesus, the NT counterpart of Joshua, teaches the substance of the song at the feast, and, as the divine Word who has become flesh, quotes the divine "I am he" as prophesied in *Tg. Ps.-J.* Deut 32:39. In *Tg. Neof.*, both the divine Word and Moses his servant predict the apostasy of Israel, and here at the feast the divine Word who has become a servant predicts the ultimate apostasy, the lifting up of the Son of Man (John 8:28).

Means: The category of means, while not at the forefront in the "I am he" sayings of this chapter, is brought out in John 8:12, 24. In saying that he is the light of the world whom believers may follow (v. 12), a certain destination is in view, to which Jesus promises to bring them. In the wilderness, that destination was the promised land, and analogous to that in the present age is heaven and eternal life. Similarly, in v. 24 Jesus warns of the consequences of not believing "that I am he," i.e., they will die in their sins. Conversely, this verse shows that believing in Jesus is the way to life.

---

[17] The MT is problematic; see *BHS*, 345; Martin McNamara, *Targum Neofiti 1: Deuteronomy* (ArBib 5A; Collegeville, Minn.: Liturgical Press, 1997), 150 n.17.

John 10:7, 9, 11, 14

Means: The first two of these ἐγώ εἰμι sayings (v. 7: "I am he, the gate for the sheep"; v. 9: "I am he, the gate") are clearly in the category of means, as is made explicit in v. 9: "If anyone *enters through me*, that one shall be saved, and shall go in and out, and find pasture."

Human: The other two ἐγώ εἰμι sayings (vv. 11, 14: "I am he, the good shepherd") constitute a claim to be a particular human. Evans catalogued the parallels between John 10 and the OT expressions of human leaders as shepherds.[18] The two primary background passages are Num 27:15–23, concerning Joshua as the successor needed to answer the prayer of Moses that the LORD's people not be as sheep without a shepherd (v. 17, echoed in Matt 9:36; Mark 6:34), and Ezek 34, where the LORD promises to raise up "David my Servant" (vv. 23–24) to be their shepherd (in contrast to the religious leaders of Judah condemned in that chapter), to feed them, and to be prince among them. It seems clear, then, this is another "I am he" claim to be the Messiah.

Divine: Evans claims that the fact that many passages depict God himself as Israel's shepherd "could have significance for the Johannine image, when it is remembered that in the Prologue the *logos* has been identified as God."[19] Ezekiel 34 is one of those places, for in addition to promising to raise up David as their shepherd, God says, "I myself will search for my sheep . . . care for my sheep . . . feed my sheep . . . make them lie down," etc. (vv. 11–22). *Targum Ezek.* 34:11 explicitly says, "Behold, I am about to reveal myself, and I will search . . ." (also v. 20). Based on analogy with *Tg. Onq.* and the *Pal. Tgs.*, where a passage in *Tg. Onq.* might speak of God revealing himself and a corresponding *Pal. Tg.* passage might speak of his Word being revealed (or of God being revealed in his Word; e.g., compare *Tgs. Onq.* and *Neof.* Exod 3:8), we may speculate that a *Pal. Tg.* of Ezek 34:11 might have read something like, "Behold, I will be revealed in my Word, and search . . ." In such a hypothetical Targum passage, the shepherds would be both the eschatological David (i.e., the Messiah) and the divine Word, who are actually one when "the Word became flesh."

The MT of Ezek 34:30 reads, "Then they will know that I, the LORD their God, am with them" (*Tg.*: "my Word is their help"). The divine shepherd described in these verses of Ezek 34 illuminates the miracle of the feeding of the five thousand as John describes it. Besides the general idea of divine feeding, "I will make them lie down" (Ezek 34:15) can be compared to John 6:10: "Have the people recline." The same verse says that "there was much grass in that place," an incidental detail that may have significance as explained by *Tg. Ps.* 23. Psalm 23 is no doubt the best known passage depicting the LORD as shepherd. Interestingly, *Tg. Ps.* 23:1 looks back to the LORD's wilderness provision for his people (as does John 6), speaks of grass, and looks to future provision along the same lines: "The LORD fed his people in the wilderness. . . . In a place of thirst he *makes me dwell in pleasant grass*. . . . He will restore my soul with manna."

---

[18] Evans, *Word and Glory*, 29–31.
[19] Ibid., 29.

The briefer passage Mic 2:12–13 should also be mentioned, because here there is mention of the sheep in the fold as well as the pasture, and going through the gate with the divine King going before them:

> I will surely gather all of you, Jacob,
>   I will surely assemble the remnant of Israel.
> I will put them together like sheep in the fold,
>   like a flock in the midst of its pasture, people will throng.
> The one breaking through goes up before them,
>   they break through and pass through the gate and go out by it.
> And their king passes through before them,
>   the LORD at their head.

The last two lines could be interpreted as referring to the LORD leading his people as shepherd, or one could see a reference to both the LORD and the human king leading his people. *Targum Jonathan* reads as follows:

> In the end I will indeed gather all of you of the house of Jacob. I will surely bring your exiles near, the remnant of Israel as one. I will make them like sheep in the pen, like a flock inside a sheepfold, noisy because of the multitude of people. The survivors shall go up as in the beginning, and a king shall go up leading at their head, and he shall break the enemy [*beʿēl debābā*] oppressing them and conquer the mighty cities; they shall take possession of the cities of the nations, and their king shall lead at their head, with the Word of the LORD for their help.

The Targum interprets the Hebrew text eschatologically but does not identify the king as the Messiah, though such an interpretation is found in rabbinical literature, and there is a parallel to the fourth night of *Pal. Tgs.* Exod 12:42, where the Messiah and Moses are said to lead the flock of Israel along with the divine Word.[20] In Jesus leading his flock, the ideas of the human king and the divine Word leading Israel come together, because "the Word became flesh." The divine Word as Shepherd is also found in *Tg. Onq.* Gen 49:24 (the blessing of Joseph). In MT, Jacob says that God ("the mighty one of Jacob") is "the Shepherd, the Stone of Israel." In *Tg. Onq.* he is described as "God, the mighty one of Jacob, who by his Word fed their fathers." "Fed" is from זון, used elsewhere in shepherding contexts (such as *Tg. Ps.* 23:1) but also more broadly with the idea of sustaining, nourishing people.

As we saw in ch. 8, Jesus in John 10 also makes a claim that, while not utilizing the expression "I am he," is based on two OT passages which contain the divine "I am he," namely, Deut 32:39 and Isa 43:13; in both of these God says, "There is no one who delivers from my hand." "Delivers" is Hebrew הַצִּיל, which has the literal meaning "snatch away." "No one shall snatch them out of my hand" (John 10:28) may thus be derived from these two key "I am he" passages that are so important to understanding the "I am he" sayings of John 8.

---

[20] Cathcart and Gordon (*Targum of the Minor Prophets*, 117 n.38) note the messianic interpretation of this passage in *Genesis Rabbah* 48.10, *Leviticus Rabbah* 32.8, and *Qoheleth Rabbah* 4.1, 1 and that Le Déaut noticed the parallel to the fourth night (*La nuit pascale*, 269). Recall that the Four Nights in *Frg Tg. P* is found at Exod 15:18.

The immediate contexts of Deut 32:39 and Isa 43:13 have nothing to suggest the imagery of God as shepherd and his people as sheep. But Ps 95:7 could be seen as a bridge between the shepherd/sheep figure and the statements that "no one shall snatch them out of my hand" from Deut 32:39 and Isa 43:13:

| My sheep hear my voice. (John 10:27) | For we are his people, the flock of his pasture, *the sheep of his hand*. Today, if you *hear his voice* (*Tg.*: "if you receive his Word"). (Ps 95:7). | No one shall snatch *them* (my sheep) out of *my hand*. (John 10:28, based on Deut 32:39; Isa 43:13) |

A few verses later in John is another saying which seems to borrow from an OT divine "I am he" saying in the same context as Isa 43:13, namely, Isa 43:10, which we have seen is so important for understanding other ἐγώ εἰμι sayings, though the "I am he" portion is not completely carried over:

> If I do them (the works of my Father), though you do not believe me, believe the works, so that you may know and understand that *I am* in the Father and the Father is in me. (John 10:38)

> So that you may know and believe me, and understand that *I am he*. (Isa 43:10)

So once again, in the "I am he" sayings of John 10, we have the same threefold message concerning the person of the Son: he is God, he is man, he is the way to the Father and eternal life.

John 11:25–26

> I am he, the resurrection and the life. He who believes in me shall live, even if he dies. And everyone who lives and believes in me shall never die. Do you believe this?

Means: This ἐγώ εἰμι saying most obviously belongs in the category of means. As the one who raises from the dead, Jesus is the means of bringing believers to eternal life.

Human: Martha testifies to the human category in answer to the Lord's question, "Do you believe this?" "Yes, Lord, I have believed that you are the Christ, the Son of God, even he who comes into the world" (11:27). The humanity of Jesus is also perhaps no better demonstrated than in v. 35, "Jesus wept," though in view of the deity of Christ we should perhaps also think of Ps 116:15, "Precious in the sight of the LORD is the death of his saints."

Divine: For the divine category, our attention should again be called to *Tg. Neof.* and *Frg. Tg. V* Deut 32:39: "See now that I, *I in my Word*, am he, and there is no other God besides me. *I am he* who puts to death the living in this world, and brings to life the dead in the world to come." Again we note that the MT of Deut 32:39 is not in itself a very likely background to John 11:25, but the *Pal. Tg.* readings have two features that the MT does not have that make such a connection more plausible: (1) the MT's "I make alive" is interpreted eschatologically; (2) "I am he" is rendered "I *in my Word* am he." A third relevant factor is the clause in John 10:28, "No one can snatch from my hand," which agrees with the literal meaning of the Hebrew of Deut 32:39 (and Isa 43:13) and also has application to eternal life, as in the Targum of Deut 32:39.

Targum Isaiah 26:19, addressed to God, uses the second person equivalent of "I am he": "You are he [את הוא] who makes alive the dead, you raise the bones of their bodies." The previous verse is of interest in light of Martha's confession of Jesus as "he who comes into the world": "Those who reside in the world have not brought deliverance to the earth, and they have not done wonders, neither will they be able to do so." Yet though he has come into the world, Jesus does not really belong to the category of "those who reside in the world" (and who therefore cannot do miracles), as this "I am he, the resurrection and the life" claim and its fulfillment make clear.

Targum Pseudo-Jonathan Exod 13:17 expands on the MT's statement that the LORD did not lead the Israelites from Egypt by the way of the land of the Philistines, lest the people fear when they see war, explaining that 200,000 Ephraimites had left Egypt thirty years before the time for the exodus and consequently were slain in battle by the Philistines. *Targum Pseudo-Jonathan* goes on to say, "These were the dry bones which the Word of the LORD brought to life by the hand of Ezekiel the prophet in the valley of Dura. If they had seen that (i.e., all the slain), they would have been afraid, and returned to Egypt." *Targum Ezekiel 37* has no mention of the divine Word in connection with this raising from the dead, though one could imagine a Palestinian Targum version of Ezek 37:13, based on analogies from Exodus noted above: "And you shall know that I am he, the LORD, when I in my Word open your graves and raise you up from the midst of your graves, O my people" (cf. *Tg. Neof.* Exod 8:22: "That you may know that I am he, the LORD, whose Word dwells in the land"). The raisings accomplished by Jesus in the Synoptics do not involve the opening of the graves and so could not be so readily related to Ezek 37 as the raising of Lazarus.

The Upper Room: John 13:19; 14:6; 15:1, 5

The four ἐγώ εἰμι sayings John preserves from the upper room discourses cover the three categories we have been noting: John 13:19, of all the ἐγώ εἰμι sayings, is most clearly dependent on the divine "I am he" of Isa 43:10. John 14:6 clearly belongs to the category of means. John 15:1, 5 suggests that Jesus is the true son of David, or Messiah, as seen from the OT background to these sayings.

Divine: John 13:19 is another ἐγώ εἰμι saying that echoes the wording of Isa 43:10:

Isa 43:10	John 13:19
"You are my witnesses," declares the LORD, "and my servant whom I have chosen, so that you may know and believe me and understand *that I am he*. Before me there was no God formed, and there will be none after me."	From now on, I am telling you before it comes to pass, so that when it does occur, you may believe *that I am he*.

The context of both passages is that of predictive prophecy that proves that the LORD is the one true God, so Jesus is clearly making a much greater claim than merely that of being a true prophet.[21] Such a conclusion would seem to be reinforced by the fact that the final ἐγώ εἰμι sayings (John 18:5, 8) occur when the prediction made in John 13:18 is fulfilled. We have also noted that the MT's "Before me there was no god formed" is rendered in *Tg. Isa.* as "I am he who is from the beginning," which John says of Jesus in 1 John 2:13–14, which, assuming common authorship, confirms this interpretation.

At the same time, there is a striking contrast between the predictions of Isa 43 and its context and the prediction of John 13:18. In Isaiah, the LORD is predicting what he will do in the future, in raising up Cyrus to set his people free from the Babylonian captivity and in sending the Servant of the LORD to redeem his people from sin. In John 13, however, Jesus is predicting that the fate of a human will befall him, as he uses the words of David from Ps 41 to apply to what will soon be his own fate, betrayal. The foot washing incident that precedes this prediction also graphically portrays Jesus as servant, reinforcing the human category. The category of means is also brought out in that event, as Jesus says, "Unless I wash you, you have no part in me" (v. 8).

Means: John 14:6, "I am he, the way, the truth, and the life; no one comes to the Father but through me," clearly belongs to the category of means. As we have seen, the near context in which this claim is made shows Jesus as both man (Servant of the LORD) and God. "Believe in God, believe also in me" (v. 1) can be related both to Exod 14:31 (Israel "believed in the LORD, and in his servant Moses") and to Deut 1:32–33 (Israel "did not believe in the LORD [*Tg. Neof.*: in the name of the Word of the LORD] your God, who goes before you on your way, to search out [Targums: prepare] a place for you").

Human: In connection with John 15:1, 5, three OT passages are of special interest. Interpreters often cite Ps 80 first in this respect.[22] The psalm describes Israel as a vine taken from Egypt and planted in Canaan, whose branches spread

---

[21] Ball comments, "In the fulfillment of the Scripture about betrayal, Jesus will be seen to be identified with the 'Lord' of the Old Testament" (Ball, *"I Am" in John's Gospel*, 200). He further observes, "In the most unlikely of situations of betrayal and crucifixion, Jesus' sovereignty will be seen and his identity revealed" (ibid.). Some interpreters relate Isa 43:10 to John 8:24 and miss the closer connection to John 13:19; so Bernard, *John*, 2:301 (Bernard also relates John 13:19 to Isa 48:5, but not to 43:10 [ibid., 2:468]); also J. C. Coetzee, "Jesus' Revelation in the EGO EIMI Sayings in Jn 8 and 9," in *A South African Perspective on the New Testament: Essays by South African New Testament Scholars Presented to Bruce Manning Metzger during His Visit to South Africa in 1985* (ed. J. H. Petzer and P. J. Hartin; Leiden: E. J. Brill, 1986), 173. Carson states that ἐγώ εἰμι in John 13:19 is "an everyday expression that can be devoid of theological overtones . . . or can call to mind the ineffable name of God, . . . the I AM HE of Is. 41:4; 43:10" (*John*, 471). It seems clear that the latter is the case here, since ἐγώ εἰμι is not used as an "everyday expression" because there is no antecedent or predicate. Further, the similarity to Isa 43:10 is too striking to be coincidence.

[22] E.g., Ball, *"I Am" in John's Gospel*, 241; Dodd, *Fourth Gospel*, 411; Morris, *John*, 593; Carson, *John*, 513; Gerald L. Borchert, *John 12–21* (New American Commentary 25B; Nashville: Broadman & Holman, 2002), 139.

out to the borders of the promised land (v. 11). But the vineyard walls have been broken down, foreigners pluck its fruit, and in a general plea for restoration the psalmist in effect asks God to be their vinedresser again: "Look down from heaven and see; have regard for this vine, the stalk that your right hand planted, and the son whom you strengthened for yourself" (vv. 14–15). While "son" here seems to be a personification of the nation, *Tg. Ps.* interprets it as the Messiah. Verse 17 seems to be a plea specifically for the restoration of the Davidic king, with parallelism between "man" and "son of man" possibly inspired by Ps 8 and David's role as heir to the theme of the new Adam: "Let your hand be on the man of your right hand, the son of man whom you strengthened for yourself." There are several parallels with John 15:1–8: (1) God is viewed as vinedresser. (2) The figure speaks of Israel as both vine and branches (the same words are used in John 15 and the LXX) and refers to fruit from the vine. (3) *Targum Psalms* 80:11 translates קָצִיר both literally as "branches" (שבשה) and figuratively as "disciples" (תלמיד, which can also mean "scholars"), and it translates "shoots" (which can also mean "nursling") with the Aramaic cognate that means "children" (which Jesus called the disciples in 13:33): "You made branches grow, you sent out her (Jerusalem's) disciples to the Great Sea, and her children to the river Euphrates." The previous verse indicates that the disciples are connected to the academies of Jerusalem. Yet the disciples of Jesus were considered "unlearned" (the opposite of תלמיד) by the graduates of such academies (Acts 4:13). Jesus says that it is by bearing fruit (as branches do), rather than getting credentials, that his followers would prove to be his disciples (John 15:8). (4) The fate of the branches that do not remain in Jesus is to be burned (v. 6), which is the fate suffered by both vine and branches in Ps 80:16. (5) The psalm has a dual focus on the nation and on the king in its petition for restoration. Another way of maintaining this dual focus would be to say that the vine is the king (Jesus) and the branches the nation (the church). In the case of Jesus as the true vine, the issue is not the success of the vine, which is not in doubt. "The 'vine' in this *mashal* is hardly in any danger of judgment as in the Old Testament texts."[23] Nor is there doubt that the vine will spread and "fill the whole world with its fruit" (Isa 27:6). The issue Jesus addresses is that of the success of those who profess to be his disciples, the fate of the individual branches. The vine in Ps 80 is Israel, and Israel is the name of the Servant of the LORD in Isa 49:3. Israel was the progenitor of the nominal people of God; Jesus "the Son of Man" is the true progenitor of the true people of God (see ch. 4). (6) Psalm 80:4 asks, "How long will you be angry with the prayer of your people?" Jesus twice specifies that by remaining in the vine, his followers may ask in his name and their prayers will be answered (John 15:7, 16).

In Jer 2:20–23, Israel is likewise depicted as a vine planted after the exodus, but it has been transformed into a foreign, unclean vine. Here the specific connection to John 15 is the idea of cleansing from unfaithfulness: "Though you wash yourself with lye . . . the stain of your guilt is before me. . . . How can you say, 'I am not unclean, I have not gone after the Baals'?" (Jer 2:22–23). Jesus tells

---

[23] Borchert, *John 12–21*, 139.

his disciples that they are already clean because of the word he has spoken, and that the Father prunes (lit., "cleans") branches that bear fruit. One of the concerns of Jesus in the upper room discourse and in his prayer of consecration is that the disciples not go after the "Baals" (or in NT language, "the world"; John 14:27; 16:33; 17:14–16). Another possible connection between these two passages is that in Jer 2:21, the vine was said to be planted of "seed of faithfulness" (or, truth: אֶמֶת), in the LXX, "entirely true" (ἀληθινός), and Jesus calls himself the true (ἀληθινός) vine (John 15:1). *Targum Jeremiah* 2:21 paraphrases, "all of you were doers of the truth," to which Hayward compares John 3:21 and 1 John 1:6 (ποιεῖν τὴν ἀλήθειαν).[24]

Ezekiel 17 is a parable about a vine planted by Nebuchadnezzar after he had taken king Jehoiachin captive to Babylon and installed Zedekiah in his place. Like Ps 80, it speaks of both vine and branches (for which the LXX has the same words as John 15), and in this case the vine is king Zedekiah and his officials are the branches. Nebuchadnezzar took "some of the seed of the land" and planted it (Ezek 17:5), which is interpreted as the installation of Zedekiah as king (v. 13), and this seed became a low, spreading vine, whose branches turned toward Nebuchadnezzar (v. 6); that is, Judah under Zedekiah was for a while a loyal vassal state, as Israel was originally supposed to be towards God. Judah was meant to live in this humbled state as a penalty for their unfaithfulness (v. 14), a situation in which the Jews found themselves again under the Romans. But then they rebelled, as Zedekiah looked to Egypt for help: "and behold, this vine bent its roots toward (Pharaoh) and shot forth its branches toward him . . . that he might water it" (v. 7). God considers Zedekiah's treachery against Nebuchadnezzar, the breaking of his covenant and violation of his sworn oath of allegiance (vv. 13, 16, 18), to be treachery against God (vv. 19–20). The branches spreading toward Pharaoh (v. 7) seem to be interpreted as Zedekiah sending envoys to Pharaoh (v. 15), which again makes Zedekiah the vine, and his men the branches. Zedekiah is the false vine, not accepting God as his Father (who put Nebuchadnezzar over him as "vinedresser"), and his "branches" likewise defect to Egypt. Zedekiah is a vine that will be uprooted and will dry up (vv. 9–10; cf. John 15:6). Zedekiah certainly could not be considered the answer to the psalmist's plea, "Let your hand be on the man of your right hand, the son of man whom you strengthened for yourself" (Ps 80:17). Jesus is the true vine, and acknowledges, "my Father is the vinedresser." In Jer 23:6, the LORD gives the Messiah the name "The LORD our righteousness," a play on the name Zedekiah (the LORD is my righteousness); that is, the Messiah is the true Zedekiah. He is the true vine, and his disciples, the branches, must remain in him and not go towards Egypt (the world) for water.

Means: The category of means is suggested in v. 3, "You are already clean because of the word I have spoken to you."

Divine: We noted in ch. 7 that Jesus speaks as the divine lawgiver in vv. 10, 12, 14, and 17. In addition, the idea of vine branches being removed as an act of divine judgment may also be found in Jer 5:10–12:

---

[24] Hayward, *Targum Jeremiah*, 52, 53 n.30.

¹⁰Go up among her walls and destroy, but do not do so completely. Take away her branches, for they are not the LORD's. ¹¹For the house of Israel and the house of Judah have dealt very treacherously against me, declares the LORD. ¹²They have lied about the LORD, for they have said "Not he! [אֵין הוּא לֹא cf. אֲנִי הוּא] Disaster will not come upon us, and we will not see sword or famine."

The walls are often taken to be vineyard walls because of the reference to branches. *Targum Jeremiah* 5:11–12 says they "have acted deceitfully against my Word, they have lied about the Word of the LORD," and the rest of v. 12 is changed to "they have said, 'Not from before him do good things come upon us.'" The Targum renders "walls" as "cities" and "branches" as "fortresses," so one could relate this Targum passage to John 15 only by knowing both the Hebrew and the Aramaic (the LXX is similar to *Tg.*) and by taking the figure as that of a vineyard. If we do so, then we see that the branches are taken away for dealing treacherously against the divine Word.

The Betrayal and Arrest: John 18:5, 6, 8

Human: When Jesus says "I am he" in John 18:5, 8 (v. 6 is John's narrative repetition), the clear antecedent is "Jesus of Nazareth." Any man could say "I am he" when someone has mentioned his name as one who is being sought, and certainly those who sought Jesus to arrest him were looking only for a man.

Divine: Yet, as Ball notes, these "I am he" sayings are directly related to that of John 13:19, since they mark the fulfillment of the prediction of betrayal by which the disciples would "know that I am he." Thus while the surface meaning of "I am he" in these verses seems merely to identify Jesus as a particular man, the connection to John 13:19 shows him to be YHWH, who proves himself by predicting the future. Ball comments, "The threefold repetition of ἐγώ εἰμι [including John's repetition in v. 6] emphasizes the importance of the expression."[25]

The other indication that there is something extraordinary in these words is that "when he said 'I am he,' they (the soldiers) drew back and fell to the ground" (v. 6). Interpreters note that this incident is another demonstration that Jesus went willingly to the cross, giving himself up for his people, and such significance would be sufficient reason for John's mentioning it. However, the sequence, "they drew back and fell to the ground" agrees with something David wrote about the fate of his enemies as a consequence of the presence of God: "When my enemies *turn back, they will stumble* and perish at your presence" (Ps 9:3). In the upper room, Jesus described his friends as those who keep his commandments, who love one another, and who remain in him. Judas has left him, breaking this great command of love, and thus falls under the category of enemy, as do those to whom he is betraying Jesus. Jesus described Judas as one who has perished (John 17:12), and John reminds us of this in 18:9. The fact that the arresting officials draw back and fall to the ground at the "I am he" thus indicates, when read against the backdrop

---

[25] Ball, *"I Am" in John's Gospel*, 201.

of Ps 9:3, the presence of the Lord. In David's experience, the presence of the Lord refers to the Lord's personal intervention on his behalf. *Targum Psalms 9:7* has David say, "As for the Word of the Lord, his seat is in the highest heavens forever; he has established his throne for judgment." But from heaven the Lord could help David only temporally, against temporal enemies. To save David (and all believers) forever, the Word of the Lord came down from his throne and became a man, to face his enemies personally, as David did. At the saying "I am he," spoken by the Word who became flesh, they turned back and stumbled, though they thought they had come to make him perish. Once Jesus ultimately prevails, Psalm 9:7, as interpreted by the Targum (though in a deeper sense than that intended by the targumist) will be true again: "The Word of the Lord sits enthroned forever" (at the right hand of the Father).

We can also look at this incident from the perspective of the disciples. Christ's enemies are also the enemies of the disciples (John 15:18–19). They experienced deliverance, much as David writes about in Ps 9:3, because of the presence of the Lord among them. Also recall the prayer of Moses as embellished in *Tg. Ps.-J.* Num 10:35: "Let the Word of the Lord be now revealed in the power of your anger, and let the enemies of your people (e.g., the disciples) be scattered, and let those who hate them *not have a foot to stand on before you.*"

Conclusions

We have seen three categories of claim or self-disclosure in the twenty-two ἐγώ εἰμι sayings of Jesus, which match the interpretation of John 1:47–51 given above. That is, these sayings portray Jesus from three different perspectives: (1) divine, (2) human, and (3) the means to eternal life, or the way to the Father. We saw that the divine use of "I am he" by Jesus matched the ot claims of YHWH that "I am he" (YHWH the one true God), but also that in such claims Jesus always asserted at the same time his servanthood or his subordination to the Father and made clear that he became a man to bring humans to the Father and eternal life. Thus the three categories are not completely separable, but together describe the incarnate Son of God. Thus it would be helpful to translate ἐγώ εἰμι uniformly as "I am he," as I have done here. These three perspectives do not depend entirely on the readings of the Targums, but we observed that often the sayings are illuminated by the Targums in general, and that the divine perspective was often illuminated by the use of the "Word of the Lord" in particular. These results support the conclusion that the Logos title is based on the targumic *Memra* and that in John's adaptation, "the Word" means "YHWH the Son," the one who is with the Father and shares the divine name with him. This is seen in the "I am he" sayings that coincide with the "I am he" sayings of YHWH in the ot and therefore characterize the Father.

Targum Neofiti and *Frg. Tg. V* Deut 32:39 are of particular interest because they add reference to the divine Word to this important "I am he" language: "I in my Word am he." Since this verse goes on to say, "there is no god besides me," it is clear that in calling Jesus the Word as a way of stressing the full deity of the Son, John is not advocating belief in another god; rather, he is advocating the notion that Jesus is One with the Father. Further, accepting that the Logos title has the targumic divine Word as background allows us to make a clear connection between the Prologue, where John calls Jesus the Word, and the body of the Gospel, where Jesus repeatedly makes the divine claim "I am he." The dozens of "I am he" sayings added in the *Pal. Tgs.* to the Pentateuch provide many additional potential conceptual parallels with the "I am he" sayings of Jesus in John and should therefore be taken into account in any study undertaken of the Johannine "I am he" sayings.

10

Unwitting Prophecies in the Targums

INTRODUCTION

John 11:51 tells us that Caiaphas prophesied that Jesus would die for the nation, when he advised the council that it was expedient for Jesus to die in order to avoid Roman action against the Jewish leadership and the temple. This kind of prophecy is obviously quite different from what one is used to from the OT. The meaning John takes from it is quite different from what Caiaphas meant, for Caiaphas was hostile to Christ, speaking not for the will of God but against it, in contrast to a prophet like Moses (Deut 18:15–22). This raises the question, why call this a prophecy at all?

Interpreters tend to focus on two features of Judaism in explanation: (1) the principle of unwitting (or unconscious) prophecy was accepted in Judaism, and (2) the high priest was believed to have prophetic powers. Brown explains:

> We can see that such an unconscious prophecy on the lips of a Jewish high priest would make an effective argument in the Jewish-Christian circles to whom (in part) the Fourth Gospel was addressed. . . .

> The principle of unconscious prophecy was accepted in Judaism (examples in StB [= Str-B], II, p. 546). In particular, the gift of prophecy was associated with the high priesthood. Josephus, *Ant.* [11.327] tells how the high priest Jaddua received an enlightenment that Alexander the Great would spare Jerusalem. Even high priests whose lives were far from perfect had the privilege, for example Hyrcanus in *Ant.* [13.299]. Therefore, John's outlook on the powers of Caiaphas was very much at home in 1st-century Judaism.[1]

Brown's comments are accurate; however, the examples Brown cites in Josephus are not actual examples of unwitting prophecy. The high priests were indeed said to accurately tell the future, and in the case of Jaddua, the prediction resulted from a dream. However, Alexander the Great also was said to have had a prophetic dream. Likewise, Hyrcanus was said to have the gift of prophecy, even to the extent of conversing with God (*Ant.* 13.282–283).

Bernard noted that the idea of the high priest's prophetic powers could be grounded in the OT:

---

[1] Brown, *John*, 1:442–44.

The Jews associated a measure of prophetic faculty to the high priest when, after being duly vested, he "inquired of Yahweh" (Ex. 28[30], Lev. 8[8], Num. 27[21]). Josephus had left on record that he, as a priest, claimed to have power to read the future [*J. W.* 3.350–354]. And Philo says that the true priest is always potentially a prophet [*On Special Laws* 4.192].[2]

Dodd noted that in Philo "the Logos is the true priest–prophet" and "Moses is a type of the Logos," but "it is clear that our present passage is moving in a different world of thought."[3] C. K. Barrett gives examples of unwitting prophecy as indicated by Philo (*Moses* 1.274, 277, 283, 286), but these deal with Balaam, who not only was not a high priest, but who also was aware that he was prophesying, though according to Philo he did not know the meaning of what he was saying.[4]

Strack-Billerbeck 2:546 refers to *b. Soṭah* 12b, where there are two alleged examples of unwitting prophecy by Pharaoh's daughter. According to R. Jochanan, when she said "Of the Hebrew children is this" (Exod 2:6) "she unwittingly prophesied that '*this*' one will fall [into the river] but no other will fall." This was a prophecy "because on that day the decree to drown the males was rescinded." According to R. Chama b. Chanina on Exod 2:9, "She prophesied without knowing what she prophesied—*Heliki* ['take away']—behold what is thine [*ha shaliki*]." Substantively, there is little here that is similar to the prophecy of Caiaphas (the second generates two differently-pronounced Aramaic words out of a single Hebrew word).

Mekilta to Exod 15:17 makes unwitting prophecy common to true prophets as well, saying that of all the prophets, only Moses and Isaiah knew what they prophesied. The verse says, "You will bring them in and plant them in the mountain of your inheritance." That it says "them," not "us," "teaches that they prophesied and knew not what they prophesied" (*b. Baba Batra* 119b). That is, they unwittingly prophesied that they themselves would not enter the land, but their children would. Rashi disagreed, saying the wording is due to Moses' foreknowledge that they would not enter.[5]

Genesis 22:8 could be viewed as an example of unwitting prophecy by Abraham: "God will provide for himself the lamb for the burnt offering, my son." Perhaps one could also point to the threat Pharaoh made to Moses, "In the day you see my face you shall die," to which Moses responds, "Rightly you have spoken! I will never see your face again" (Exod 10:28–29). Likewise Caiaphas speaks "rightly," but the true meaning is quite different from what he intends. In this respect, the prophecy of Caiaphas lacks the foreknowledge said to be possessed by other high priests, in which they did know what they were foreseeing.

These examples show us that that it is not necessary to refer to the Targums in order to suggest a plausible reason for John's interest in the unwitting prophecy of Caiaphas. Nevertheless, when one reads the Targums in light of John's

[2] Bernard, *John*, 2:405.

[3] C. H. Dodd, "The Prophecy of Caiaphas: John 11:47–53," in *More New Testament Studies* (Grand Rapids: Eerdmans, 1968), 64.

[4] Barrett, *John*, 407.

[5] M. Rosenbaum and A. M. Silbermann, *Pentateuch with Targum Onqelos, Haphtaroth and Sabbath Prayers and Rashi's Commentary* (5 vols.; London: Shapiro, Vallentine & Co., 1946), 2:78–79, 241.

identification of Jesus as the divine Word, it appears that there are a number of rather striking unwitting prophecies, analogous to that of Caiaphas in four distinct ways: (1) The meaning, according to a Christian reading of the Targum passage, is quite different from that intended by the authors. We may safely assume that in speaking of the divine Word, the targumist never intended to refer to the expected Messiah. (2) There is some expectation that the source is capable of such prophetic speaking. Above we noted this expectation in the case of the high priest. Likewise, the targumists seemed to have a "quasi-prophetic status" as they attempted to speak the word of God to their own generation.[6] (3) The source may be considered hostile to the Christian teaching of the incarnation of Christ. In the case of Caiaphas, this is obvious. In the case of the Targums, we take note again that the very theological/philosophical mind-set that led to the appropriation of the concept of the divine Word seems to have arisen out of a need to avoid or downplay the idea of the immanence of God and anthropomorphic representations of God, which would presumably be hostile to the idea of the incarnation, as an ultimate expression of immanence, the ultimate anthropomorphism. In ch. 1 we noted McIvor's statement that the targumist worked to ensure that God remains "high and lifted up," and for that reason he avoided translating Isa 52:13 to the effect that the Servant of the LORD was also "high and lifted up." Similarly, Keener noted that in translating Isa 9:6, the targumist reworded the passage "to avoid the idea that the royal child is God" and "deliberately alter[ed] the grammar to distinguish the Davidic king from the Mighty God."[7] (4) Just as Caiaphas was not "a prophet like Moses," and thus could not be counted upon to speak for God on other occasions, likewise, a recognition of the phenomenon of unwitting prophecy in the Targums need not lead to the conclusion that the Targums are inspired in the same sense as the Scriptures they are meant to explain, in the sense that they are completely reliable in their interpretations or teachings.

CATEGORIZING UNWITTING PROPHECIES IN THE TARGUMS

One could go about listing targumic unwitting prophecies in a number of different ways. One could just go through the Targums in canonical order and list

---

[6]"The usage of 'the prophet said' suggests the meturgeman took his quasi-prophetic status quite seriously" (Chilton, *Isaiah Targum*, xiii). According to the Talmud (*Megillah* 3a), Jonathan (putative author of *Tg. Jon.*) was said to have worked under the guidance of Haggai, Zechariah, and Malachi. Chilton says this "statement may be taken to illustrate in a creative way the prophetic claim which the meturgeman makes" (ibid., xxi). "Since the destruction of the Temple [according to rabbinic understanding], prophecy has been taken from the prophets and given to the wise. As we have seen, such a derivative notion of prophetic authority seems to be claimed by the meturgeman" (ibid., xxiii). Hayward concludes: "It is possible that the Targumists saw themselves as having a quasi-prophetic part to play in the communities of their own day" (Hayward, *Targum Jeremiah*, 32).

[7]Keener, *John*, 203 n.312, 295 n.135. This example would be pertinent whether such alteration took place specifically as a reaction against Christianity or was current during the ministry of Jesus.

relevant passages. One could try to categorize them thematically. Or one could go through John's Gospel sequentially and relate various Targum passages to various specific incidents in the Gospel. I am going to follow a combination of the second and third approaches. The reason for this is that there seem to be two broad categories of unwitting prophecies: (1) those which speak in general terms of the consequences to Israel of not receiving the divine Word, dealing falsely with the divine Word, etc., consequences similar to those experienced by Israel in the Roman conquest of c.e. 70 (defeat in battle, destruction of Jerusalem and the temple, exile, the withdrawal of the *Shekinah*, etc.); (2) those that can be related to specific incidents in the Gospel.

THE CONSEQUENCES OF NOT RECEIVING THE WORD OF THE LORD

Again we note the wording of *Tgs. Onq.* and *Ps.-J.* Exod 19:5–6, "If you indeed receive my Word, . . . you will be to me . . . a holy nation." As in the first century, the majority of those who came out of Egypt did not receive the divine Word, and died in the wilderness: those "who have seen my glory and my signs . . . yet have put me to the test these ten times and have not received my Word shall by no means see the land which I swore to their fathers" (*Tgs. Onq.* and *Ps.-J.* Num 14:22–23). Above we noted that "my glory" and "my signs" can be related to "his glory" and "his signs" in John 2:11, 23.

In Deut 9:23, Moses looks back at this rebellion and says, "You did not believe him or listen to his voice." The way the Targums render this is distinctly reminiscent of John 1:11–12: "You did not believe in the holy name of the Word of the LORD" (*Tg. Neof.*) and "you did not receive his Word" (*Tgs. Onq.* and *Ps.-J.*).

The covenant curses

This idea of not receiving the divine Word is found in the covenant curses. *Targum Onqelos* Lev 26:14, 18, 21, 27 and *Tgs. Onq.* and *Ps.-J.* Deut 8:20; 28:15, 45, 62 all state that various calamities—the covenant curses—will befall the people if they do not receive the Word of the LORD. Jews who believed that their Scriptures came from God, that Moses was a true prophet, would, of course, agree that there must have been some great sin that resulted in the conquest of Jerusalem, the destruction of the temple, and the exile of the Jews. "Oh how serious are these sins and how great the sins that caused our fathers in Jerusalem to eat the flesh of their sons, and the flesh of their daughters they ate" (*Tg. Neof.* Lev 26:29). Josephus suggested that the sins of the rebels themselves were a sufficient explanation (e.g., *J.W.* 1.10). By identifying Jesus as that Word that they did not receive, John gives an alternate explanation in the language commonly heard by worshippers in the synagogues.

After the destruction of the temple and the city of Jerusalem by the Romans, observant Jews would ask the same question posed in the time of Jeremiah: "Why is the land ruined?" (Jer 9:12), to which the answer must be the same, "They did not listen to my voice" (9:13), which the targumist has rendered, perhaps quasi-prophetically, as, "they did not *receive my Word*." In Deut 31:17, God says that the people will conclude after experiencing God's judgments, "Is it not because my God is not in my midst that these disasters have come upon us?" to which God says, "I will surely hide my face on that day on account of all the evil they have done" (v. 18). In *Tgs. Onq.* and *Ps.-J.*, they conclude that these disasters have come upon them because "the *Shekinah* of my God" (*Tg. Neof.*: "the glory of the LORD's *Shekinah*") is not in their midst. In *Tg. Neof.*, this future was revealed when "the Word of the LORD was revealed in the tent" (31:15), and "the Word of the LORD spoke to Moses" (v. 16 [mg.]); v. 18 says, "I, in my Word, will hide the face of my good pleasure from them in that day." The Targum prediction that the LORD's people will conclude that the *Shekinah* has departed from them can be related to the tradition preserved in the Talmud, which we have noted several times, that the regular miracles indicating the presence of the *Shekinah* in Israel ceased forty years prior to the destruction of Jerusalem.

Of course, John would not only be interested in explaining the reason for the disasters experienced by his fellow Jews, but would want to point them to the remedy, which is also how the curse section in Lev 26 ends: "But if they confess their iniquity and the iniquity of their fathers, their treachery with which they acted treacherously against me, and (how) they walked in hostility to me, . . . then I will remember my covenant with Jacob," etc. (vv. 40–42). The rendering in *Tg. Ps.-J.* makes the passage more specifically applicable to the time John is writing, identifying Jesus as the divine Word: "But if in the time of their distress they confess their sins, and the sins of their fathers, their falseness with which they acted falsely against my Word, . . . then I will remember with mercy the covenant which I made with Jacob in Bethel" (cf. *Pal. Tgs.* Gen 28:10, in which "the Word" [*Dibbura/Dibbera*] desired to speak with Jacob at Bethel).

Numbers 14

Mention was made above of *Tgs. Onq.* and *Ps.-J.* Num 14:22, which states that Israel had tested God ten times and failed to receive his Word. Consequently, they would die in the wilderness and not enter the promised land. They would die in their sin, to use the expression of Num 27:3, which Jesus also used in John 8:24: "Unless you believe that I am he, you will die in your sin." Numbers 14:40–45 goes on to describe how the Israelites changed their mind and decided to go fight the Canaanites anyway, and Moses warned them not to, since the LORD was no longer among them.

A parallel may exist between the wilderness situation and that which existed between the crucifixion of Jesus and the Jewish rebellion against Rome. In the Olivet discourse, which predicted the destruction of Jerusalem and the temple, there was an implicit warning against fighting the Romans (Luke 21:20–21), just as Jeremiah had warned against fighting the Babylonians. *Targum Neofiti* Num 14:42 could be applied to the first-century situation, especially if the belief was current that the *Shekinah* had departed from the temple: "Do not go up, for the glory of the *Shekinah* of the LORD does not rest upon you, lest you be struck down before your enemies. . . . You shall fall by the sword because you have turned back from (following) the Word of the LORD." Thus the MT of Num 14:42 specifically addressed the situation in the wilderness, but later interpreters could use it to address the situation of the first century by analogy. The Targum wording makes such an application easier, and, one could argue, was providentially so ordered by God in the same manner as was the unwitting prophecy of Caiaphas.

Targum Isaiah 1:19–20

> If you are willing and *receive my Word*, you shall eat of the good of the land; but if you refuse and *do not receive my Word*, by the adversary's sword you shall be killed; for *by the Word of the LORD it has been so decreed.*

Aramaic-speaking Jewish Christians would readily see a specific fulfillment of this threat in the destruction of Jerusalem and the temple by the Romans, and perhaps even relate "by the Word of the LORD it has been decreed" to the prophecy of such destruction by Jesus in the Olivet discourse in the Synoptic Gospels.

The temple sermons of Jeremiah and Jesus

One of Jeremiah's temple sermons (Jer 26) gives us a striking example of how an apologetic based on Targum readings might be developed. This sermon repeats some of the themes expressed in Jer 7 and culminates in Jeremiah's arrest. Standing in the temple, Jeremiah warns the people that if they do not listen to the voice of God, walk in his law, and heed the prophets he has sent, the temple and the city will be destroyed. In *Tg. Jer.* 26:4–6, his words read, "*If you do not receive my Word* . . . I will make this house like Shiloh, and this city I will make into a cursing for all the nations of the earth."

The Targum goes on to say that the priests and the scribes (MT: "prophets") and all the people seized Jeremiah and demanded that he be put to death (vv. 7–9). The priests and the scribes went to the officials to have the sentence carried out, and Jeremiah's defense was that "the LORD sent me" (v. 12). He then repeats his call for the people to "receive the Word of the LORD your God" (v. 13) and warns them that if they kill him, they will bring innocent blood upon Jerusalem and its inhabitants (vv. 14–15).

The officials and the people then say to the priests and the scribes that Jeremiah does not deserve to die, and Jeremiah is spared. That "the people" are said to be both in favor of (vv. 7–8) and against (v. 16) Jeremiah's execution indicates a division of the people, not a change of mind, since v. 24 again has "the people" in favor of his execution.

Much of John's Gospel consists of temple sermons by Jesus, and it is not difficult to see Jeremiah's history repeating itself in the Gospels, with a more serious rejection of the Word of God: (1) The religious leadership in both cases takes the initiative to seize God's prophet and hand him over for execution. John specifically quotes the high priest Caiaphas as calling for Jesus' death. (2) The secular power judges the prophet as unworthy of the death penalty. In the case of Jeremiah, it is Jewish officials who save his life. In the case of Jesus, it is a pagan Roman who recognizes his innocence, but who is unwilling to stand up against a united Jewish leadership calling for his death. (3) The people, in both cases, are divided, a theme that John mentions on several occasions (John 7:12, 40–44; 9:16; 10:19–21). (4) Jeremiah's defense is that the Lord sent him (Jer 26:12, 15); Jesus' defense is that the Father has sent him (see John 3:34; 5:36, 38; 6:29, 38, 57; 7:29; 8:42; 10:36; 11:42; 17:3, 8, 18, 21, 23, 25; 20:21). (5) The issue of innocent blood and the consequences for Jerusalem occur in both episodes: "Only know for certain that if you put me to death, you will bring (the guilt of) innocent blood on yourselves, and on this city and on its inhabitants; for in truth the Lord has sent me to you to speak all these words in your hearing" (Jer 26:15). Jeremiah's warning would apply to the judicial execution of any innocent man, not just a prophet (or the Messiah), according to Deut 21:1–9, which also warns that the same consequences would result from the failure to execute a known murderer such as Barabbas (Matt 27:25; Luke 23:19; Acts 3:14).

If one recognizes the targumic background to the Logos title, then one can see in the ministry of Jesus a re-enactment of the temple sermon of Jeremiah, except that the Word (whom Israel must receive) has become flesh (a real man such as Jeremiah, yet without sin).

Targum Ezekiel 39:23

> And the nations shall know that the house of Israel was exiled because of their sins, because they *dealt falsely with my Word*, so that *I removed my Shekinah* from them, and delivered them into the hands of their enemies, and they were slain by the sword, all of them.

This example was cited at the end of ch. 1. We note again that what the Targum says of the Babylonian exile parallels the exile later caused by the Romans, when combined with the belief that the *Shekinah* departed Jerusalem forty years before the destruction of the temple, which according to *Tg. Ezek.* 39:23 would have been the time that Israel dealt falsely with the divine Word.

Targum Hosea 5:6, 7, 15

> They will go with their sheep and their cattle to seek instruction from before the Lord, but they shall not find it. He will *withdraw his Shekinah* from them; *against the Word of the Lord* they have dealt falsely. . . . I will remove my *Shekinah*, I will return to my holy dwelling in heaven, until they realize they are guilty, and petition me.

We noted this text in ch. 2 (p. 60, no. 50) for its use of both "Word" and "*Shekinah*," and again in ch. 8 in connection with Jesus' saying "You shall seek me, but not find me" (John 7:34). Again, this passage would have been quite suggestive in light of the belief that the withdrawal of the *Shekinah* took place forty years prior to the destruction of the temple, which must therefore have been when, in Targum language, Israel was believed to have dealt falsely with the divine Word.

Targum Zechariah 1:3–4

> Return to my service, . . . and *I will return by my Word* to do good for you. . . . Do not be like your fathers. . . . They *did not receive my Word*. . . . Your fathers, where are they?

The first part of this passage is also found in *Tg. Mal.* 3:7. John had a similar message to his contemporaries, many of whom would have been children of exiles, to whom he would likewise say, "Do not be like your fathers." In this context, John 14:23 gives a promise of the Father and Son coming to those who love the Son and keep his commandments.

Targum 2 Chronicles 30:7–9

In this passage, Hezekiah appeals to the survivors in the northern kingdom after their defeat by the Assyrians, that they should come to celebrate the Passover in Jerusalem. His words in the Targum could easily have been adapted by Aramaic-speaking Jewish Christians to appeal to their brethren after c.e. 70. Hezekiah says that they should not be like their ancestors and contemporaries who acted unfaithfully against the Word of the Lord, the God of their fathers, and were handed over to those who hated them and given up to desolation. Speaking of the captives, he says, "If you return to the fear of the Lord, your brethren and your sons, . . . he will return in his Word to restore them to this land; . . . he will not take up his *Shekinah* from you."[8]

Passages Relating to Specific Incidents in John's Gospel

John 2:19–22

> "Destroy this temple and in three days I will raise it up." . . . But he (Jesus) was speaking of the temple of his body. When he was raised from the dead, his disciples remembered that he had said this, and they believed the Scripture and the word which Jesus had spoken.

Targum Isaiah 53:5, speaking of the Messiah (52:13), says, "And he *will build the sanctuary which was profaned for our sins*, handed over for our iniquities; and by his teaching his peace will increase upon us, and in that we long for his words,

---

[8]There is no evidence that Chronicles was ever recited in the synagogue, but perhaps the Targum was made of it so that it would be available to serious Bible students on a more popular level.

our sins will be forgiven us." The next verse says, "We have gone into exile, every one his own way." Targumic references to the destruction of the sanctuary and exile would presumably refer to the Roman, not Babylonian, conquest, thus would not be current during the ministry of Jesus. But by the time John wrote his gospel, the Targum may have read as above. If so, John might look back on the words of Jesus about the destruction and rebuilding of the temple, that is, his body, and notice that the targumist had unwittingly done the same thing, as the MT reference to the piercing and crushing of the Servant is changed into a promise that the Messiah will rebuild the temple.

John 8:24, 28, 58

> Unless you believe that *I am he*, you will die in your sins. . . . Then you will know that *I am he*. . . . Before Abraham was born, *I am he*.

We have discussed in some detail already how this passage can be viewed as a fulfillment of *Tg. Ps.-J.* Deut 32:39 (see chs. three, eight, and nine): "When the Word of the LORD shall be revealed to redeem his people, he shall say to all the nations, 'See now that I am he who is and was, and I am he who will be in the future. . . .'" This is followed in v. 43 by "and he, by his Word, will make atonement for the sins of his land and of his people." The threefold "I am he" of John 8:24, 28, 58, past, present, and future, mark the revelation of the divine Word at the Feast of Booths.

Other passages connected with the Song of Moses are suggestive of the NT situation. Deuteronomy 31:21 says that when Israel experiences calamities, "this song will testify before them as a witness" (because it predicts the apostasy which leads to those calamities). Ironically, the targumist's alterations make this an even more poignant witness. In *Tg. Neof.* Deut 31:27, Moses exclaims, "While I am still alive you have refused to follow the Word of the LORD; how much more after my death!" The ultimate fulfillment of that statement could easily have been understood by early Christians as occurring in the events that followed the revelation of the Word of the LORD, Jesus Christ, to redeem his people: they will put him to death, and he will be followed by only a remnant of faithful disciples.

John 8:18

> I am he who testifies concerning myself.

The witness of Jesus, the divine Word, at the Feast of Booths (and throughout his ministry) could be related to the oath of *Tg. Jer.* 42:5-6. In vv. 1–4, Jeremiah agrees to ask for the LORD's guidance for the remnant that has survived the destruction of Jerusalem. They promise, "*May the Word of the LORD be among us as a faithful and true witness*, if we do not act according to every word in which the LORD your God has sent you to us. Whether good or evil, *we will receive the Word* of the LORD our God before whom we are sending you, so that it will be well for us *when we receive the Word* of the LORD our God." They do not keep their promise; they do not receive the divine Word, and in the incarnation their invocation comes true, the divine Word is among them as a true and faithful witness of their apostasy. Again they do not receive him (John 1:11), and it does not go well for them.

Again we cite *Tg. Mic.* 1:2–3: "Let the Word of the Lord God be a witness against you, the {Word of the} Lord from his holy temple; for the Lord will be revealed from the place of the house of his *Shekinah*" (discussed in ch. 9 with respect to John 8:18). While the context of the Targum passage relates to OT times, mentioning the transgressions of Israel in Samaria (as well as those of Judah in Jerusalem), the wording would be especially applicable when the Word became flesh and testified against his people from the temple.

John 18:20, 23

> I have spoken openly to the world; I always taught in the synagogues and in the temple, where all the Jews come together, and *I spoke nothing in secret.* . . . If I have spoken wrongly, testify of the wrong, but *if (I have spoken) rightly*, why do you strike me?

John's narration of the earthly trial of Jesus can be compared to the heavenly trial which is a recurring theme of Isa 40–55, in which the Lord is giving evidence that "I am he." In John 18:20, 23, Jesus borrows wording from Isa 45:19 in the course of this trial: "*I have not spoken in secret*, in some dark land; I did not say to the offspring of Jacob, 'Seek me in some waste place.' I, the Lord, *speak what is right*, declaring things that are upright" (Isa 45:19). The Targum of this passage reads similarly, but goes on to say "turn to my Word (MT: turn to me) and be saved, all the ends of the earth" (v. 22). God says, "I have not spoken in secret" again in Isa 48:16: "Come near *to me*, hear this: From the beginning I have not spoken in secret." In the Targum it reads, "Come near *to my Word*, hear this: from the beginning *I have not spoken in secret*." John presents this as literally fulfilled when Jesus' accusers literally drew near to the divine Word-become-flesh at his trial and heard him say, "I spoke nothing in secret."

Caiaphas, as an instigator of the arrest of Jesus, was particularly involved in fulfilling the targumic injunction to draw near to the divine Word, though its fulfillment actually took place before his father-in-law, Annas (John 18:13), who had heard Jesus give the divine apologia for why they should believe his "I am he." Ironically, the man who said to others, "You know nothing at all," was quite unaware of his involvement. Perhaps this incident in particular led John to notice that there were Targum passages analogous to the statement of Caiaphas that it was expedient for them that one person die for the nation.

John 19:14–15

> And (Pilate) said to the Jews, "Behold, your king!" So they cried out, "Away with him, away with him. . . . We have no king but Caesar."

In *Frg. Tg. V* Exod 15:18 (*Tg. Ps.-J.* Exod 15:18 reads similarly), the proper response to the miracles the Israelites witnessed is interesting in light of the presentation of Jesus by Pilate with a crown of thorns, and in light of Jesus' statement that his kingdom is not of this world:

> When the children of Israel saw the signs and wonders which the *Holy One*, blessed be he, had done for them by the shore of the Sea—may his name be blessed forever and ever—they gave glory and praise and exaltation to their God. The children of Israel answered and said one to the other, "*Come, and let us set the crown on the head of the Redeemer* (*Tg. Ps.-J.*: "Come, let us set the crown of anointing on the head of our redeemer"), who causes to pass, but is not himself made to pass (away), who changes but is not himself changed; who is King of kings in this world, and to whom also belongs *the crown of kingship in the world to come* (cf. John 18:36: "my kingdom is not of this world"), and his it is forever and ever."

Forty years later, according to *Tg. Neof.* Deut 26:17, Moses says, "This day you have made *the Word of the LORD your God* to be *King over you*, so that he may be for you a savior God, (promising) to walk in ways that are right before him." By way of contrast, in *Tg. Isa.* 30:11, disobedient Judah, intent on going to Pharaoh for help, instead of to this divine King, says to Isaiah, "*Remove from before us the Word of the Holy One of Israel*" (MT: "cause to cease from our presence the Holy One of Israel").

From John's perspective, one might argue that since the Jews had not responded to the miracles as in *Pal. Tgs.* Exod 15:18, recognizing Jesus as their redeemer king, setting a crown of anointing on his head, Pilate nevertheless on behalf of God the Father set the crown of anointing upon his head and declared him to be king. Yet they responded as their fathers had done in the days of Isaiah, by crying out, "Away with him."

APOLOGETIC USES OF UNWITTING PROPHECIES

The primary and most obvious audience to whom the apologetic approach of Targum-based unwitting prophecy would have been directed would have been Aramaic-speaking Jews familiar with the Targums. According to the usual date assigned the Gospel, John writes between the first and second destructions of Jerusalem by the Romans. While the reason for the recent exile was given generally in the Hebrew Scriptures (i.e., it must have been due to some apostasy such as that which led to the forty-year wilderness wanderings or the Babylonian exile), John appeals to a more specific answer as given in the Targums: Israel has not received the divine Word, nor believed in his name; they have dealt falsely with the divine Word.

In Deut 30, after predicting the eventual exile of Israel, Moses addressed the post-exilic situation, the same situation from which John writes his gospel. If Israel turns to the LORD and obeys him with a whole heart and soul, the LORD will regather them as his people and bless them (vv. 1–10). In *Tg. Onq.*, the condition is "*if you receive his Word* with your whole heart and your whole soul" (v. 2), "*You will again receive the Word* of the LORD . . . the LORD (*Tg. Ps.-J.*, "the Word of the LORD") will again rejoice over you for good, as he rejoiced over your fathers *because you receive the Word* of the LORD your God to observe his commandments" (vv. 8–10). By calling Jesus the divine Word, and by speaking of those who did not receive this Word (John 1:11), writing from an historical perspective in which the consequences of not receiving the divine Word would have been well understood, John gives a Christian interpretation to the words later codified by the school of Akiba, just as he has given a Christian interpretation to the unwitting prophecy of Caiaphas.[9] Akiba, of course, went in a different direction, encouraging another rebellion against Rome, which led to another exile. John's apologetic would have influenced a remnant at best, the size of which is today unknown.

Today the Targums are little known. The Aramaic-speaking, Targum-conscious audience of the first century no longer exists. Does this mean that the apologetic based on unwitting Targum prophecies is just a historical curiosity? In answer, I would say that my study of the Targums has convinced me that in order to appreciate more fully the meaning of John's Gospel, both Jew and Gentile need to be familiar with the Targums, for the simple reason that so many points of interpretation in John seem to hinge on them. John must have expected Aramaic-speaking Jewish Christians to help their Gentile brothers in understanding the Jewish background to the Gospel, in order to grasp its full meaning. This means that John's appeal to these unwitting prophecies was intended not just for first-century Aramaic-speaking Jews, but also for Gentiles. By extension, the same holds true today. Such unwitting prophecies are part of understanding the Gospel, which means that they serve as both a testimony and a warning to the largely Gentile church. Perhaps we could say that they were a witness to the emerging Gentile church in second and third generation Christianity and in subsequent generations. The Targum rendering of the OT helps us see how the OT warnings to Israel apply to the church. The consequences of not receiving the divine Word will be equally serious for the largely Gentile church. Indeed, the letters to the churches in Asia Minor in Rev 2–3 anticipate such consequences.

---

[9] *Tgs. Onq.* and *Jonathan* are ascribed to the school of Akiba based on the *halakah* found in them (see, e.g., Leivy Smolar and Moses Aberbach, *Studies in Targum Jonathan to the Prophets*; Pinkhos Churgin, *Targum Jonathan to the Prophets* [Library of Biblical Studies; New York: Ktav, 1983], 1–3).

11

"The Word Became Flesh"
Elsewhere in the New Testament

INTRODUCTION

Since enlightenment times it has been suggested that John's Christology is "high" compared to the rest of the NT. Some would argue, in fact, that it is too high to have been penned by a first-generation disciple of Christ. William Hendriksen responds to this argument as follows:

> But this is not even an argument. It amounts to begging the question. It is a bold assertion when proof is wholly lacking. Besides, the question may well be asked: Is the Christology of Paul any lower? Read Col. 2:9 or Phil. 2:6 or that very tantalizing passage Rom. 9:5. . . . And indeed, is the Christology of the Synoptics any lower? Read Matt. 11:27, 28.[1]

I seek to make the same point in the present chapter, not by discussing all the passages outside of John's writings that have relevance to the doctrine of Christ's deity, but rather by showing that there are many passages that can be interpreted along the lines of the statement, "the Word became flesh," where "the Word" is taken from the Targums. That is, if we examine the OT passage that seems to provide background to a saying of Jesus (or about Jesus), suggesting by comparison that Jesus is divine, and then we look in the corresponding Targum passage, we find reference to the divine Word.

We will look at two types of passages, which may or may not overlap. In one type, the message "the Word became flesh" comes through by both human and divine OT typology that is reinforced by Targum reference to the divine Word (e.g., Matt 11:27–28—one of the texts referred to above by Hendriksen). A second type occurs where there may not be any human typology involved, but where an OT background text used in a way that suggests that Jesus is YHWH has a corresponding Targum text that refers to the divine Word. Such a text in and of itself may not suggest "the Word became flesh," but since in the NT there is always the assumption that Jesus is a real man, the "became flesh" portion may be fairly implied (e.g., the baptism of Jesus as related in the Synoptics). Texts cited here are not meant to be exhaustive, but rather representative; they show that other NT writers,

---

[1] Hendriksen, *John*, 10.

had they wished, could also have written "the Word became flesh" for the benefit of their readers who were familiar with the Targums.

THE BAPTISM OF JESUS
(MATTHEW 3:13–17; MARK 1:9–11; LUKE 3:21–22)

All three of the Synoptic Gospels mention the Spirit of God descending from heaven upon the Son after his baptism (Matt 3:16; Mark 1:10; Luke 3:21) and thus could be related to *Tg. Ps.-J. Num 7:89* in the same way that we saw earlier a connection with John 1:32–33. The Targum passage says that in the holy of holies Moses heard the voice of the Spirit speaking to him as the Spirit descended from heaven over the mercy seat of the ark, and from there the Word spoke to him. Yet part of our justification for seeing a connection with the passage in John was John's explicit identification of Jesus as the divine Word, which the Synoptics do not do. Is there a similar linking feature in the Synoptics that would justify seeing the Spirit descending upon Jesus at his baptism as analogous to the Spirit descending over the ark, from where the Word spoke to Moses?

I would answer this by appealing to the fact that Jesus' baptism in the Jordan is typologically related to Israel's crossing of the Red Sea (see "Jesus in the Footsteps of Joshua and David" in ch. 5 above), which in turn is related to Israel's crossing of the Jordan. The ark had not yet been made at the crossing of the sea; the LORD's presence was manifested in the pillar of fire and cloud, and some Targum texts speak of the divine Word in that pillar (see ch. 2, p. 53, nos. 12 and 13). But in the crossing of the Jordan, the LORD's presence is indicated by the location of the ark, so in terms of *Tg. Ps.-J. Num 7:89*, the divine Word would have been present over the ark in the Jordan River as Israel crossed over.

A second typological argument concerns the succession of Moses by Joshua, and the succession of Elijah by Elisha, both of which took place when God began to magnify the successor at the Jordan River (Josh 3–4; 2 Kgs 3). This pattern is repeated in the succession of John the Baptist by Jesus at the Jordan when the Father magnifies the Son at his baptism. The Spirit of God descending upon Jesus suggests how much greater he is than John; he is not just another great human successor (like Joshua or Elisha), but is the divine Word. The "became flesh" portion of the message is not as explicit as it is in the prologue to the Gospel of John, but it is nevertheless implied in the OT background of the Father's statement following Jesus' baptism that "this is my Son," suggesting that Jesus is the promised Messiah, the son of David.

THE TRANSFIGURATION OF JESUS
(MATTHEW 17:1–8; MARK 9:2–8; LUKE 9:28–36)

On the Mount of Transfiguration, Moses and Elijah appeared, speaking with Jesus. Why Moses and Elijah? Perhaps because also in the OT both Moses and Elijah saw the glory of the LORD and spoke to him on a mountain (Sinai). Luke says they were speaking to him concerning "the exodus" he was about to accomplish. In both the OT and NT cases, this appearance in glory was in a context of apostasy.

As we have seen, the *Pal. Tgs.* of the Pentateuch of Exod 33–34 describe this incident as Moses seeing "the glory of the Word" on Mt. Sinai. Yet Jesus is also a man like Moses, going up to the mountain where his appearance is changed and his face shines (Matt 17:2; Exod 34:29–35).

John does not give an account of the transfiguration, although if one reads the Synoptics before reading John's Prologue, one might think that "we saw his glory" referred to the transfiguration. In calling Jesus the Word, John helps his readers to read the Synoptics with greater understanding, enabling them to have the same experience as the eyewitnesses to the transfiguration, that they might become "fully awake" and thus "see his glory" (Luke 9:32).

GREATER THAN JONAH
(MATTHEW 8:23–27; MARK 4:35–41; LUKE 8:22–25)

"The men of Nineveh will rise up at the judgment with this generation and condemn it. For they repented at the preaching of Jonah, and behold, a greater than Jonah is here" (Matt 12:41; Luke 11:32). The incident of Jesus asleep in the boat while a storm comes up, viewed against the background of the story of Jonah, serves to show how much greater Jesus is than Jonah.

Since Jesus is asleep in the boat during the storm in which the disciples fear for their lives, interpreters naturally wonder if we are to understand this in light of Jonah's similar experience. We have mentioned previously that the twofold mission of Jacob journeying (Gen 28) provides a paradigm for the ministry of Jesus and that the words of Jesus in John 1:51 invite us to see this paradigm. The same applies when Jesus comments that "something greater than Jonah is here" (Matt 12:41; Luke 11:32). That is, Jonah's experience in the great fish is recapitulated in Jesus' death and resurrection (Matt 12:40) as a sign to the present generation. If we combine this human parallel with the fact that Jesus stills the storm, which is what God did in the book of Jonah, we have the same message as conveyed by "the Word became flesh," that is, that Jesus is both God and man.

Neither the onset of the storm nor its stilling as experienced by Jonah is ascribed to the divine Word in *Tg. Jonah*. But in *Tg. Ps.* 107:23–24, the sailors who go in ships are interpreted as the sailors of Jonah who saw God's wonders, and v. 25 says "the Word of the LORD" raised a storm and gale, with waves lifted high, and v. 29 (like the MT) says that the LORD silenced the storm, reminding us of Mark 4:39, "Be silent! Be quiet!" Such passages suggest how a first-century Palestinian Targum of Jonah might have ascribed the sending and/or stilling of the storm experienced by Jonah to the divine Word.

Targum Jonah 2:6 takes Jonah's mention of sea weeds (סוּף) as an indication that his experience took place in the Red Sea: "The Red Sea was suspended above my head." *Targum Psalms 114:3*, speaking of Israel's crossing of the Red Sea, says that when the Word of the LORD was revealed at the sea, the sea saw this and turned back. This rich OT background provides an answer for the question of the disciples, "What kind of a man is this, that even the winds and the sea obey him?" (Matt 8:27; Mark 4:41; Luke 8:25). *Targum Jonah* 3:5 says that at the preaching of Jonah in Nineveh, "the people believed in the Word of the LORD." Those who heard "the one greater than Jonah" (Matt 12:41), the divine Word who who had become flesh and stirred up and stilled the sea, had an even greater cause to trust in the one who could save Jonah (and them) from their sins.

GREATER THAN SOLOMON (MATTHEW 11:28–30)

> Come to me, all who are weary and heavy laden, and I will give you rest. Take my yoke upon you, and learn from me, for I am gentle and humble in heart, and you shall find rest for your souls. For my yoke is easy, and my burden is light.

In Matt 12:42 and Luke 11:31, Jesus says "a greater than Solomon is here." Jesus is greater than Solomon, and his kingdom is greater than that of Solomon. But just how much greater is Jesus than Solomon?

The claim to be greater than Solomon might remind us that there was someone in OT times who also claimed to be greater than Solomon—Solomon's son Rehoboam. The Lord's words in Matt 11:28–30 appear as a contrast to the proud, foolish boaster Rehoboam. Israel came to Rehoboam at Shechem, weary and seeking rest from the hard service of Solomon. In response, he said that he would add to their yoke, because "my little finger is thicker than my father's loins" (1 Kgs 12:10; 2 Chr 10:10). In making this claim, he was in effect saying, "I am greater than my father Solomon, and I will prove it by adding to your yoke." Rehoboam was arrogant in heart; Jesus is humble in heart. Rehoboam said in effect, "no rest, more burdens, I will add to your yoke"; Jesus in contrast said, "you shall find rest for your souls, for my yoke is easy, and my burden is light." The older wise men who advised Solomon gave very good advice to Rehoboam: become a servant for just one day; please them by kindly granting their request; speak good words to them; then they will serve you forever (1 Kgs 12:7; 2 Chr 10:7). But Rehoboam was unwilling to become a servant even for a single day, and as a consequence of his "walking in the counsel of the wicked" (Ps 1:1), he lost most of his kingdom. In contrast, the Son of God humbled himself to come into the world as a servant to his people. Jesus was not just a servant for one day, but for his whole life on earth, ultimately going to the cross so that his followers might find eternal rest. The sufferings of Jesus, which were his service to Israel, included being scourged (Matt 20:19; Mark 10:34; Luke 18:33; John 19:1), which is of relevance to the account of Rehoboam in the Targum, which has him say to Israel, "My father disciplined you with whips, but I will discipline you with scourges" (מרגנין; vv. 11, 14). Rehoboam was unwilling even to "speak good words" to Israel. Jesus spoke very good words indeed, words that have brought rest to those who responded in faith.

Thus the human typology clearly shows Jesus as "flesh," namely, the true son of David in contrast to the false son, Rehoboam. But a divine typology can also be expounded, especially with help from the Targums. The most obvious evidence for this (and presumably the reason Hendriksen referred to this passage in the quote above, despite the fact that the relevant text is v. 29, not vv. 27–28), is that the promise, "you shall find rest for your souls," is what God says to Israel in Jer 6:16. Two earlier passages in Jeremiah speak of Israel's yoke in a way that is suggestive of the Lord's words in Matt 11:29–30. In Jer 2:20, the LORD says to Israel, "Long ago I broke your yoke and tore off your bonds, but you said, 'I will not serve.'" The LORD took away the hard yoke of servitude to the Egyptians and gave them the easy yoke of his law, which should lead to rest in the promised land. Although "yoke" is not used here of Israel's service which is due to God, it is used in this way a few chapters later, along with the same words for "break," "tear," and "bonds":

> Then I said, "They are only the poor; they are foolish. For they do not know the way of the LORD or the ordinance of their God. I will go to the great, and will speak to them; surely they know the way of the LORD, the ordinance of their God." But they, too, together have broken the yoke and burst the bonds. (Jer 5:4–5)

Thus, the "way of the LORD, the ordinance of their God" is also a yoke. With this background, we see that the yoke Jesus speaks of is the yoke of the divine lawgiver, not just the yoke of the true Son of David. As in the time of Jeremiah, "the great" do not serve, though in a different way than in Jeremiah's time. Though there is much talk about keeping the law, those who teach it have taken away the key of knowledge, have not entered the kingdom, and have prevented others from doing so (Luke 11:52); they teach the law in such a way as to make it a heavy burden (Matt 23:4), so that the Israelites are weary and heavy laden as in the latter days of Solomon. Jesus thus speaks here as divine redeemer and lawgiver, roles which we noted in earlier chapters are roles clearly ascribed to the divine Word in the Targums.

Further, the "come to me" of Matt 11:28 can also be related to the divine "come to me" of Isa 55:3, which we saw was so important to understanding the words of Jesus in John 5–7. Recall that in *Tg. Isa.* 55:1, "come to the waters" becomes "come and learn," and "come buy and eat" becomes "come, hear, and learn," which is also the rendering of "come buy wine and milk." We saw in ch. 8 that in John 6:45, Jesus seems to have utilized this interpretation: "Everyone who has *heard* from the Father and *learned, comes* to me" (spoken just after Jesus quotes Isa 54:13). Likewise, Matt 11:28–29, "Come to me, . . . and learn from me," could be based on this Targum interpretation. Recall that the Targum goes on to say, "receive my Word diligently" (for Isa 55:2 [MT]: "listen carefully to me") and "receive my Word" (for 55:3 [MT]: "come to me").

The promise, "I will give you rest," could also be a quote from OT divine speech, though not so obviously as "You shall find rest for your souls." For this is what God promised Moses: "My presence shall go with you, and I will give you rest" (Exod 33:14). In *Tg. Onq.,* this reads "My *Shekinah* will go with you, and I will give you rest." When Jesus says in Matt 18:20, "Where two or three have gathered in my name, there I am in their midst," in a context addressing the exercise of church discipline, he is claiming for himself what is said of the *Shekinah* in the Talmud: "If three are sitting as a court of judges, the Divine Presence [*Shekinah*] is with them" (*b. Berakhot* 6a, which also says that when two gather to study the law, the *Shekinah* is among them; similarly, *m. Avot* 6:6).

In the *Pal. Tgs.*, the promise of rest in Exod 33 occurs in the context of conversation: "the Word of the LORD would converse with (Moses); . . . he would hear the voice of the Word [*Dibbura*]" (*Tg. Ps.-J.* Exod 33:9, 11); "the Word of the LORD spoke with Moses, speech to speech, as a man speaks to his friend" (*Tg. Neof.* [mg.] Exod 33:11). When the Word came in the flesh, what was extraordinary in the history of Israel became ordinary, as Jesus spoke again as a man speaks to his friends. We might also remind ourselves that the divine promise, "I will give you rest," was spoken to Moses outside the camp. When Jesus spoke on earth, people could literally come to him and become followers. We have seen from John's Gospel that the ascension of Jesus to heaven can be viewed as a withdrawal of the *Shekinah* due to the apostasy of Israel, as happened after the golden calf incident. Therefore, for Matthew's readers, responding to the invitation, "come to me . . . and I will give you rest," involves going outside the camp (Heb 13:13), following the earlier example of Moses.

One can see therefore in this saying of Jesus the merging of both divine and human typology, as Jesus speaks not only as a man greater than Solomon, the true Son of David (in contrast with Rehoboam), but also as the God of Israel did to his people in OT times, or as the divine Word of the Targums spoke to his people. The message for those who were familiar with these Targums is that the Word has become flesh. It would appear then that in telling us that the Word became flesh, John is not just telling us how to read his gospel, but he is also giving us a key (perhaps forgotten or neglected) to interpreting the Synoptics.

JESUS WALKS ON THE WATER
(MATTHEW 14:22–33; MARK 6:45–52)

We have already discussed this miracle as it is recorded in John 6. Here it may be observed that the accounts in the Synoptics also contain the assurance by Jesus, "It is I [ἐγώ εἰμι]; do not be afraid" (Matt 14:27; Mark 6:50). The same connections shown previously between John's account and Isa 43, enhanced by the Targum of that chapter (thus suggesting this incident as a fulfillment of "my Word will be for your help"), are possible also in Matthew and Mark, as are connections to passages such as Ps 107 that have been linked to the account in John 6. Brown wrote, "In John the special emphasis on *egō eimi* in the rest of the Gospel does seem to orient this story more precisely, that is, the majesty of Jesus is that he can bear the *divine name*."[2] Another way to put it would be that John focuses his readers' attention on features of the miracle whose significance may have been overlooked by those not well versed in the OT background. John does this not only in his "special emphasis on *egō eimi* in the rest of the Gospel" (especially where ἐγώ εἰμι may be related to

---

[2] Brown, *John*, 1:255.

Isa 43:10), but also in his calling Jesus the divine Word, both features helping make the connection to Isa 43 and its Targum. John also gives a briefer account of the incident, leaving out, for example, the episode of Peter walking on the water, perhaps so as not to distract from the impression of a theophany. On the other hand, the saving of Peter from drowning in Matthew and Mark could also have targumic relevance, since *Tg. Neof.* [mg.] and *Frg. Tg. P* Exod 14:27 say that the Word of the LORD drowned the Egyptians in the sea, and we saw above that the miracles God did *for* Israel are often an opposite to the judgments of God *against* the Egyptians.

THE DIVINE WORD AS JUDGE (MATTHEW 18:20)

Where two or three have gathered in my name, there I am in their midst.

We noted above the similarity of this claim to what is said of the *Shekinah* in *b. Berakhot* 6a.[3] The concept of the divine Word could be used in a similar way. In ch. 2, we noted that in *Tg. 2 Chr. 19:6*, Jehoshaphat says to the judges whom he is sending out through Judah that they are judging before the Word of the LORD and that his *Shekinah* dwells with them when they are passing judgment. Jesus appeared to men as another man who might make up the number required to pass judgment, but he spoke as *the divine presence* promised to be with Israel when rendering judgment.

THE GREAT COMMISSION (MATTHEW 28:18–20)

There are a number of similarities between Jesus' Great Commission and the commission that was given to Joshua after the death of Moses: (1) The command, "teaching them to observe all things that I have commanded you," (Matt 28:20) can be compared to the command to Joshua to keep the whole law of Moses (Josh 1:7–9); (2) The promise, "I am with you always, even to the end of the age," can be compared to Josh 1:5, 9, "Just as I have been with Moses, I will be with you; I will not fail you or forsake you. . . . The LORD your God is with you wherever you go."

Two other similarities are not quite so obvious, but they are based on some observations already noted in ch. 5, namely, that the preaching of the gospel is a new kind of conquest (thus especially the extension of the gospel to the Gentiles) and that John's baptism (on which Christian baptism is based) took place at the Jordan River because of its historical and theological significance in Israel's history. Thus we can note additionally, that the command to make disciples of all nations

---

[3] Similarly *b. Sanhedrin* 39a: "The emperor said to Rabban Gamaliel, 'You maintain that upon every gathering of ten [Jews] the Shechinah rests. How many Shechinahs are there then?'" A skeptic might ask the same question about Matt 18:20: "How many Jesuses are there?" The rabbi answered that if the one sun shines in every house, so much more could the divine presence.

is analogous to the command to Joshua to conquer the seven Canaanite nations (Josh 1:3–5), and that the command to baptize them is analogous to the command to cross the Jordan (1:2).

Even if one is skeptical of these last two points, *Tg. Josh.* 1:5, 9 could be seen as connecting Jesus with the targumic Word: "As my Word was for the help of Moses, so my Word will be for your help. . . . The Word of the Lord your God is for your help, wherever you go." Similarly, *Tg. Ps.-J.* Deut 31:8, which also looks forward to Joshua's conquest: "The Word of the Lord, his *Shekinah*, is marching before you, and his Word will be for your help. He will not forsake you or be far from you." *Targum Neofiti* Deut 31:8 has Moses say to Joshua, "The Word of the Lord, the glory of whose *Shekinah* is leading before you, shall be for your help." *Targum Onqelos* does not mention the *Shekinah* but does render "he will be with you" as "his Word will be for your help." The targumic background thus helps us see the divine nature of the one who is commanding and promising his help in fulfillment of his command, as the Son of God goes with his people on a new kind of conquest.

The Revelation of Jesus to Saul of Tarsus
(Acts 9:3–7; 22:6–9; 26:12–15)

A human parallel can be seen in the fact that Jesus speaks to this Saul from heaven in a manner that reminds us of David speaking to Saul's namesake, King Saul. In the following comparison of texts, keep in mind that in both Greek and Hebrew, the same word can mean either "pursue" or "persecute":

Saul, Saul, why do you *persecute* [διώκω] me? . . . I am Jesus the Nazarene, whom you are *persecuting*. (Acts 9:4–5; 22:7–8; 26:14–15)

Why then does my lord *pursue* [רדף; lxx: καταδιώκω] his servant? (1 Sam 26:18)

After whom has the king of Israel come out? Whom are you *pursuing*? [רדף; lxx: καταδιώκω] A dead dog, a single flea? (1 Sam 24:14)

We can also compare Saul's question "Who are you, Lord?" with Abner's in 1 Sam 26:14, "Who are you who calls to the king?" One difference between the accounts is brought out in the fact that King Saul recognized David's voice and thus knew whom he was persecuting; he could not say, as Paul, "I acted in ignorance" (1 Tim 1:13).

In Paul's account before Agrippa, he reports Jesus' saying to him, "It is hard for you to kick against the goads" (Acts 26:14). That is, by persecuting Jesus, Saul was only hurting himself in an effort as futile as kicking against a sharp point used to prod animals. Likewise, King Saul was hurting himself by pursuing David, driving the best officer out of his army, inspiring many other defections as well, so that Saul perished in battle against the Philistines.

For the divine character of Jesus' speech, all three accounts have ἐγώ εἰμι, which might stand for Aramaic אנא הוא, though this possibility alone is not decisive.

The Nestle-Aland Greek NT cross-references Acts 9:7 with Deut 4:12, from Moses' account of Israel's experience at Mt. Sinai:

Acts 9:7 The men who traveled with him stood speechless, hearing the voice, but seeing no one.

MT Deut 4:12 You heard the sound of words, but you saw no form, only a voice.

Tg. Ps.-J. You heard the voice of the Word [*Dibbura*], but a likeness you did not see, only a voice speaking.

Tg. Neof. You heard the voice of his words [*dibber*], but you did not see a likeness, only the voice of his Word [*Memra*].[4]

If Acts 9:7 is indeed meant to allude to Deut 4:12, then we have a good example of the OT background supporting the twofold message that Jesus is both human and divine, or in John's language, the targumic Word has become flesh.

PAUL AT CORINTH (ACTS 18:9–10)

The Lord's words of assurance to Paul at Corinth are reminiscent of the LORD's words to Jeremiah when he was commissioned:

Acts 18:9–10	**Jer 1:17, 19**
Do not be afraid, but go on speaking and do not be silent. *For I am with you*, and no one will attack you in order to harm you, for I have many people in this city.	*Do not be dismayed before them*, lest I dismay you before them. . . . They will fight against you, but they will not prevail against you, *for I am with you*, declares the LORD, to deliver you.

For "I am with you," *Tg. Jer.* has "my Word is for your help," as in the case of *Tg. Isa.* 43:2, 5. By "the Lord," Luke most likely means Jesus, as would seem to be the case in the similar passage Acts 23:11 (the Lord stood by Paul and encouraged him that he would testify "about me" in Rome as he had in Jerusalem).

CHRIST IN NUM 21 (1 COR 10:9)

We must not put Christ to the test, as some of them did, and were destroyed by serpents. (ESV)

Many translations have "the Lord" instead of "Christ" due to scribes who, likely confused about the person of Christ, changed the Greek text. Like many moderns,

---

[4] McNamara translates, "You heard the voice of his utterance," suggesting other possibilities: "of the Word of"; "of my Word"; "of his word" (Aramaic: דביר). *Targum Neofiti* [mg.] reads דבירין, "words," as in the Ten Commandments (*Neofiti 1: Deuteronomy*, 36 n. "gg").

they would read Num 21 and point to the bronze serpent raised up on a standard as a foreshadowing of Christ (John 3:14), overlooking the doctrine that Jesus was both God and with God from the beginning, not just from the incarnation.[5]

Recall that in *Tgs. Ps.-J.* and *Neof.* Num 21:5, "the people spoke against the Word of the LORD" and complained against Moses (*Tg. Neof.* [mg.]: they spoke against "the name of the Word of the LORD" and against Moses). The *Tgs. Ps.-J.* and *Neof.* [mg.] and *Frg. Tgs.* P, V Num 21:6 say that "the divine Word" let loose poisonous serpents. *Targum Neofiti* Num 21:7 describes the people confessing to Moses that "we have spoken against the [name of the] Word of the LORD and against you;" *Tg. Neof.* [mg.] Num 21:8 says that "the Word of the LORD" told Moses to make a bronze serpent. In *Tg. Ps.-J.* vv. 8–9, the one who is bitten by a snake lives, "if his heart is directed toward the name of the Word of the LORD."

So, Paul could have made the point: "the divine Word has become flesh." Perhaps he did when speaking to Aramaic-speaking Jews. But if, as I suggested, identifying Jesus with the divine Word of the Targums is only a means to an end, that end being to identify Jesus as YHWH, the God of Israel, then Paul is simply taking a more direct route by telling the Corinthians that the Israelites tested *Christ* in the wilderness. That raises the question, why did John not follow Paul's example? Why complicate things by calling Jesus *the Word*? One reason might be that when John was writing years later, the presence of unwitting targumic prophecies pertaining to the destruction of Jerusalem had become evident (our subject in ch. 10), and calling Jesus the Word facilitated pointing to such prophecies.

Another thing that may have become clear by the time John wrote his Gospel is that there were many Christians who were not perceiving the christological message of the earlier NT writings (just as later scribes in their confusion may have altered texts such as this because they did not understand the implications of the doctrine of Christ's deity for a proper understanding of the OT). Perhaps the words of Jesus to Philip express John's burden as he observes the church in his day: "Have I been with you for so long Philip, and you have not come to know me?" (John 14:9).

Contemporary approaches often lack an appreciation of the close association, as seen in the Targums, between the work of God and the work of the divine Logos. Consider a modern example from an author writing on how to treat the OT as Christian Scripture: "There may indeed be sessions of studying an Old Testament passage in which there is no mention made of Jesus," meaning that mention of God in the OT does not inherently constitute mention of Jesus.[6] So when God is

---

[5] See Metzger, *Textual Commentary*, 494: "The reading that best explains the origin of the others is Χριστόν, attested by the oldest Greek manuscript ($\mathfrak{P}^{46}$) as well as by a wide diversity of early patristic and versional witnesses (Irenaeus in Gaul, Ephraem in Edessa, Clement in Alexandria, Origen in Palestine, as well as the Old Latin, the Vulgate, Syriac, Sahidic, and Bohairic). The difficulty of explaining how the ancient Israelites in the wilderness could have tempted Christ prompted some copyists to substitute either the ambiguous κύριον or the unobjectionable θεόν. Paul's reference to Christ here is analogous to that in ver. 4."

[6] Graeme Goldsworthy, *Preaching the Whole Bible as Christian Scripture* (Grand Rapids: Eerdmans, 2000), 123.

referred to in the OT, the reference is presumed to be exclusively to the Father. If this is the case, how can a sermon on such a text have Christological import without a direct reference to Christ? The author continues:

> The assumption is made [by a Christian preacher preaching the OT to Christians without mentioning Jesus] that when God is spoken of it is the God of Jesus and the apostles. When this God addresses us as his people, we have not suddenly become followers of Judaism. We remain Christians.[7]

That is, the sermon is Christian because the preacher and hearers share the assumption that the God being referred to is the Father of Jesus (but not Jesus). The Son of God is apparently seen as somewhere on the sidelines, waiting to come into the world. Paul's assumption reflected in 1 Cor 10:9 is quite different. For Paul, Christ was present in OT texts that speak of God's words and deeds.

PROVOKING CHRIST TO JEALOUSY (1 COR 10:22)

Paul warns, "You cannot drink the cup of the Lord and the cup of demons. You cannot partake of the table of the Lord and the table of demons" (1 Cor 10:21). Here the cup and table of the Lord refer to the rite of the "Lord's Supper" (cf. 10:16; 11:20) that the Lord Jesus established. The expression "table of the LORD" is an OT expression for the altar, which the prophet Malachi warned against defiling (Mal 1:7, 12). Paul contrasts the observance of the Lord's Supper with pagan observances that honor the false gods of demonically inspired pagan religion (1 Cor 10:20; echoing Deut 32:21). Such a contrast implicitly treats the Lord Jesus as the divine object of the religious observance. Paul then asks, "Or are we provoking the Lord to jealousy?" (1 Cor 10:22). This rhetorical question clearly alludes again to Deut 32:21, where Moses warned against provoking the Lord YHWH to jealousy. Paul's train of thought here makes no sense unless "the Lord" whom we should avoid provoking to jealousy (1 Cor 10:22) is the same "Lord" to whom belong the cup and the table (10:21). In short, Paul here assumes that the Lord Jesus is in fact the Lord YHWH.[8]

In Deut 32:21, the LORD says, "They have made me jealous with what is not God; they have provoked me to anger with their idols." The plausibility of connecting 1 Cor 10:22 to this verse becomes evident when we compare MT Deut 32:30 with *Tg. Neof.* and *Frg. Tg. V*:

MT	Tgs.
Their Rock sold them, *the* LORD delivered them up.	Because they sinned and provoked to anger before him, the *Strong One* has forsaken them, and the *Word of the* LORD delivered them over into the hand of their enemies.

---

[7] Ibid., 126.
[8] Bowman and Komoszewski, *Putting Jesus in His Place*, 164–65.

Paul's rhetorical question, "We are not stronger than he, are we?" (1 Cor 10:22b), comes naturally from seeing Christ as "their Rock" = "their Strong One," also equated in the *Tgs.* with "the Word of the LORD."

We have also noted that Deut 4:24, "The LORD your God is a consuming fire, a jealous God," is in *Tg. Onq.*, "The LORD your God, his Word, is a consuming fire, a jealous God." *Targum Pseudo-Jonathan* says the same and adds, "the jealous God is a fire, and takes vengeance in jealousy."

In Deut 4:3, Moses draws the people's attention to what the LORD did at Baal Peor; in *Tgs. Ps.-J.* and *Neof.* he says, "Your eyes have seen what the Word of the LORD did to the worshippers of the idols of Peor." Paul referred to this incident shortly before his discussion of the Lord's table (1 Cor 10:8). Moses refers to the incident recorded in Num 25, in connection with which *Tg. Neof.* [mg.] Num 25:10–11 says that "the Word of the LORD" said that Phinehas "was jealous with my jealousy."

THE NAME ABOVE ALL NAMES (PHIL 2:9–11)

In this passage, Paul says that God has given to Jesus the name above all names, which name is not "Jesus" but can only be the Tetragrammaton. This conclusion agrees with John 17:11–12, which says that the Father has given his name to Jesus. Paul then says that as a consequence, every knee should bow to Jesus and every tongue will confess that he is Lord, to the glory of God the Father. Since this passage draws on Isa 45:23, where the LORD swears that every knee will bow to him, it is among the clearest passages teaching the deity of Christ, so that the confession of Jesus as "Lord" means one confesses him as "LORD," that is, YHWH.

Targum Isaiah does not say that every knee will bow to the Word. However, the clause "By myself I have sworn" (MT) is rendered in the Targum, "By my Word I have sworn." Likewise in MT 45:22, where the ends of the earth are invited to "turn to me and be saved," the Targum has "turn to my Word and be saved." And vv. 17, 25 in the Targum say, "Israel is saved by the Word of the LORD with an everlasting salvation" and "In the Word of the LORD all the seed of Israel will be justified and glorified."

CREATION THROUGH THE SON (COL 1:16; 1 COR 8:6; HEB 1:2)

Colossians 1:16 says of Christ, "by him [ἐν αὐτῷ] were created all things [τὰ πάντα], in heaven and on earth, visible and invisible, whether thrones or dominions, rulers or authorities; all things were created through him [δι αὐτοῦ] and for him [εἰς αὐτόν]." This agrees quite nicely with John 1:3, 10, and as we have seen, creation is accomplished through the *Memra* in *Tg. Jon.* (Isa 44:24; 45:12; 48:13; Jer 27:5); *Tg. Onq.* Deut 33:27; *Tg. Neof.* and *Frg. Tg. P* Gen 1 (throughout); *Tg. Neof.* [mg.] Gen 3:1; 14:19, 22; *Frg. Tg. V* and *Tg. Neof.* [mg.] Gen 35:9; *Tg. Neof.* [mg.] Exod 20:11; [mg.] Exod 31:17; *Tg. Ps.* 124:8; and some mss of *Tg. Ps.* 33:6.

First Corinthians 8:6 does not use verbs such as "create," "make," etc., but says that all things are *from* God the Father and *through* one Lord, Jesus Christ. This statement is most naturally interpreted in agreement with Col 1:16.

Hebrews 1:2 speaks of Jesus as "heir of all things, through whom [δι οὗ] he also made the world." "The world" is not τὸν κόσμον, but τοὺς αἰῶνας, which, with its possible dual meaning of "world" and "ages," can be related to Hebrew עוֹלָם and Aramaic עָלְמָא, which was used in *Tg. Onq.* Deut 33:27, "through his Word the world was made."

WAITING FOR CHRIST FROM HEAVEN (1 THESS 1:9–10)

> You turned to God from idols to serve a living and true God and to wait for his Son from heaven, whom he raised from the dead, Jesus, who rescues us from the wrath to come.

It is not necessary to turn to the OT to understand this passage: Jesus promised to return and his followers wait for him. But this passage does have a number of features in common with Isa 25:9 and 26:8:

> And it will be said in that day, 'Behold, this is our God, for whom we have waited, that he might save us. This is the LORD, for whom we have waited. Let us rejoice and be glad in his salvation. . . .'

> We have waited for you eagerly. Your name, even your memory, is the desire of our souls.

Besides the idea of waiting, both passages are focused on eschatological deliverance. Paul also speaks about turning from idolatry, which may allude to the exclusion of Moabites from the eschatological banquet of Isa 25:6–12. Earlier the Moabites were condemned for their sins of pride and idolatry (Isa 16:6, 12), which were also sins of Judah (Isa 2:11–18), so their exclusion from the banquet is likely a symbolic indication that the proud and idolatrous are excluded. For MT "This is the LORD, for whom we have waited," *Tg. Isa.* 25:9 reads, "This is the LORD; we were waiting for his Word."

TASTE AND SEE THAT THE LORD IS GOOD (1 PET 2:3; HEB 6:5)

Robert M. Bowman Jr. and J. Ed Komoszewski note, "Two passages in 1 Peter refer to Jesus as 'Lord' in a way that identifies or equates him with the Lord YHWH." We will consider these verses in this section and the next.[9] Peter encourages Christians to be like newborn children longing for spiritual milk whereby we might grow up to salvation, "if indeed you have tasted that the Lord is good" (1 Pet

---

[9] Bowman and Komoszewski, *Putting Jesus in His Place*, 168. The discussion of both verses is on pp. 168–70.

2:3). Verse 4 indicates that "the Lord" refers to Jesus: "As you come to him, a living stone, rejected of men. . . ." But the idea of tasting that the Lord is good is from Ps 34:8, where Lord is LORD (YHWH). That Peter is quoting Ps 34 is confirmed by the fact that he quotes again from the Psalm in the next chapter (1 Pet 3:10–12; Ps 34:12–16). In *Tg. Ps. 34:8*, a personal pronoun referring to the LORD is rendered with *Memra*. Note the following comparison:

1 Pet 2:3	**Ps 34:8**	**Tg.**
if indeed you have tasted that the Lord (Jesus) is good.	Taste and see that the LORD is good. Happy is the man who takes refuge *in him!*	Recognize and see that the LORD is good. Happy is the man who trusts *in his Word!*

In the Targum, "happy" is the noun טוב (pl.), related to the adjective "good" (טב; cf. Heb. טוב). Interestingly, Heb 6:5 speaks of those who have "tasted the goodness of the word of God" (θεοῦ ῥῆμα). We have seen that there is good reason to believe that the author of Hebrews was aware of the paraphrase of "I am he" from *Tg. Ps.-J.* Deut 32:39, so possibly he was familiar with the Targums more broadly. If one allows that Heb 6:5 may be influenced specifically by *Tg. Ps. 34:8*, or generally by the targumic practice of substituting "the Word of the LORD" for "the LORD," then it is possible that "the word of God" in this verse is a targumic equivalent of "the LORD." In context, the author also says they have tasted the heavenly gift, and shared in the Holy Spirit, which would support the view that he is talking about tasting the goodness of God personally, not just in his spoken or written word. Hebrews 4:12 also speaks of God's word in terms that could be just as well used of God himself, as "living and active, sharper than a two-edged sword, . . . able to judge the thoughts and intentions of the heart." The author does not identify the targumic Word specifically and exclusively with Christ (if in fact he is using a targumic expression), but, as we have seen, John makes such an identification in his adaptation of the targumic Word.

THE LORD AND HIS WORD AS STONE OF STUMBLING (1 PET 2:8)

As with Ps 34, Peter quotes from Isa 8 in both ch. 2 and ch. 3 in a way that equates Christ with YHWH. First Peter 3:14–15 is based on Isa 8:12–13:

Isa 8:12–13	**1 Pet 3:14–15**
Do not fear what they fear, or be in dread. *The LORD of Hosts, him shall you regard as holy.* He shall be your fear, he shall be your dread.	Do not fear their fear, and do not be troubled, but *hallow Christ as Lord* in your hearts.

Isaiah goes on to say, "He (i.e., the LORD) will become a sanctuary and a stone of offense and a rock of stumbling to both houses of Israel." Again, what is said of the LORD is said of Christ by Peter, as he quotes this verse after quoting several passages interpreted as speaking about Christ as a stone or rock: a choice and precious cornerstone (1 Pet 2:6, from Isa 28:16), the stone rejected by the builders which became the cornerstone (v. 7, from Ps 118:22), and a stone of stumbling, a rock of offense (v. 8, from Isa 8:14). *Targum Isaiah 8:14* says, "And if you do not listen [lit.: receive], his Word will become among you an avenger, and a stone of striking and a rock of stumbling." Thus, while it is true that Peter equates Christ with "the LORD" in Isa 8:14, the corresponding passage from the Targums speaks of his Word as the stone of stumbling. This is not to suggest that Peter had the Targum on his mind (certainly the Targum did not regard the *Memra* as equivalent to the Messiah), but if he had, he could have identified Jesus as the Word who became flesh, as John did, without having to elevate his Christology.

JESUS SAVED HIS PEOPLE FROM EGYPT (JUDE 5)

Jude reminds his readers "that Jesus, who saved a people out of the land of Egypt, afterward destroyed those who did not believe" (v. 5 ESV). For "Jesus," some MSS read "Lord" (so most editions and versions), others "God." 𝔓72 has θεὸς Χριστός. As Metzger notes, the reading "Jesus" is favored by several principles of textual criticism:

> Critical principles seem to require the adoption of Ἰησοῦς, which admittedly is the best attested reading among Greek and versional witnesses. . . . Struck by the strange and unparalleled mention of Jesus in a statement about the redemption out of Egypt (yet compare Paul's reference to Χριστός in 1 Cor 10.4), copyists would have substituted (ὁ) κύριος or ὁ θεός.[10]

According to *Tg. Neof.* Exod 14:30, "On that day the Word of the LORD saved and delivered Israel from the hands of the Egyptians." We also saw frequent association of the divine Word with the death of the Egyptian firstborn in the Targums. I suggested that early Aramaic-speaking Jewish Christians would have understood the symbolism of the baptism of Jesus in light of *Tg. Ps.-J.* Num 7:89, identifying Jesus as the divine Word, but that this was a means to an end, not an end in itself. The end was to identify Jesus as YHWH the Son, the God of Israel. Jude's language is thus natural.

As for Jude's assertion that Jesus "afterward destroyed those who did not believe," the extant Targums do not ascribe this destruction to the divine Word in Deut 2:15, the most comprehensive description of this judgment: "Also the hand of the LORD was against them, to destroy them from within the camp until they

---

[10] Metzger, *Textual Commentary*, 657. Thus the reading "Jesus" is best attested, is the more difficult reading, and best explains how the others came about. The committee majority, however, "was of the opinion that the reading was difficult to the point of impossibility, and explained its origin in terms of transcriptional oversight ($\overline{KC}$ being taken for $\overline{IC}$)" (ibid.). Allen Wikgren shared Metzger's minority opinion.

perished." But in *Tg. Ps.-J.* Num 16:11, 26, Korah and his company are gathered together against the divine Word, and in *Tg. Neof.* [mg.] Num 16:30 the swallowing up of those who followed Korah is a work of the divine Word. Similarly, in *Tg. Neof.* [mg.] Num 16:44–45, the Word of the LORD says he will destroy the congregation; in *Tg. Neof.* [mg.] Num 21:6 the Word of the LORD let loose the poisonous serpents; and in *Tg. Neof.* Num 25:10 [mg.], 11, the Word of the LORD says that Phinehas in his zeal has kept him from destroying the whole nation. If the point of identifying Jesus as the divine Word was to identify him as YHWH the Son, there would be no need to confine Jesus' divine activity to OT passages where the Targums happen to employ *Memra*. The divine Word is commonly used in passages speaking of divine warfare, including warfare against his own people (e.g., *Tg. Isa.* 63:10: "His Word turned to be an enemy to them; he himself fought against them), which is also an activity of the Son in the NT era (Rev 2:16).

CONCLUSIONS

In his study of John's Gospel, A. T. Hanson said, "The truth is that Jesus did not claim to be God, and in representing him as making no such claim the other three evangelists were being faithful to history. John is not just bringing out into the open what was always implicit. He is creating his own christology."[11] We have seen that, to the contrary, just as there can be no name higher than the Tetragrammaton, so there can be no higher Christology than one finds in the Synoptic Gospels, Acts, or NT letters. The Christology found in the rest of the NT is completely consistent with "the Word was with God, and the Word was God, and the Word became flesh." Only John's manner of expressing this Christology, and his emphasis on it, are unique.

---

[11] Hanson, *Prophetic Gospel*, 259.

12

The Superiority of the Targum View

Introduction

We saw in ch. 1 that several views of the origin and background to the Logos title in John are plausible. Examined in isolation, the case for each might seem rather compelling. Now that I have made as compelling a case as I can for the Targum view, it is time to make the case for why the Targum view is to be preferred quite decisively over the other views. My focus here will be on (1) the conceptual overlap between the various views, which may account in part for why the Targum view has been overlooked (i.e., interpreters citing evidence for other views are unaware that such evidence also fits with the Targum view); and (2) methodological and other types of errors made by those arguing against the Targum view. The first subject involves ignorance of or insufficient attention to evidence for the Targum view; the second involves misdirected arguments by those who do pay attention to the Targum view.

Common Features between the Targum View and Other Proposed Views

The Old Testament Word of the Lord

As we saw in ch. 1, Dodd acknowledged that a fairly strong case could be made for the view that the Logos title was derived simply from the concept of "the word of the Lord" in the OT. We also noted Köstenberger's four reasons why this view should be preferred to either Wisdom or Philo's Logos:

> (1) the evangelist's deliberate effort to echo the opening words of the Hebrew Scriptures by the phrase "in the beginning"; (2) the reappearance of several significant terms from Gen 1 in John 1 ("light," "darkness," "life"); (3) the Prologue's OT allusions, be it to Israel's wilderness wanderings (1:14: "pitched his tent") or to the giving of the law (1:17–18); and (4) the evangelist's adaptation of Isa. 55:9–11 for his basic christological framework.[1]

---

[1] Köstenberger, *John*, 27.

We can see now that the first three reasons, while they may show the superiority of the OT word view over proposed backgrounds in the Wisdom literature or Philo, do not favor OT word over the Targum view at all, since the Prologue's allusions to Gen 1 and other OT passages such as Exod 34 are allusions to passages where in the Targums (especially the *Pal. Tgs.* of the Pentateuch) the targumic Word (whether *Memra* or *Dibbera/Dibbura*) figures prominently. The fourth argument, as acknowledged previously, appears to be a strong argument. Yet if there is some degree of conceptual overlap between the targumic Word of the LORD and OT word of the LORD, interpreters need not be in an either-or situation. Both backgrounds could find support in various passages in John.

Against the idea of such overlap, Moore pointed to the fact that for "the word of the LORD" and related expressions in the MT, "word" is usually Heb. דָּבָר, and in *Tgs. Onq.* and *Jon.* it is translated by *pithgam* or *milla*, not *Memra* or *Dibbera.*[2] But the picture is not so clear-cut elsewhere. In Gen 15:1, "the word of the LORD" which came to Abram is rendered as "a word [מימר] from before the LORD" in *Frg. Tg. P.* In Ps 119:42, "I trust in your word [דְּבָרֶךָ]" is translated with מימרך in one MS. Similarly, "I shall praise his word" [דְּבָרוֹ] of Ps 56:4, 10 (*2x*) is in the Targum "I will praise his *Memra*." We have already noted that in the MT of Ps 106:12, "they believed his words [דְּבָרָיו]" becomes "they believed in the name of his Word [מימריה]." Also "You heard the sound of words" (Deut 4:12) is in *Tg. Ps.-J.* "You heard the voice of the Word [*Dibbura*]."

Also of interest is Ps 106:24, not because of how it is rendered in the Targum, but because of how it alludes to Num 14:11, where in MT, God asks, "How long will they not believe in me?" Referring back to this event, Ps 106:24 says, "They did not believe his word" [דְּבָרוֹ], which could be taken as precedent for *Tgs. Onq.* and *Ps.-J.* Num 14:11, "How long will they not believe in my Word" [מימרי], which was further developed by *Tg. Neof.* to "How long will they not believe in the name of my Word?" Recall that John 12:37 makes excellent sense as a paraphrase of Num 14:11, even without John's designation of Jesus as the divine Word. *Tg. Ps.* 106:24 is translated literally (they did not believe בפתגמיה), which is somewhat surprising because of the Targum reading from earlier in the Psalm (v. 12) that we have just noted.

In addition, there are other Hebrew words used for the word of God besides דָּבָר. When the MT has the Hebrew noun אֵמֶר or אִמְרָה—both etymological relatives of Aramaic מֵימַר—about two thirds of the time they are translated with מֵימַר in the Targums. If we make the reasonable assumption that there were Targums (whether written or oral) before the development of the *Memra* theology, then it follows that there could be several Aramaic words used to render the several Hebrew words for "word." Based on our extant Targums we could posit that פִּתְגָּם was regularly used to translate דְּבַר and מֵימַר was regularly used to translate אֵמֶר and אִמְרָה. With the adoption of the "Word" theology into the Targums, the question would have arisen as to which Aramaic word for "word" would be best to use when rendering the Tetragrammaton by "the Word of the LORD." There would be a number of reasons to use the term that was (presumably) already in use to translate אֵמֶר and אִמְרָה:

---

[2] Moore, "Intermediaries in Jewish Theology," 46.

1. In the MT of Ps 105:19, there would already be what could be viewed as a ready-made exemplar for the targumic usage: "Until the time of his word [דְּבָרוֹ; *Tg.* פתגמיה] came, the word of [אִמְרַת] the LORD tested (Joseph)." The NLT understands "the word of the LORD" here as metonymy, translating it as "the LORD tested Joseph's character." This is a reasonable interpretation, as it is clear from Genesis that it was the LORD who tested Joseph. Such an interpretation would appear just as reasonable to the targumists. If "the word of the LORD tested Joseph" can be used to mean "the LORD tested Joseph" in Ps 105:19, why not also substitute "the word of the LORD" for "the LORD" elsewhere? *Targum Psalms* 105:19 has the familiar מימרא דיהוה for "the word of the LORD"; presumably this was also how it read in an earlier, more literal stage of the Targums, and this expression could be readily extended to other passages, modifying the Tetragrammaton to "the Word of the LORD" in situations where God was described as interacting with his creation. Such modifications eventually numbered in the hundreds. *Targum Psalms* 105:19 is an example showing that targumic phraseology that differs from the MT may have precedent elsewhere in Scripture.[3]

Similarly, *Tg. Ps.* 107:11 says, "They rebelled against the *Memra* of God" for Hebrew אִמְרֵי־אֵל, "the words of God." Again we can posit an intermediate stage, prior to the development of the *Memra* theology, where the Targum used the plural of מֵימַר as a literal translation of the plural of Hebrew אֹמֶר. With the development of the *Memra* theology, only a slight change would make the plural (and literal) "words" into the singular (and metonymic) "Word."

2. Since אֹמֶר and אִמְרָה are fairly rare words (less than one hundred total uses), the "common" (literal) meaning of מֵימַר would also be fairly rare. On the other hand, דְּבָר in the MT is very common; therefore its translation by פִּתְגָּם in the Targums would also be very common. The use of מֵימַר in the Targums for the Word who is God would allow listeners in the synagogue who were not fluent in Hebrew to distinguish between "the word of the LORD" as a literal translation of the Hebrew and "the Word of the LORD" as a way of referring to God himself. Capitalizing Word in translation accomplishes the same purpose for modern readers, at least in English. Note, for example, the following from *Tg. Jer.* 17:20–27:

Say to them: "Listen to [lit.: receive] the word [פִּתְגָּם] of the LORD, O kings of the house of Judah. . . . Sanctify the Sabbath day, as I commanded your fathers. . . . But they did not receive. . . . But if you will certainly receive my Word [מֵימְרִי] . . . . But if you will not receive my Word [מֵימְרִי] . . . .

3. אִמְרָה in particular refers to God's word in a high percentage of cases, primarily because so many of its occurrences are in Ps 119. דְּבָר, on the other hand, often does not even mean "word" at all.

---

[3]Levine makes the same point concerning the substitution of "the glory of the LORD" for "the LORD" when MT says the LORD appeared to someone. The MT itself often says that people saw "the glory of the LORD." As Levine concludes, this way of speaking is not a targumic invention (*Aramaic Version of the Bible*, 58).

Looking more generally at the idea of God's written word, whatever word is used to describe it, one can observe that in one place in the MT the psalmist writes of trusting in the LORD (e.g., Ps 37:3, 5, 9, 34, 40), while in another place he writes of trusting in his word (e.g., Ps 119:42). One can see how the idea of God's word as a surrogate for God could develop in loose translations like the Targums (*Tg. Ps.* 37:3, 5, 9, 34, 40) and eventually be extended to all facets of divine interaction with the creation.

Above we noted the targumic expression "a word [מימר] from before the LORD." Evans noted that this expression can be compared to John's statement "the Word was with God."[4] "A word from before the LORD" is often personified: a word from before the LORD (or God) took Enoch away (*Tgs. Neof., Frg. Tg. V,* and *Ps.-J.* Gen 5:24) and cursed the earth (*Tgs. Neof.* and *Ps.-J.* Gen 5:29), struck Pharaoh (*Tg. Ps.-J.* Gen 16:1), came to Abimelech and Laban in a dream (*Tgs. Onq.* and *Ps.-J.* Gen 20:3; 31:24), caused the deaths of Er and Onan (*Tg. Neof.* Gen 38:7, 10), spoke to Moses at the burning bush (*Tg. Ps.-J.* Exod 10:29), and met, came to, or was heard by Balaam (*Tg. Onq.* Num 22:9, 20; 23:3, 4, 16; 24:4, 16). In Gen 20:3 as well as five of the seven passages mentioned above dealing with Balaam (all but the last two), *Tg. Neof.* uses "the Word of the LORD" rather than "a word from before the LORD." *Targum Pseudo-Jonathan* usually agrees with *Tg. Onq.* in its use of this expression. In *Frg. Tgs.* P, V Num 24:4, 16, מלל is used. In *Tg. Mic.* 2:7, the question, "has the LORD grown impatient?" is rendered (presumably to avoid the anthropopathism) "has a word [מימר] from before the LORD been shortened?" Clearly, this "word [מימר] from before the LORD" is personified as much as is the OT word of the LORD.

One could posit the following development in targumic thought: (1) The "word from before the LORD" is personified as is "the word of the LORD" in the MT, as a way of describing how God intervenes in the world; (2) the term is simplified to "the Word of the LORD," initially meaning the same as (1) but later used as metonymy to refer to God himself. Therefore, as noted above, Balaam can be "met" by either "a word from before the LORD" in one Targum or "the Word of the LORD" in another. The following "parallels" give another illustration:

MT Gen 12:17	*The LORD struck* Pharaoh . . . with great plagues. (similarly *Tg. Neof.*)
Tg. Ps.-J. Gen 16:1	Her name was Hagar, a daughter of Pharaoh, whom he gave to (Abram) . . . being *struck by a word from before the LORD* (referring back to Gen 12:17).
Tg. Ps.-J. Gen 12:17	The Word of the LORD sent great plagues against Pharaoh.

It is natural to suppose that these three examples represent a general chronological development in targumic practice: (1) literal—Pharaoh was struck by the LORD; (2) specification of the agency—Pharaoh was struck by a word/decree going forth from the LORD; (3) a rewording of (2)—the word (taken literally) of the LORD

---

[4] Evans, *Word and Glory,* 115.

struck Pharaoh; (4) metonymy—"the Word of the LORD struck Pharaoh" as a way of saying "the LORD struck Pharaoh," while guarding the transcendence of God.

Alternatively, one could suppose that "a word from before the LORD" is a development from "the Word of the LORD." Chester takes this position, stating that this phraseology was used particularly for encounters between God and unbelievers/Gentiles as an accommodation to rabbinic doctrine, which limited the possibility of God's revelation to pagans.[5] But Chester only discussed examples that came up in his investigation of Targum passages speaking of revelation using the verb אתגלי; thus he did not take note of passages which cannot be explained this way, such as *Frg. Tg. P* Gen 15:1 ("a word from before the LORD came to Abram") and *Ps.-J.* Exod 10:29, where Moses says, "It was told me [at the burning bush] by a word from before the LORD."

Whether there was such a development from "a word from before the LORD" to "the Word of the LORD" or not, we can observe that the Targums have both "the Word" who *is* God ("the Word of the LORD" as a way of referring to "the LORD") and the (personified) word which is *with* God ("a word from before the LORD") and goes forth from before him to accomplish his will, which is how Jesus describes himself (John 8:42; also 13:3; 16:27–30; 17:8). Thus "Word" in the latter sense could have been taken by John and applied as a title to Christ in exactly the same way as proposed for the OT word of the LORD (or for Wisdom, for that matter). That the Targums have a word who is *with* ("from before") God and the Word who *is* God means that the Targums provide background material that is closer conceptually to John's description of the Logos than any other proposed source material.

As for the word of God in Isa 55:9–11 as a summary of the work of Jesus, there are no clear allusions to this passage in the Gospel. Of far greater christological significance, we have seen clear dependence of the words of Jesus on the divine invitation "come to me" from earlier in the chapter (vv. 1–3) which, in the Targum, is an invitation to receive the divine Word (John 5:40; 7:37).

Further, even if one wants to focus on the OT word of the LORD as a basis for the Logos title, one could point to Aramaic דִּבּוּר/דִּבְּיר, meaning divine speech in the Targums, which can be highly personified as well. The first and second commandments in the *Pal. Tgs.* of the Pentateuch are much like the word of God in Isa 55:10–11 and would be just as attractive to adapt to the person of Christ.

> The first word [דביר], when it came forth from the mouth of the Holy One, may his name be blessed, was like shooting stars, like lightning, and like flames of fire; a fiery torch on its right, and a fiery torch on its left, flying and floating in the air of the sky; it returned and was seen over the camps of Israel; it turned round and was engraved on the tablets of the covenant that had been given into the palm of Moses' hands, and it was changing from side to side on them. Then he cried out and said, "My people, children of Israel, I am the LORD your God who redeemed and brought you out redeemed from the land of the Egyptians, from the house of bondage of slaves." (*Tg. Ps.-J.* Exod 20:2)

---

[5] Chester, *Divine Revelation*, 129, 136.

Tg. Ps.-J. Exod 32:19 says that when Moses broke the tablets at the foot of the mountain, the holy writing upon them began flying and circling in the sky again, and pronounced a woe on the people who heard the second commandment and just forty days later made a useless molten calf. Thus דִּבֵּיר in its literal sense comes forth from God and speaks to his people (supporting "the Word was with God" and providing an analogy with the incarnation and ministry of Jesus) but also functions as metonym for God (supporting "the Word was God"). Note that this first and second "word" were also light which illumined men.

One could argue, then, that both מימר and דביר, in their literal meanings in the Targums, could provide background for the Logos title in the same way that OT word (דבר) is thought to do, supporting "the Word was with God." But the targumic Word is closer to the Logos of the Prologue because it also gives background to "the Word was God."

The Targumic Word and Wisdom or Philo's Logos

Some targumic usages of *Memra* are suggestive of the Wisdom/Logos idea. The *Pal. Tgs.* of the Pentateuch have a long refrain describing the disposition of four cases brought to Moses in the wilderness; two of them capital cases (Lev 24:10–14; Num 15:32–36), and two civil (Num 9:6–13; 27:1–11). According to *Pal. Tgs.* Num 7:89, the decision would have been communicated to Moses by "the Word" speaking to Moses from above the mercy seat, between the cherubim. Part of the refrain in all four cases in *Tg. Ps.-J.* is the statement that Moses judged these cases "according to _____."[6] The terms which fill in the blank in the four cases are (1) "the *Memra* which is above" (מימרא דלעיל; Lev 24:12); (2) "the *Memra* of the Holy One" (מימרא דקודשא; Num 9:8; 15:34); and (3) "the understanding/mind which is above" (דעתא דלעיל; Num 27:5; also *Tg. Neof.* and *Frg. Tg. P* Lev 24:12). The use of מימרא with such parallels is perhaps reminiscent of Philo's Logos as the mind of God or rational principle.[7] Also note James' reference to "the wisdom that comes from above" (Jas 3:17; cf. Wis 9:17: "And who could ever have known your will, had you not given Wisdom and sent your holy Spirit from above?" [NJB]) and Jesus' statement "I am from above" (John 8:23). A word (מֵימַר) from before the LORD (i.e., from above; MT, "words of God") is also used in parallel with knowledge (דֵּיעָה) from before the Most High in *Tg. Neof.* Num 24:16 (Balaam "heard a word (מימר) from before the LORD, and acquired

---

[6]"There are no real parallels in rabbinic literature to this Targumic midrash" (Maher, *Pseudo-Jonathan: Leviticus*, 197 n.30).

[7]Harry A. Wolfson wrote, "the term Logos is used by Philo in the sense of Nous, both as the mind of God which is identical with His essence and as a created mind which is distinct from His essence. . . . He wanted to have a special term to designate the divine mind, or the incorporeal mind created by God, in order to distinguish it from the human mind." Wolfson also thought that Philo justified his use of Logos because of its use in LXX in the same way that Philo wanted to use it—for creation, government of the world, prophecy, and revelation (*Philo: Foundations of Religious Philosophy in Judaism, Christianity, and Islam* [Cambridge: Harvard University Press, 1968], 253–54).

knowledge (דיעה) from before the Most High"). The passage in *Frg. Tg. V* is the same except it has מלל instead of מימר.

In these passages and many others, דיעה has the sense of "knowledge," but in others it means "mind." In *Tg. Neof.* Num 16:28, Moses says that in the sign of Korah's death, Israel would know that what has happened is "not from my own mind" (לא מדעתי; *Tg. Neof.* [mg.] and MT have "my heart"). Similarly, in *Tg. Neof.* Num 24:13 Balaam says, "If Balak should give me his house full of silver and gold, I would not be able to go beyond the decree of the Word of the LORD to do either good or evil from my own mind."[8]

The difference of opinion over whether the *Memra* of the Targums has anything to do with the Logos of Philo is about as wide as it could be. Most today would agree with Alfred Edersheim's conclusion, if not his reasoning, of 125 years ago: "The Logos of Philo is *not* the *Memra* of the Targumim. For, the expression *Memra* ultimately rests on theological, that of *Logos* on philosophical grounds."[9] It seems doubtful that Philo and other ancients would make such a complete separation between philosophy and theology.

In contrast to Edersheim, Daniel Boyarin states that Philo's Logos and the targumic *Memra* represent variations in detail of "the Logos theology [which] was a virtual commonplace" (and into which John's Prologue fits comfortably).[10] Levey writes, "The *Memra* is the most versatile literary device in our Tg.'s [i.e., Ezekiel's] theological exegesis, similar to Philo's *logos*."[11] Israel Abrahams, after acknowledging Philo's dependence on Greek philosophy, comments, "On the other hand, Philo's Logos is rooted in the biblical idea of the creative word of God, the Targum's *Memra*, the mystical concepts of the *merkavah* ('divine chariot'), the *Shekinah*, the name of God, and the names of angels."[12] Unlike Boyarin, however, who sees John's Prologue as an understandable development from the current "Word theology," Abrahams states that the idea of the incarnation of the Word "created an impossible [*sic*; impassible?] gulf between Judaism and its daughter faith."[13] Similarly, Westcott: "No one . . . who had accepted [Philo's] teaching could without a complete revolution of thought accept the statement 'the Logos became flesh.' The doctrine of the personality of the Logos, even if Philo had consistently maintained it, would not have been in reality a step towards such a fact."[14] A key purpose of targumic *Memra* and Philo's Logos was to guard the transcendence of God— to keep God up in heaven, so to speak, and out of contact with the world. Thus, to accept the idea that the Word (defined as God) became flesh, one would have to

---

[8] *Tgs. Ps.-J.* and *Onq.* read "my own will." Díez Macho suggests emending *Tg. Neof.* to this reading, but he himself points to Num 16:28 as a parallel (*Neophyti 1*, 4:598).

[9] Edersheim, *Life and Times of Jesus the Messiah*, 1:48.

[10] Daniel Boyarin, "The Gospel of the *Memra*: Jewish Binitarianism and the Prologue to John," *HTR* 94 (2001): 249. Boyarin suggests that first-century Judaism had thoroughly absorbed central Middle Platonic ideas (ibid., 248).

[11] Levey, *Targum Ezekiel*, 15.

[12] Israel Abrahams, "Word," *EncJud* 16:635.

[13] Abrahams, "Word," 16:635.

[14] Westcott, *St. John*, xvii.

repudiate the *Memra*/Logos theology. In fact, if Palestinian Judaism had absorbed Middle Platonic ideas (as indicated in the use of *Memra*), it would raise the interesting question as to what extent these foreign ideas played a role in the fact that the Jews by and large did not recognize Isa 9:6 as a prophecy of the incarnation, and hence would not consider the possibility of its fulfillment in Jesus of Nazareth. "The Word became flesh" is a clear refutation of, not a development from, the Logos/*Memra* theology. It could be that first-century Judaism (or elements of it) had the opposite problem addressed in Jer 23:23, where God asks Judah, "'Am I a God near at hand,' says the LORD, 'and not a God afar off,'" which could be interpreted, "Am I only immanent, and not also transcendent?" The question (and thus the suggestion of God's immanence) is totally avoided in *Tg. Jer.*, which has in common with the MT only "I", "God" (2*x*), and "says the LORD": "'I, God, created the world from the beginning,' says the LORD; 'I, God, am going to renew the world for the righteous.'" In the Targum, "afar off" is evidently taken as activity in the distant past (creation), and "near" as activity in the near future.

Beyond the discussion of general conceptual similarities between Philo's Logos and the Targums' *Memra*, one can point to cases where Philo speaks of the Logos in connection with a certain biblical passage in a way that is similar to the *Memra* in one or more of the Targums of that passage. Explaining the Passover ceremony, Philo says, "They make the Passover sacrifice while changing their dwelling-place in accordance with the commands of the Logos," and "The divine Word gives the command . . . to keep (the festival)" (*Questions and Answers on Exodus* 1.4, 5). Likewise, the first Passover instructions are given by "the Word of the LORD" in *Tg. Neof.* [mg.] Exod 12:1, and the command to keep the festival in the wilderness is given by the Word of the LORD in *Tg. Neof.* [mg.] Num 9:1, as are the supplementary instructions for the keeping of the feast in the second month (*Tg. Neof.* [mg.] Num 9:9).

Philo's explanation of the idea of God meeting with/speaking to Moses from between the cherubim is interesting in light of our discussion above of *Pal. Tgs.* Num 7:89, which records the fulfillment of Exod 25:22; 29:42; 30:6, 36. Recall that in the Exodus passages the Targums (including *Tg. Onq.*) use *Memra* for God meeting/speaking with Moses from above the mercy seat, between the cherubim, while at Num 7:89, *Tgs. Neof.* and *Ps.-J.* say that from there the *Dibbera* spoke with Moses.

Philo also employed the agency of the Word for God's presence between the cherubim. In *Questions and Answers on Exodus* 2.68, Philo puts the question, "What is the meaning of the words, 'I will speak to thee above from (= from above) the mercy-seat, between the two cherubim'?" Philo then describes the situation in the holy of holies: "directly above them (the cherubim), in their midst, (is) the voice and the Logos, and above it, the Speaker [ὁ Λέγων]" and "there appears as being in their midst the divine Logos and, above the Logos, the Speaker."[15]

Philo's description differs in various details from *Tgs. Neof.* and *Ps.-J.* Num 7:89, but *Tg. Ps.-J.* Num 7:89 is like Philo in employing two concepts (the Spirit

---

[15] Presumably, Hanson meant to refer to this section of Philo, but he actually cited §78 (*Prophetic Gospel*, 76).

and the Word) to explain the situation in the most holy place, and Philo has the Speaker above the Word, just as *Tg. Ps.-J.* has the Spirit (whom Moses hears) descending to the place from which the Word spoke to him. Philo also quotes Exod 25:22 in *On Flight and Finding* 101, where he says that the divine Logos (λόγος θεῖος) is above the cherubim. Here Philo does not make a distinction between Logos and Speaker, but rather the invisible Logos, the image of God, is in closest possible proximity to the only truly existing God.

Philo's *On Dreams* 1.70–71, 229–230 is also of interest in light of the reading of *Pal. Tgs.* Gen 28:10 that the Word desired to speak with Jacob at Bethel. Philo has Jacob meeting the Logos and implying that Moses also took the people out to meet the Logos (Exod 19:17), whereas the Targums of Exod 19:17 say that Moses brought them to meet the Word of the LORD (*Tg. Onq.* and *Frg. Tg. P*), the glory of the LORD's *Shekinah* (*Tg. Neof.* and *Frg. Tg. V*), or the *Shekinah* of the LORD (*Tg. Ps.-J.*).[16] *On Dreams* 1.70 also implies that Abraham met the divine Word in Gen 18, which we saw (in ch. 2, p. 52, no. 5) was a revelation of the divine Word in *Tg. Neof.* and *Frg. Tgs. P, V* Gen 18:1, etc.

Philo also allegorizes the rescue of Lot and the destruction of the cities of the Plain as a work of the Word (*Logos*) of God: "For the Word of God, when it arrives at our earthly composition, in the case of those who are akin to virtue and turn away to her, gives help and succour, thus affording them a refuge and perfect safety, but sends upon her adversaries irreparable ruin" (*On Dreams* 1.85). Likewise, *Tgs. Neof.* and *Ps.-J.* Gen 19:24 and *Tg. Neof.* Gen 19:29 say that the cities were destroyed by the Word of the LORD, and *Tg. Neof.* [mg.] 19:13 says the Word of the LORD sent the angels to destroy Sodom (so, presumably, the divine Word also sent the angels to rescue Lot).

The importance of the *Memra* to the name of God in the *Pal. Tgs.* of the Pentateuch ("the name of the Word of the LORD") suggests another possible connection to Philo's Logos. As noted in ch. 2, Philo considered the concept of the Logos "identical with the Name."[17]

Since the Word and the glory of the *Shekinah* are related concepts in the Targums, we should not be surprised to also find connections between Philo's Logos and the *Shekinah* of the Targums, if in fact Philo's Logos is conceptually similar to the Word of the Targums. Hanson notes that Exod 24:10, "they saw the God of Israel," was rendered in the LXX as "they saw the place where the God of Israel stood,"

---

[16]"Meet and right then is it that Jacob . . . meets not now God but a word of God, even as did Abraham. . . . For we are told that 'the Lord departed, when He ceased speaking to Abraham, and Abraham returned to his place' (Gen. xviii. 33). . . . Thus should the divine Word, by manifesting Itself suddenly and offering Itself as a fellow-traveller to a lonely soul, hold out to it an unlooked-for joy—which is better than hope. For Moses too, when he 'leads out the people to meet God' (Ex. xix. 17), knows full well that He comes all unseen to the souls that yearn to come into His presence" (*On Dreams* 1.70–71). Maclean, in discussing John 1:51, noted Philo's point about Jacob meeting the Logos at Bethel ("Tale of Two Weddings," [n.p.] n.12).

[17]Meagher, "John 1 14 and the New Temple," 57 (citing *On the Confusion of Tongues* 146).

and that Philo explains somewhat tentatively in *Questions and Answers on Exodus* 2.37 that "this place is that of His Logos."[18] *Targum Onqelos* says that they saw "the glory of the God of Israel"; *Tgs. Ps.-J.* and *Neof.* [mg.] "the glory of the *Shekinah* of the God of Israel"; *Tg. Neof.* "the glory of the *Shekinah* of the LORD."

In light of these parallels, it hardly seems persuasive to say that we should ignore the similarities between Philo and the Targums on the basis of a generalized claim that Philo's concerns were philosophical and the Targums' theological.

Conclusion

Conceptual similarities between the OT word of the LORD, Wisdom of the Wisdom literature, and Philo's Logos have been noted and addressed by interpreters arguing for their preferred views. This overlap is certainly part of the reason that each of these views has a measure of plausibility. Yet there is also considerable conceptual overlap with a fourth view, the targumic Word. When interpreters favoring one of the first three views interact only with the other two, they miss their mark, since proving that one of them is better than the other two does not prove that any of them is better than the Targum view.

EVALUATION OF ARGUMENTS USED AGAINST THE TARGUM BACKGROUND

Some of this section will include review, since along the way in earlier chapters some objections against the targumic explanation have been noted.

Memra Is Not Used for Creation

Moore claimed that in contrast to Philo's Logos, "in the Targums *memra* . . . is not the creative word in the cosmogony of Genesis or reminiscences of it."[19] To make such a claim, Moore had to overlook the many cases in the *Frg. Tgs.* of Genesis, *Tg. Onq.* Deut 33:27, variant readings in *Tg. Ps.*, as well as several passages from *Tg. Jon.* (Isaiah and Jeremiah). These are summarized in ch. 1 (pp. 21–24). Even if Moore's comment had actually been true when he wrote it, the discovery of *Tg. Neof.* would nevertheless have overthrown this objection.

Memra Is Not a Hypostasis

Moore summarizes the argument as follows: From the thirteenth to eighteenth centuries,

---

[18] Noted by Hanson, *Prophetic Gospel*, 76.
[19] Moore, "Intermediaries in Jewish Theology," 54.

a vast amount of testimony was uncritically accumulated, and conclusions drawn which obtained general assent and continue to be accepted in some quarters to the present time. In the *Memra* of the Targums, the Word (Logos) was recognized, so to speak, in his own name and character; the Skekinah [*sic*] was sometimes taken for the Second Person of the Trinity, sometimes for the Third.

. . .

The sum of the whole matter is that nowhere in these Targums is *memra* a "being" of any kind or in any sense, whether conceived personally as an angel employed in communication with men, or as a philosophically impersonal created potency, . . . or God himself in certain modes of self-manifestation . . . . The appearance of personality which in many places attaches to the *memra* is due solely to the fact that the phrase "the *memra* of Y.," or, with pronouns referring to God, My, Thy, His *memar*, is a circumlocution for "God," "the Lord," or the like, introduced out of motives of reverence precisely where God is personally active in the affairs of men. . . .

It is an error . . . when, by association of the Christian doctrine of the Logos and by abuse of a technical term of Christian theology, the *Memra* is described as "an hypostasis." . . .

Like *memra*, *shekinah* acquires what semblance of personality it has solely by being a circumlocution for God in contexts where personal states or actions are attributed to him.[20]

A number of observations are in order: (1) Moore restricts himself to considering the official Targums *Onqelos* and *Jonathan*; as we have seen, the most impressive points of contact with John are found in the other Targums. It is true that in *Onqelos* and *Jonathan* a large number of uses of *Memra* could be taken literally, if one is so inclined; the same is not true of the *Pal. Tgs.*, as the expression "name of the Word of the LORD," which must denote the Tetragrammaton, is sufficient to prove. (2) The claim that "nowhere in these Targums is *memra* a being in any sense" or "God himself in certain modes of self-manifestation" is at odds with the admission that *Memra* is a "circumlocution for 'God,' 'the Lord,' or the like, introduced out of motives of reverence precisely where God is personally active in the affairs of men," unless one denies that God is "a being in any sense." (3) That *Memra* is a circumlocution for God should count in favor of, rather than against, the idea that John has adapted the Logos title from *Memra*, for John begins his Gospel by telling us "the Word was God." Likewise, Elizabeth Harris, arguing for a Wisdom background and against a Targum background, says that the targumic Word is "a mere periphrasis for God in order to avoid naming him."[21] Again, why does the fact that *Memra* is a "periphrasis for God" not count in its favor as the concept underlying John's Logos title?

---

[20] Moore, "Intermediaries in Jewish Theology," 42, 53–55, 59.

[21] Elizabeth Harris, *Prologue and Gospel: The Theology of the Fourth Evangelist* (JSNT-Sup 107; Sheffield: Sheffield Academic Press, 1994), 197.

McNamara notes Billerbeck's claim that "the expression '*Memra* of Adonai' was an empty, purely formal substitution for the Tetragrammaton and is consequently unsuitable to serve as a starting-point for the Logos of John."[22] McNamara writes elsewhere that "neglect of the targumic evidence in this regard is chiefly due to the writings of P. Billerbeck."[23] As evidence for this opinion one could cite Rudolf Schnackenburg, who in his commentary spends six pages discussing the evidence for a gnostic background to the Logos title but deals with the targumic view in two dismissive sentences, referring to Billerbeck.[24]

Vinzenz Hamp's view is often quoted: "neither the Logos, Philonian or Johannine, nor the preexistent Christ of Paul could be explained by the *Memra*."[25] "The formula has practically nothing to do with the prologue of John or with Christianity."[26] Philo scholar Harry A. Wolfson is also often quoted: "as for the *memra* of the Targum, no scholar nowadays will entertain the view that it is either a real being or an intermediary."[27]

Israel Drazin states that *Memra* should be translated "command," "will," "teaching," "inspiration," "power," "protection," etc. (i.e., it should be understood literally). In his translation of *Tg. Onq.* of Deuteronomy, he writes, "the retention of the Aramaic [transliteration *Memra*] should not lead anyone to suppose that *Memra* is a supernatural being." Yet in Drazin's own translation of *Tg. Onq.* Deut 4:24 the *Memra* "is a consuming fire, a zealous God."[28]

The old argument that targumic Word is a "hypostasis," meaning a being *distinct* from God, certainly overstretches the evidence, though this view is not without advocates today.[29] But showing that *Memra* is not a "hypostasis" in this sense does not settle the question; throughout this book I have sided with McNamara in viewing the *Memra* not as a hypostasis but as an instance of metonymy; targumic *Memra* is suitable for John's use precisely because it is a way of referring to God

---

[22] Str-B 2:333, quoted in McNamara, *Targum and Testament*, 101.

[23] McNamara, *Palestinian Judaism*, 237 n.46.

[24] "We may exclude completely, as is now sufficiently obvious, the appeal to the *Memra* d^eAdonai (the word of the Lord) in the Aramaic translations of the Bible. This has nothing to do with speculation on hypostasization, but merely a periphrasis for God, to avoid irreverence (Rudolf Schnackenburg, *The Gospel according to St. John* [trans. Kevin Smyth; London: Burns & Oates, 1980], 485; trans. of *Das Johannesevangelium* [Freiburg: Herder, 1965]). The gnostic view is discussed on pp. 488–93. Schnackenburg refers on p. 485 n.14 to the Str-B excursus on "*Memra* Jahves" for support, and cites Middleton, "Logos and Shekinah in the Fourth Gospel," 129 (see above, ch. 1 n. 79), for the view that John's Logos is connected to a personified divine word.

[25] L. Sabourin, "The *MEMRA* of God in the Targums," *Biblical Theology Bulletin* 6 (1976): 79 n.2. Sabourin is summarizing Hamp, *Der Begriff "Wort."*

[26] Forestell, *Targumic Traditions*, 19. Forestell also summarizes Hamp, *Der Begriff "Wort."*

[27] Wolfson, *Philo*, 287; also quoted by McNamara in "*Logos* of the Fourth Gospel and *Memra* of the Palestinian Targum," 115, and in *Targum and Testament*, 101.

[28] Israel Drazin, *Targum Onkelos to Deuteronomy: An English Translation of the Text with Analysis and Commentary, Based on A. Sperber's Edition* (New York: Ktav, 1982), 34, 90.

[29] Boyarin, "Gospel of the *Memra*," 248–49 n.19, 255. Though I do not agree with Boyarin's conclusion regarding the *Memra* as a being distinct from God, I would concur with him that the argument of Billerbeck, Moore, et al. "collapses logically upon itself" (ibid., 255).

under certain circumstances (generally speaking, in his interaction with the creation, especially his people, and when God is represented anthropomorphically). Granting that targumic *Memra* is not a being distinct from God, "It by no means follows that John was not influenced by targumic usage in his choice of Logos as a designation for Christ."[30] Similarly, Morris writes against this sort of objection: "But this is hardly the point. The point is that wherever people were familiar with the Targums, they were familiar with 'the Word' as a designation of the divine."[31] Evans adds, "The simple fact that 'Word' appears as a periphrasis or name for God in [some Targums of] Gen 1–2 and elsewhere in reference to creation and to God's *Shekinah* dwelling among his people means that it could easily have been adopted by the Fourth Evangelist for his own use."[32] Likewise, Brown reasons, "If the Aramaic expression for 'word' was used in the Targums as a paraphrase for God in his dealings with men, the author of the Prologue hymn may have seen fit to use this title for Jesus who pre-eminently incorporated God's presence among men."[33]

Some critics of the Targum view find it more convenient to argue against the nineteenth-century hypostatic *Memra* view, as it is always easier to knock down the straw man. For example, in 1990 Tobin (a Philo advocate, as noted above) mentioned McNamara's *Expository Times* article (in which he argued that Memra was used as metonymy; see ch. 1, n. 45) in a footnote, noting that another view was that the use of Logos in John was derived from targumic usage (he provided no explanation or discussion).[34] In his 1992 *ABD* article, Tobin included a brief discussion of McNamara's view, but seems to have entirely missed the point, criticizing McNamara's view as if he had argued for the old hypostatic *Memra* view, when in fact McNamara had himself rejected that view. Tobin writes, "*Memrā'* (word) as used in the Targums is basically a buffer term to preserve the transcendence of God; it has no reality of its own."[35] This was Hamp's point in refutation of the nineteenth-century view, and McNamara dealt with it. Yet Tobin inappropriately cited Hamp as a refutation of McNamara instead of addressing McNamara's view.

Bruce Chilton notes that "a significant, perhaps disproportionate, influence upon commentators has been exerted by Kittel's remark in the *Theologische Wörterbuch* [*TWNT* 4:132] that 'all attempts to explain the λόγος statements of John 1 in terms of the targumic מימרא have failed, since this is never a personal hypostasis, but only a substitute for the tetragrammaton.'"[36] Kittel's statement is inaccurate in the sense that the word "Lord" was already substituted for the Tetragrammaton as

---

[30] McNamara, *Targum and Testament*, 102–3; similarly in "*Logos* of the Fourth Gospel and *Memra* of the Palestinian Targum," 115.

[31] Morris, *John*, 120.

[32] Evans, *Word and Glory*, 128.

[33] Brown, *John*, 1:524.

[34] Tobin, "Prologue of John," 255 n.12.

[35] Tobin, "Logos," 4:352.

[36] Bruce Chilton, "Typologies of *Memra* and the Fourth Gospel," in *Textual and Contextual Studies in the Pentateuchal Targums* (vol. 1 of *Targum Studies*; ed. Paul V. M. Flesher; Atlanta: Scholars, 1992), 93 n.9. Kittel's comment is derivative of Billerbeck (*TWNT* 4:132 n.224).

in the LXX, for example; adding "the Word" to this substitution serves other purposes. "The Word of the LORD" is used specifically to refer to God as he interacts with his creation. John begins by telling us that Jesus the Word is God, and then tells us this Word became flesh—surely the ultimate in divine interaction with the creation. Kittel is correct, however, that the targumic Word implies the Tetragrammaton in the sense that it is used to refer to YHWH the God of Israel, a fact that is vital to the understanding of the full christological significance of the Logos title.

Chilton also notes Barrett's remark that the targumic *Memra* is "a blind alley in the study of the biblical background of John's logos doctrine."[37] Barrett bases his conclusion on the idea that targumic *Memra* "was not truly a hypostasis but a means of speaking about God without using his name."[38] However, since the Jews already used the substitute "Lord" or "God" to avoid speaking his name, Barrett's explanation is not persuasive. Barrett cites only a single passage from the Targums (*Tg. Onq.* Gen 3:8) to explain why targumic *Memra* "might erroneously be taken as a hypostasis." He then mentions McNamara for "a different view," without providing any discussion.[39]

More recently, Keener, though he cites McNamara's work and admits that his argument is different from the old hypostasis argument, continues to make the issue revolve around the question of whether the *Memra* represents a hypostatization.[40]

To conclude, the anti-hypostatic argument seems to depend on an arbitrary constraint. Scholars seem to want to force John to have taken some concept that was distinct from God and to have adapted it so that he could say that it was not only with God, but was in fact God. Why could not John have gone in the other direction, taking a concept that was recognized as a way of referring to God under certain circumstances and adapting that concept so that it applied both to the one who *is* God and to the one who is *with* God? To require that John must have adapted in one direction and not the other is arbitrary.

Memra Is Not Used in an Absolute Sense

We noted Moore's argument in ch. 1: "it is to be observed that *memra* does not occur without a genitive—'the word of the Lord,' 'my word,' etc., or a circumlocution for the genitive, 'a *memar* from before the LORD.' 'The *Memra*,' 'the Word,' is not found in the Targums, notwithstanding all that is written about it by authors who have not read them."[41] This argument assumes that targumic *Dibbera/Dibbura*, which is used in this absolute sense, "the Word," is too late to be of interest. Yet we have seen rather compelling cases where John's Gospel seems to be illuminated by Targum passages that have this more restrictively used "Word," especially John's allusions to the revelation of God to Moses in Exod 34, which in

---

[37] Chilton, "Typologies of *Memra*," 93 n.8.
[38] Barrett, *John*, 153.
[39] Barrett, *John*, 153; McNamara, *Targum and Testament*, 101–4.
[40] Keener, *John*, 349–50. Keener concludes by endorsing Barrett's "blind alley" comment.
[41] Moore, "Intermediaries in Jewish Theology," 61 n.24.

the *Pal. Tgs.* Exod 33:23 is described beforehand as a revelation of the *Dibbera/Dibbura*, and which included God's self description as "full of grace and truth." We also noted the isolated use of *Dibbura* in *Tg. Jon.* (Ezek 1), which can most reasonably be ascribed to the work of Johanan ben Zakkai, who was a contemporary of the apostle John. The argument that *Memra* is not used in an absolute sense, then, loses its force, since a number of targumic passages involving "the Word" (*Dibbera/Dibbura*) can be related to various passages in John. To summarize these: (1) Exodus 34 can be compared to John 1:14–18 (ch. 1, pp. 32–34; ch. 2, pp. 62–68). Various roles in which God appears in Exod 34 are also roles of Jesus in John (he comes down, reveals his name, fights for his people, etc., as described in chs. three through eight). (2) *Targum Pseudo-Jonathan* Num 7:89 can be compared to John 1:32–33, the account of the baptism of Jesus as recalled by John the Baptist. The same Targum passage (and the version found in *Tg. Neof.*) and various *Pal. Tg.* passages dealing with the giving of the law through the *Dibbera/Dibbura* also relate to the theme of Jesus as divine lawgiver in the body of the Gospel, as described above in ch. 7. (3) The revelation of the *Dibbera/Dibbura* to Jacob in *Pal. Tgs.* Gen 28:10 has certain points of contact with John 1:43–51, the revelation of Jesus to Nathanael. (4) The *Dibbera* speaking to Moses from the pillar of fire at the Red Sea in *CTg. T* Exod 14:30 relates to John 1:4–5, 9, which show the Word as light shining upon men and in victorious conflict with darkness (ch. 1, pp. 24–28).

Memra Is Only Used in the Targums

Keener suggests that the targumic usage is "too isolated to suggest that the language was used widely in early Judaism."[42] This comment seems to reflect a view of the Targums in which they occupy a small portion of the shelf space in a rabbinical academy library compared to that of the rest of rabbinic literature. It overlooks what should be of greater significance, namely, that the Targums (or at least major portions of them) were meant for public recitation in the synagogue on Sabbaths and feast days. They thus would be by definition "widely used in early Judaism" and are more likely to have been familiar to John and his readers than material meant primarily for scholars. It seems to me that scholars are actually starting with the question, "What is important for modern Judaism?" in deciding what John might or might not have been influenced by. If we ask such a question, then the Targums would not be high on the list. I suggest, however, that that is not the right question to ask.

Memra in the Targums Is Late

"All our extant targumic evidence is too late to allow us to be certain that *Memra* was used in a particular manner in the first century."[43] Such an argument

---

[42] Keener, *John*, 349–50.
[43] Ibid., 350.

is fine to make in theory, but it is answered in practice by the pervasive evidence for how John's Gospel is illuminated by passages in the Targums that feature the divine Word, which we saw over the course of the first ten chapters of the present work. In fact, we could say that John's Gospel itself constitutes compelling evidence "that *Memra* was used in a particular way in the first century."

Here too there seems to be a double standard at work. Dodd, for example, devoted just two sentences (one in a footnote) to a discussion of the targumic background to the Logos title, in part because of its supposed lateness: "[Philo's] use of the term Logos itself has some affinity with the (probably later) use of the term מֵימְרָא as a periphrasis for the divine name."[44] Dodd's double standard is evident in that although he acknowledged that most of the *Corpus hermeticum* was later than John, he nevertheless devoted an entire chapter to considering its potential relevance to John's Gospel. Should not the same approach be taken with the Targums, even if one suspects that the *Memra* theology in them is later than John? One can argue for an early date by showing conceptual similarities between *Memra* and Philo's Logos (acknowledged by Dodd, as noted above), since Philo dates from the first half of the first century. These similarities have already been noted.

Similarly, there are some references to the word of God in intertestamental Wisdom literature that sound like things in the Targums, and such similarities would obviously make an intertestamental development of the *Memra* theology more plausible. Brown cited two passages from the Wisdom of Solomon that could be used to support the OT word as background for the Logos title, but I mention them here because one can also make connections between them and the Targums (Wis 16:5–13; 18:14–15).[45]

Wisdom of Solomon, commenting on the bronze serpent incident, says, "For the one who turned toward it (the bronze serpent) was saved, not by the thing that was beheld, but by you, the Savior of all. . . . For neither herb nor poultice cured them, but it was your word [λόγος], O Lord, that heals all people" (16:7, 12 NRSV). We see in this passage similar concerns evident also in *Tg. Ps.-J.* Num 21, which we looked at above in connection with John 3:14, particularly, the desire to avoid the impression that the Israelites were saved from death by the mere act of looking at the bronze serpent. The Targum says that the one who looked would live "if his heart was directed towards the name of the Word of the LORD." Hayward links this passage with *Tg. Neof.* [mg.] and *Frg. Tgs.* Exod 15:26: "I am the LORD who in my Word heals you."[46] John might have seen the healing ministry of Jesus as further fulfillment of this promise when the Word became flesh.

Wisdom of Solomon 18:14–15 describes the death of the Egyptian firstborn, saying that at midnight the Lord's all-powerful Word leapt down from the

---

[44] Dodd, *Fourth Gospel*, 68, 12. At p. 68 n.1 Dodd cites Str-B and G. F. Moore to the effect that "מימרא in the Targums is never the name of a personal mediating hypostasis," a fact which, as we have seen, does not settle the question of whether or not the Logos title arose from the Targums.

[45] Brown, *John*, 1:521.

[46] Hayward, *Divine Name and Presence*, 118–20. Both *Frg. Tg.* traditions have this reading.

heavenly royal throne carrying the divine command to strike the Egyptian firstborn like a sword. Various Targum passages also ascribe the death of the firstborn to the *Memra*:

***Tg. Neof.* Exod 11:4**	In the middle of the night my Word will be revealed in the midst of Egypt.
***Tg. Neof.* Exod 12:12–13**	And I, in my Word [mg.: And I will be revealed in my Word], will pass through the land of Egypt this night. . . . And I, in my Word, will defend you [mg.: my Word will defend you].
***CTg. AA* Exod 12:12–13**	My Word will pass through the land of Egypt. . . . My Word will see the blood.
***CTg. AA* Exod 12:23**	And the Word of the LORD will pass through to slay the Egyptians.
***Tg. Neof.* [mg.] Exod 12:29**	At midnight the Word of the LORD killed all the firstborn in the land of Egypt. (similarly *Tg. Ps.-J.*, *CTg. AA*)
***Frg. Tg. V* Exod 12:42**	The third night: when the Word of the LORD was revealed against the Egyptians in the middle of the night.

What the two Wisdom texts have in common with the Targum texts is that they add "the Word" where the MT account does not have it. In the case of Exod 12:29, both Wis 18:15 and *Tgs. Ps.-J.* and *Neof.* [mg.] Exod 12:29 ascribe to the Word what the MT ascribes to the LORD. Such examples certainly make it plausible that the targumic *Memra* theology developed in intertestamental wisdom circles rather than in post-first-century rabbinic Judaism, in which there is no trace of its development. Based on Wis 16:10, 12; 18:14–16, Hayward concludes "*Memra* was known in Alexandria in the second half of the first century BC."[47]

Along similar lines, the Hellenistic Jewish tragedian Ezekiel, who wrote a play reenacting the exodus sometime during the third to first centuries B.C.E., depicted the voice from the burning bush (emanating from behind a curtain) saying to Moses (v. 99), "And the divine Word [Logos] shines out from the bush upon you."[48] Note the association of the Word with shining light, as in John's Prologue, as well as the repeated use of *Memra* in the Targums of the burning bush scene: "The Word of the LORD called to him from the midst of the bush" (*Tg. Neof.* Exod 3:4; see also *Tg. Neof.* [mg.] Exod 3:14, 15; 4:2, 6, 11, 21, 30; *Frg. Tgs. P, V* Exod 3:14); "I have been revealed in my Word to deliver them" (*Tg. Neof.* Exod 3:8); "I, in my Word, will be with you, and this will be a sign that my Word has sent you" (*Tg. Neof.* Exod 3:12; similarly *Tg. Neof.* Exod 4:15); "they will say to me, 'The Word of the LORD was not revealed to you'" (*Tg. Neof.* [mg.] Exod 4:1); "that by my Word they may be delivered" (*Tg. Ps.-J.* Exod 3:8); "it was told me (at the burning bush) by a word [*memar*] from before the LORD that the men who had sought to kill me had fallen" (*Tg. Ps.-J.* Exod 10:29).

---

[47] Hayward, *Divine Name and Presence*, 121.

[48] Noted by Hanson, *Prophetic Gospel*, 31, citing J. Jeremias, "Zum Logos-Problem," *ZNW* 59 (1968): 84.

Eliezer Segal does not hesitate to relate Ezekiel the Tragedian to Philo, and Philo to targumic *Memra*:

> Philo preferred to minimize God's direct involvement with the created world by applying the Stoic concept of the "Logos," an emanated entity that furnished the rational structure that regulates the physical world. In Philo's interpretations, it was this Logos, not God himself, that was heard or seen by the prophets of the Bible. This usage was adopted by the standard Aramaic translation of the Torah (where the Logos appears as the *Memra*, the word of God) and continued to influence Jewish philosophers in later generations.

> And so, while striving to fashion a literary representation of God's appearance to Moses, the tragedian Ezekiel was scrupulous in eschewing all references to the "voice" of God. Instead, he consistently makes reference to the "word of God," namely the divine "Logos," in a manner reminiscent of Philo.[49]

So targumic *Memra* theology/philosophy seems to fit right in with intertestamental Hellenistic Judaism. This makes the refusal to consider a Targum background to the Logos title on the supposition that *Memra* theology is later than John precarious, to say the least. Those who put the Targums out of bounds for consideration of the background of the Logos title based on date need to consider these facts.

The Targum View Is Not Even Worth Investigation

Such is the implication of Barrett's "blind alley" comment. And to quote Wolfson and Moore again, "as for the *memra* of the Targum, no scholar nowadays will entertain the view that it is either a real being or an intermediary."[50] (So *Memra* is God but not "a real being"?) "'The Memra,' 'the Word,' is not found in the Targums, notwithstanding all that is written about it by *authors who have not read them*."[51] The attitude expressed by such statements carries the implication that those who investigate the Targum background to the Logos title may not only be wasting their time; they might be putting their scholarly reputations at risk.

---

[49] Eliezer Segal, "Staging the Exodus," *Jewish Free Press*, April 21, 1997, 18–19; repr. as "Who Staged the First Biblical Epic?" in *Holidays, History and Halakah* (Northvale, N.J.: Aronson, 2000), 169–72. Online: http://www.ucalgary.ca/~elsegal/Shokel/970421_Ezek Trag.html.

[50] Wolfson, *Philo*, 287. Wolfson's comment sounds a bit like the Pharisees who sent officers to arrest Jesus at the Feast of Booths: "No one of the rulers or Pharisees has believed in him, has he? But this crowd which does not know the law is cursed" (John 7:48–49).

[51] Moore, "Intermediaries in Jewish Theology," 61 n.24 (emphasis added). Moore's comment sounds a bit like Caiaphas: "You know nothing at all" (John 11:49). This is the same Moore who said, "In the Targums *memra* . . . is not the creative word in the cosmogony of Genesis or reminiscences of it" (ibid., 54).

Conclusions

The Gospel of John provides plenty of clues, beginning with the first verse of the Gospel, that make a targumic origin of the Logos title likely. Because of the conceptual similarity between targumic *Memra/Dibbura* and other, better known concepts such as Philo's Logos, and because of the relative neglect of Targum study in Johannine scholarship, it has been easy to miss these clues and find other plausible explanations for the Logos title, explanations that are not necessarily unrelated to Targum usage. Naturally, it is difficult to find something if one is looking in the wrong place, no matter how much light there is in the location being investigated. The twentieth century should have been a period in which scholarship went forward to more fully uncover the evidence for the targumic backgrounds to John's Gospel. This is especially true subsequent to the rediscovery, halfway through the century, of a complete *Pal. Tg.* of the Pentateuch, *Tg. Neof.* Instead, due to rather reactionary essays focused only on the misguided question of whether the targumic *Memra* was a hypostasis, scholarship has regressed; believing that targumic *Memra* is a "blind alley," scholars have not ventured very far into this path and have ended up going down various truly blind alleys. While I expect it that current trends will continue for some time, it is hoped that scholars will at least be persuaded to carefully consider the Targums when trying to explain John's Logos title.

Summation and Implications
for Johannine Scholarship

John's Adaptation of the Targumic Word

Since all of our extant Targums seem to date from a time later than John, whenever we observe a potential correlation between a text and a passage from John, a measure of uncertainty is warranted. This is augmented by the fact that we are dealing with likely allusions rather than direct quotations. It seems to me, however, that the cumulative weight of evidence strongly supports the conclusion that the Logos title is adapted from the Targums. Since Logos is a christological title, it is important to be clear on just how John has adapted this title. It is *adapted* (not simply carried over) in at least three ways:

(1) In the Targums, the divine Word is distinguished from the Messiah, and the idea of the divine Word seems to come from a philosophical mind-set in which "the Word became flesh" would be inconceivable.

(2) Whereas the targumic Word seems to be employed as a way of safeguarding the transcendence of God, it does not follow that Jesus as "Word" is immanent, in contrast to the Father who is transcendent. Jesus is "God with us," not merely a projection of God, and Jesus says that the Father is with him (John 16:32), that both he and the Father will come to his disciples and make their dwelling with them (14:23), and that the Holy Spirit "will be in you" (14:17). The triune God is both transcendent and immanent.

(3) In the Targums, the divine Word is employed to refer to God especially in contexts where he is interacting with his creation, and particularly his people; the divine Word is not a Person distinct from God. Thus if the targumic Word were simply carried over from the Targums unchanged and applied to the Son, the theological result would be more like the heresy of modalism. In the Targums, the Word *is* God (Father, Son, and/or Spirit), not merely *with* God. The Word in John's Gospel is specifically YHWH the Son. John employs this adaptation of the targumic Word in his opening sentence.

The Unity of John's Gospel

Seeing John's Logos title as derived from a background in the Targums is consistent with a greater readiness to see unity between the Prologue and the body of the Gospel. A targumic interpretation of the Logos title would permit a great deal of progress in connecting the Prologue to the rest of the Gospel: (a) "The Word became flesh" is programmatic for John's Gospel, once we understand that "the Word" is a way of saying "YHWH the Son." Throughout the body of the Gospel, we see Jesus speak and act in the flesh in a manner that echoes the ways in which the God of Israel acted in OT times, ways that the Targums used the concept of the divine "Word" to describe. (b) "The Word" as a targumic divine title is complemented by Jesus' repeated "I am he" sayings in the Gospel. These two are joined in *Tg. Neof.* and *Frg. Tg. V* Deut 32:39, where God says, "I, in my Word, am he." Added confirmation comes from the fact that the various *Pal. Tg.* renderings of Deut 32:39 figure prominently in many of these "I am he" sayings, and that the many "I am he" sayings added in the *Pal. Tgs.* of the Pentateuch are spoken by the divine Word according to *Tg. Neof.* main text or glosses. (c) The connection between the targumic Word and the name of God helps us see the ministry of Jesus as a multifaceted revelation of the name of God along the lines of God's revelation of his name to Moses after the Israelites' worship of the golden calf. In proclaiming his name, God revealed himself as "full of grace and truth." This was a revelation of the divine Word according to *Tg. Neof.* and *Frg. Tgs. P, V* Exod 33:23, and it fits well with the overall mission of Jesus, described as manifesting, or revealing, the divine name to God's people (John 17:6, 26).

UNITY OF AUTHORSHIP IN THE JOHANNINE LITERATURE

Elucidating the targumic background of John's writings adds significantly to evidence for the unity of authorship of the NT writings traditionally ascribed to John. Not only does the Logos title feature in John, 1 John, and Revelation, but in each of these books a targumic background to this title makes excellent sense. A characteristic common to the Johannine literature emerges, that John takes the language of the Targums applied to the God of Israel and applies it to Jesus, while Jesus uses the equivalent language from the MT. John calls Jesus "the Word," while Jesus says "I am he." John calls Jesus the one who is from the beginning (1 John 2:13–14), while Jesus says "I am the first and the last" (Rev 1:17; 2:8; 22:13). The divine claim, "I am the first and the last" of Isa 44:6; 48:12 is rendered in *Tg. Isa.*, "I am he who is from the beginning" (which is also included in *Tg. Isa.* 43:10). Jesus says "I have come down from heaven" (John 6:38), which follows the divine language of the MT (Exod 3:8, etc.), whereas John uses targumic language (or an adaptation) to describe the same event: "the Word became flesh" (John 1:14); "the Son of God was revealed" (1 John 3:8). Jesus says "come to me" in a context which shows it is dependent on God's "come to me" of Isa 55:1–3 (John 5:40; 7:37), whereas John uses the language of the equivalent expression in the Targums, "receive my Word" in John 1:11–12.

JOHN'S AUDIENCE AND PURPOSE

It is clear from John 1:38, 41–42, where John gives some very elementary translation lessons to his readers (Rabbi = teacher, Cephas = Peter, Messiah =

Christ), that at least one segment of John's intended audience consists of Gentile converts with little or no background in Hebrew or Aramaic. From the extensive evidence of Targum influence on the Gospel, with the implication that to get the fullest possible meaning of what John has written one needs to become familiar with the Targums, it follows that Aramaic-speaking believers should follow John's example set in these verses, instructing their fellow Gentile believers in this rich background in order to receive everything John has put on their table. The present book (ironically, written by a Gentile) is an attempt to make at least a good start towards that goal. It is indeed lamentable that the first-century Targums have not been completely preserved in our extant Targums, although the evidence suggests that the extant Targums preserve an earlier interpretive tradition. Considering relatively recent finds (e.g., *Tg. Neof.* and *CTgs.*), we have reason to hope for further discoveries that will close the gap between us and the first century.

I suggested above that John had two motives for calling Jesus "the Word." The first was christological, to address the "Philips" in the church, who, so to speak, have spent so much time with Jesus (i.e., being instructed in the church) yet do not really know who Jesus is. There is still a need for this emphasis in modern times, since many Christians are unable to defend their faith against the christological heresies represented in the contemporary cults, and there is a tendency for Christians to read the OT as though God were not then triune. The second motive I suggested was apologetic, based on the existence of "unwitting prophecies" in the Targums, which would be particularly applicable to the situation of the Jews towards the end of the first century, but would have continuing applicability to Gentile Christians as warnings that, as Paul put it, "If God did not spare the natural branches, neither will he spare you" (Rom 11:21).

John is commonly accused of anti-Semitism because of his pejorative references to "the Jews" and especially because of the words of Jesus in John 8:44, "You are of your father the devil." However, "offspring of the serpent" is simply a way of saying they are unregenerate, which is the natural state of all people, not just Jews. (Cain, the prototype of the offspring of the serpent, was obviously not Jewish). The need for regeneration was also an issue that needed to be addressed in the largely Gentile church in second and third generation Christianity for whom John was writing (so he warns professing Christians that they, too, are children of the devil if they are like Cain; 1 John 3:8–15). Thus we can see that if there were people in the church (mostly Gentile) who remind John of "the Jews" of a previous generation, he would write in such a way as to make these parallels evident as well as to make clear the Lord's sharp denunciation of such false professors who oppose the truth and its true adherents; people who, like Caiaphas, put their own place ahead of all other considerations.[1] Subsequent church history shows that such concerns were clearly warranted. In such circumstances, believers today should be willing to follow Jesus "outside the camp," whether that unbelieving camp be Jewish or nominally Christian. And as John shows his original hearers as well as Christ's followers today, this is the place where Moses his servant saw his glory, and where they, too, can see his glory.

---

[1] I have already pointed to Diotrephes as another example; 3 John 9–10;

Bibliography

Abrahams, Israel. "Word." Pages 634–35 in vol. 16 of *Encyclopaedia Judaica*. Editor-in-chief, Fred Skolnik. Executive editor, Michael Berenbaum. 16 vols. Jerusalem: Keter, 1971.

Alcalay, Reuben. *The Complete English-Hebrew Dictionary*. Hartford, Conn.: Prayer Book, 1965.

Alexander, Philip S. *The Targum of Canticles*. The Aramaic Bible 17A. Collegeville, Minn.: Liturgical Press, 2003.

Archi, Alfonso. "Les textes lexicaux bilingues d'Ebla." *Studi Eblaiti* 2 (1980): 81–89.

Ashton, John. *Understanding the Fourth Gospel*. Oxford: Clarendon, 1991.

Ball, David Mark. *"I Am" in John's Gospel: Literary Function, Background and Theological Implications*. Journal for the Study of the New Testament: Supplement Series 124. Sheffield: Sheffield Academic Press, 1996.

Barrett, C. K. *The Gospel According to St. John*. 2d ed. Philadelphia: Westminster, 1978.

Beasley-Murray, George R. *John*. Word Biblical Commentary 36. Dallas: Word, 1987.

Berg, Werner. "Nochmals: Ein Sündenfall Abrahams—der erste—in Gen 12, 10–20." *Biblische Notizen* 21 (1983): 7–15.

———. "Der Sündenfall Abrahams und Saras nach Gen 16, 1–6." *Biblische Notizen* 19 (1982): 7–14.

Bernard, J. H. *A Critical and Exegetical Commentary on the Gospel According to St. John*. 2 vols. International Critical Commentary. New York: Charles Scribner's Sons, 1929.

Black, Matthew. *An Aramaic Approach to the Gospels and Acts*. 3d ed. Oxford: Clarendon, 1967.

Boismard, M. -É. "Aenon, près de Salem." *Revue biblique* 80 (1973): 218–29.

———. "Les citations targumiques dans le quatrième évangile." *Revue biblique* 66 (1959): 374–78.

Bonneau, Normand R. "The Woman at the Well: John 4 and Genesis 24." *The Bible Today* 5 (1973): 1252–59.

Borchert, Gerald L. *John 12–21*. New American Commentary 25B. Nashville: Broadman & Holman, 2002.

Boring, M. Eugene, Klaus Berger, and Carsten Colpe, eds. *Hellenistic Commentary to the New Testament*. Nashville: Abingdon, 1995.

Borsch, Frederick Houk. *The Son of Man in Myth and History*. New Testament Library. London: SCM, 1967.

Bowman, Robert M., Jr., and J. Ed Komoszewski. *Putting Jesus in His Place*. Grand Rapids: Kregel, 2007.

Boyarin, Daniel. "The Gospel of the *Memra*: Jewish Binitarianism and the Prologue to John." *Harvard Theological Review* 94 (2001): 243–84.

Brady, Christian M. M. *The Rabbinic Targum of Lamentations: Vindicating God*. Studies in the Aramaic Interpretation of Scripture 3. Leiden: Brill, 2003. Cited 23 October 2008. Online: http://targum.info/meg/tglam.htm.

Brown, Raymond E. *The Gospel according to John: Introduction, Translation, and Notes*. 2 vols. Anchor Bible 29–29A. Garden City, N.Y.: Doubleday, 1966, 1970.

Burkett, Delbert. *The Son of Man Debate: A History and Evaluation*. Society for New Testament Studies Monograph Series 107. Cambridge: Cambridge University Press, 2000.

———. *The Son of the Man in the Gospel of John*. Journal for the Study of the New Testament: Supplement Series 56. Sheffield: JSOT Press, 1991.

Burney, Charles F. *The Aramaic Origin of the Fourth Gospel*. Oxford: Clarendon, 1922.

Burton, Ernest de Witt. *A Critical and Exegetical Commentary on the Epistle to the Galatians*. International Critical Commentary. Edinburgh: T&T Clark, 1921.

Calvin, John. *Commentaries on the Epistles of Paul: Galatians and Ephesians, Philippians*. Grand Rapids: Eerdmans, 1957.

Cappel, Jacques. *Observationes in novum testamentum. Una cum eiusdem Ludovici Cappelli Spicilegio*. Amsterdam: Elzevir, 1657.

Caragounis, Chrys C. *The Son of Man: Vision and Interpretation*. Wissenschaftliche Untersuchungen zum Neuen Testament 38. Tübingen: J. C. B. Mohr, 1986.

Carson, Donald A. *The Gospel according to John*. Grand Rapids: Eerdmans, 1991.

Cathcart, Kevin K., and Robert P. Gordon. *The Targum of the Minor Prophets*. The Aramaic Bible 14. Collegeville, Minn.: Liturgical Press, 1989.

Chester, Andrew. *Divine Revelation and Divine Titles in the Pentateuchal Targumim*. Texte und Studien zum antiken Judentum 14. Tübingen: J. C. B. Mohr (Paul Siebeck), 1986.

Chilton, Bruce D. *The Isaiah Targum*. The Aramaic Bible 11. Wilmington, Del.: Michael Glazier, 1987.

———. "Typologies of *Memra* and the Fourth Gospel." Pages 89–100 in *Textual and Contextual Studies in the Pentateuchal Targums*. Vol. 1 of *Targum Studies*. Edited by Paul V. M. Flesher. Atlanta: Scholars Press, 1992.

Churgin, Pinkhos. *Targum Jonathan to the Prophets*. New York: Ktav, 1983.

Clark, Rosemary. *The Sacred Tradition in Ancient Egypt: The Esoteric Wisdom Revealed*. Saint Paul, Minn.: Llewellyn, 2000.

Clarke, Ernest G. *Targum Pseudo-Jonathan: Deuteronomy*. The Aramaic Bible 5B. Collegeville, Minn.: Liturgical Press, 1998.

Coetzee, J. C. "Jesus' Revelation in the EGO EIMI Sayings in Jn 8 and 9." Pages 171–77 in *A South African Perspective on the New Testament: Essays by South*

African New Testament Scholars Presented to Bruce Manning Metzger during His Visit to South Africa in 1985. Edited by J. H. Petzer and P. J. Hartin. Leiden: E. J. Brill, 1986.

Coloe, Mary L. *God Dwells With Us: Temple Symbolism in the Fourth Gospel.* Collegeville, Minn.: Liturgical Press, 2001.

———. "Like Father–Like Son: The Role of Abraham in Tabernacles—Jn 8:31–59." *Pacifica* 12 (February 1999): 1–11. Accessed 5 November 2007. Online: http://www.cecs.acu.edu.au/coloe/Pacifica_Abraham_word.pdf.

Cook, Edward M. "The Psalms Targum: An English Translation." Accessed 27 June 2009. Online: http://targum.info/?page_id= 11.

Dalman, Gustaf. *The Words of Jesus Considered in the Light of Post-biblical Jewish Writings and the Aramaic Language.* Edinburgh: T&T Clark, 1902. Translation of *Die Worte Jesu: mit berücksichtigung des nachkanonischen jüdischen Schrifttums und der aramäischen Sprache.* Leipzig: J. C. Hinrichs, 1898.

Dalman, Rodger Wayne. "The Theology of Israel's Sea Crossing." Th.D. diss., Concordia Seminary, Saint Louis, 1990.

Day, Peggy L. *An Adversary in Heaven: śāṭān in the Hebrew Bible.* Harvard Semitic Monographs 43. Atlanta: Scholars Press, 1988.

Delitzsch, Franz. *Psalms.* Vol. 5 of *Commentary on the Old Testament.* London, Hodder and Stoughton, 1887. Repr. Grand Rapids: Eerdmans, 1986.

Díez Macho, Alejandro. "El Logos y el Espíritu Santo." *Atlántida* 1 (1963): 381–96.

———. *Neophyti 1: Targum Palestinense MS de la Biblioteca Vaticana.* 5 Vols. Madrid: Consejo Superior de Investigaciones Científicas, 1968-1979.

Dodd, C. H. *The Interpretation of the Fourth Gospel.* Cambridge: Cambridge University Press, 1953.

———. "The Prophecy of Caiaphas: John 11:47–53." Pages 58–68 in *More New Testament Studies.* Grand Rapids: Eerdmans, 1968.

Dods, Marcus. "The Epistle to the Hebrews." Pages 219–381 in volume 4 of *The Expositor's Greek Testament.* Edited by W. Robertson Nicoll. 5 vols. New York: Hodder and Stoughton, 1912. Repr. Grand Rapids: Eerdmans, 1983.

Drazin, Israel. *Targum Onkelos to Exodus: An English Translation of the Text with Analysis and Commentary (Based on A. Sperber's Edition).* New York: Ktav, 1990.

———. *Targum Onkelos to Deuteronomy: An English Translation of the Text with Analysis and Commentary (Based on A. Sperber's Edition).* New York: Ktav, 1982.

Driver, S. R. *Treatise on the Use of the Tenses in Hebrew and Some Other Syntactical Questions.* 3d ed. Oxford: Clarendon Press, 1892.

Duke, Paul D. *Irony in the Fourth Gospel.* Atlanta: John Knox, 1985.

Edersheim, Alfred. *The Life and Times of Jesus the Messiah.* 3d ed. 2 Vols. London: Longmans, Green, and Co., 1883. 3d ed. 2 vols. London: Longmans, Green & Co., 1886. Rep. 1901.

Ellis, Earl A. *Paul's Use of the Old Testament.* Grand Rapids: Baker, 1981.

Etheridge, J. W. *The Targums of Onkelos and Jonathan Ben Uzziel on the Pentateuch, with Fragments of the Jerusalem Targum from the Chaldee.* 2 Vols. London: Longman, Green, Longman, 1862, 1865. Repr. 2 vols. in 1, New York: Ktav, 1968.

Evans, Craig A. *Word and Glory: On the Exegetical and Theological Background of John's Prologue.* Journal for the Study of the New Testament: Supplement Series 89. Sheffield: JSOT Press, 1993.

Flesher, Paul V. M., ed. "Palestinian Targum to the Prophets." Page 467 in volume 2 of *Dictionary of Judaism in the Biblical Period: 450 B.C.E. to 600 C.E.* Edited by Jacob Neusner and William Scott Green. 2 vols. New York: Simon & Schuster Macmillan, 1996. Repr. Peabody, Mass.: Hendrickson, 1999.

Forestell, J. T. *Targumic Traditions and the New Testament: An Annotated Bibliography with a New Testament Index.* Society of Biblical Literature Aramaic Studies 4. Chico, Calif.: Scholars Press, 1979.

Funk, R. W. "Papyrus Bodmer II ($\mathfrak{P}^{66}$) and John 8, 25." *Harvard Theological Review* 51 (1958): 95–100.

Gage, Warren Austin. *The Gospel of Genesis: Studies in Protology and Eschatology.* Winona Lake, Ind.: Carpenter Books, 1984.

Glasson, Thomas Francis. *Moses in the Fourth Gospel.* Studies in Biblical Theology 40. Naperville, Ill.: Allenson, 1963.

Godet, F. *Commentary on the Gospel of St. John.* 3 vols. Edinburgh: T&T Clark, 1899.

Goldsworthy, Graeme. *Preaching the Whole Bible as Christian Scripture.* Grand Rapids: Eerdmans, 2000.

Gordon, Cyrus H. "Near East Seals in Princeton and Philadelphia." *Orientalia* 22 (1953): 243–44.

Grossfeld, Bernard. *The Targum Onqelos to Exodus.* The Aramaic Bible 7. Collegeville, Minn.: Liturgical Press, 1988.

Hamp, Vinzenz. *Der Begriff "Wort" in den aramäischen Bibelübersetzungen: Ein exegetischer Beitrag zum Hypostasen-Frage und zur Geschichte der Logos-Spekulationen.* Munich: Neuer Fiber-Verlag, 1938.

Hanson, Anthony Tyrell. "John I.14–18 and Exodus XXXIV." *New Testament Studies* 23 (1976): 90–101.

———. *The Prophetic Gospel: A Study of John and the Old Testament.* Edinburgh: T&T Clark, 1991.

Harner, Phillip B. *The "I Am" of the Fourth Gospel: A Study in Johannine Usage and Thought.* Facet Books, Biblical Series 26. Philadelphia: Fortress, 1970.

Harrington, Daniel J., and Anthony J. Saldarini. *Targum Jonathan of the Former Prophets.* The Aramaic Bible 10. Collegeville, Minn.: Liturgical Press, 1987.

Harris, Elizabeth. *Prologue and Gospel: The Theology of the Fourth Evangelist.* Journal for the Study of the New Testament: Supplement Series 107. Sheffield: Sheffield Academic Press, 1994.

Harris, J. Rendel. *The Origin of the Prologue to St. John's Gospel.* Cambridge: Cambridge University Press, 1917.

Hayward, Robert. *Divine Name and Presence: The Memra.* Totowa, N.J.: Allenheld, Osmun, 1981.

———. *Targum Jeremiah.* The Aramaic Bible 12. Collegeville, Minn.: Liturgical Press, 1987.

Heil, John Paul. *Jesus Walking on the Sea: Meaning and Gospel Functions of Matt 14:22–33, Mark 6:45–52 and John 6:15b–21.* Analecta biblica 87. Rome: Biblical Institute Press, 1981.

Hendriksen, William. *The Gospel of John.* Edinburgh: Banner of Truth Trust, 1954.

Higgins, A. J. B. *Jesus and the Son of Man.* London: Lutterworth, 1964.

Hunter, A. M. *Paul and His Predecessors.* London: SCM, 1961.

Jastrow, Marcus. *A Dictionary of the Targumim, the Talmud Babli and Yerushalmi, and the Midrashic Literature.* New York: Putnam, 1903.

Jeremias, Joachim. "Zum Logos-Problem." *Zeitschrift für die neutestamentliche Wissenschaft und die Kunde der älteren Kirche* 59 (1968): 82–85.

Josephus. Translated by H. St. J. Thackery et al. 10 vols. Loeb Classical Library. Cambridge: Harvard University Press, 1926–1965.

Kasher, Menachem M. *Genesis.* Vol. 3 of *Encyclopedia of Biblical Interpretation: A Millennial Anthology.* Translated under the editorship of Harry Freedman. New York: American Biblical Encyclopedia Society, 1957.

Kasher, Rimon. "Eschatological Ideas in the Toseftot Targum to the Prophets." *Journal for the Aramaic Bible* 2 (2000): 25–59.

———. *Toseftot Targum to the Prophets* [Hebrew Title, תוספתות תרגום לנביאים]. Sources for the Study of Jewish Culture 2. Jerusalem: World Union of Jewish Studies, 1996.

Keener, Craig S. *The Gospel of John: A Commentary.* 2 vols. Peabody, Mass.: Hendrickson, 2003.

Keil, Karl Friedrich. *The Pentateuch.* Vol. 1 of *Biblical Commentary on the Old Testament.* 1864. Repr., Grand Rapids: Eerdmans, 1949.

Keiser, Thomas A. "The Song of Moses: A Basis for Isaiah's Prophecy." *Vetus Testamentum* 55 (2005): 486–500.

Kerr, Alan R. *The Temple of Jesus' Body: The Temple Theme in the Gospel of John.* Journal for the Study of the New Testament: Supplement Series 220. New York: Sheffield Academic Press, 2002.

Khouri, Rami. "Where John Baptized." *Biblical Archaeology Review* 31, no. 1 (January/February 2005): 34–43.

Klein, Michael L. *The Fragment-Targums of the Pentateuch according to Their Extant Sources.* 2 Vols. Analecta biblica 76. Rome: Biblical Institute Press, 1980.

———. *Genizah Manuscripts of Palestinian Targum to the Pentateuch.* 2 vols. Cincinnati: Hebrew Union College, 1986.

———. "The Preposition *qdm* ('before'), a Pseudo-anti-anthropomorphism in the Targum." *Journal of Theological Studies* 30 (1979): 502–7.

———. "The Translation of Anthropomorphisms and Anthropopathisms in the Targumim." Vetus Testamentum Supplements 32 (1979): 162–77.

Kline, Meredith G. *Images of the Spirit.* Grand Rapids: Baker, 1980.

Koester, Craig R. *Symbolism in the Fourth Gospel: Meaning, Mystery, Community.* Minneapolis: Fortress, 1995.

Köstenberger, Andreas J. *John.* Baker Exegetical Commentary on the New Testament. Grand Rapids: Baker, 2004.

Kysar, Robert. *The Fourth Evangelist and His Gospel: An Examination of Contemporary Scholarship.* Minneapolis: Augsburg, 1975.

———. *Voyages with John: Charting the Fourth Gospel.* Waco, Tex.: Baylor University Press, 2005.

Le Déaut, Roger. "The Current State of Targumic Studies." *Biblical Theology Bulletin* 4 (1974): 3–32.

———. *La nuit pascale: Essai sur la signification de la Pâque juive à partir du Targum d'Exode XII 42.* Analecta biblica 2. Rome: Biblical Institute Press, 1963.

Lehrman, S. M. *Midrash Rabbah: Exodus.* London: Soncino, 1939.

Levey, Samson H. *The Messiah: An Aramaic Interpretation. The Messianic Exegesis of the Targum.* Cincinnati: Hebrew Union College, 1974.

———. *The Targum of Ezekiel.* The Aramaic Bible 13. Collegeville, Minn.: Liturgical Press, 1987.

Levine, Etan. *The Aramaic Version of the Bible: Contents and Context.* Beihefte zur Zeitschrift für die alttestamentliche Wissenschaft 174. Berlin: de Gruyter, 1988.

Lightfoot, John. *A Commentary on the New Testament from the Talmud and Hebraica; Matthew–I Corinthians.* Oxford: Oxford University Press, 1859. Repr., Grand Rapids: Baker, 1979.

Longman, Tremper III. *How to Read the Psalms.* Downers Grove: InterVarsity, 1988.

Longman, Tremper III, and Daniel G. Reid. *God Is a Warrior.* Grand Rapids: Zondervan, 1995.

Maclean, Jennifer K. Berenson. "A Tale of Two Weddings: The Divine Trickster in John." Paper presented at the annual meeting of the Society of Biblical Literature. Boston, Mass., November 21, 1999. Accessed December 11, 2007; no longer available. Online: http://www.roanoke.edu/religion/Maclean/SBL/DivineTrickster.htm.

Maher, Michael. *Targum Pseudo-Jonathan: Genesis.* The Aramaic Bible 1B. Collegeville, Minn.: Liturgical Press, 1992.

Manson, William. *Jesus the Messiah: The Synoptic Tradition of the Revelation of God in Christ: With Special Reference to Form-Criticism.* London: Hodder & Stoughton, 1943.

McGrath, James F. *John's Apologetic Christology: Legitimation and Development in Johannine Christology.* Society for New Testament Studies Monograph Series 111. Cambridge: Cambridge University Press, 2001.

McNamara, Martin. "*Logos* of the Fourth Gospel and *Memra* of the Palestinian Targum (Ex 12^{42})." *Expository Times* 79 (1968): 115–17.

———. *The New Testament and the Palestinian Targum to the Pentateuch.* Analecta biblica 27A. Rome: Biblical Institute Press, 1978.

————. *Palestinian Judaism and the New Testament*. Good News Studies 4. Wilmington, Del.: Michael Glazier, 1983.

————. *Targum and Testament: Aramaic Paraphrases of the Hebrew Bible: A Light on the New Testament*. Grand Rapids: Eerdmans, 1972.

McWhirter, Jocelyn. *The Bridegroom Messiah and the People of God: Marriage in the Fourth Gospel*. Society for New Testament Studies Monograph Series 138. Cambridge: Cambridge University Press, 2006.

Meagher, John C. "John 1 14 and the New Temple." *Journal of Biblical Literature* 88 (1969): 57–68.

Mellon, Brad. "The 'Son of Man' in Hebrews 2:1–10." Master's thesis, Biblical Theological Seminary, Hatfield, Pa., 1985.

Metzger, Bruce. *A Textual Commentary on the Greek New Testament*. Second Edition. Stuttgart: German Bible Society, 1994.

Middleton, R. D. "Logos and *Shekinah* in the Fourth Gospel." *Jewish Quarterly Review* 29 (1938–1939): 101–33.

Miscall, Peter D. "Literary Unity in Old Testament Narrative." *Semeia* 15 (1979): 27–44.

Moffatt, James. "The Revelation of St. John the Divine." Pages 279–494 in vol. 5 of *The Expositor's Greek Testament*. Edited by W. Robertson Nicoll. 5 vols. Grand Rapids: Eerdmans, 1956.

Moore, George Foot. "Intermediaries in Jewish Theology: *Memra, Shekinah*, Metatron." *Harvard Theological Review* 15 (1922): 41–85.

Morris, Leon. *The Gospel according to John*. Rev. ed. New International Commentary on the New Testament. Grand Rapids: Eerdmans, 1995.

————. *The Word Was Made Flesh: John 1–5*. Vol. 1 of *Reflections on the Gospel of John*. 4 vols. Grand Rapids: Baker, 1986.

Motyer, Alec. *The Prophecy of Isaiah*. Leicester: InterVarsity, 1993.

Muñoz-León, Domingo. *Dios–Palabra. Memrá en los Targumim del Pentateuco*. Granada: Institución San Jerónimo, 1974.

Neyrey, Jerome H. "The Jacob Allusions in John 1:51." *Catholic Biblical Quarterly* 44 (1982): 586–605.

————. "Jacob Traditions and the Interpretation of John 4:10–26." *Catholic Biblical Quarterly* 41 (1979): 419–37.

Niccacci, Alviero. "Esodo 3,14a 'lo sarò quello che ero' e un parallelo egiziano." *Liber annuus Studii biblici franciscani* 35 (1985): 7–26.

Nickelsburg, George W. E. "Son of Man." Pages 137–50 in vol. 6 of *The Anchor Bible Dictionary*. Edited by David Noel Freedman. 6 vols. New York: Doubleday, 1992.

Nöldeke, Theodore. *Compendious Syriac Grammar*. Translated by James A. Chrichton. London: Williams and Norgate, 1904.

Pearl, Chaim. *RASHI, Commentaries on the Pentateuch*. New York: W. W. Norton & Company, 1970.

Philo. Translated by F. H. Colson et al. 10 vols. and 2 supplementary vols. Loeb Classical Library. Cambridge: Harvard University Press, 1956–1962.

Reim, Günter. *Studien zum alttestamentlichen Hintergrund des Johannesevangeliums.* Cambridge: Cambridge University Press, 1974.

———. "Targum und Johannesevangelium." *Biblische Zeitschrift* 27 (1983):1–13.

Ronning, John L. "The Curse on the Serpent: Genesis 3:15 in Biblical Theology and Hermeneutics." PhD diss., Westminster Theological Seminary, Glenside, Pa., 1997.

———. "The Naming of Isaac: The Role of the Wife/Sister Episodes in the Redaction of Genesis." *Westminster Theological Journal* 53 (1991): 1–27.

———. "The *Targum of Isaiah* and the Johannine Literature." *Westminster Theological Journal* 69 (2007): 247–78.

Rosenbaum, M., and A. M. Silbermann. *Pentateuch with Targum Onkelos, Haphtaroth and Sabbath Prayers and Rashi's Commentary.* 5 vols. London: Shapiro, Vallentine & Co., 1946.

Sabourin, L. "The *Memra* of God in the Targums." *Biblical Theology Bulletin* 6 (1976): 79–85.

Sahlin, Harald. *Zur Typologie des Johannesevangeliums.* Uppsala: Lundequistska Bokhandeln, 1950.

Schnackenburg, Rudolf. *The Gospel According to St. John.* Translated by Kevin Smyth. 3 vols. London: Burns & Oates, 1980. Translation of *Das Johannesevangelium.* Freiburg: Herder, 1965.

Scott, Martin. *Sophia and the Johannine Jesus.* Journal for the Study of the New Testament: Supplement Series 71. Sheffield: JSOT Press, 1992.

Segal, Eliezer. "Staging the Exodus." *Jewish Free Press*, April 21, 1997, 18–19. Repr. as "Who Staged the First Biblical Epic?" pages 169–72 in *Holidays, History and Halakah.* Northvale, N.J.: Aronson, 2000). Online: http://www.ucalgary.ca/~elsegal/Shokel/970421_EzekTrag.html.

Slotki, Judah. *Midrash Rabbah Numbers II.* London: Soncino, 1951.

Smelik, Willem F. *The Targum of Judges.* Leiden: Brill, 1995.

Smith, Morton. *Tannaitic Parallels to the Gospels.* Journal of Biblical Literature Monograph Series 6. Philadelphia: Society of Biblical Literature, 1951.

Smith, Robert Houston. "Exodus Typology in the Fourth Gospel." *Journal of Biblical Literature* 81 (1962): 329–42.

Smolar, Leivy, and Moses Aberbach. *Studies in Targum Jonathan to the Prophets.* Pinkhos Churgin. *Targum Jonathan to the Prophets.* Library of Biblical Studies. New York: Ktav, 1983.

Smothers, E. R. "Two Readings in Papyrus Bodmer II." *Harvard Theological Review* 51 (1958): 109–22.

Strack, Hermann L., and Paul Billerbeck. *Kommentar zum Neuen Testament aus Talmud und Midrasch.* 6 vols. Munich: C. H. Beck, 1922–1961.

Stec, David M. *The Targum of Psalms.* The Aramaic Bible 16. Collegeville, Minn.: Liturgical Press, 2004.

Targum Neofiti 1: Exodus. Translated by Martin McNamara. *Targum Pseudo-Jonathan: Exodus.* Translated by Michael Maher. The Aramaic Bible 2. Collegeville, Minn.: Liturgical Press, 1994.

Targum Neofiti 1: Deuteronomy. Translated by Martin McNamara. The Aramaic Bible 5A. Collegeville, Minn.: Liturgical Press, 1997.

Targum Neofiti 1: Genesis. Translated by Martin McNamara. The Aramaic Bible 1A. Collegeville, Minn.: Liturgical Press, 1992.

Targum Neofiti 1: Leviticus. Translated by Martin McNamara. *Targum Pseudo-Jonathan: Leviticus.* Translated by Michael Maher. The Aramaic Bible 3. Collegeville, Minn.: Liturgical Press, 1994.

Targum Neofiti 1: Numbers. Translated by Martin McNamara. *Targum Pseudo-Jonathan: Numbers.* Translated by Ernest G. Clarke. The Aramaic Bible 4. Collegeville, Minn.: Liturgical Press, 1995.

The Targum of Chronicles. Translated by J. Stanley McIvor. *The Targum of Ruth.* Translated by D.R.G. Beattie. Collegeville, Minn.: Liturgical Press, 1993.

Tobin, Thomas H. "Logos." Pages 348–56 in vol. 4 of *The Anchor Bible Dictionary.* Edited by David Noel Freedman. 6 vols. New York: Doubleday, 1992.

———. "The Prologue of John and Hellenistic Jewish Speculation." *Catholic Biblical Quarterly* 52 (1990): 252–69.

Treat, Jay C. "The Aramaic Targum to Song of Songs." Cited 15 December 2007. Online: http://ccat.sas.upenn.edu/~jtreat/song/targum/.

Usteri, Johann Martin. "Die Selbstbezeichnung Jesu als des Menschen Sohn." *Theologische Zeitschrift aus der Schweiz* 3 (1886): 1–23.

Weber, Ferdinand. *System der Altsynagogalen palästinischen Theologie aus Targum, Midrasch, und Talmud.* 1880. Repr. in *Jüdische Theologie auf Grund des Talmud und verwandter Schrifen.* Edited by Franz Delitzsch and Georg Schnedermann. 2d ed. Leipzig: Dörfling & Francke, 1897.

Westcott, B. F. *The Gospel according to St. John: With Introduction and Notes.* 1880. Repr., London: James Clarke & Co., 1958.

Wolfson, Harry A. *Philo: Foundations of Religious Philosophy in Judaism, Christianity, and Islam.* Cambridge: Harvard University Press, 1968.

Wright, Christopher J. *Deuteronomy.* New International Biblical Commentary on the Old Testament. Peabody, Mass: Hendrickson, 1996.

Young, Franklin W. "A Study of the Relation of Isaiah to the Fourth Gospel." *Zeitschrift für die neutestamentliche Wissenschaft und die Kunde der älteren Kirche* 46 (1955): 215–33.

Zurro, Eduardo. "Disemia de *brḥ* y paralelismo bifronte en Job 9,25." *Biblica* 62 (1981): 546–47.

Index of Modern Authors

Index of Ancient Sources

Scriptures are cited according to the English numbering system, even when the discussion is exclusively about the passage in Hebrew, and/or the Targums, or the LXX. The Targums are indexed separately.

Index to the Targums

Since for a passage in the Pentateuch there may be as many as six different Targums (three full length Targums, covering the entire Pentateuch, and three fragmentary), the Pentateuch Targum index consists of two sets of three parallel indexes. The first set has the full length *Tgs. Onq.*, *Ps-J.*, and *Neof.* The order reflects the fact that *Tg. Ps.-J.* sometimes has the character of *Tgs. Onq.*, and sometimes that of *Tg. Neof.* (as well as often having its own unique readings). *Targum Neofiti* glosses are not indexed separately in this first index. The second index has *Frg. Tg. P*, *Frg. Tg. P*, and MS fragments from the Cairo Genizah. In the case of the latter, MS identifiers are used for the particular verses cited.

Frequently in the text I make general references to the reading of a particular passage in the "*Pal. Tgs.*," meaning that the reading is supported by two or more of *Tg. Ps.-J.*, *Tg. Neof.* (including glosses), *Frg. Tg. P*, *Frg. Tg. V*, and *CTg.* In the Pentateuchal Targum indexes I have resolved these general references to indicate which specific Targums support the reading(s) in question. The same procedure is followed if reference is made to "the Targums" of a passage (which may include *Tg. Onq.*).

FULL-LENGTH TARGUMS OF THE PENTATEUCH

	Targum Onqelos	Targum Pseudo-Jonathan	Targum Neofiti
Genesis			
1	21, 22	21	247
1:1			21n54
1:3			21, 21n54, 24
1:4–6			21n54
1:7			21
1:8			21n54
1:9			21, 21n54
1:10			21n54

	Targum Onqelos	*Targum Pseudo-Jonathan*	*Targum Neofiti*
1:11			21, 21n54
1:15			21
1:16			21n54
1:17			21n54, 51
1:20			21n54
1:22			21n54
1:24			21, 21n54
1:25			21n54
1:27			21n54, 106
1:28–29			21n54, 51
1:30			21
2:2			21n54
2:3			21n54, 51
2:8			108, 108n36
2:18			106
2:23			106
3:1			21, 247
3:8	51, 265	14	14, 51
3:9			51
3:10	51	14, 51	14, 51
3:15	xv	xv	xv
3:22			108n36
3:24		51–52	52
4:26		30n77	30n77
5:2		30n77	30n77
5:24		255	255
5:29		255	255
6:7			106
8:20			30n77
8:21			106
9:5			106
9:6			106
11:5	86	86	86
11:7		86	86
12:7–8			30n77

	Targum Onqelos	*Targum Pseudo-Jonathan*	*Targum Neofiti*
12:17		255	255
13:4			30n77
13:18			30n77
14:19			21, 247
14:22			21, 247
15:6	19, 31n78, 193	19, 31n78, 193	19, 30n77, 31n78, 193
16:1		255	255
16:13		52	30n77, 52
17:1			52, 89–90, 211
17:3			52, 90
17:7–8			20
17:9			52, 90
17:15			52, 90
17:22	52, 89	52, 89	52, 89
18:1		52	52, 260
18:3		52	52
18:5		30n77	30n77
18:17		52	52
18:33	52	52	52
19:13			260
19:24		260	260
19:29			260
20:3	255	255	255
21:33		30n77	30n77
22:1		52	52
22:14			30n77, 52
22:16	18n48	18n48	30n77
24:3		30n77	30n77
26:24			211
26:25			30n77
27:15		108n36	108n36
28:10	40	39, 39n85, 40, 42, 52, 149–50, 198, 228, 260, 266	39, 40, 42, 52, 149–50, 198, 228, 260, 266
28:10–21		200	200

	Targum Onqelos	Targum Pseudo-Jonathan	Targum Neofiti
28:13	52	52	
28:15	52	52	52
28:16	52	39, 52	39, 52
28:20	39	39	39
28:21	20, 21n53, 40	20, 21n53, 40	40
31:13		199–200	199–200
31:24	255	255	255
35:1			30n77
35:7		52	52
35:9		30n77	21, 52, 247
35:11			90
35:13		52, 90	52, 90
35:15			52
38:7			255
38:10			255
40:23		179	106, 179, 187
45:3		195	195
48:22			108n36
49:24	215		
Exodus			
3:4			52–53, 268
3:4–6			211
3:6	53	53	53
3:8	86	86, 268	52, 86, 268
3:12			268
3:14		72, 74, 83, 86, 208	52–53, 72, 74, 208, 268
3:15			268
4:1			52, 268
4:2			52–53, 268
4:6			52–53, 268
4:11		106, 108n36, 108n38	52–53, 106, 108n38, 268
4:15			268
4:21			52–53, 268
4:30			268

	Targum Onqelos	*Targum Pseudo-Jonathan*	*Targum Neofiti*
4:3			30n7
5:23			30n77
6:2			196
6:2–3			211
6:2–7			209
6:7			20
7:1			209
7:5		210	209
7:17			209
8:20–22			209
8:22			53, 66, 217
9:4		66	
10:2			209
10:29		255, 256, 268	
11:4			53, 268
12:1			259
12:12		53	53, 210
12:12–13			268
12:13			53
12:23		53	53
12:29		53, 268	53, 268
12:42			24–25, 215
13:17		217	
13:21		53	53
13:21–22			26, 134, 171, 189
14		203	203
14:1			210
14:4		210	210
14:13–14			53
14:15			210
14:18			210
14:20	26n68	26n68	26n68
14:24			53, 182
14:25		53, 182	
14:27			53, 242

	Targum Onqelos	Targum Pseudo-Jonathan	Targum Neofiti
14:30			250
14:31	31, 160	29, 30n77, 31n78, 160, 176	29, 30n77, 31n78, 160, 176
15:8			141
15:12		xv	xv
15:18	178	141, 234	
15:26		178	178, 267
16:4	204	204	204
16:11			204
16:12		204	204, 210
16:15			204
17			155, 201, 202
17:1	16	16	
17:6			53, 151
17:7	53	53	53
17:15			30n77
18:4	40n86	40n86	40n86
19:3			157
19:5	147, 157	147, 157	
19:5–6	32, 227	32, 227	
19:8			147, 158
19:9		53	53, 158
19:11	91	91	53, 91, 158
19:17	21, 21n53, 53, 260	53, 260	53, 260
19:20	91	91	53, 91, 158
20:1	33	33	15
20:2		256	
20:7		30n77	
20:11			21, 247
20:22			163
23:17			13n32
23:20	132	132	132
23:21			30n77
24:3			147
24:7	147	147	147

	Targum Onqelos	*Targum Pseudo-Jonathan*	*Targum Neofiti*
24:10	261	261	261
25:22	14, 161, 163, 259	14, 161, 163, 259	14, 14n34, 161, 163, 259
26:28		30n77	
29:42	259	259	259
29:43	54	54	14n34, 54, 210
29:45			20
29:45–46	54	54	54, 210
29:46		210	
30:6	259	259	14n34, 259
30:36	259	259	14n34, 259
31:17			21–22, 247
32:13			30n77
32:19		257	
32:25			78
33–34			42, 238
33:1			54
33:3	54	54	54
33:5	54	54	54
33:6		78	78
33:9		186, 241	
33:11		65, 186, 241	65, 186, 241
33:14	240		
33:14–16	65	65	65
33:19		30n77	
33:19–23	66	67	66
33:20	54		
33:21			54
33:22	16		
33:22–23	54		54
33:23	66n17, 67	54, 67n19	34, 67, 186, 201, 266, 272
34			253
34:5	86	30n77, 54, 86	16, 30n77, 54, 86
34:5–6	68	68	68
34:6	54	54, 67, 70	54

	Targum Onqelos	Targum Pseudo-Jonathan	Targum Neofiti
36:33		30n77	
Leviticus			
1:1		14	14
5:21		31n77	
9:4	55	55	55
9:6	55	55	55
9:22		192	
9:23	55	55, 192	55
10:20		195	
11:45			20
16:2	55	55	55
16:8–9			31n77
18:5			106
22:32			154
22:32–33			19
22:33			20
24:11		78	
24:12		257	257
25:38			20
25:55	28	28	
26:11			20
26:11–12	55, 169	55, 169	55, 169
26:12		20	20
26:14	227		
26:18	227		
26:21	227		
26:27	227		
26:27–31	32		
26:29			227
26:40–42		228	
26:44		169	
26:45			20
Numbers			
6:2		31n77	
6:27			19

	Targum Onqelos	**Targum Pseudo-Jonathan**	**Targum Neofiti**
7:89		14, 15, 35, 35n80, 36, 37, 41, 42–43, 135, 161, 163, 170, 237, 250, 257, 259, 266	14, 15, 41, 42, 161, 163, 170, 257, 259–60, 266
9:1			259
9:8		257	
9:9			259
10:13	170	170	170
10:33	175	175	175
10:35		55, 130, 137, 222	130
10:35–36		133, 134, 175	55, 133, 134, 175
10:36	55		
11:17	56	56	56, 91
11:20	56	56	56
11:25	56, 91	56, 91	56, 91
12:5	56, 56n10	56	56
14:9	56		56
14:11	30, 31n78, 43, 177, 253	30, 31n78, 43, 177, 253	29–30, 30n77, 31n78, 43, 177, 253
14:14	56	56	56
14:20			192
14:21			22
14:22	29, 64, 177, 228	29, 64, 177, 228	
14:22–23	227	227	
14:24			64, 190
14:40–42	178	178	178
14:41–43	56–57	56–57	56–57
14:42			228–29
14:42–43	186	186	186
15:34		257	
15:41			20
16:11		251	
16:19	57	57	
16:20			57
16:28			258, 258n8

	Targum Onqelos	*Targum Pseudo-Jonathan*	*Targum Neofiti*
16:30			251
16:44–45			251
17:4	14, 161	14, 161	14, 161
18:9			30n77
20:6	57	57	
20:6–7	99	99	57
20:8		78	
20:11		145n5, 202	
20:12	31n78	31n78	30n77, 31n78
21:5	57, 203	57, 203, 245	30n77, 57, 203, 245
21:6		245	251
21:7	57, 57n11	57	57, 57n11
21:7–8			245
21:8–9		31n77, 180, 245, 267	
22:9	255		255
22:20	255		255
23:3	255		255
23:4	255		255
23:16	255		255
23:21	57	57	57
24:4	255		
24:13	258n8	258n8	258
24:16	255		257–58
25:10			251
25:10–11			247
25:11			251
27:5		257	
32:11–12			190
Deuteronomy			
1:30	57	57	57
1:32	31n78, 176n2	31n78, 176n2	30n77, 31n78, 176
1:32–33	132	132	132, 218
1:32–36			176
1:33	218	218	
1:36	187		187, 190

	Targum Onqelos	*Targum Pseudo-Jonathan*	*Targum Neofiti*
4:3		247	247
4:4			30n77
4:7		31n77, 33, 59, 187	
4:12		158, 244, 253	158, 244
4:12–13		15	
4:13		15n38	
4:24	21, 247, 263	21, 247	
4:32			108n36
4:36	158	158	158
5:5	158	158	158, 195
5:11		31n77	
5:23–28			158
5:24	57	33, 50, 51, 57	57
6:13		31n77	
7:4			190
8:3			106
8:20	227	227	
9:23	31, 31n78, 58, 227	31, 31n78, 57, 227	30n77, 31, 31n78, 57–58, 227
10:8			30n77
11:12		132	
11:22		58	30n77
12:5	58		58
12:11	71	58, 71	71
12:14			58
12:21	71	71	71
13:5			30n77
14:1–2		32	
14:2	7	7	7
16:2	71	71	71
16:6	71	71	71
16:11	71	71	71
18:5			30n77
18:7		31n77	30n77
18:19		18n48	18n48

	Targum Onqelos	*Targum Pseudo-Jonathan*	*Targum Neofiti*
18:19–20			30
18:22			30
21:5			30
23:14	58	58	58
26:2	71	71	71
26:17			20, 234
28:2	169	169	169
28:15	227	227	
28:45	227	227	
28:62	227	227	
30:2	235		
30:4		41	
30:8–10	235		
30:9		235	
31:3–8		58	58
31:6–8	58		
31:8	243	243	243
31:15	58	58, 212	58, 212, 228
31:16			228
31:17	228	212, 228	212, 228
31:17–18	58	58	58
31:18			185, 212–13, 228
31:27			190, 213, 232
32:3		73	73, 247
32:6	28	31n77	
32:9		31n77	
32:15	23	23, 24	23, 24
32:18		23, 24	23, 24
32:30			246
32:32–33		213	
32:39	196	72, 73, 73n5, 74, 78, 79, 81, 82, 83, 86, 87, 194, 195, 197, 204, 210, 211, 213, 232, 249, 272	22, 76, 81, 83, 151, 191, 195, 197, 213, 216, 217, 222–23, 272
32:39–40	77		194

	Targum Onqelos	*Targum Pseudo-Jonathan*	*Targum Neofiti*
32:40		88	22, 78, 88, 204
32:43		194, 204, 232	
32:51			30
33:2			158
33:27	22, 24, 247, 248, 261		
33:29		31n77	

FRAGMENTARY TARGUMS OF THE PENTATEUCH

	Fragment Targum P	*Fragment Targum V*	*Cairo Genizah Targums*
Genesis			
1	247		
1:3	21, 21n54, 24		
1:4	21n54		
1:5	21n54		
1:6	21n54		
1:7	21, 21n54		
1:8	21n54		
1:9	21, 21n54		
1:10	21n54		
1:11	21, 21n54		
1:14	21n54		
1:15	21		
1:16	21n54		
1:17	21n54, 51		
1:20	21n54		
1:21	21n54		
1:22	21n54		
1:24	21, 21n54		
1:25	21n54		
1:26	21n54		
1:27	21n54	21	
1:28	21n54, 51	21	
1:29	21n54, 51		

	Fragment Targum P	*Fragment Targum V*	*Cairo Genizah Targums*
2:2	21n54		
2:3	21n54, 51		
3:8	14, 51		
3:9	51	51	
3:10	14, 51	51	
3:15	xv	xv	
3:24	52	52	
5:24		255	
15:1	253, 256		
16:13	52	52	
18:1	52, 260	52, 260	
18:17	52	52	
22:14	52	52	
28:10	39, 40, 42, 52, 149–50, 198, 228, 260, 266	39, 40, 42, 52, 149–50, 198, 228, 260, 266	
28:10–21	200	200	
28:21			40 (e)
31:1			199–200 (e)
35:1			52 (c)
35:9	21	21, 51, 52, 247	52 (c)
40:23	179, 179n5, 187	179n5, 187	
48:22	108n36	108n36	108n36 (z)
Exodus			
3:14	72, 74, 52–53, 268	52–53, 268	
6:2			196 (d)
6:2–3			211 (d)
6:2–7			209 (d)
7:17			209 (d)
12:2	117, 196		
12:12			53 (aa)
12:12–13			268 (aa)
12:13			53 (aa)
12:23			53, 268 (aa)
12:29			53, 268 (aa)
12:42		24–25, 211, 215	24–25 (ff)

	Fragment Targum P	Fragment Targum V	Cairo Genizah Targums
14:20		192	
21:6	245	245	
23:21	57	57	
24:4	255	255	
24:16	255	255, 258	
Deuteronomy			
5:24			57 (d)
26:17		20	20 (aa)
32:3	73	73, 247	
32:15		23, 24	
32:18		23, 24	
32:30		246	
32:39		22, 81, 83, 88n4, 191, 195, 197, 204, 216, 217, 222–23, 272	
32:39–40		194	
32:40		22, 78	
33:2	158	158	

TARGUMS OF THE PROPHETS AND WRITINGS

Tg. Josh.
1:5   243
1:9   243
4   119
5:6   31
22:31   59

Tg. Judg.
6:12–13   59
13:18   78

Tg. 1 Sam.
2:35   18n48
4:4   59
4:8   59

Tg. 2 Sam.
6:2   59
6:7   59

Tg. 1 Kgs.
11:36   71
12:11   239
12:14   239

Tg. 2 Kgs.
18:5   131
18:12   31
18:22   131
18:30   131
19:28   131
19:31   131
21:4   71
21:7   71

Tg. Isa.
1:15   185
1:19–20   229
6:1   33, 187
6:1–8   35, 50, 59
6:5   33
6:8   33
8:14   250
10:17   130
11:1   106
11:2   35
25:9   248
26:13   71

26:19   217
30:11   234
30:20   59
30:31   130
31:4   130
31:8   131
33:10   130
33:11   130
36:7   130–31
36:15   131
40:5   86
41:4   28, 74
42:1   36, 41
43   26, 242
43:1   23, 28, 182
43:2   181–82, 202–3, 244
43:5   181, 203, 244
43:10   28, 74–75, 76, 191, 196, 201n7, 201, 211, 218, 272

43:12   210, 211
43:13   75, 210
43:25   75, 191–92, 196
44:6   75, 76, 196, 208, 272
44:24   18n48, 22, 23, 24, 247
45:12   22, 24, 247
45:15   185
45:17   247
45:22   233, 247
45:23   18n48, 247
45:25   247
46:3   28
46:4   76
48:11   19
48:12   28, 70–71, 76, 196, 208, 211, 272
48:13   22, 24, 76, 247

9 780801 047596